Information Networking in Asia

Advanced Information Processing Technology

A series edited by Tadao Saito, *Department of Information and Communication Engineering, School of Engineering, The University of Tokyo, Japan*

Volume 1

Domain Oriented Systems Development: Principles and Approaches
edited by Kiyoshi Itoh, Toyohiko Hirota, Satoshi Kumagai and Hiroyuki Yoshida

Volume 2

Designing Communication and Collaboration Support Systems
edited by Yutaka Matsushita

Volume 3

Information Networking in Asia
edited by Hiroaki Higaki, Yoshitaka Shibata and Makoto Takizawa

Volumes in Preparation

Advanced VLSI CAD Systems and Algorithms
T. Fujita

Advanced High Performance Database System Technology
M. Kitsuregawa

Advanced Parallel Knowledge Processing Technology: Fifth Generation Computer Technology
S. Uchida and T. Chikayama

Information Networking in Asia

Edited by

Hiroaki Higaki

Department of Computers and Systems Engineering
Tokyo Denki University, Japan

Yoshitaka Shibata

Department of Software and Information Science
Iwate Prefectural University, Japan

Makoto Takizawa

Department of Computers and Systems Engineering
Tokyo Denki University, Japan

GORDON AND BREACH SCIENCE PUBLISHERS
Australia • Canada • France • Germany • India • Japan
Luxembourg • Malaysia • The Netherlands • Russia
Singapore • Switzerland

Amsteldijk 166
1st Floor
1079 LH Amsterdam
The Netherlands

British Library Cataloguing in Publication Data

Information networking in Asia. – (Advanced information
    processing technology ; v. 3)
    1. Computer networks – Asia – Congresses 2. Information
    networks – Asia – Congresses 3. Electronic data processing –
    Asia – Distributed processing – Congresses
    I. Higaki, Hiroaki II. Shibata, Yoshitaka   III. Takizawa,
    Makoto
    004.6′095

    ISBN: 90-5699-306-2
    ISSN: 1028-0049

Contents

Preface to the Series

The Information Processing Society of Japan (IPSJ) is the top academic institution in the information processing field in Japan. It has about thirty thousand members and promotes a variety of research and development activities covering all aspects of information processing and computer science.

One of the major activities of the society is publication of its transactions containing papers covering all the fields of information processing, including fundamentals, software, hardware, and applications. Some of the papers are published in English, but because the majority are in Japanese, the transactions are not suitable for the non-Japanese wishing to access advanced information technology in Japan. The IPSJ therefore decided to publish a book series entitled Advanced Information Processing Technology.

The series consists of independent books, each including a collection of top quality papers, from mainly Japanese sources of a selected area in information technology. The book titles were chosen by the International Publication Committee of the IPSJ so that they enable easy access to information technology for international readers. Each book contains original papers and/or those updated or translated from original papers appearing in the transactions or internationally qualified meetings. Survey papers to aid understanding of the technology in Japan in a particular area are also included.

As the chairman of the International Publication Committee of the IPSJ, I sincerely hope that the books in the series will improve communication between Japanese and non-Japanese specialists for their mutual benefit.

Tadao Saito

Chairman
International Publication Committee
The Information Processing Society of Japan

Preface

The 12th International Conference on Information Networking (ICOIN) was held at the Communication Research Laboratory, Tokyo in January 1998.

In this conference, 170 high-quality technical papers on communication networks and distributed systems were presented and very active and fruitful discussions were held with more than 220 attendants. Not only academic research papers on hot topics like high-speed communication ATM, multimedia communications and systems, and distributed algorithms but also industrial papers, especially on Internet-based electronic commerce network systems, were presented. These papers show the state-of-the-art of communication networks and the distributed systems area in Asia.

Researchers in communication networks and distributed systems are so active and successful in Asia that new technologies and products like digital TV and high speed networks with PCs are used not only in industries but also modern society. The program committee selected 27 distinguished papers out of the 170 papers presented at ICOIN-12. The selection was difficult because of the many excellent papers submitted. The papers were rewritten based on discussions and comments given at the conference and then reviewed by at least three experts.

Hiroaki Higaki
Yoshitaka Shibata
Makoto Takizawa

A Routing Strategy for Self-Healing ATM Networks Based on Virtual Path

Ardian Greca

Kiyoshi Nakagawa

Leonard Barolli

Yamagata University

ABSTRACT

A highly reliable network which can restore itself from failures is an important concept for the future high capacity broadband network. In this paper we propose a self-healing scheme for ATM Networks based on virtual path, taking advantages of backup restoration method and dynamic restoration algorithm in order to meet different requirements of service classes of survivability under minimum cost. The performance evaluation by simulations shows that the proposed algorithm can restore VPs quickly and it uses the network resources very efficiently.

1 Introduction

Today, many end users have an absolute dependence on telecommunication networks. They require fully reliable services and high-quality performance, assured service continuity, and transparency to failures. This desired quality is called network survivability performance. A major benefit of setting survivability performance objectives will be to ensure that, under given failure scenarios, network performance will not degrade below predetermined levels. Furthermore, reliability in telecommunications networks is a measure which is both hard to define and to evaluate.

ATM network, as a future powerful network, support multimedia traffic with diverse service characteristics and various Quality-of-Services (QoS) requirements. Routing strategies play an important role in meeting these requirements.

The proposed [1, 2, 3, 5] restoration strategies can be classified in two groups, link restoration and path restoration. Furthermore, two types of algorithms have been proposed to provide network restoration under failure. The dynamic restoration are capacity search algorithms that try to reroute the affected traffic to the extended possible on facilities with spare capacity [5]. Another class of restoring algorithms are the algorithms that use the preassigned backup VP (B-VP) to restore the affected traffic [2, 3]. The precomputed backup routes are stored in the network nodes.

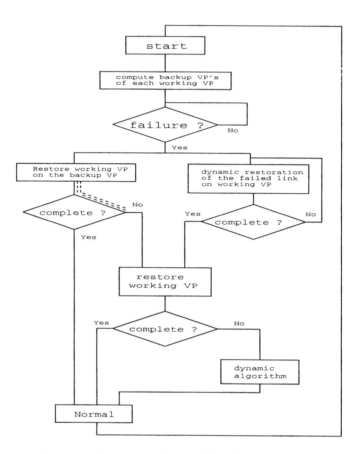

Figure 1: Flowchart of the self-healing algorithm.

The advantages and disadvantages of the two algorithms are not one sided. The dynamic restoration algorithm requires less capital investment in the network, but on the other hand requires a considerable time for restoration. The B-VP is a high speed restoration algorithm, but for large scale networks it may turn out to be fairly expensive to plan for all possible failure scenarios and precompute backup paths. Therefore, compromises for both algorithms exist.

In this work, we propose a new routing strategy to restore the multiple failures in ATM networks. This new routing algorithm consist on the coordination of the B-VP algorithm and dynamic algorithm in order to meet different requirements of survivability service classes.

This paper is organized as follows. In Section 2 a new rerouting strategy is proposed. In Section 3 the features for classification of service classes and cell format are adopted for the proposed algorithm. The simulation results are treated in Section

4. The conclusions are given in Section 5.

2   The proposed rerouting strategy

In this section a new routing algorithm in order to improve the survivability parameters is proposed. This algorithm coordinate both, the B-VP and dynamic algorithms to reroute the affected traffic when a failure happen.

The conventional algorithms [2, 5] have mainly studied only a single link or single node failure. On the other hand the proposed rerouting algorithm is able to recover multiple failures. Furthermore, this rerouting algorithm can be used for both link failure and node failure cases. Here only the link failure is considered for two reasons: a) the nodes are well enough protected from many factors, and b) the node failure can be considered as a failure of all links that are connected on this node. The flowchart of the proposed self-healing algorithm is shown in Figure 1.

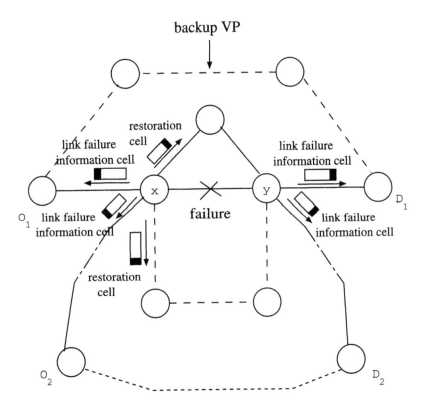

Figure 2: Basic behavior of the activation phase.

First, the B-VPs are precomputed for each working VP (W-VP) on the network.

The B-VP establishment of the W-VP depend on these parameters: the survivability performance requirements (see Sec. 3.A), the current capacity, and the current available VPI number in the network. The route for B-VP should be completely different from W-VP. The centralized control of the backup assignment for each VP on the network is used. (For more information see [6].)

Let suppose that a link failure happens on the network. Two adjacent nodes on the failed link detect the failure and enter in the activation phase.

Activation phase. When a failure happens, two nodes that connect the failed link (x,y) inform every termination node of the VPs which share the failed link by sending the information cells (see Sec. 3.B). At the same time they (x,y) start broadcasting the connection messages, by sending the restoration cells, to restore the failed link on the shortest route (the time is considered as the only parameter). This is shown in Figure 2. The parallel activation is used, because it fulfills the requirements for a fast restoration.

Recover and switching phase. This phase is connected with recovering of B-VP of the failed W-VP. The destination (D) nodes of each VP which are shared on the failed link, after receiving the information messages, send a recover message along the B-VP as is shown in Figure 3(a). The cross-connect (C-C) nodes of the B-VP that receive the restoration message occupy the appropriate bandwidth on the link and then transmit the message to the next node (see Figure 3(b)). If the origin O node receives the restoration message, it will switch the traffic from the failed W-VP to the B-VP and the procedure is completed.

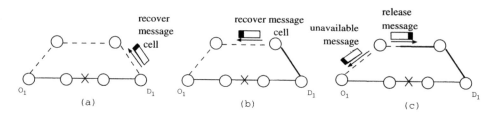

Figure 3: Basic behavior of the recover and switching phase.

When the bandwidth of the link is not enough for that VP, the C-C nodes send an unavailable message to the O node and the release message is sent back to release the occupied bandwidth (see Figure 3(c)).

Under the multiple failure, it may occur that two or more B-VPs use the same link. But maybe the capacity of this link is not enough to support the B-VPs (see Figure 4).

The O-D nodes in which a failure has happened try to use the B-VP. The B-VPs of these nodes may use the same link (a,b). Let suppose in this case that, the capacity of this link is not enough to support both B-VPs. The C-C node (a,b) will decide which B-VP will use the shared link based on the priority of the services

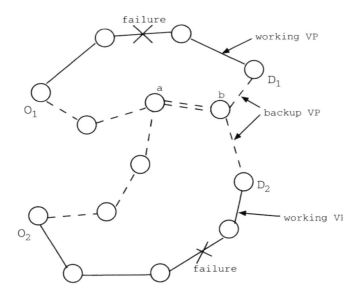

Figure 4: Unanticipated failure.

classes. Then one of the (a,b) nodes will send an unavailable message to the O node to inform that the B-VP can't use this link.

Search phase. This phase is connected with dynamic restoration of the failed link. One node becomes sender and the other becomes chooser. The sender will broadcast the restoration messages to the neighbour nodes to find the shortest path (time is considered as the only parameter). Each node will add in the restoration cell the information about the spare capacity and its identity. The message wall is used in order to prevent the useless cells [7].

Acknowledgment phase. When the chooser node receives several restoration messages from the sender node, the chooser node transmits the response message to the sender node on the founded paths. Each C-C node that receives response message will update the bandwidth information for the route and transmit it to next node on the route. When the sender node will receive the response messages from different routes, based on their information will select the route that is shorter and possess more bandwidth. Then will send the acknowledgment message to the chooser node on the selected route. The acknowledgment message will occupy the free bandwidth of the selected path.

Connection phase. All O nodes which received the unavailable messages will transmit a waiting message to the sender node (see Figure 5(a)). After the restoration of failed link by dynamic restoration, the sender node will choose the appropriate O-D node pairs to use the restored VP (see Figure 5(b)). The all O nodes that received the connection message will switch their traffic on the recovered path.

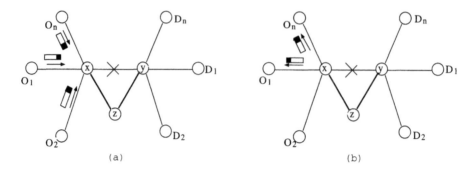

Figure 5: Connection phase.

The remained VP's that are still not restored will use dynamic algorithm to find a new VP route for their traffic.

A number of cells are exchanged between network nodes for each restoration algorithm (B-VP and dynamic restoration algorithms). Figure 6 illustrates the timing sequence for these algorithms. As is shown there the dynamic restoration has always greater restoration time than the backup algorithm ($t_d > t_b$). Therefore, the conflicts between cells of different algorithms are avoided.

3   Features of self-healing algorithm

The main purpose of proposed self-healing scheme is to improve the restoration time after failures occurs in network. In this Section the classification of service classes and cell format are adopted for this algorithm.

A. Classification of service classes.

This hybrid mechanism can fast restore failed VP's based on their assigned priority in case of failures. According to restoration time requirements and sensitivity of services, we adopt three service classes of survivability at ATM VP level, in order to optimize the economics and survivability. In the first class can be classified together higher survivability services, like emergency services, real time processing, access to distributed database, national banking services etc. In the second class can be classified medium speed services like hifi sound, video telephony, high speed data, etc. The services of class 1 and class 2 will be maintained by minimum impact in the case of failures. And in the third class can be classified services where the delay is not an important parameter, like e-mail etc. Each survivability class of W-VP will be determined by the compromise between survivability performance and cost.

B. Cell format.

The self-healing messages can use ATM layer Operation and Maintenance (OAM) cells. ITU-T has proposed a management scheme using OAM cells for the VP layer. VP-AIS (VP Alarm Indication Signal) cells are generated and transmitted as soon as

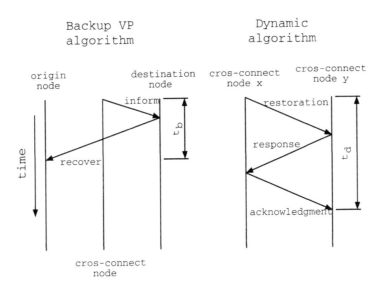

Figure 6: Timing diagram for two restoration algorithms.

possible after observing a defect indication, and transmitted periodically during the defect's existence in order to indicate an interruption of cell transfer capability at the VP level. A VP-RDI (VP Remote Defect Indicator) cell is sent to the far-end from a VP termination point as soon as it has declared a VP-AIS state. Therefore, C-C nodes along the failed VP can detect the failure very rapidly. The self-healing cell format is shown in Figure 7. These cells will have the same format as OAM cells with the following determinations. In the OAM cell type we propose using of 0100 code that is not used by ITU-T, to identify the self-healing messages from the other OAM messages. OAM function type field will contain the type of self-healing message, e.g. recover message, connect message, etc. According to the self-healing message type, the information field of the OAM cell will contain the necessary information carried from these messages. Furthermore, the self-healing message is expected to need only one cell to transfer the self-healing parameters. This will make cells to be transferred quickly through the nodes.

4   Simulation results

The performance evaluation of the proposed algorithm is investigated by simulation for one- and two-links failure. The network model which has 15 nodes and 25 links is the existing middle-distance network in Japan and is shown in Figure 8. The link labels denote the number and delay (ms) of the link. We assume that there are 36 active VPs in the network and the bandwidth of them varies from 10 Mb/s to 45

Parameters	Volume	Use
Self healing message	4 bits	Identification of self-healing message (e.g., recover message, connect message, etc.)
Source node ID	2 bytes	Identification of O node of the affected W-VP
Destination node ID	2 bytes	Identification of D node of the affected W-VP
Affected W-VP	2n bytes	Identification of the affected W-VP between O and D
Failed link or node ID	2 bytes	Identification of the failed link or node between O and D node
Required capacity	2 bytes	Capacity required for the affected W-VP
Link ID's on the alternative route	2n bytes	Identification of the alternative route, link ID is added when the message passes through each node
Available spare capacity	2 bytes	Identification of minimum available spare link capacity accommodated the alternative route
VP priority	2 bits	Priority restoration to solve the connection in the case of multifailure
Hop count limit	4 bits	Restriction on broadcasting of self-healing messages

Mb/s. The node processing time is considered 4 ms/message. The capacity of all links is considered 150Mb/s, and the average spare capacity ratio is considered 45%.

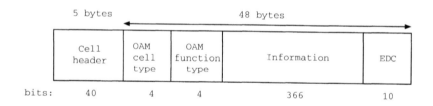

Figure 7: Self-healing cell format using OAM cell.

The network survivability is studied for the following survivability measures: 1) average traffic survivability ratio $S_t = \frac{(L_t - l_{ti})}{L_t}$, where S_t is the traffic survivability ratio, L_t is the load of network on all links, and l_{ti} is the load on the failed link i; 2) the average fraction of VPs which remain connected after the failure $C_N = \frac{(C_N - n_{ci})}{C_n}$, where C_N is the average connectivity ratio, C_n is the total connection on the network, and n_{ci} is the number of connections which go through the link i; and 3) the average time restoration t_r [4].

The results of the survivability measures obtained by simulations are shown in Table 1. The results show the average of the traffic which remain after one- or two-links failure happen, the average connectivity, and the average restoration time, respectively.

For one link failure $S_t = 0.858$, $C_N = 0.792$ and for two links failure $S_t = 0.771$, $C_N = 0.657$, respectively. The traffic affected and connectivity for two links failure

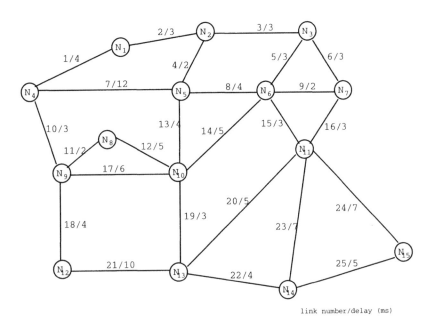

Figure 8: Simulated network model.

is lower than for one link failure. This is because in the two links failure scenario the number of affected links is greater than for one link failure scenario. On the other hand, the average restoration time for two links failure is greater than for one link failure, but there is not a big difference. The difference is less than 5 ms. This means, the proposed algorithm has a good restoration time even for two links failure.

The restoration speed for the one- and two-links failure scenario is shown in Figure 9. They have nearly the same restoration speed up to 32 ms and then for two links failure case the restoration speed is growing slowly because the affected traffic is greater.

The restoration time after failure of each link happened in network is shown in Figure 10. The bigger restoration time is when failure happen on links that connect node N3 with node N7 and node N9 with node N12, and the lower restoration time is when failure happen on link that connect node N6 with node N7. This graph show that the restoration time is depended from the topology and the traffic on the network.

In the two links failure case, since the amount of bandwidth affected is greater than in the one-link failure case the restoration time is greater, but this difference is not so big, because the algorithm can use spare capacity more effectively.

The restoration speed for two links failure is shown in Figure 11. The algorithm in Ref. [2] has a fast restoration time until 60 ms of the restoration time. This

Table 1: Results of the survivability measures.

Survivability measures	One link failure	Two links failure
S_t	0.858	0.771
C_N	0.792	0.657
t_r	38.66 ms	43.15 ms

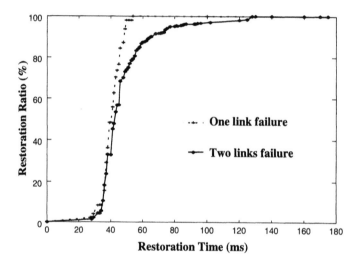

Figure 9: One- and two-links failure restoration speed.

happens because this algorithm is using only the B-VPs restoration method. But after 60 ms the curve of the proposed algorithm increases faster and recovering ratio is almost 100%. This is because the proposed algorithm coordinate the B-VP and dynamic restoration algorithms, so the resource utilization is better than the algorithm proposed in Ref. [2].

5 Conclusions

In this paper, we proposed a new self-healing algorithm based on VP for building-up survivable ATM networks. The proposed algorithm coordinates the B-VP and dynamic algorithms to reroute the affected traffic when a failure happens. The proposed algorithm has many advantages versus a simple combination method, which will suffer from inefficient resource utilization. This means that some resources are not utilized either from backup or dynamic algorithm. It may happen, for soft

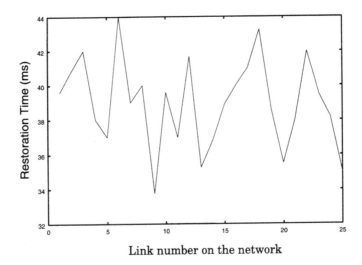

Figure 10: Restoration time for each link under failure.

failure, that two algorithms will ocucpy more resources that are needed. This will degrade the effectiveness of network. The proposed algorithm solve the problem of conflicts between cells of different algorithms and assure high speed node's processing of cells because they belong to the same algorithm. These reasons will influence on restoration time. The large number of cells passing the network is the drawback of the proposed algorithm. The performance of the proposed algorithm was investigated by simulation. From the simulation results we conclude that the restoration time was evidently improved. The proposed algorithm has almost 100% restoration ratio. This means, the proposed algorithm uses the resources very efficiently. In a case where the spare capacity is not enough, the restoration time is getting longer and restoration ratio is not so good but nevertheless the services of first and second class will suffer less from this.

Bibliography

1) Veitch, P., Hawker, I., and Smith, G. "Administration of Restorable Virtual Path Mesh Networks", *IEEE Communication Magazine*, pp. 96–101 (1996).

2) Kawamura, R., Sato, K., and Tokizawa, I., "Self-Healing ATM Networks Based on Virtual Path Concept", *IEEE Journal on Selected Areas in Communications*, Vol. 12, No. 1, pp. 120–127 (1994).

3) Chen, Sh., Cheng, Sh., and Chen, J., "A backup VP Assignment Method for ATM Survivable Networks", *Proc. IEEE ICCS/ISPACS '96*, pp. 805–809 (1996).

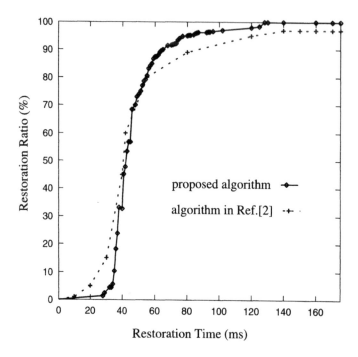

Figure 11: Two links failure restoration.

4) Zolfaghari, A., and F. J. Kaudel, F. J., "Framework for Network Survivability Perfor-mance", *IEEE Journal on Selected Areas in Communications*, Vol. 12, No. 1, pp. 46–51 (1994).

5) Fujii, H. and Yoshikai, N., " Restoration Message Transfer Mechanism and Restoration Characteristics of Double-Search Self-Healing ATM Network", *IEEE Journal on Selected Areas in Communications*, Vol. 12, No. 1, pp. 149–158 (1994).

6) Greca, A., Nakagawa, K., and Barolli, L., "A Self-Healing Scheme for ATM Networks Based on Virtual Path", *Proc. IEEE ICOIN-12*, pp. 77–81 (1998).

7) Wipusitwarakun, K., Tode, H., and Ikeda, H., "Fast Failure Restoration Algorithm with Reduced Messages Based on Flooding Mechanism", *IEICE Trans. Commun.*, Vol. E-80-B, No. 4, pp. 564–572 (1997).

8) Chen, Sh., Cheng, Sh., and Chen, J., "A Network Survivability Management System and Its Global Survivability Control for ATM/SDH Networks", *IEEE ICCS/ISPACS '96*, pp. 810–814 (1996).

2

A Multiple-Class Buffer Allocation Scheme for ATM Networks with VBR Traffic

Tsang-Ling Sheu

Kuo-Fu Lee

National Sun Yat-Sen University

ABSTRACT

A multiple-class buffer allocation scheme for ATM networks with VBR (Variable Bit Rate) traffic is presented in this paper. The dynamic buffer allocation scheme consists of two parts. The first part is used to estimate the buffer size required for each class of traffic. The second part is used to dynamically rearrange the buffer space among different priorities of traffic classes. For the purpose of evaluation, we develop a mathematical model to analytically estimate the buffer size required for each stage of switch node. In addition, a simulation model is built. In the simulation study, the analytical results from the mathematical model are verified with the simulation.

Keywords: ATM, Buffer Allocation, Cell Loss Ratio, Queuing Delay, VBR .

1   Introduction

This paper presents a dynamic buffer allocation scheme for various types of VBR (Variable Bit Rate) traffic over ATM networks. It is critical that an ATM switch have the sufficient bandwidth to allocate its buffer space dynamically to meet the stringent QoS (Quality of Service) requirements for real-time VBR traffic. Previous work [1] has pointed out that the importance of automatically determining the minimal resources necessary to satisfy a specified QoS measure. Wu and Huang [2] proposed a dynamic priority scheme to improve QoS requirements in ATM network. Their work mainly uses two pointers, one for data and another for real-time stream, to adjust the buffer space for reducing the overall delay and cell loss rate. Comparison of buffer allocation scheme in ATM switches with complete sharing and dedicated allocation can be found in [3]. A complete sharing with virtual partition strategy for buffer management was proposed in [4]. The total buffer space is partitioned based on the relative traffic loads. This virtual partition allows a newly arriving cell belonging to an oversubscribed type to occupy the spare space of an underscribed type. Two optimal buffer sharing schemes can be found in [5-6], where the authors have proved that the optimal policy can be achieved by dropping (pushing out) packets based on a predefined buffer threshold. Separate buffer schemes for real-time and non-real time streams were proposed in [7], where they assumed the buffer size is invariable. By considering only non-uniform traffic, an improved buffer sharing scheme, called Hot-Spot-Push-Out (HSPO), for ATM network was recently proposed [8].

The buffer allocation scheme presented in this paper mainly focuses on the reduction of the end-to-end queuing delay and the overall cell loss ratio by dynamically reallocate the switch's buffer space for different classes of traffic with different levels of QoS requirements. We have developed two algorithms to dynamically rearrange the buffer space for each class of traffic. The first algorithm is used to estimate the buffer size required for each class of traffic based on the average cell loss ratio, and to determine the total number of cells arrived at the switch for each class of traffic between two bursty intervals. The second algorithm is developed to dynamically rearrange the buffer space among different classes of traffic. Here, we have assumed that a higher-priority class of traffic, such as real-time VBR video and audio traffic, has the privilege to occupy the buffer size originally reserved to a lower-priority class of traffic, such as non-real time data traffic, up to 80%. This dynamic buffer allocation scheme is generalized to be able to support any number of traffic classes.

The proposed buffer allocation scheme is evaluated through an analytical model first. From the analytical modeling, we can deterministically estimate the buffer size required for each class of traffic at each stage of switch node. We then build a simulation model based on the IBP (Interrupted Berroullii Process) cell arrival process to verify the analytical results. The IBP process can completely capture the behavior of bursty traffic based on two cell generation states; the state of peak cell rate and the state of zero cell rate. From the simulation results, we observe that the buffer size required for each class of VBR traffic calculated from the analytical model is only 5%-7% apart from the results generated by the simulation model. This confirms the correctness of our analytical analysis. The simulation also demonstrates two significant improvements: (1) The end-to-end queuing delay and the queuing delay at each switch node for a specific traffic class have been largely decreased; (2) At each switch node, the cell loss ratio for a higher-priority traffic as a function of the burst probability (BP) has been greatly reduced as compared to those of the lower-priority traffic.

The rest of this paper is organized as follows. Section 2 describes the dynamic buffer allocation scheme. In Section 3, a network topology is introduced and a VBR traffic source based on the IBP model is established. In Section 4, a mathematical model for estimating the buffer space required for each switch node under different VBR traffic is introduced. In addition, a simulation is performed to verify the analytical results. Finally, we conclude this paper in Section 5.

2 Dynamic Buffer Allocation

2.1 Traffic Class with Priority

We divide the VBR traffic into different classes with each class having a priority level. For example, the following shows 4 different classes of VBR traffic used in our simulation study: Class 1 : Sensitive to both cell loss and cell delay. Class 2 : Sensitive to cell delay but insensitive to cell loss. Class 3 : Sensitive to cell loss but insensitive to cell delay. Class 4 : Insensitive to cell loss and cell delayc.

Note that in the above, we have assumed that class 1 has the highest priority, while class 4 (also referred to as the reserved class) has the lowest priority. In general, for the same traffic load, the more occupancy of buffer space, the smaller of the cell loss ratio. In other words, when the cell loss ratio of a traffic loss has exceeded the QoS requirement, the buffer size required for that traffic class should be increased. On the other hand, when the cell loss ratio of a traffic class is much lower than its QoS requirement, some portion of the buffer space can be reallocated to other traffic classes such that the entire buffer utilization can be increased.

2.2 The Buffer Estimation Algorithm

Figure 1 shows the pseudo code of the Buffer Estimation (BE) algorithm. The core of the BE algorithm is right in the following equation[1].

$$T(n, t + 1) = T(n, t) + K(n, t)log(P(n, t)/Q(n)) \qquad (2.1)$$

Where T(n,t+1) and T(n,t) represent the buffer size required at time t+1 and t, respectively, for a specific traffic class n, P(n,t) is the measured cell loss ratio for class n of a switch node at time t, Q(n) is the average cell loss ratio for class n, and K(n,t) represents the buffer re-adjustment factor for class n at time t. When P(n,t)$\geq$ Q(n) (that is, log(P(n,t)/Q(n)) is positive), the buffer space should be increased to meet the QoS requirements. On the other hand, when P(n,t)<Q(n) (that is, log(P(n,t)/Q(n)) is negative), the buffer space should be decreased to increase the entire buffer utilization. As long as P(n,t) is not equal to Q(n), the buffer size is dynamically adjusted (increased or decreased) as a function of time t.

Note that Interval[n,t] in the pseudo code represents the cycle of changing buffer sizes. There are two modes in the BE algorithm. At mode = 1, the cycle of changing buffer size (Interval[n,t]) is fixed, but K(n,t) is increased as the increase of time t. Hence, the QoS requirements for the cell loss ratio can be quickly satisfied, since the buffer size is re-adjusted every time when K(n,t) is changed. K(n,t) is linearly increased or decreased till the sign of log(P(n,t)/Q(n)) is changed. After that, K(n,t) keeps to reducing to its half till K(n,t)$\leq$ [n,∞], where mode = 2 is initiated. At mode = 2, since the algorithm is converged to the average cell loss ratio, K(n,t) will be fixed and the interval of changing buffer sizes is varied as the increase of time t.

```
//Initial values: inc_flag = TRUE, mode = 1,
//Q = average cell loss ratio of each class.
//P( n , t ) = (the number of lost cells of class n ) /
//the total number of cells arrived at time t.
curr_error ← log(P( n , t )/Q( n ));
prev_error ← log(P(n−1,t )/Q( n ));

if (mode = 1) {
   Interval [ n , t ] ← Interval [ n , t−1 ];
   if ((curr_error * prev_error > 0)&&(inc_flag = TRUE))
       K( n , t ) ← K( n , t ) + K ( n , 0 );
   else {
       inc_flag ← FALSE;
       K( n , t ) ← K( n , t−1 )/2;
       if (K( n , t ) ≤ K( n , ∞ )){
          K( n , t ) ← K( n ,∞ );
          mode ← 2;
          }
      }
   }
else {            /*mode=2*/
      K( n , t ) ← K(n , t−1 );
      if (curr_error * prev_error < 0 )
          Interval[ n , t ] ← 2 * Interval[ n , t−1 ];
      else
          Interval[ n , t ] ← Interval[ n , t−1 ];
   }
```

Figure 1: The Buffer Estimation Algorithm.

2.3   The Buffer Rearrangement Algorithm

As shown in Figure 2, the Buffer Rearrangement (BR) algorithm is developed to re-adjust the buffer space for the VBR traffic classes with different priorities. For a higher-priority traffic class, if its buffer size, calculated from the BE algorithm, is found to be too small, the buffer size should be incremented and obtained immediately from the lowest-priority class (or the reserved class). On the other hand, if its buffer size is determined to be too large, the extra buffer space will be returned to the reserved class. Moreover, if the increment of buffer size of a higher-priority class exceeds the amount of the reserved buffer space, the higher-priority class has the privilege to obtain the required buffer space from all the lower-priority classes. However this buffer occupancy by the higher-priority class is limited to be only 20% of the initially allocated buffer spaces of those lower-priority classes.

As shown in the figure, each buffer size has two values, the estimated buffer size $B_{estimated}(n,t)$, which is estimated from the BE algorithm, and the actual buffer size $B_{actual}(n,t)$, which is initially allocated by the BR algorithm. The difference between $B_{estimated}(n,t)$ and $B_{actual}(n,t)$ is the increment and decrement of the buffer space required for each traffic class. This buffer increment or decrement will be appropriately adjusted either from the reserved class or from the lower-priority classes. Note that a while-loop is used in the BR algorithm. The while-loop allows a higher-priority traffic class keeps occupying another 20% of buffer space from the next lower-priority class, if the 20% occupancy from the first lower-priority class is not enough. This buffer occupancy will not stop until all the lower-priority traffic classes have donated their 20% of initially allocated buffer spaces.

```
//Buffer size has two values: the estimated buffer size, Bestimated(n,t),
//and the actual buffer size, Bactual(n,t)
difference ← K( n , t ) * curr_error;
Bestimated(n,t) ← Bestimated(n,t−1) + difference;
If ( difference < reserved buffer size )
 //The increment of buffer size is larger than
 //the reserved class.
 {
  reserved buffer sizes ← ( reserved buffer size − difference );
  Bactual(n,t) ← Bactual(n,t−1) + difference;
}
else//The increment of buffer size is smaller than
the buffer size of the reserved class.
 {
  Bactual(n,t) ← Bactual(n,t−1) + reserved buffer size;
  difference ← ( difference−reserved buffer size );
  I = priority of the lowest class;
  while (( difference > 0 ) and ( I < priority of present class ))
  {
   obtain buffer space from class I, until Bactual(n,t) of class I
has reached 0.8*( Bestimated(n,t) of class I );
   difference ← ( difference − buffer size ), obtained from class I;
   Interval [ n , t ] of class I ← ∞;
   I ← I − 1;
  }
 }
if ( difference > 0 )    Interval[ n , t ] ← ∞;
```

Figure 2: The Buffer Rearrangement Algorithm.

3 Network Topology and IBP Model

3.1 Network Topology

A famous parking lot configuration [9] is adopted as our network topology. The source station is assumed to be able to generate n classes (where n = 1 to N) of VBR traffic with different priorities. There are 5 switch nodes (SW1 to SW5) between the source and the destination stations. In addition to foreground traffic generated by the source, background traffic are injected to each switch node. Each background traffic is assumed to enter into switch k and leave after passing switch k + 1.

3.2 IBP Traffic Model

The VBR traffic of the source station is generated through an IBP (Interrupted Bernoulli Process) model, where two cell-generation states are assumed, the bursty state with peak cell rate (PCR) and the silent state with zero cell rate. The state transition diagram of the IBP model is shown in Figure 3, where x and y represent the silent state and the bursty state, respectively, and P_1, P_2, P_3, and P_4 are the conditional probability.

Not that P_1= P(y|x), P_2= P(x|y) , P_3= 1 − P_1 and P_4= 1 − P_2. By Baye's theorem, $P(x|y) = \frac{P(x \bigcap y)}{P(y)}$, we have $P_1 P(x) = P_2 P(y)$. Since P(x) + P(y) = 1, we have $P(y) = \frac{P_1}{P_1 + P_2}$. If we let P_1+ P_2= 1, then the burst probability, P(y) = P_1.

4 Performance Evaluation

4.1 Buffer Size Estimation

Based on the network topology presented in Section 3, a switch node receives two inputs, the foreground traffic and the background traffic. Hence, we have

Lost cells = (foreground traffic cells + background traffic cells) − output cells.

Now, let us define,

n = Number of traffic classes, n = 1 to N,
k = Number of switch nodes, k = 1 to K,
R = Link cell rate (cells/sec),
T = Simulation interval (seconds),
P_{fore} = Prob. of foreground traffic at burst state,
P_{back} = Prob. of background traffic at burst state,
LC(n,k) = Lost cells of class n at switch k,
CLR(n,k) = Cell loss ratio of class n at switch k,
P(n,k) = Cell pass ratio of class n at switch k = 1 - CLR(n,k),
B = Total buffer size,
B(n,k) = Buffer size of class n at switch k,
$F(n, k) = \frac{B(n,k)}{B}$.

For time interval T at switch 1, we have

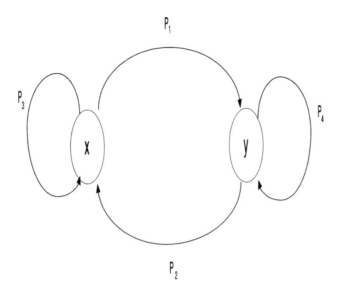

Figure 3: The IBP Model.

$$LC(n,1) = RTP_{fore}/N + RTP_{back}/N - RTF(n,1).$$

$$CLR(n,1) = \frac{RTP_{fore}/N + RTP_{back}/N - RTF(n,1)}{RTP_{fore}/N + RTP_{back}/N} = 1 - \frac{NF(n,1)}{P_{fore} + P_{back}}.$$

$$P(n,1) = 1 - CLR(n,1) = \frac{NF(n,1)}{P_{fore} + P_{back}}.$$

At switch 2, we have

$$LC(n,2) = RTP_{fore}P(n,1)/N + RTP_{back}/N - RTF(n,2).$$

$$CLR(n,2) = \frac{RTP_{fore}P(n,1)/N + RTP_{back}/N - RTF(n,2)}{RTP_{fore}P(n,1)/N + RTP_{back}/N} = 1 - \frac{NF(n,2)}{P_{fore}P(n,1) + P_{back}}.$$

$$P(n,2) = 1 - CLR(n,2) = \frac{NF(n,2)}{P_{fore}P(n,1) + P_{back}}.$$

At switch k, we have

$$LC(n,k) = [RT P_{fore} P(n,1) P(n,2)....P(n,k-1)]/N + RT P_{back}/N - RTF(n,k).$$

$$= [RT P_{fore} \prod_{i=1}^{k-1} P(n,i)]/N + RT P_{back}/N - RTF(n,k).$$

$$CLR(n,k) = 1 - \frac{NF(n,k)}{P_{fore} \prod_{i=1}^{k-1} P(n,i) + P_{back}}.$$

Let us replace P(n,1),P(n,2),.....,P(n,k-1) with P_{fore}, P_{back},F(n,k), and N, we have

$$CLR(n,k) = 1 - \frac{NF(n,k)[P_{fore} \sum_{j=1}^{k-2}[P_{back}^{k-j-i} \prod_{i=1}^{j} NF(n,i)] + P_{fore} P_{back}^{k-2} + P_{back}^{k-1}]}{P_{fore} \sum_{j=1}^{k-1}[P_{back}^{k-j-1} \prod_{i=1}^{j} NF(n,i)] + P_{fore} P_{back}^{k-1} + P_{back}^{k}]}$$

$$(2.2)$$

Substitute equation(2) into equation(1) presented in Section 2.2 and by assuming that CLR(n,k) = P(n , t) at switch k and at time t , we have derived the buffer size required for class n at switch k and at time t+1, given that a buffer size (T(n,k,t)) for class n at switch k and at time t is known.

$$T(n,k,t+1) = T(n,k,t) + K(n,t) log(\frac{CLR(n,k)}{Q(n)}) \qquad (2.3)$$

4.2   Evaluation and Simulation

A simulator is built with a VBR traffic source based on the IBP model. As we have introduced in Section 3.2, the burst probability (BP) is the probability of traffic state that remains at the peak cell rate (PCR). In the following simulation, a "raw" system, used as a reference model, is defined as the same parking lot topology without applying the DBA scheme. The traffic load of the background traffic is fixed to 0.533 and the initially allocated buffer size for each traffic class is 15 cells (that is, the total buffer size at a switch node = 60 cells). Based on equation (2), we can calculate CLR(n,k) for traffic class n at switch k. In the calculation, we have assumed the following initial conditions: N = 4, K = 5, B = 60, P_{fore} = 0.9, P_{back} = 0.533, and F(n,k) = B/N = 15. Substitute CLR(n,k) into equation(3), and by assuming that an initial condition T(n,k,0) = 15, the buffer size required for class n at switch k and at time t+1, T(n,k,t+1), can be calculated.

Figure 4 shows the difference of CLR by the calculation from equation (3) and by the simulation model. As can be seen, the estimation results are very close to the simulation results at switch 1, no matter how the traffic load is increased. However, the two curves (estimation and simulation) become gradually separated for switch 3, when traffic load is increased to 0.6. There are two reasons to explain this deviation. First, accumulated error due to the CLR of the next stage is derived from that of the previous stage. Second, cell slots are assumed to be full in estimation, but they may be empty in simulation when neither background traffic nor foreground traffic sending cells.

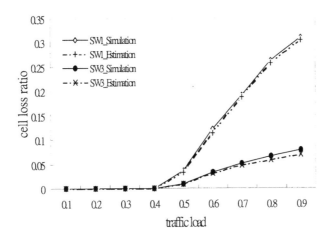

Figure 4: Cell Loss Ratio Between Estimation and Simulation.

Figure 5 shows the buffer sizes required for different traffic classes at different switch nodes. It is observed that the results from the calculation are about 5%-7% apart from the simulation for traffic class = 1, 2, and 3. However, the differences become bigger for the reserved class (that is, class 4), since the buffer size required for class 4 is calculated by subtracting the buffer sizes of classes 1, 2, and 3 one by one from the total buffer size. This also explains why the calculation results are larger than the simulation results only for class 4.

Figure 6 shows the cell loss ratio (CLR) as a function of the BP. As can be seen, class 1 has the lowest CLR, while class 4 has the highest. The raw system has the CLR, which is slightly higher than class 3, but is much lower than class 4. When BP = 0.6, the CLR is largely increased, since the total traffic load of the foreground plus the background has exceeded one.

Figure 7 shows the end-to-end queuing delay as a function of the BP. As can be observed from the figure, the raw system has the longest queuing delay, while class 4 has the shortest one. The reason is because that the buffer size of class 4 is decreased as the increase of BP. As a result, the number of cells that can go into the buffer is largely reduced. Note that class 1 has the queuing delay that is slightly higher than class 4, but still lower than the raw system.

Figure 8 shows the buffer size required at switch 1 for each traffic class as a function of the simulation time by assuming that BP = 0.9. As can be observed, class 1 quickly occupies the largest buffer size (about 29 cells) and class 4 gradually

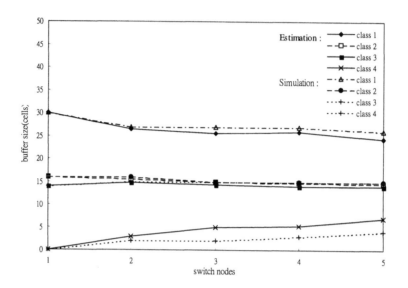

Figure 5: Estimated Buffer Size vs Simulation.

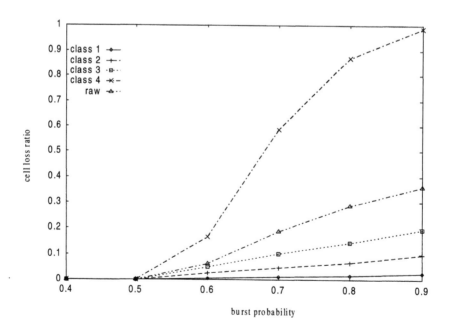

Figure 6: Cell Loss Ratio vs Burst Probability.

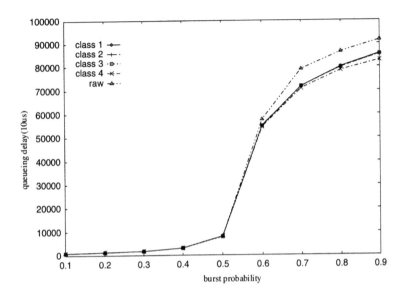

Figure 7: End-to-End Queuing Delay vs the Burst Probability.

lost its buffer size to approach to zero eventually. Note that classes 2 and 3 occupy 17 cells initially, but saturate to 15 cells finally, due to the dynamic buffer adjustment.

5   Conclusions

In this paper, we have presented a multiple-class buffer allocation scheme for ATM networks with VBR traffic. We have developed two algorithms, the BE and the BR algorithms, to initially estimate the buffer size required for each traffic class and to dynamically adjust the buffer sizes based on the QoS requirements. The proposed buffer allocation scheme was first evaluated through a mathematical model, through which the buffer size required for each traffic class based on the average cell loss ratio can be calculated. For the purpose of verification, we have built a simulator, through which we have proved that the analytical results are only 5%-7% apart from the simulation results. In addition, the simulation also demonstrates two significant improvements provided by this buffer allocation scheme. That is, the cell loss ratio and the end-to-end queuing delay for a higher-priority traffic class have been greatly reduced, as compared to a system where buffer sizes can not be dynamically adjusted.

Bibliography

1)   Sanjeev Rampal, Dougal S. Reeves and Ioannis Viniotis, "Dynamic Resource Allocation

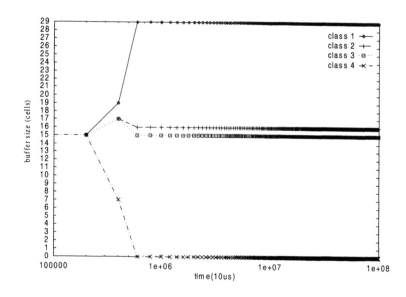

Figure 8: Buffer Size Required as a Function of Simulation Time When BP =0.9.

Based on Measured QoS," Technical Report TR 96-2, Center for Advanced Computing and Communication, North Carolina State University, Raleigh, NC.

2) Jean-Lien C. Wu and Trien-Yu Huang, "Dynamic Priority Scheme to Improve the QoS in ATM Networks," Proc. IEEE GLOBECOM'94, pp.1195-1199.

3) Jeffery W. Causey and Hyong S. Kim, "Comparison of Buffer Allocation Schemes in ATM Switches: Complete Sharing, Partial Sharing, and Dedicated Allocation," Proc. IEEE ICC'94, pp.1164-1168.

4) Guo-Liang Wu and Jon W. Mark, "A Buffer Allocation Scheme for ATM Networks: Complete Sharing Based on Virtual Partition," IEEE/ACM Transaction on Networking, vol. 3, no. 6, December 1995, pp.660-670.

5) Israel Cidon, Leonidas Georgiadis, Roch Guerin and Asad Khamisy, "Optimal Buffer Sharing," IEEE Journal on Selected Area in Communications, vol. 13, no. 7, September 1995, pp.1229-1239.

6) Israel Cidon, Leonidas Georgiadis, Roch Guerin and Asad Khamisy, "Optimal Buffer Sharing," Proc. IEEE INFOCOM'95, pp.24-31.

7) Marwan Krunz, Herman Hughes, and Parvis Yegani, "Design and Analysis of a Buffer Management Scheme for Multimedia Traffic with Loss and Delay Priorities," Proc. IEEE ICC'94, pp.1560-1564.

8) Simon Fong and Samar Singh, "An Improved Buffer Sharing Scheme for ATM Switches under Bursty Traffic," Proc. Of 19th ACSC Conference 1996.

9) David Ginsburg, ATM Solution for Enterprise Internetworking. Addison-Wesley1996.

3

Performance Evaluation of Self Detective Congestion Control Scheme for ATM Networks

Akio Koyama, Leonard Barolli,

Said Mirza and Shoichi Yokoyama

Yamagata University

ABSTRACT

In this paper, we propose an adaptive Self Detective Congestion Control (SDCC) scheme for Available Bit Rate (ABR) service in Asynchronous Transfer Mode (ATM) networks. We show that the SDCC scheme can achieve good fairness performance among connection classes existing in the network. In transient behavior, the SDCC scheme offers fast access to available bandwidth, which is a sensible requirement, particularly in LAN environment. Also, by allocating control cells based on networks scales, the SDCC scheme is able to control a number of greedy sources with moderate size buffers. Furthermore, the comparison between the rate-based congestion control schemes show that the SDCC scheme has a better behavior than existing schemes.

1   Introduction

The ATM networks are recommended as a transfer mode for future B-ISDN. To cope with congestion control of the ABR services in ATM networks a rate-based scheme is considered to be the best [1]. There are several rate-based scheme proposed by the ATM Forum, such as FECN [2], BECN [3], and PRCA [4]. The FECN scheme uses Explicit Forward Congestion Indication (EFCI) as a single-bit to indicate congestion in the forward direction of the Virtual Connection (VC). In the BECN scheme, the notification cell is sent directly from the congested points to the source. Both the FECN and BECN schemes are based on a negative feedback rate control paradigm. That is, a source will reduce the cell transmission rate when it receives congestion notification cells. If, within a predetermined period of time, the source does not receive congestion notification cells, it will increase the current transmission rate until it reaches the peak cell rate. But, if all notification cells in the backward direction will experience extreme congestion, all sources will increase the rate to the peak cell rate, so the overall network congestion collapse may occur.

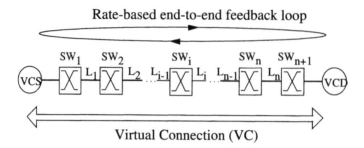

Figure 1: Network element of a VC.

The PRCA uses a positive feedback rate control paradigm instead of the negative feedback. However, unfair distribution of available bandwidth among VCs may occur because data cells from a VC passing through more congested links will be marked more often than those passing through fewer congested links. Thus, VCs with more congested links in their path will suffer from starvation, because their Allowed Cell Rate (ACR) is lower than others.

To resolve the problems of the existing rate-based schemes, we propose an adaptive scheme based on two basic concepts: 1) positive feedback rate control which resolves the problems of the FECN and BECN schemes; 2) intelligent holding of the Resource Management (RM) cells which resolves the problems of the PRCA.

The organization of this paper is as follows. In Section 2, the SDCC scheme is described. The simulation results are discussed in Section 3. The Enhanced SDCC (ESDCC) scheme is introduced Section 4. The comparison for different rate-based schemes is shown in section 5. The conclusions are given in Section 6.

2   SDCC Scheme

In this section, we describe the network elements and the SDCC basic operation.

2.1   Network Elements

The network elements of a VC are the Virtual Connection Source (VCS), Virtual Connection Destination (VCD) and ATM Switch (SW). The rate-based end-to-end feedback loop control scheme is shown in Figure 1.

The VCS and VCD generate and receive ATM cells. The VC is a bidirectional connection. The forward and backward connections have the same virtual connection identifiers and pass through identical transmission facilities. The VCS must have the ability to transmit cells into the network at a variable and controlled rate from a predetermined minimum cell rate to peak cell rate. On the other hand, the VCD must return every received RM cell to the VCS in the backward connection in order

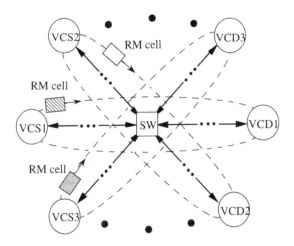

Figure 2: VCs with their RM cells.

to support the closed loop control scheme.

ATM switches route ATM cells from the VCS to the VCD, and each ATM switch has an identifier in the form of an address number. We assume that the ATM switch has output buffers divided into two parts: one for data cells and the other one for RM cells. Each part of the buffer implements a FIFO cell queuing discipline. The buffer service algorithm always serves the RM cells in preference to the data cells. That is, the RM cells have a higher service priority than the data cells.

2.2 Basic Operation

The basic SDCC scheme, in which every VC has one RM cell for congestion control purpose, is shown in Figure 2. We refer to this scheme as the self detective congestion control scheme because the VCS itself generates and sends out the RM cell to detect congestion which may occur at its bottleneck switch. The bottleneck switch is the switch which has the narrowest bandwidth between the switches in a VC. The bottleneck switch is considered to be known from the initial routine and its address is written in the SWI field of the RM cell.

The VCS starts a timer every time it transmits a RM cell. The timer starts to count down from a predetermined value, CD_Time (Congestion Detection Time), until it reaches 0. The CD_Time is a variable of the VCS, which is determined before the RM cell is sent out for the first time. The parameters and variables of the VCS are shown in Table 1 and Table 2, respectively (for more information about specifications of the SDCC scheme see ref.[5]).

The VCD returns the received RM cell to the VCS in backward connection. If the output buffer of the bottleneck switch is congested, the bottleneck switch will hold the RM cells flowing in the backward direction until it recovers from the congestion state.

Table 1: VCS parameters.

Name	Full name	Units	Comments
PCR	Peak Cell Rate	Cells/s	The maximum cell rate will be policed by the network
MCR	Minimum Cell Rate	Cells/s	The minimum cell rate guaranteed by the network
ICR	Initial Cell Rate	Cells/s	Start up rate
MAX_AIR	Maximum Additive Increase Rate	Cells/s	The increment of cell rate ranging from MIN_AIR to MAX_AIR
MIN_AIR	Minimum Additive Increase Rate	Cells/s	
MDF	Multiplicative Decrease Factor	None	To decrease the cell rate
NC	Number of Cells	Cells	RM cell is forwarded, if the number of data cells sent out at the previous round are NC or more
DTP	Decrease Time Period	Cell time	Time period to decrease the cell rate if congestion occurs
DTT	Delay Tolerance Time	Cell times	To tolerance the queueing delay of RM cell.
no_of_RM	Number of RM cell	None	Number of RM cell allocated to the VC

The bottleneck switch will pass all received RM cells without considerable delay if no congestion is detected, since the RM cells have higher priority. When the timer expires and the RM cell has not returned back yet, the VCS considers its bottleneck switch to be congested, therefore decreases the cell rate at regular predetermined intervals until receives the RM cell. On receiving the RM cell, the VCS considers its bottleneck switch decongested if the timer is still on, or if its bottleneck switch has been recovered from congestion state. The VCS will then increase its cell rate proportional to the current rate. The RM cell will be sent out to the network again if the VCS has transmitted a Number of Cell (NC) or more data cells since the RM cell was sent out during the previous round. This procedure reduces the amount of RM cell traffic when the cell rate of the VC is low or when the VC enters an idle state. The VCS is considered idle if at the current rate it isn't transmitted any data cell in an interval of length corresponding to NC interval.

By implementing intelligent holding, the VCs having the same bottleneck link will share the available bandwidth fairly. The intelligent holding means, all RM cells belonging to the VCs are selected only by the bottleneck switch when it is congested.

Table 2: VCS variables.

Name	Full name	Units	Calculation
AIR	Additive Increase Rate	Cells/s	$\text{MIN\_AIR} + \left(\frac{\text{PCR-CCR}}{\text{PCR-MCR}}\right)(\text{MAX\_AIR} - \text{MIN\_AIR})$
ADR	Additive Decrease Rate	Cells/s	$\frac{\text{CCR}}{2\text{MDF}}$
CCR	Current Cell Rate	Cells/s	Increase: CCR + AIR Decrease: CCR - ADR
RD_Time	Round_trip Time	Sec.	At initialization procedure
CD_Time	Congestion Detection Time	Sec.	$(\text{RD\_Time} + \text{DTT})/\text{no\_of\_RM}$

3   Simulation Results

In this section, we present simulation results which demonstrate the performance of the SDCC scheme.

The queuing model of the simulations is shown in Figure 3. The transmitter (T) always serves the RM cells in preference to the data cells. In the simulations, we assume that all VCSs are persistently greedy i.e., all VCSs will attempt to transmit the data cells at their peak cell rate. Each transmitter (T/R) will independently removes the data cells from the VCS buffer and transmits to the receiver (R). The intelligent holding will be performed by a bottleneck switch if the number of cells queued in the buffer (data cells) in the forward direction exceeds a threshold value. In all simulations, the threshold value is considered 50 cells. The VCS parameters used in the simulations are listed in Table 3.

3.1   Fairness Performance

The Generic Fairness Configuration (GFC) is used as a benchmark for the assessment of the fairness performance [6]. The GFC model is shown in Figure 4. There are 23 connections, grouped into 6 classes (A-F). The number of connections belonging to class A, B, C, D, E, F are 3, 3, 3, 6, 6, 2, respectively as specified in parenthesis after the class label. The network consists of 5 switches with links of various capacities. We consider fairness performance in a LAN environment. The distance between VCS/VCD and its nearest switch is about 100 meters and the distance between two switches is about 400 meters.

Let consider two connections, class B and E, which share the same bottleneck link L4. Since the VCS of class E is closer to the link L4 and passes less congested switches than that of class B, class E will get more of the link bandwidth than class B. This is analogous to a parking lot scenario in which E is closer than B from the exit. However, in a good ATM network with separate VCs for class B and E, they should share the available bandwidth of the link fairly (100 Mbps). Thus, each connection

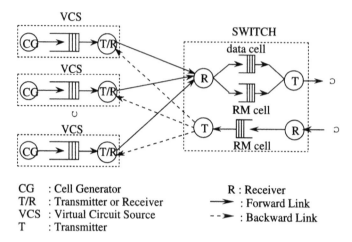

CG   : Cell Generator   R : Receiver
T/R : Transmitter or Receiver   ──➤ : Forward Link
VCS : Virtual Circuit Source   --➤ : Backward Link
T   : Transmitter

Figure 3: Queuing model.

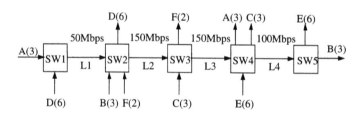

Figure 4: GFC model.

in class B and class E should take about 1/9 of the bandwidth (11.1 Mbps).

Considering the above fairness objective, the bandwidth of each link to each connection is allocated as follows: 1) the VCs on the most congested link will share the link bandwidth equally (this determines the rates to be set for these VCs); 2) apply the procedure to the other VCs with the remaining bandwidth of the network; 3) continue repeating the procedure until rates for all VCs have been assigned.

Using the above fair rate-setting procedure, the bandwidth assigned to the individual connection classes are shown in Table 4. The bandwidth allocated to each connection in the SDCC scheme is shown in Figure 5. It is clear that the SDCC scheme can achieve fair bandwidth allocation among connections in a class.

3.2 Transient Performance

In LAN environment, the fast access to available bandwidth is a sensible requirement. Therefore, the transient behavior of the SDCC scheme is considered in order to show

Table 3: VCS parameters used in the simulations.

Parameter	Fig. 5	Fig. 7	Fig. 8	Fig. 9
PCR (Mbps)	150	150	150	150
MCR (Mbps)	0.15	0.15	0.15	0.15
ICR (Mbps)	7.5	20	0.5	0.5
MAX_AIR (Mbps)	2	8	1	1
MIN_AIR (Mbps)	0	0	0	0
MDF	4	4	5	5
NC	32	32	32	32
DTP (cell times)	128	64	128	128
DTT (cell times)	16	16	16	64
no_of_RM	1	1	1	4

Table 4: Expected bandwidth for connection classes in GFC.

Connection class	Allocated bandwidth	Bottleneck link	Bottleneck switch
A	5.56 Mbps	L1	SW1
B	11.1 Mbps	L4	SW4
C	33.3 Mbps	L3	SW3
D	5.56 Mbps	L1	SW1
E	11.1 Mbps	L4	SW4
F	50.0 Mbps	L2	SW2

how the ABR connections will respond to the available bandwidth during an interval of time.

To evaluate the transient behavior of the SDCC scheme, we consider the model shown in Figure 6. This model has two switches with a single bottleneck link. Five connections start in a staggered sequence with a new connection starting every 10 ms. We consider here the transient performance in LAN environment. The distance between VCS/VCD and the switch is 100 meters, whereas the distance between the two switches is 400 meters.

In Figure 7 is shown the transient performance of the SDCC scheme. The SDCC scheme can ramp up quickly to the fair rate. That is, when a new connection comes, connections which have already existed in the network will reduce their cell rate immediately to give the new connection a chance to get available bandwidth until all connections have approximately the same cell rate. Furthermore, there are no

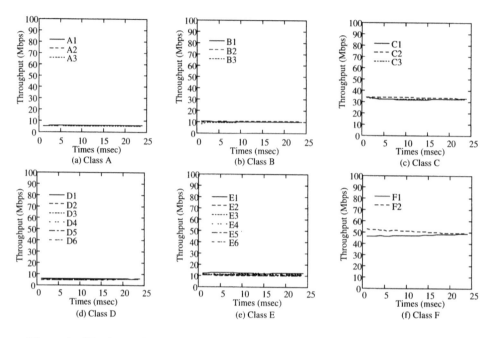

Figure 5: The basic SDCC scheme performance in GFC for LAN environment.

noticeable oscillations in the rate allocation. Thus, the SDCC scheme can improve bandwidth efficiency and reduces the oscillation rate.

3.3 Buffer Length

In the SDCC scheme, the VCS detects congestion using a timer. The longer the distance between VCS and VCD, the higher the CD_Time value. That is, the longer the distance between VCS and VCD, the slower VCS will react to the congestion. Therefore, it is necessary to observe the maximum and mean buffer length.

We consider the network configuration in Figure 6 for observing buffer length in different network scales. The simulation are carried out with up to 40 greedy VCSs, each attempting to transmit at 100 percent of the output line. The results are shown in Figure 8. In LAN environment (the distance up to 50 km or 100 cell times), for up to 40 VCs the mean and maximum buffer length remains below 100 cells, and approximately constant with respect to the distance. In MAN and WAN environments (the distance from 50km up to 1000 km or 1800 cell times), the mean buffer length remains below 200 cells. The buffer length is approximately constant with respect to the distance and approximately proportional to the number of connections. For up to 40 VCs, the maximum buffer length remains below 600 cells growing slowly with the network distance.

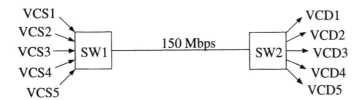

Figure 6: Two-switches with a single bottleneck link model.

4   Enhanced SDCC (ESDCC) Scheme

In LAN environment, the basic SDCC scheme is able to control a large number of greedy sources with a moderate buffer length. However, in MAN and WAN environments the buffer length becomes longer. In order to reduce buffer size in MAN and WAN environments, we propose a new scheme called ESDCC scheme. The key idea of the ESDCC scheme is to reduce the CD_Time (or the timer) value of the VCS. The smaller the CD_Time value, the faster the congestion detection of the VCS. To realize the idea, we allocated two or more RM cells (maximum four RM cells) to each VC. The operation of ESDCC scheme is quite similar with the SDCC scheme.

The performance results of the ESDCC scheme are shown in Figure 9. The ESDCC-4 indicates that every connection has four RM cells. In MAN and WAN environments, the maximum buffer length of ESDCC-4 remains below 300 cells. The buffer length of the ESDCC-4 is less than the basic SDCC scheme.

5   Comparison Between Rate-Based Schemes

The comparison between rate-based congestion control schemes is made based on the network problems, switch complexity, responsiveness and smoothness. The results are shown in Table 5.

(1) Network Problems

Network congestion collapse problem occurs in the FECN and BECN schemes because both schemes use a negative feedback rate control. In the PRCA, the network congestion collapse problem do not occur because the PRCA uses the positive feedback rate control instead the negative feedback. However, unfair distribution of bandwidth among connections may occur because the congested switch marks all data cells. The network problems do not occur in SDCC and ESDCC scheme because they use a positive feedback rate control and an intelligent holding of RM cells.

(2) Switch Complexity

In the FECN and PRCA, a congested switch needs to mark the data cells to inform the sources of the congestion state. Therefore, the switch complexity of two schemes is low. The switch complexity of the BECN scheme is high because the switch needs to generate the congestion notification cells and to filter the cells. The

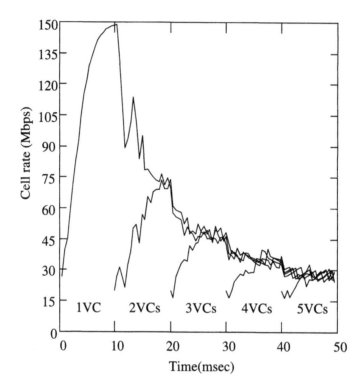

Figure 7: Transient performance of the basic SDCC scheme in LAN environment.

switch complexity of the SDCC and ESDCC scheme is considered to be medium because the switch needs the priority and intelligent holding functions.

(3) Responsiveness and Smoothness

The responsiveness and smoothness of FECN scheme is the worst between the existing schemes. This is because, the FECN scheme uses a feedback mechanism in forward direction, therefore the sources respond to the congestion state slowly. The BECN scheme uses a backward feedback notification. That is, a congestion notification is sent directly from the congested point to the source. Therefore, the responsiveness and smoothness of BECN scheme are better than the FECN scheme. In PRCA, the responsiveness and smoothness depend on N, where the N is the number of the data transmitted by the source. The smaller N the better responsiveness and smoothness. However, the smaller N the smaller link utilization. The responsiveness and smoothness of the SDCC and ESDCC scheme depend on parameters NC and no_of_RM. The smaller NC value (or the bigger no_of_RM), the better responsiveness and smoothness is. But the smaller NC value, the smaller link utilization is. Considering the trade-off between the NC and link utilization, the SDCC and ESDCC schemes have very good responsiveness and smoothness in the simulation.

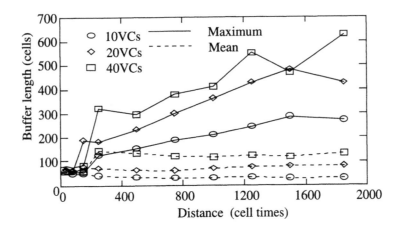

Figure 8: Buffer length versus the distance for basic SDCC scheme.

Table 5: Comparison between rate-based schemes.

Scheme	Network problems		Switch complexity	Responsiveness	Smoothness
	Network congestion collapse	Unfairness bandwidth distribution			
FECN	occur	occur	low	adequate	bad
BECN	occur	occur	high	good	good
PRCA	not occur	occur	low	depend on N	
SDCC (ESDCC)	not occur	not occur	medium	very good	very good

6 Conclusion

In this paper, we proposed the SDCC and ESDCC schemes for coping with congestion control in ATM networks. The performance evaluation via simulations showed that, in GFC, the SDCC scheme can achieve fair bandwidth allocation among connections in a class. In transient behavior, the SDCC scheme ramps up quickly to the fair rate and there are not noticeable rate oscillations. This means, the SDCC scheme improves bandwidth efficiency and reduces the buffer length. In LAN environment, the basic SDCC scheme offers very good performance. The maximum and the mean buffer length remain below 100 cells. In MAN and WAN environments, the ESDCC scheme with 4 RM cells in each VC offer adequate performance. The comparison between the rate-based congestion control schemes showed that the SDCC and ES-

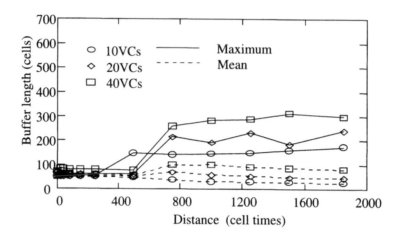

Figure 9: Buffer length versus the distance for ESDCC-4 scheme.

DCC schemes have a better behavior than existing schemes. In future, we plan to implement the proposed scheme in a real environment.

Acknowledgment.

The authors would like to thank Japan Society for the Promotion of Science (JSPS) for awarding Dr. Leonard Barolli a Post-doctor Fellowship.

Bibliography

1)   F. Bonomi and K. W. Fendick, "The Rate-Based Flow Control Framework for the Available Bit Rate ATM Services", *IEEE Network*, Vol. 9, No.2, pp. 25–39 (1995).

2)   M. Hluchyj and N. Yin, "On Closed-loop Rate Control for ATM Networks", *Proc. INFOCOM'94*, pp. 99–108 (1994).

3)   P. Newman, "Backward Explicit Congestion Notification for ATM Local Area Networks", *Proc. IEEE GLOBECOM'93*, Vol. 2, pp. 719–723 (1993).

4)   K. Y. Siu and H. Y. Tzeng, "Adaptive Proportional Rate Control for ABR service in ATM Networks", *Proc. IEEE INFOCOM'95*, pp. 529–535 (1995).

5)   A. Koyama, L. Barolli, S. Mirza and S.Yokoyama, "An Adaptive Rate-Based Congestion Control Scheme for ATM Networks", *Proc. ICOIN-12*, pp. 14–19 (1998).

6)   ATM Forum, "ATM User-Network Interface Specification Ver. 3", *Prentice Hall*, (1993).

4

On LLR Routing in Circuit-Switched Networks

Huang-Leng Chang

Ren-Hung Hwang

National Chung-Cheng University, Taiwan, R.O.C.

ABSTRACT

In the circuit-switching literature, the Least Loaded Routing (LLR) concept has been shown to be very simple and efficient. However, there is no unique definition for the "least busy" path. In this paper, we examine six ways of defining the least busy path and a random policy. The performance of these policies is evaluated via both simulation and analysis. Our numerical results show that all policies, include the random policy, have almost the same performance under most of the network configurations. Only under extremely low traffic load conditions, the difference between the policies becomes significant. However, the magnitude of the difference is still very small (about 0.001). Therefore, we conclude that how to select the alternate path does not affect the performance of LLR-based routing algorithms significantly. Instead, we found that the trunk reservation level affects the performance of LLR-based routing algorithms significantly.

1 Introduction

Due to the advance of switching technology, it has become feasible to implement sophisticated routing algorithms in the modern telephone network to minimize the network blocking probability. In particular, since the early 1980's, considerable research has focused on the design of adaptive routing algorithms which select a route for a call based on the state of the network at the time of call-arrival. Among these adaptive routing algorithms, algorithms based on the Least Loaded Path Routing(LLR) concept have been shown to be very simple and efficient. The LLR-based algorithms try to route an incoming call to the direct link first. If the call is blocked (because of no free circuits), the "least busy" path is then tried.

Although the LLR routing concept seems to have been well defined, there is no unique definition for the "least busy" path. For example, in [1], the "least busy" path is defined as the alternate path that has the maximum number of free circuits (MFC). In [2], the "least busy" path is defined as the path that has the minimum occupancy. Yet, in [3], the "least busy" path is selected at random, with selection probabilities proportional to the residual capacity of all candidate paths. To our knowledge, no research effort has been made to show which of these definitions yields the best performance.

In LLR-based routing algorithms, trunk reservation was introduced to prevent too many calls carried on alternate paths. In this paper, based on the Markov decision theory, we propose an algorithm that will set the trunk reservation level adaptively, dependent on the offered traffic to the link. In our simulation results, we will show that the proposed algorithm is able to find the optimal trunk reservation level under various traffic conditions.

Seven routing algorithms are studied in this paper. They differ from each other in the way how they select an alternate path as the "least busy" path. Our simulation results show that these seven algorithms yield almost the same performance under both symmetric and asymmetric networks. Based on these simulation results, we then form a conjecture that with the proper setting of trunk reservation levels, different LLR-based algorithms can yield almost the same performance.

In order to verify our conjecture, both mathematical models and simulations are developed to evaluate the performance of three algorithms: random, MFC, and M^2. M^2 was proposed in [4] and showed to yield better performance than MFC. We find that the analytical results agree with the simulation results very well when blocking probability is not too small (larger than 0.01). Furthermore, the performance of MFC, M^2, and random is very competitive. However, when the blocking probability is less than 0.01, the analytical model tends to underestimate the blocking probability by several orders of magnitude. Our simulation results indicate that although MFC and M^2 yield better performance than the random algorithm when blocking probability is very small, the magnitude of the difference between the performance of these algorithms is not as significant as predicated by the analytical models.

This observation is slightly different from the results of [2] in which the authors, based on analytical results, claimed that the random algorithm (called ABLA-2 in [2]) yields a much worse performance than MFC (called ABLA in [2]) when blocking probability is less than 0.01. This observation is also contradictory to the results shown in [4] in which the authors showed that the M^2 routing algorithm yielded a better performance than the MFC policy. However, we will show that the improvement is insignificant in large networks with large link capacity.

The remainder of the paper is organized as follows. In section 2, we describe the network model and define the routing problem. Section 3 describes the algorithm for setting the optimal trunk reservation level on a link. In section 4, seven routing algorithms are proposed. The performances of these routing algorithms are compared in section 5. Section 6 concludes our study and discusses some of our future work.

2   Network Model and Problem Definition

We model a circuit-switched network as a fully connected, undirected graph. For a N-node network, there are $N(N-1)/2$ Origin-Destination pairs and $N(N-1)/2$

links. Each link is associated with a link capacity, C_ℓ.

The routing problem of circuit-switched networks is defined as follows. Upon a call arrives at an O-D pair, the routing algorithm either routes a call to a path or blocks the call. If the call is routed to a path, a circuit on each link of the path is reserved for the call. The goal of routing is to find a "good" path to route the call such that the call blocking probability can be minimized.

One of the most commonly used routing algorithms in circuit-switched networks is the Least Loaded Path Routing (LLR) algorithm. When a call arrives to the network, following steps are performed by LLR routing algorithms:

1. First try to set up the call on the direct path, i.e., the direct link that connects the source node to the destination.

2. If there is no free circuit available on the direct path, route the call to the least busy alternate path among the candidate alternate paths.

3. If there is no candidate path can be selected, block the call.

The trunk reservation level on a link is a threshold used to restrict the usage of the alternate traffic. An alternate path is considered as a candidate path only if its current occupancy does not exceed the threshold. In the next section, we describe a near optimal algorithm for setting trunk reservation level on a link.

3   Near Optimal Trunk Reservation Level

The optimal trunk reservation problem has been studied in [5, 6]. In this paper, we solve the optimal trunk reservation problem based on Markov decision theory, as proposed in [5]. However, we formulate the Markov decision process slightly different from that of [5] and, thus, obtain a different set of expressions for computing the optimal trunk reservation level.

Let us formally define the trunk reservation level first. Let t_ℓ be the trunk reservation level for link ℓ such that an alternate call can be carried on link ℓ only if the current occupancy of link ℓ, x_ℓ, is less than $C_\ell - t_\ell$. We also define the "available" capacity on link ℓ to be $C_\ell - t_\ell - x_\ell$.

Calls offered to a link are classified into two types: direct calls and alternate calls. In order to make the problem tractable, following assumptions are made: (1) a call carried on an alternate path with two links is assumed to behave like two independent calls; (2) the reward for carrying a call on an alternate path is evenly distributed to each link of the path; (3) both direct calls and alternate calls arrive to any link ℓ according to a Poisson process with rate λ_1^ℓ and λ_2^ℓ, respectively.

Based on these assumptions, the optimal trunk reservation problem is formulated as a Markov decision process on each link. Let $r_1 = 1$ be the link reward for carrying a direct call and $r_2 = 0.5$ be the link reward for carrying an alternate call. Let us focus on link ℓ, let π be a trunk reservation policy which sets the trunk reservation level to t_ℓ^π. That is, define $\pi : X \to \{0, 1\}$ where $X = \{0, ..., C_\ell\}$ is the set of all feasible states and $\pi(x)$ is the action taken by policy π for an incoming alternate call when the link occupancy is x. If $\pi(x) = 0$, the incoming alternate call is rejected. Otherwise, the alternate call is accepted. Specifically,

$$\pi(x) = \begin{cases} 1 & \text{if } x < C_\ell - t_\ell^\pi, \\ 0 & \text{otherwise.} \end{cases}$$

Let $q(x, \pi(x))$ be the revenue loss rate when the Markov decision process is in state x and action $\pi(x)$ has been chosen for an incoming alternate call. Define

$$q(x, \pi(x)) = \begin{cases} \frac{1}{2}\lambda_1^\ell & \pi(x) = 0, \\ 0 & \text{otherwise.} \end{cases}$$

Now we can define the expected revenue loss for policy π. We only consider the infinite horizon problem with no reward discounting case [5]. Since all trunk reservation policies are stationary and completely ergodic, the expected revenue loss for a policy π, $V_x(t, \pi)$, is given by [7]:

$$V_x(t, \pi) = g(\pi)t + v(x, \pi)$$

where $g(\pi)$ is called the loss rate of policy π and $v(x, \pi)$ is the relative value of state x under policy π.

An optimal policy, π^*, is the policy such that $V_x(t, \pi^*) = \min_\pi \{V_x(t, \pi)\}$ for all x. According to Markov decision theory, an optimal policy can be found by a policy iteration procedure based on the following iteration cycle [7]:

- **Value Determination Step:** for a given policy during the ith iteration, $\pi^{(i)}$, solve the following set of equations

$$g(\pi^{(i)}) = 0 + \sum_{j=1}^{2} \lambda_j^\ell (v(1, \pi^{(i)}) - v(0, \pi^{(i)})),$$

$$g(\pi^{(i)}) = 0 + \sum_{j=1}^{2} \lambda_j^\ell (v(x+1, \pi^{(i)}) - v(x, \pi^{(i)}))$$
$$\qquad\qquad -i(v(x, \pi^{(i)}) - v(x-1, \pi^{(i)})), \quad 0 < x < C_\ell - t_\ell^{\pi^{(i)}},$$

$$g(\pi^{(i)}) = \frac{1}{2}\lambda_2^\ell + \lambda_1^\ell (v(x+1, \pi^{(i)}) - v(x, \pi^{(i)}))$$
$$\qquad\qquad -i(v(x, \pi^{(i)}) - v(x-1, \pi^{(i)})), \quad C_\ell - t_\ell^{\pi^{(i)}} \le x < C_\ell,$$

$$g(\pi^{(i)}) = \lambda_1^\ell + \frac{1}{2}\lambda_2^\ell - C_\ell (v(C_\ell, \pi^{(i)}) - v(C_\ell - 1, \pi^{(i)})), \qquad (4.1)$$

for all relative values $v(x, \pi^{(i)})$ and policy loss rate $g(\pi^{(i)})$.

Solutions to the set of equations (4.1), in terms of $\mathcal{W}(x) = v(x+1, \pi^{(i)}) - v(x, \pi^{(i)})$, are given as follows. For convenience, we omit $\pi^{(i)}$ in our notations.

$$g = E(\bar{\lambda}, C_\ell)(\lambda_1^\ell + \frac{1}{2}\lambda_2^\ell + C_\ell \cdot f(C_\ell - 1)),$$

$$\mathcal{W}(x) = \frac{g}{\bar{\lambda}_x E(\bar{\lambda}, x)} - f(x), \quad 0 \le x < C_\ell,$$

where

$$\bar{\lambda}_x = \begin{cases} \lambda_1^\ell + \lambda_2^\ell & \text{if } 0 \leq x < C_\ell - t_\ell, \\ \lambda_1^\ell & \text{if } C_\ell - t_\ell \leq x < C_\ell, \end{cases}$$

$$E(\bar{\lambda}, x) = \frac{\frac{1}{x!} \prod_{j=0}^{x-1} \bar{\lambda}_j}{\sum_{n=0}^{x} \frac{1}{n!} \prod_{j=0}^{n-1} \bar{\lambda}_j},$$

and the function $f(x)$ is defined as follows:

$$f(x) = \begin{cases} 0 & \text{if } 0 \leq x < C_\ell - t_\ell, \\ \frac{r_2 \lambda_2^\ell + x \cdot f(x-1)}{\lambda_1^\ell} & \text{if } C_\ell - t_\ell \leq x < C_\ell, \end{cases}$$

- **Policy Improvement Step:** find the policy, which will be used for the next iteration, that minimizes the right hand side of equations (4.1) for each state x using the relative values obtained from the previous step. Equivalently, the improved trunk reservation policy is to set a trunk reservation level such that

$$\mathcal{W}(C_\ell - t_\ell^{\pi^{(i+1)}} - 1) \leq 0.5 < \mathcal{W}(C_\ell - t_\ell^{\pi^{(i+1)}})$$

Initially, let $t_\ell^{\pi^0} = 0$. The iteration procedure then iterates until the policy obtained in the policy improvement step is equivalent to the previous iteration policy.

4 Routing Policies

In this section, we examine six policies for selecting the least busy alternate path and a random policy.

- **Maximum Free Capacity (MFC)**
  Define the available capacity of an alternate path to be the minimum of the available capacities of the two links of the alternate path. Let us denote the available capacity of the ith alternate path by F_i. The alternate path which has the maximum available capacity in the candidate set is selected as the least busy path.

- **Proportional to Free Capacity (PFC)**
  In this policy, alternate paths are selected at random, with selection probabilities proportional to the available capacity of all candidate paths. That is, the least busy path is chosen randomly with probability proportional to the path's available capacity. For example, the probability for choosing the ith alternate path is $F_i / \sum_{j=1}^{m} F_j$, where m is the total number of alternate paths.

- **Minimum State (MS)**
  The MS policy defines the degree of busy of an alternate path as the number of busy circuits of the path. The number of busy circuits of a path is the maximum of the number of busy circuits of the links of the path. The least busy path is defined as the alternate path with minimum number of busy circuits.

- **Minimum Traffic Load (MTL)**
  Let us define the traffic load of a link as current occupancy divided by the link capacity and the traffic load of a path as the maximum of the traffic load of the links of the path. The MTL policy defines the least busy path as the path with minimum traffic load.

- **Proportional to Traffic Load (PTL)**
  As in the PFC policy, the PTL policy also selects the least busy path randomly, with selection probability inversely proportional to the traffic load. However, the selection probability of an alternate path is defined as follows. Let P_i be the traffic load of the ith alternate path in the set of candidate routes. Let $\bar{P}_i = 1 - P_i$. The least busy path is then selected randomly with probability proportional to $\bar{P}_i$.

- M^2
  This policy differs form the MFC policy only when there are more than one alternate path have the same maximum number of available capacity. In such a case, M^2 chooses the path that has the minimum number of total occupied capacity, which is the sum of busy circuits of the links on that path. If there are more than one alternate path that have the same total occupied capacity, an alternate path is randomly selected.

- **Random**
  The random policy selects the least busy path randomly from the set of candidate alternate paths, independent of the current state of each path.

5   Numerical Results

In this section, the performance of the routing policies is evaluated via analytical models and simulations. The analytical models for MFC, M^2, and random policies can be found in [2], [1], [8], respectively. The numerical results presented are based on three network configurations: (1) 10-node symmetric network with all O-D pairs have the same arrival rates; (2) 10-node asymmetric network with all O-D pairs have the same arrival rates; (3) 10-node asymmetric network in which the arrival rate of an O-D pair is proportional to the capacity of the direct link. The detailed link capacity assignment for the asymmetric network is given in [8]. In all simulations, the arrival process of each O-D pair is assumed to be a Poisson process and the call holding time of each call is assumed to be exponentially distributed.

We first conduct the sensitivity analysis of the trunk reservation level. Figure 1 shows the effect of trunk reservation level on the performance of MFC under the first configuration. The vertical lines about each point in the figure indicate the 95 percent confidence interval. From this figure, we can observe that the performance of MFC is very sensitive to the setting of trunk reservation level, which should be set according to the arrival rate. We can also observe that the proposed algorithm is able to find the optimal trunk reservation level under most of the traffic conditions.

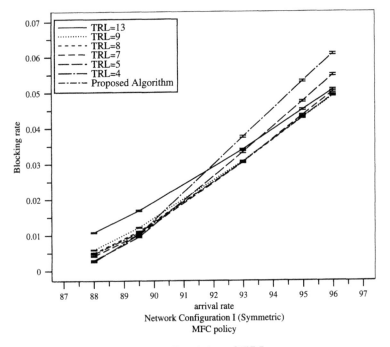

Figure 1: Sentivity of TRL

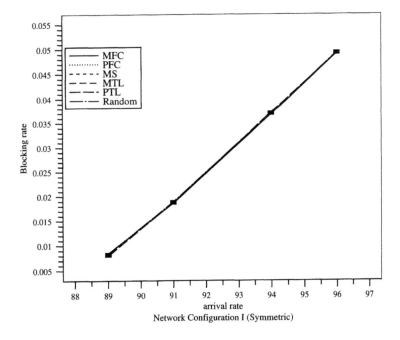

Figure 2: Performance of six LLRalgorithms

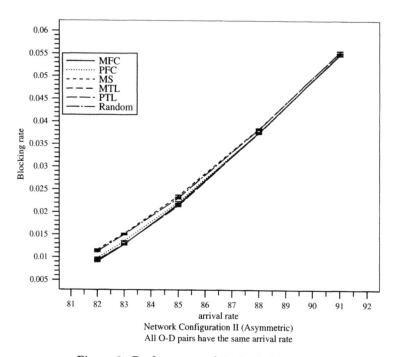

Figure 3: Performance of six LLRalgorithms

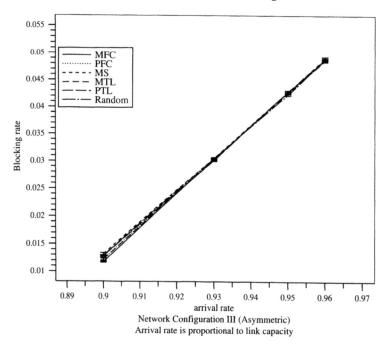

Figure 4: Performance of six LLRalgorithms

Figures 2, 3, and 4 show the performance of six routing policies. As we can see that all policies have almost the same performance, except that the MS and random policies perform slightly worse than the other four policies under the second network configuration. From these figures, we observe that how to select a path as the least busy path does not affect the performance of LLR routing algorithms significantly.

Let us compare the performance of the M^2 policy with that of the MFC policy, which is shown in figure 5. In [4], the authors proposed the M^2 policy and claimed that it outperforms the MFC policy. However, such a conclusion was drawn from analytical results based on very small networks with small trunk size. We are interested to see whether M^2 also outperforms MFC under large networks with large trunk sizes. As shown in figure 5, M^2 and MFC yield almost the same performance in a symmetric network with reasonable trunk size.

Table 1: Some mismatches of simulation results and analytical results.

(C_ℓ, m, λ, r)	MFC		Random	
	Simulation	Analysis	Simultaion	Analysis
(120, 20, 107, 6)	2.260146e-04	1.044028e-07	1.133258e-03	8.398794e-05
(120, 8, 104, 1)	3.147895e-05	5.956085e-12	7.097741e-03	3.249820e-10
(120, 8, 105, 2)	1.538443e-04	1.931460e-09	1.838663e-03	1.597586e-07
(120, 8, 106, 3)	9.542240e-04	2.651917e-07	2.858687e-03	4.871182e-05

Analytical models were developed in [4] and [2] to predict the performance of M^2 and MFC policies under symmetric networks. In [2], the authors concluded that the MFC policy outperforms the random policy under low traffic load by several order of magnitude, based on analytical results. In the following, we present the performance of the three policies based on analytical models. Figure 6 and 7 compare the analytical results with the simulation results for the MFC and random policies, respectively. We can see that the analytical results match the simulations results reasonably well if trunk reservation level is not too small. Figure 8 compares the performance of MFC and M^2 based on analytical models. As we can observe that they yield almost the same performance, as indicated by simulation results.

Finally, let us compare the simulation results with analytical results under extremely low blocking probabilities. In [2], based on analytical results, the authors found that the MFC outperforms the random policy by several order of magnitude. However, we find that the analytical results do not match the simulation results very well when blocking probability is very low. As shown in table 1, we can observe that when the blocking probability is less than 0.01, the analytical results may differ from the simulation results by several order of magnitude. Furthermore, the lower the blocking probability, the larger the difference. The inaccuracy of analytical model is due to some assumptions made. For example, the traffic overflowed from the direct link to alternate paths is assumed to be a Poisson process which is not true.

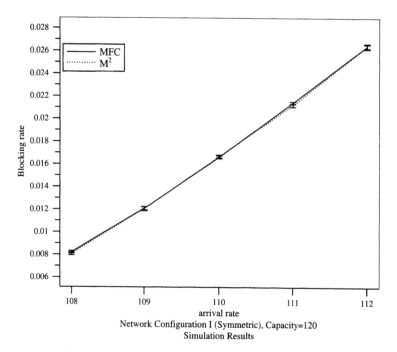

Figure 5: Performance of MFC and M^2 policies.

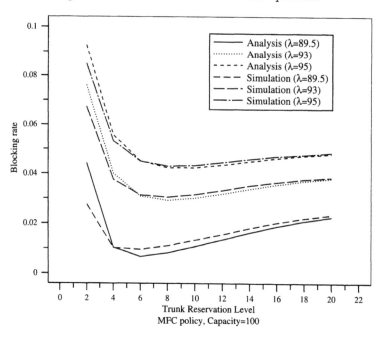

Figure 6: Analysis vs. simulationresults (MFC policy).

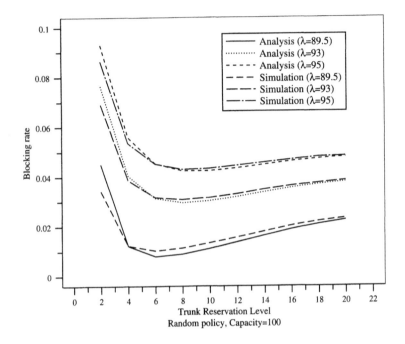

Figure 7: Analysis vs. simulationresults (Random policy).

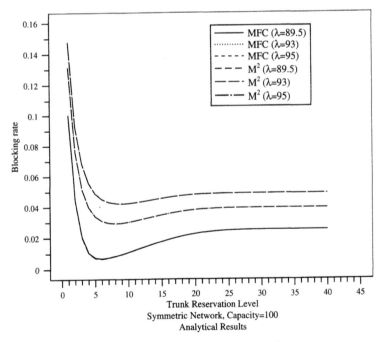

Figure 8: Performance of MFC and M^2 policies.

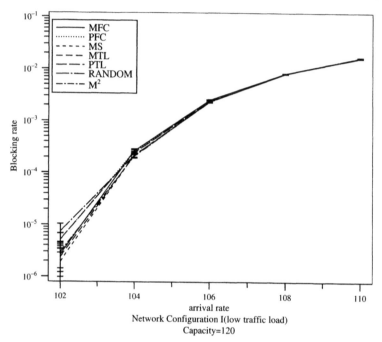

Figure 9: Performance of sevenLLR policies.

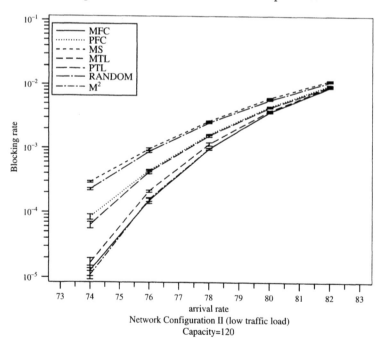

Figure 10: Performance of sevenLLR policies.

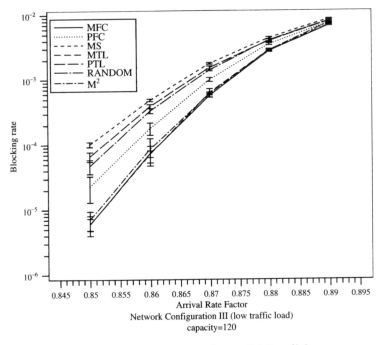

Figure 11: Performance of sevenLLR policies.

Although the analytical results exaggerate the performance of the MFC policy at extremely low blocking probability, the simulation results do show that the MFC policy outperforms the random policy. Therefore, we re-examine the performance of the six LLR-based policies and the random policy under extremely low traffic load conditions. Figures 9, 10, and 11 show the

results for different network configurations. In symmetric networks, as shown in figure 9, the performance difference among them is not very significant. However, in the asymmetric networks, as shown in figure 10 and 11, performance difference among them becomes more significant. Among these policies, the MFC policy consistently yields very good performance.

6   Conclusion

In this paper, we have studied six LLR-based routing policies and a random policy. From our simulation results and analytical results, we conclude that, with proper setting of trunk reservation level, how to select the least busy path does not affect the call blocking probability if the blocking probability is larger than 0.01. However, at very low blocking probability, the MFC and M^2 policy yield better performance. On the other hand, the performance of MFC and M^2 obtained from analytical models differs from the simulation results by several order of magnitude. Thus, the MFC policy may not outperform the random policy as much as reported in [2]. Finally, the

M^2 policy does not improve the MFC policy as significant as reported in [4].

Bibliography

1) Wong, E. and Yum, T.-S., "Maximum Free Circuit Routing in Circuit-Switched Networks," *proc. IEEE INFOCOM'90*, pp. 934–937, 1990.

2) Mitra, D., Gibbens, J. R.,and Huang, B. D., "State-Dependent Routing on Symmetric Loss Networks with Trunk Reservations, I," *IEEE Transactions on Communications*, vol. 41, pp. 400–411, Feb., 1993.

3) Cameron, W. H., Galloy, P., and Graham, W., "Report on the Toronto Advanced Routing Concpet Trial," in *Telecommunication Networks Planning Conference*, (Paris), 1980.

4) Wong, E., Yum, T.-S., and Chan, K. M., "Analysis of the M and M^2 Routings in Circuit-Switched Networks," *GLOBECOM'92*, pp. 1487–1492, Dec. 1992.

5) Key, P. B., "Optimal Control and Trunk Reservation in Loss Networks," *Probability in the Engineering and Informational Sciences*, vol. 4, pp. 203–242, 1990.

6) Nguyen, V., "On the Optimality of Trunk Reservation in Overflow Processes," *Probability in the Engineering and Informational Sciences*, vol. 5, pp. 369–390, 1991.

7) Howard, R. A., *Dynamic Programming and Markov Processes*. John Wiley & Sons, Inc., 1960.

8) Chang, H.-L., "On LLR Routing in Circuit-Switched Networks," Master's thesis, Department of Computer Science and Information Engineering, National Chung Cheng University, June 1997.

5

Backup Path Sharing for Survivable ATM Networks

Hoyoung Hwang

Sanghyun Ahn[*]

Yanghee Choi

Chong Sang Kim

Seoul National University, University of Seoul[*]

ABSTRACT

As survivability has become a critical issue in high-speed networks, it is highly needed to provide mechanisms to restore lost connections. This paper proposes a new backup restoration mechanism for ATM networks. Conventional backup recovery method provides fast and simple reaction to connection failure using predefined alternate routes and reserved spare bandwidth. However, it requires quite large spare resource redundancy and management cost to maintain backup connections. So far, the effort to improve the spare resource utilization efficiency in backup recovery methods is concentrated to optimal spare bandwidth allocation and sharing. In this paper, we consider backup route sharing as well as spare bandwidth sharing. The proposed shared backup route scheme provides a virtual backup network that can be shared by multiple working connections, rather than one backup path per working connection. The simulation results show that the new backup mechanism provides: 1) efficient spare resource utilization, 2) flexible and robust restoration path routing.

1 Introduction

In ATM networks, even a single link failure may cause an adverse effect on a large number of connections. For example, a single ATM link may contain a large number of virtual paths (VPs), and a VP, in turn, may contain a large number of virtual channels (VCs). This gives rise to a highly reliable mechanism to restore lost connections. We consider a VP as a basic restoration unit, since the VP concept has many advanced features such as enhanced network reliability, simple routing, fast switching, and multiplexing gain [2, 3]. The basic procedure of VP restoration follows three steps: failure detection, alternate VP setup, and traffic switching (from the failed VP to the alternate VP). The first and the last steps may be identical in

Restoration method	Dynamic	Backup
Resource overhead	low	high
Flexibility	high	low
Management cost	low	high
Message complexity	high	low
Restoration speed	slow	fast
Optimality	low	high

Table 1: Comparison of dynamic on-demand approach and predefined backup approach

most restoration schemes. Failure detection and propagation can be performed using OAM functions [1], and traffic switching is performed by updating the VPI field in the ATM cell header. The differences between restoration schemes are found in the second step; when and how to setup backup VPs.

To date, various restoration techniques have been proposed. According to the alternate VP setup policy in the second step, we can classify them into two main approaches: dynamic on-demand approach and predefined backup approach. There are trade-offs between these two approaches as shown in Table 1. The dynamic on-demand approach [4, 5, 8], provides high flexibility since all the possible alternate paths for a failed VP can be found by the distributed flooding mechanism, even against multiple links or nodes failure. However, it suffers from slow restoration speed and complex run-time operation that generates a large number of restoration messages. Therefore, the dynamic approach is generally applied to line (local) restoration rather than path (end-to-end) restoration. As illustrated in Figure 1, the path restoration provides more optimal solution than the line restoration.

The predefined backup approach [6, 7] provides fast and simple restoration since only traffic switching is performed at run-time while a backup VP with reserved bandwidth has already been established per each working VP. In addition, optimal end-to-end backup path can be preplanned using global network information. However, the backup approach has two main disadvantages that are opposite to the dynamic approach. First, it wastes spare resources reserved for backup connections which are in idle state in most cases. Second, it shows less flexibility against multiple failures. A predefined backup VP may be lost simultaneously with the working VP.

Until now, the effort to improve the performance of the backup restoration method is concentrated to reduce spare bandwidth requirement by optimal bandwidth allocation and sharing. Other resources including VPI has been less considered. Moreover, the inflexibility problem has not been solved, thus conventional backup methods cannot handle the simultaneous failure of a working VP and its backup VP. In this paper, we propose a new VP backup mechanism for ATM mesh networks that centers around the concept of *shared backup route*, a virtual backup

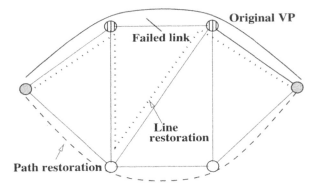

Figure 1: Line restoration and Path restoration

network that can be shared by multiple working VPs for restoration purposes. Our key idea is that the efficient spare resource utilization can be obtained by backup path sharing as well as spare bandwidth sharing. Also, the flexibility problem can be solved by the backup path sharing.

This paper is organized as follows. Section 2 gives a brief review on the previous works to enhance the performance of backup restoration techniques. Section 3 describes the conceptual model of backup path sharing and the restoration protocol. Section 4 presents simulation results to show the effectiveness of the proposed mechanism. Section 5 is the summary of our work.

2   Previous Works

To reduce the large overhead cost for backup recovery, Kawamura et al. [7] proposed a shared bandwidth allocation scheme for backup VPs. This scheme exploits an important feature of ATM networks, separation of path setup and bandwidth allocation. In this scheme, backup paths are established with zero bandwidth, and the required spare bandwidth is allocated during restoration procedure. Although several backup VPs may be routed along a same link, if they are not activated simultaneously, the spare bandwidth on the link can be shared by multiple backup VPs. This zero bandwidth allocation can largely reduce the spare bandwidth overhead. However, the number of backup paths and backup management overhead is the same as those of the dedicated bandwidth backup scheme.

To enhance the flexibility of backup recovery, Landegem et al. [11] proposed a multilink-based self-healing scheme. In their scheme, the cells of an ATM connection are distributed over several physical links. If a physical link supporting the multilink fails, the cells are distributed among the remaining physical links thus providing self-healing bandwidth. This scheme can support flexible restoration against multiple failures by increasing the load of the remaining physical links. However, very complex operations should be performed to setup multilink connections and to manage the

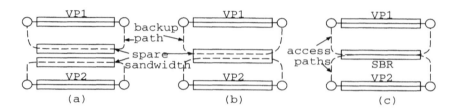

Figure 2: Spare bandwidth sharing and backup path sharing

proper cell order. Ahn [9] proposed sharable backup path scheme which accepts multiple backup connections in a single ring-like backup route. This scheme provides flexible line restoration against multiple link or node failure.

In this paper, we propose a new backup path sharing that supports end-to-end path restoration to achieve both spare resource efficiency and flexible backup path routing.

3 Backup Path Sharing

3.1 Conceptual model

Figure 2 shows our motivation considering resource sharing to achieve end-to-end VP restoration with low resource overhead and flexible backup path routing.

Conventional dedicated bandwidth backup scheme, shown in Figure 2 (a), establishes one backup VP per each working VP and allocates same amount of bandwidth to both. In this scheme, the required bandwidth and path management overhead are twice of those in working VP networks.

The shared bandwidth backup scheme, shown in Figure 2 (b), also establishes one backup path per each working VP. However, spare bandwidth on the path can be shared by multiple backup VPs. Thus, this scheme can largely reduce the bandwidth overhead. But, the backup path management overhead is the same as that of dedicated bandwidth backup scheme.

One step further, the backup path as well as the spare bandwidth can be shared by multiple VPs as shown in Figure 2 (c). There exists a shared backup route (SBR) with a preassigned path and spare bandwidth, and each VP end node establishes access paths to the shared backup route. The path and bandwidth on shared backup route can be used to restore any failed working VP. Thus, both spare bandwidth overhead and backup path management overhead can be reduced.

As an extension of the shared backup route, we can consider a backup network rather than 1:1 backup path as shown in Figure 3. There are three components: shared backup route (SBR), backup route server (BRS), and access path. vSBR is a collection of possible backup routes and available spare bandwidth that can be shared by multiple VPs for restoration purposes. The routes on SBR (also the access paths) are preestablished meta VPs that can be generated using the residual network. If

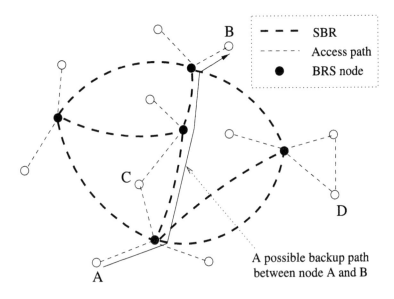

Figure 3: Shared Backup Route Example

a working VP fails, for example between node A and node B in Figure 3, then a backup VP is established by concatenating the two access paths from A and B via the most preferred route on SBR.

A BRS is a distributed server that performs SBR setup, reconfiguration, and backup route concatenation. There are a number of BRSs in a network, and each BRS has connections to adjacent BRSs along one or more possible routes. These connections between BRSs and the spare bandwidth on them construct SBR. A BRS can be thought as a switch node on SBR, and also an access point to SBR. BRSs perform the following functions.

- maintain BRS list in the network
- maintain access path list from VP end nodes
- make connections and routing table to other BRSs
- configure/reconfigure SBR
- activate (assign VPI/bandwidth) paths on SBR
- deactivate (release VPI/bandwidth) paths on SBR
- perform backup path selection on SBR
- join the backup path on SBR with access paths
- generate restoration confirm/fail mesasges

Access paths provide VP end nodes with spare routes to the appropriate BRSs. An access path should be disjoint with the working VP that would be restored. The number of access paths from a VP end node to SBR can be variable; a VP end node may have multiple access paths to different BRSs, or may have multiple access paths to a single BRS. Multiple connectivity is important to avoid simultaneous failures of

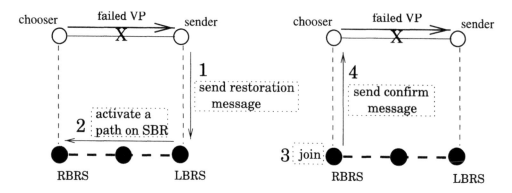

Figure 4: Basic restoration protocol

a working VP and the backup path.

This model provides a simpler backup architecture than the conventional 1:1 backup methods. Each VP end node has only several access paths to SBR rather than managing a backup VP for each working VP. Thus the number of backup connections is not proportional to the number of working VPs, but is dependent of the network diameter or the number of nodes. This feature enables a scalable backup architecture.

3.2 Restoration Procedure

VP restoration is performed semi-dynamically by a backup VP that is not predefined but determined after a failure. A backup VP is constructed by connecting the two access paths from the VP end nodes along a part of SBR. The main operation is joining the three already prepared parts (two access paths and a part of SBR). Therefore, though a backup VP is established on demand, the cost for searching the path and the bandwidth is low.

Upon a failure detection, the VP destination node becomes sender, and the originating node becomes chooser. We call the BRS accessed by the sender local BRS (LBRS), and the one accessed by the chooser remote BRS (RBRS). Figure 4 illustrates the following restoration protocol.

Phase 1: The sender activates an access path to LBRS and sends a restoration message. A restoration message contains information fields such as failed VPI, failed link ID, sender, chooser, LBRS, RBRS, and required bandwidth.

Phase 2: On receiving a restoration message, LBRS selects and activates an appropriate route on SBR and forwards the restoration message to RBRS. Then, join the activated path on SBR with the access path from the sender, which results in a seamless partial backup VP. If all the trials to activate a path to RBRS fail, LBRS sends a restoration fail message to the sender, which will initiate a new trial to other BRSs.

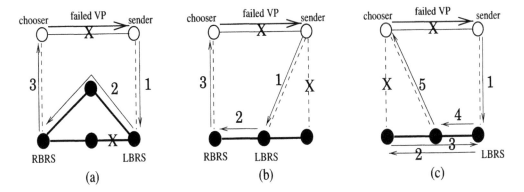

Figure 5: Restoration of multiple link failures

Phase 3: On receiving a restoration message, RBRS activates the access path to the chooser and join the access path with the partial backup VP, which results in complete backup VP. If the activation fails, RBRS sends a restoration fail message to LBRS and deactivates the backup path on SBR.

Phase 4: RBRS sends a restoration confirm message to the chooser along the access path. Then, the chooser performs traffic switching.

Fast restoration is performed by this protocol. Although this protocol consists of four phases, VP restoration is performed with one-way message transmission from the sender to the chooser.

Multiple failures can be handled with the restoration protocol. We can consider several different multiple link-failure cases. The working VP may be lost simultaneously with the preferred backup route on SBR, or one of the access paths from the sender or the chooser. In these cases, the backup VP can be established using another safe route on SBR as shown in Figure 5 (a), or via another safe access path as shown in Figure 5 (b) and (c). These alternatives are possible since a BRS has a routing table to other BRSs and a VP end node has multiple access paths to SBR. In case that the first trial to activate the most preferred route is failed, the second preferred route is tried. If all the trials fail, a restoration fail message is generated and sent back to the prior BRS or the sender, which initiates the alternate route selection. The extension of the protocol to node-failure cases is trivial since a node failure can be thought as a set of link failures.

4   Simulation

We performed simulations to see the feasibility and effectiveness of the proposed mechanism. The simulations were performed on two mesh topology networks as shown in Figure 6, one with 49 nodes and 84 links and the other with 11 nodes and 23 links.

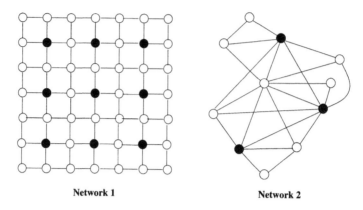

Network 1   Network 2

Figure 6: Example networks

Each working VP has integer bandwidth within a restricted range, 1 to 3 unit, and a disjoint backup VP is computed by shortest path algorithm.

First, we report the spare resource overhead and the backup path optimality to perform 100% restoration for any single link failure with number of working VPs, assuming infinite bandwidth on communication links. Figure 7 and 8 depict the spare bandwidth overhead for different numbers of primary VPs. Comparisons are performed for the three backup restoration schemes: the dedicated bandwidth backup scheme, the shared bandwidth backup scheme, and the shared backup route scheme (virtual backup network). The proposed mechanism shows a significant improvement of bandwidth efficiency up to 50% compared with dedicated bandwidth backup, and a marginal improvement up to 15% compared with the shared bandwidth backup. The gap becomes larger as the number of VPs grows.

Figure 9 and 10 show the backup VPI overhead that indicates the complexity of backup connections. We compared the proposed scheme with the conventional 1:1 backup. The VPI overhead is largely reduced up to 70% by using the shared backup route.

In Figure 11 and 12, we compared the backup path optimality described by the average hop-count between 1:1 backup and the proposed mechanism. The backup path generated by the proposed scheme shows a little bit longer but tolerable delay than that of the 1:1 backup, since a backup path via the SBR is generally longer than the shortest backup path without considering the SBR.

The simulation results tell that the resource efficiency of the shared backup ro ute scheme is better than that of the conventional 1:1 backup scheme. If we consider all the nodes as BRSs as an extreme case, then the shared backup route scheme produces identical result as that of the shared bandwidth backup sc heme. This means that the proposed mechanism can show at least the same overhead as shared bandwidth backup scheme. If carefully designed considering the number of BRSs and their locations, the shared backup route can provide better resource efficiency in mo st cases.

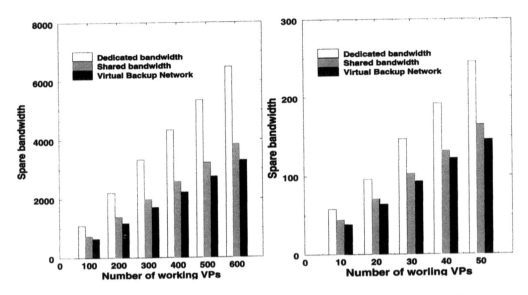

Figure 7: Bandwidth overhead: Network 1

Figure 8: Bandwidth overhead: Network 2

Double-failure cases	total	1	2	3	4	5
Number of failed VPs	3299	55	57	49	85	63
Conventional backup	94.9	83.6	89.4	85.7	63.5	65.0
Shared backup route	99.6	100	100	100	100	100

Table 2: Restoration ratio against double-link failures

Next, we report the restoration ratio of failed VPs in double-link-failure cases. We assumed that two links are failed simultaneously, and tried to restore the failed VPs first with predefined backup VPs and second with the shared backup r oute. 100 different cases were tested in 49 node networks under the assumption that th ere are 300 working VPs and 3-connectivity is provided for accessing SBR. As listed in Table 2, the proposed mechanism shows 99.6% restoration ratio on the average while the conventional backup mechanism shows 94.9%. In some selected cases (the two link failures are not far from each other), the conventional backup scheme showed 63% - 89% restoration ratio while the proposed scheme could find restoration routes for all the failed VPs.

5 Summary

The backup method provides simple, fast, and guaranteed VP restoration. However, it shows large resource overhead and inflexibility against multiple failures. Some

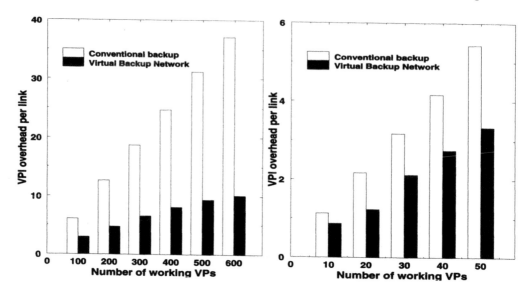

Figure 9: Connection overhead: Network 1

Figure 10: Connection overhead: Network 2

previous works achieve the performance improvement either on resource efficiency by spare bandwidth sharing, or on flexibility by using multi-link path or hybriding backup approach and dynamic approach. However few of them achieved both.

We propose a new restoration mechanism that provides backup network rather than 1:1 backup connections. The proposed mechanism provides several contributions. First, it provides an efficient way to share spare resources, backup paths as well as spare bandwidth, thus can reduce both spare bandwidth overhead and backup path management overhead. Second, it provides flexible backup path routing against multiple failure. There are several alternate routes to be selected on SBR and multiple access paths to SBR, thus the simultaneous failure of a working VP and its backup VP can be handled. Finally, it provides a simple and scalable backup architecture. The backup network with shared backup route maintains much smaller number of backup connections that is not proportional to the number of working VPs.

Bibliography

1)   ITU-T DRAFT Recommendation I.610, "B-ISDN operation and maintenance principles and functions" (1994).

2)   Sato, K., Hadama, H., and Tokizawa, I., "Network Reliability Enhancement with Virtual Path Strategy," *In Proceedings of GLOBECOM'90*, pp. 464–469 (1990).

3)   Ayanoglu, E. and Gitlin, R. D., "Broadband Network Restoration," *IEEE Communications Magazine*, Vol. 34, No. 7, pp. 110–119 (1996).

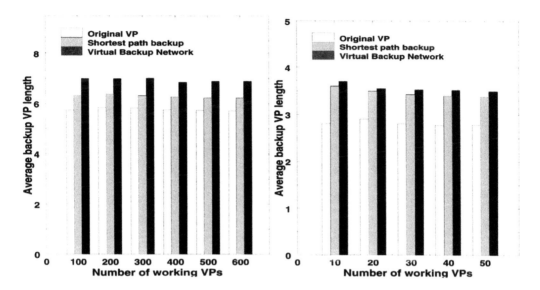

Figure 11: Backup path delay: Network 1

Figure 12: Backup path delay: Network 2

4) Grover, W. D., "The Selfhealing network: A fast distributed restoration technique for networks using digital cross-connect machines," *In Proceedings of GLOBECOM'87* pp. 1090–1095 (1987)

5) Lin, L. D., Zolfaghari, A., and Lusinan, B. "ATM Virtual Path Self-Healing Based on a New Path Restoration Protocol," *In Proceedings of GLOBECOM'94*, pp. 794–798 (1994)

6) Anderson, J., Doshi, B. T., Dravida, S., and Harshavardhana, P., "Fast Restoration of ATM Networks," *IEEE Journal of Selected Areas in Communications*, Vol. 12, No. 1, pp. 128–138 (1994)

7) Kawamura, R. and Tokizawa, I., "Self-healing Virtual Path Architecture in ATM Networks," *IEEE Communications Magazine*, Vol. 33, No. 9, pp. 72–79 (1995)

8) Fujii, H. and Yoshikai, N., "Restoration Message Transfer Mechanism and Restoration Characteristics of Double-Search Self-Healing ATM Network," *IEEE Journal on Selected Areas in Communications*, Vol. 12, No. 1, pp. 149–158 (1994)

9) Ahn, S., "A Fast VP Restoration Scheme using Ring-Shaped Sharable Backup VPs," *In Proceedings of GLOBECOM'97*, pp.1383–1387 (1997)

10) Murakami, K. and Kim, H. S., "Comparative Study on Restoration Schemes of Survivable ATM Networks," *In Proceedings of INFOCOM'97*, pp. 345–352 (1997)

11) Landegem, T. V., Vankwikelberge, P., and Vanderstraeten, H., "A Self-Hesling ATM Network Based on Multilink Principles," *IEEE Journal of Selected Areas in Communications*, Vol. 12, No. 1, pp. 139–148 (1994)

6

A Flexible Communication Architecture to Support Multimedia Services in High Speed Network

Jaesung Park, Sangheon Lee, Seungcheon Kim
†Junho Lee, Jaiyong Lee and Sangbae Lee

Department of Electronic Engineering, Yonsei University
†Department of Electronic Engineering Seoul National Polytechnic University

ABSTRACT

There have been research works on supporting *Quality of Service(QoS)* in a distributed multimedia systems. These researches can be categorized as follows; system platform, real-time operating system, transport protocol, communication architecture. In distributed multimedia environment, QoS must be guaranteed in end systems, but much less progress has been made in addressing these problems. As the processing power of end systems increases, most of the bottleneck occur in communication protocol, especially transport protocol. To meet an end-to-end QoS, overall QoS architectures must be integrated. In this paper, we propose a new QoS architecture and control mechanisms(group control, and media control) to guarantee an end-to-end QoS for distributed multimedia services. We also verify proposed architecture by applying them to a multimedia conferencing system in LAN.

1 Introduction

From early 1990s, there have been research works on supporting Quality of Service(QoS) in distributed multimedia environments. There has been considerable progress in the separate areas of Open Distributed Processing(ODP)[1], end systems[2] and network[3] to support QoS. In end-systems, most of the progress has been made in the areas of scheduling[4], flow synchronization[5] and transport support[6]. In networks, researches have focused on providing suitable traffic models[7] and service disciplines[8], as well as appropriate admission control and resource reservation protocols[9]. Meeting QoS is an end-to-end problem, but most of the researches address QoS from a provider's point of view and analyze network performance, failing to comprehensively address the QoS needs of applications.

As the processing power of end-systems increases, most of the bottleneck occurs in communication protocols. Current transport protocols, such as TCP, UDP, TP4, are designed for the text data applications such as e-mail, ftp. When applied to a real-time multimedia applications, these protocols cause some problems. For example, TCP supports only one-to-one communication service. It doesn't have the concept of the multicast, and accordingly, multicast group management. Also, TCP supports only fully-reliable data transfer. It doesn't care end-to-end transfer delay. Because multimedia streams, such as audio and video stream, can tolerate error to some extent, it is not appropriate to use TCP to deliver real-time stream data. Moreover, data control mechanism is determined by a protocol, applications must follow the embedded mechanisms. It ignores the application's characteristics.

Current state of QoS provision in architectural framework can be summarized as follows. First, each multimedia service has its own requirements, but most of the current interfaces do not support QoS configuration. For example, in socket interfaces user can specify only local address and port, remote address and port. It needs interfaces by which users can specify their own QoS requirements. Second, as new applications emerge and they require their own QoS requirements, it is impossible for a fixed data control mechanism predetermined by a protocol to meet the required QoS effectively. It needs to configure data control mechanisms according to user's requirements. Third, to support QoS optimally, it needs several functions such as QoS negotiation and re-negotiation, QoS monitoring, QoS maintenance, but these functions are not supported by most of current communication protocols. Fourth, there is lack of an overall QoS architecture that integrates separate functions, mechanisms, policies for multimedia communications.

In this paper, we propose a new QoS architecture and control mechanisms(group control, and media control) to support an end-to-end QoS for a distributed multimedia services. We also verify proposed QoS architecture and control mechanisms by applying them to a multimedia conferencing system in high speed LAN.

This paper is organized as follows; we present a general QoS principles in section 2. In section 3, we present a new QoS architecture that can support end-to-end QoS for distributed multimedia services. In section 4, we present group and media control mechanisms-group control, media control, and verify the proposed mechanism by applying them to a multimedia conferencing system in high speed LAN. In section 5, conclusions follow.

2   General QoS Principles

Because each multimedia application has its own QoS requirements, multimedia system must provide a method for a user to configure his own QoS requirements to reflect the features of an application. QoS mapping which translates user's QoS requirements into communication protocol's parameters is necessary. In designing a QoS architecture, we consider the following principles.

2.1 QoS Specification

A QoS specification can be classified into two levels; user level and protocol level. User level QoS specification is somewhat abstract. Users can specify the type of service, management policy, and application characteristics. They do not specify control mechanisms and the exact threshold values of performance parameters. User level QoS specification is translated into protocol level QoS specification by a configuration entity. This process is called QoS mapping. QoS mapping occurs in two ways. Configuration entity converts user specified service type into flow performance parameter values, such as delay, jitter, frame rate etc. and selects the adequate functions from a function pool to make an optimal protocol per flow. A management entity translates user specified management policy and application characteristics into actual management mechanisms and uses them to meet the requested QoS. We can categorize service type according to applications, because of the error tolerance and performance parameter controllability of multimedia data[10].

Generally, there are more than three participants in multimedia applications such as teleconferencing, computer supported cooperative work(CSCW). If there are more than three participants in an application, we must manage the participant group. Because the feature of a group is one of important characteristics of an application which affects the behavior of an application, a user shall specify group features.

2.2 QoS Mechanism

To meet a requested QoS, appropriate control mechanisms are required. In LANs, especially where resources can't be reserved, we can't guarantee requested QoS when congestion occurs. As mentioned previously, each multimedia service has its own requirements, a fixed control mechanism predetermined by an underlying protocol can't satisfy various user's requirements. A control mechanism must be dynamically configured according to the user level QoS specification. Because continuous media data can tolerate errors to some extent, and there are some differences between user perception QoS and parameter level QoS, we can control performance parameters without user perception QoS degradation.

A control mechanism is instantiated by a management entity. A management entity can be classified according to the time it applies to, and objects it manages. In multimedia applications, management entity must manage media flows and user groups. A media manager performs call admission control, environment status monitoring, and flow QoS management. A user requested QoS specfication is translated into an underlying layer's QoS specification by a configuration entity. A media management entity decides if a requested call can be accepted by comparing its QoS requirements with the monitoring results at the time the call is requested. After call setup, media management entity monitors whether a requested QoS is guaranteed at every specific interval. If it is violated for a certain amount of time, media management entity starts data control mechanism to handle the violation according to the specified management policy. Media stream is transmitted in packets, but it is not effective to start data control mechanism at every time violation packets are detected. Because it takes processing and adaptation time to use data control mechanism, if we apply data control mechanism to every violation packet, it may deteriorate system performance.

3   A Flexible QoS Architecture

In past years, protocol designers have little QoS concept, they just considered reliable data transfer. Yet, as we get to meet various kinds of application and each application has different requirements, we need a method by which we can configure different QoS. Also, with the previous one fixed policy or mechanism, various QoS requirements can't be satisfied. Therefore, the optimized policy or mechanism for each QoS requirements should be dynamically configured.

In this paper, we suggest a new QoS architecture, which mainly consists of the management part, the configuration part, and data transfer part as shown in figure 1.

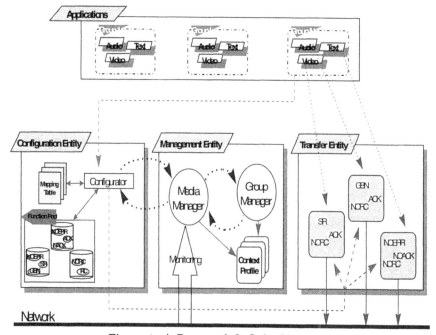

Figure 1: A Proposed QoS Architecture

Like a multimedia conferencing system and CSCW, recent multimedia communication is, by nature, multicast communication rather than one-to-one. So, a group management function is highly important. The group management functions include the role management for participant authentication and group attribute, and the status change management of participants' group. A group attribute determines a group management function, and affects data transfer mechanisms. The roles of participants and their relationship also affect the mechanism. For example, a key member's reception quality degradation should be treated in advance than that of normal participants. Each entity can run in parallel.

4 Management Mechanisms

To meet an end-to-end QoS, it needs management mechanisms. The management entity can be divided according to objects it manages; group, and media. A group manager controls participant groups. It is related with overall management principles. According to the user specified management policy, a media manager monitors the requested QoS, and controls data sending rate to meet the requested QoS. We propose a group management mechanism and media management mechanism to meet an end-to-end QoS. To verify management mechanisms and, the QoS architecture proposed in the previous section, we implement the multimedia conferencing system in LAN.

4.1 Group Manager

A group is classified according to its configuration char acteristics, duration period and, *Active Group Integ rity(AGI)*[12] condition. AGI condition specifies the minimum number of participants, key members who must participate in the conference and so on. It is the criteria, which determines for a service to sustain for a while, or to be terminated immediately when something illegal happens. A group manager checks if AGI conditions are met at connection setup time, and at every group state transitions time. For example, when participants join or leave a group, and if AGI conditions are violated, group manager takes an adequate measure according to *integrity condition(IC)*[12]. If IC is hard, data transfer is stopped. Connection is released and an application is terminated. On the contrary, if IC is soft, only data transfer is terminated. After some period, if AGI conditions are met again, data transfer is restarted. A group can also be classified according to the degree of membership control. A group is called open, if everyone can join a conference without any explicit control. On the contrary, a group is called closed, if there is a strict mem bership control.

In conferences, participants can be classified according to their roles: manager and participant. A manager's group manager coordinates a conference according to AGI con ditions. Figure 2 shows a state transition diagram of a group manager. If IC is soft, normal state transition is as follows. After receipt of conference creation request, group manager waits for participants' replies. If AGI con dition is met, a group manager constitute an active group profile which records participant's information, and allo cate an unique identifier to the conference. After this, a group manager manages the group using the identifier. Users can join and/or leave a group during data transfer phase. In tightly-coupled conferences, a manager checks AGI condition at every time a user leaves and/or joins a group, but in loosely-coupled conference any members can participate in a conference at any time. This attribute is specified

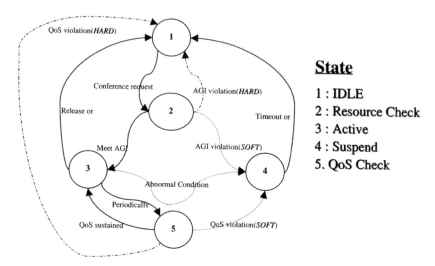

Figure 2: State Transition Diagrem of a Group Manager

at the conference setup time in the argument attribute. We can verify proposed state transition diagrams by reachability analysis mechanism[14]. Because there are only control flows in proposed state transition diagrams, we can verify it in finite time. As a result of reachability analysis, we can verify that there are no dead-lock, and live-lock at any states, and there is no unused state transi tion.

4.2   Media Manager

A media manger manages data transfer to meet an end-to- end QoS. It performs environmental status monitoring, and data rate control. The media manager performs call admission control using monitoring information such as host capacity and network load. After call admission, media manager checks if the requested QoS is met by comparing reported performance parameters with the requested performance parameters at every specified interval. If the requested QoS is violated for some time, media manger controls data sending rate to meet the end- to-end QoS. Figure 3 shows the architecture of the media manager

4.2.1   Call Admission Control Mechanism

Applications such as teleconferencing require the establishment of multiple participants, multiple sessions. To orchestrate the multiparty multimedia connections, we propose a connection management scheme. The emphasis of our scheme is to provide transmission across LANs such as Ethernet that cannot guarantee the reliable communication bandwidths. Ethernet protocol has some identical transfer-delay

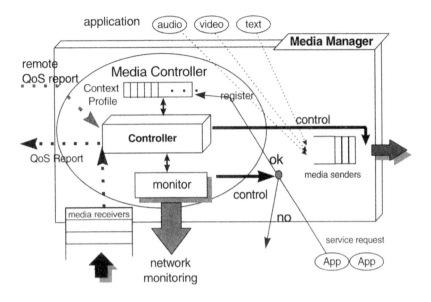

Figure 3: An architecture of the Media Manager

characteristics[15]. This protocol is affected tremendously by overall network load. As the network load is increased, relatively more collisions take places and the performance deteriorates to relatively low throughputs. Some experimental analysis shows that efficient transmission can be provided under 40% of its maximum transmission ability[15]. So, network overload can be prevented, with the management of participation. At this point of view, we consider a call admission control mechanism. Before starting new communication session, the current network load should be examined by monitoring underlying network. A communication session can be admitted only when overall network load is under 40% of maximum transmission throughput. With this mechanism we can prevent network overload and guarantee real-time requirements.

4.2.2 Media Control Mechanism

To meet an end-to-end QoS, the media manager controls data sending rate whenever there is QoS degradation. At every predetermined interval, the media manager checks if the requested QoS is met. If the requested QoS is not guaranteed, the media manager controls data rate. In general, video stream has higher bit rates than audio, furthermore audio stream has higher priority than video stream in multimedia conference. If there is QoS degradation due to network congestion, it is more effective to reduce video data sending rate than audio data sending rate.

In multiparty environment, each participant may have different capabilities. In multimedia conference, it is not desirable to sacrifice QoS of many participants for an inferior participant. How to control data rate is affected by the group characteristics. Because participants play different roles in a conference, a key member's QoS must be met in advance.

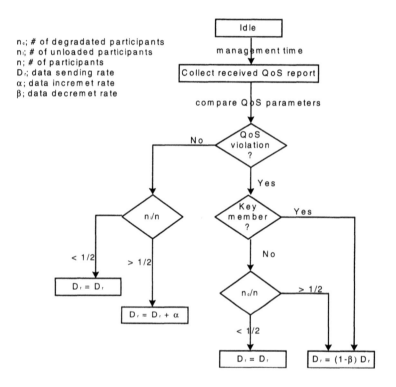

Figure 4: data Sending Rate Control Algorithm

A proposed data sending rate control algorithm is described in figure 4. We must consider AGI condition and receiver's QoS report to decide whether to control data rate or not. The decision is made at the manager side.

4.2.3   Verification: Desktop Conferencing System

To verify the proposed QoS architecture and management mechanisms, we implement the multimedia conferencing system in LAN. Table 3 shows the Development environment.

We select received frame rate and end-to-end delay as video performance parameters. A real-time multimedia conference service requires a received frame rate to

Table 1: Desktop Conferencing System Development Environment

End Host	Sparc 2(3), Sparc20(1)
Operating System	Solaris 2.3
Audio Codec	Sun audio board
Video Codec	Parallax board
Network Protocol	IP multicast
Network medium	10B-ethernet,100B-Fast Ethernet

be at least 5 frames/sec, and average end-to-end delay to be in the range of 200-300ms[10].

Image size varies as window size and compression algorithm used. There are two ways to control video bit rate. One is to control image resolution, and the other is to control video frame rate. Using parallax video board, we can control image resolution by varying Q factor. The more we increase Q factor, the higher image resolution is. We use image window size of 160x180 pixels in the experiment.

4.2.4 Empirical Results

Image size changes as window size varies. We used window size of 120x160 in which case average image size was 5495 bytes. End-to-end transfer delay is measured at media playback time. To increase network load, we generate 30 bytes packets using "ping" utility at every 3 second. Since there are time-random variance in network load, all the experiments were performed simultaneously to guarantee the fair comparison.

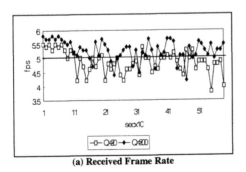

(a) Received Frame Rate

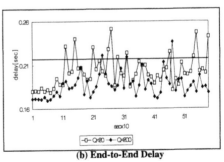

(b) End-to-End Delay

Figure 5: Distribution of Received Frame rate and End-to-End Delay When Controlled Data Bit Rate

Figure 5(a) and figure 5(b) respectively shows the distribution of received frame rate and end-to-end transfer delay to network load when we control data bit rate using Q factor. They say that received frame rate goes lower, and end-to-end transfer delay is getting longer as an image resolution goes higher.

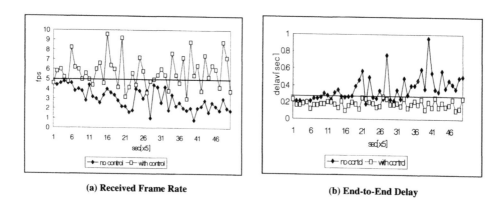

(a) **Received Frame Rate**   (b) **End-to-End Delay**

Figure 6: Distribution of Received Frame rate and End-to-End Delay When Controlled Frame Sending Rate

Figure 6(a) and figure 4(b) respectively shows the distribution of received frame rate and end-to-end transfer delay to network load when we control frame sending rate. When there is no explicit data control mechanism, average received frame rate is 3.0, but when we apply the proposed data control mechanism, average received frame rate becomes 5.7. In the case of end-to-end delay, we can get twice increments in performance. Especially, when we use a proposed frame rate control, delay variation is almost flat. It means the jitter is small, so we can achieve better video playback quality.

5   Conclusions

We have proposed and implemented QoS architecture and control mechanism to guarantee end-to-end quality of service. Since, different media flows have their own characteristics, different management policies and control mechanism should be provided for each media. In the proposed structure, users may request suitable QoS policy depending on the application service type. To satisfy user's request, optimal control policies have to be configured, monitored, and guaranteed while conference is maintained.

Applications that require the establishment of multiple participants have to be controlled by a group manager. A group manager has to generate some primitives maintaining participants and provides group integrity condition to media manager for efficient quality of service control. A media manager executes some important role such as call admission control and congestion control with monitoring network traffic. Considering shared medium LAN system like Ethernet, the performance is affected tremendously by network bandwidth usage. So, we apply call admission control mechanism for it. Requested call is accepted only when overall quality of service can be guaranteed.

To validate proposed QoS architecture and control mechanism, we have implemented desktop conference system. Considering conference environment, audio data have higher priority than video data. If network experience congestion, video data transmission rate should be reduced. We used received frame rate and end-to-end transmission delay as evaluation parameters. At lower and upper bound of the parameter values, QoS control mechanism may regulate its transmission rate. With proposed QoS control mechanism, end-to-end transmission delay and received frame rate can be improved by two. Especially the uniform distribution of transmission delay can be obtained.

Bibliography

1) Nicolaou, C., "An Architecture for Real-Time Multimedia Communications Systems," *IEEE Journal on Selected Areas in Communications*, Vol. 8, No. 3, (1990).

2) Coulson, G., et al., "Design of a QoS Controlled ATM Based Communication Systems in Chorus," *IEEE JSAC special issue on ATM LANs: Implementation and Experience with Emerging Technology*, May, (1995).

3) Guerin, R., el al., "Equivalent Capacity and its Application to Bandwidth Allocation in High Speed Networks," *IEEE JSAC*, Vol. 9, No. 7, Sept., (1991).

4) Stankovic, el al., "Implications of Classical Scheduling Results for Real-Time System," *IEEE Computer, Special Issue on Scheduling and Real-Time Systems*, Jun, (1995).

5) Little, T.D.C, and A. Ghafoor, "Synchronization Properties and Storage Models for Multimedia Objects", *IEEE JSAC*, Vol. 8, No. 3, pp229-238, Nov., (1990).

6) W. Doneringer, et al., "A Survey of Light-Weight Transport Protocols for High Speed Networks", *IEEE Transactions on Communications*, Nov., (1990).

7) Kurose, J.F., "Open Issues and Challenges in Providing Quality of Service Guarantees in High Speed Networks", *ACM Computer Communication Review*, Vol., 23, No. 1, pp6-15, Jan., (1993).

8) H. Zhang, S. Keshav, "Comparison of Rate-Based Service Disciplines", *ACM SIG-COMM*, (1991).

9) Zhang, L., et al., "RSVP Functional Specification", *Working Draft*, draft-ietf-rsvp-spec-10.txt, (1996).

10) MMCF Working Document, "Arch/QoS/94-001, Rev.1.5", *Multimedia Communications Forum, Inc.*, May, (1994).

11) Francois Fluckiger, "Understanding Networked Multimedia:Application and Technology", *Prentice Hall*, pp321-381.

12) ISO/IEC JTC1/SC6, "Second Draft on Multi-Peer Taxonomy", (1994).

13) M. Handley, et al., "The Internet Multimedia Conferencing Architecture", *Internet Draft draft-ietf-mmusic-confarch-00.txt*, IETF, July, (1997).

14) West C. H., "An Automated Technique of Communication Protocol Validation", *IEEE Transactions on Communication*, Vol. COM-26, pp1271-1275, (1978).

15) Mischa Schwartz, "Telecommunication Networks, Protocols, Modeling and Analysis", *Addison-Wesley*, pp453-467, (1987).

Efficient Protocols for Multimedia Streams on WDMA Networks

Lixin Wang

Mounir Hamdi

The Hong Kong University of Science and Technology

ABSTRACT

This paper introduces a new approach to integrate different types of medium access (MAC) protocols into a single wavelength division multiplexing (WDM) network system so as to efficiently accommodate various types of multimedia traffic streams with different characteristics and quality of service (QoS) demands. The proposed WDM network, which is termed *multimedia wavelength multiple access* (M-WDMA), considered three types of multimedia traffic streams: a constant-bit-rate (CBR) traffic and two classes of variable-bit-rate (VBR) traffic. Accordingly, three tunable transmitters and one fixed home channel receiver for data transmission are used . The transmitters transmit the three types of multimedia traffic streams in a pipeline fashion so as to overcome the tuning time overhead. We further incorporate a *dynamic bandwidth allocation* scheme that dynamically adjusts the portions of bandwidth occupied by the three types of traffic streams according to their QoS demands. The performance of M-WDMA is evaluated through a simple analytical model and extensive simulations. It is shown that M-WDMA can satisfy the QoS requirements of various mixes of multimedia traffic streams even under very stringent requirements.

1 Introduction

It is widely believed that the multimedia communication is one of the most important features in the new generation of the computer networks. That is, in a single network, video, audio, data streams should be able to be transmitted in a expected quality. To support this, high capacity transmission system and multimedia oriented media access protocols are needed. The development of the fiber optical technology supplies with extremely high bandwidth transmission system. The wave-length division multiplexing (WDM) is the one of the promising techniques which comes up with the occurance of the fiber techniques. In a WDM architecture, a transmitter and a receiver have to tie onto the same wavelength (i.e., channel) to communicate to each other. Due to the limitation of the number of transceivers at each node, the complete connectivity of a WDM network requires the use of *tunable transceivers* which can tune their working wave-length across all channels in the network. Unfortunately one has to make a compromise between the tuning time and the tuning range. As a result, dealing with the tuning time overhead, together with the consideration of multimedia communication requirements, becomes a crucial design issue in *broadcast-and-selection* WDM networks (single-hop or star-coupled networks) [5].

A plethora of MAC protocols have been proposed for star-coupled WDM networks [6]. However, most of these MAC protocols are not suited for an integrated services environment because they have been designed with just one *generic* traffic type in mind. They perform quite well for the traffic streams they have been designed for, but poorly for other traffic streams with different characteristics. All traffic can be classified into three categories. The isochronous traffic, such as video/audio, require guaranteed bandwidth and low variance services, so *pre-assigned time slot* protocols (e.g. TDM protocol [1]) are the best choice for this types of traffic. The generic reservation based protocols can not well match the requirements since extra reservation penalty is unnecessarily high for isochronous traffic. While unbalanced traffic and long bursty traffic need the feature of reservation based protocols [8, 5], the TDM protocols cause very low utilization. Many applications need very fast response such as interactive gaming, remote control panel operation, etc. the TDM and the reservation based protocols can not supply this types of services in the senses that they are both not *immediate access* protocols and their non-neglect-able scheduling overhead are inevitable. However, the contention based protocols (random access protocols) can reduce the access delay to almost close to the signal propagation delay. But random access protocol suffers collision and retransmission penalty when the traffic load become higher.

As can be seen, none of these MAC protocols serves all types of traffic well although each one of them is ideal for certain types of traffic streams. This observation lead us to propose an efficient scheme of integrating different MAC protocols into a single MAC protocol for WDM networks, each serves best for certain type of the traffic streams.

In this chapter, we propose a novel WDM MAC protocol which integrates different types of MAC protocols into a single physical WDM network and efficiently supports multimedia traffic streams. This MAC protocol is termed *Multimedia-WDMA*, or M-WDMA, for short. In the study of the M-WDMA, we consider the following environment: 1) three types of traffic streams: a Constant Bit Rate (CBR), a Variable Bit Rate with large burstness (VBR1), and a Variable Bit Rate with longer inter-arrival times (VBR2); 2) the importance of the deadline associated with each traffic stream; and 3) nonzero tuning time of the transmitters/receivers. In addition, a dynamic bandwidth allocation strategy is designed to further improve the utilization of our M-WDMA, which is named M-WDMA+.

This chapter is organized as follows. section 2 introduces the M-WDMA architecture. section 3 presents the operation of the M-WDMA, and the M-WDMA+. In section 4, simple mathematical model for the M-WDMA architecture is discussed. section 5 shows the results of the performance evaluation of M-WDMA networks using extensive computer simulations. section 6 concludes this chapter.

2 The M-WDMA Architecture

Let us consider a M-WDMA network with N nodes which are connected by a star-coupler and having C channels. Each node has a fixed channel (*home channel*) with wave-length λ_i ($i = 1, 2, .., C$) which is used to receive the packets designating to the node. The M-WDMA MAC protocol has three integrated *MAC sub-protocols*: a TDMA protocol (named TDM sub-protocol), a reservation-based protocol (RSV), and a random-access protocol (CNT). Correspondingly in a M-WDMA network, each node has three tunable transmitters used to serve three classes of traffic streams according to the corresponding *sub-protocols*. The transmitters are named TDM transmitters, RSV transmitters, and CNT transmitters. With employing three transmitters on each node, we can reduce the tuning time overhead by pipelining the transmission and tuning process. More details on the operation of these *sub-protocols* are discussed in section 3.

There are multiple queues on each node to eliminate the *head-of-line-blocking* problem, each of them stores the packets for each channel. The whole network is assumed synchronized with respect to time-slots and the synchronization is relative to the center of the hub of the star coupler. The tuning time, Γ, is chosen in such a way that tunable transmitters can access all of the given C channels [2, 7]. In addition, pair of extra transmitter and receivers are set on each node, tying on a shared control channel λ_0, to exchange the control information such as reservation requests, or transmission acknowledgment.

3 M-WDMA Frame Structure and Protocol

3.1 M-WDMA Frame Structure

Because the three transmitters can operate in a pipeline fashion, the three transmitters can not send packets at the same time. This observation has led us to organize the three types of transmissions into a time *frame*. A frame consists of three *segments*: a TDM segment with length L_{TDM} slots, a RSV segment with length L_{RSV} slots and a CNT segments with length L_{CNT} slots. Each of the segments are further divided into slots with length b. The TDM transmissions can only be started in a TDM segment, and so do the CNT and RSV transmissions, respectively. To make sure that the TDM segments appear in periodic constant intervals, the frame length, L_{frame} is fixed. A transmission example of our M-WDMA MAC protocol is illustrated in Figure 1. In this figure, the horizontal direction denotes time and the vertical direction denotes space

The frame length can have an implication on the operation and performance of a M-WDMA network. Hence, it should be properly chosen so that the multimedia communication requirements can be satisfied and the tuning time can be efficiently covered. That is: $L_{TDM} + L_{RSV} > \Gamma$, $L_{TDM} + L_{CNT} > \Gamma$, and $L_{CNT} + L_{RSV} > \Gamma$. Since $L_{frame} = L_{TDM} + L_{RSV} + L_{CNT}$, then $L_{frame} > 3\Gamma/2$

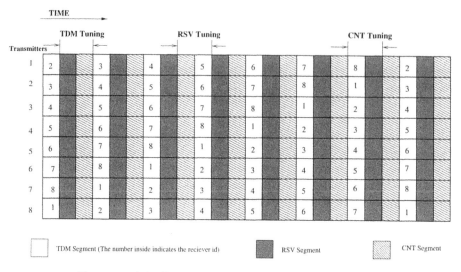

Figure 1: A M-WDMA transmission schedule example.

3.2   M-WDMA sub-protocols

The M-WDMA protocol consists of the TDM sub-protocol, the RSV sub-protocol and the CNT sub-protocol. The operation of the TDM sub-protocol is basically an *interleaved TDMA* MAC protocol [1]. The major difference is that in a M-WDMA network, we take tuning time into consideration . Since the tuning order is prefixed, no extra information exchange is needed in the control channel.

The RSV packet transmission is controlled using a *multiple token* method [8]. Each channel is assigned with a *token*. A node can send its packets onto the destination channel only when it holds the token of the destination channel. In the M-WDMA, the tokens are not explicitly issued. In each cycle of the control channel, the M-WDMA nodes broadcast their transmission requests to all nodes. At the end of the cycle, all nodes synchronously execute a distributed *token rotation algorithm* (TRA) to determine the token distribution in the coming frame. The TRA guarantees that all tokens are held by one node and each node can not hold more than one token.

The CNT sub-protocol of our M-WDMA MAC protocol is similar to the *interleaved slotted ALOHA* [1]. The active nodes compete for the slots in the current CNT segment. In case there is a collision, retransmission is scheduled according to a binary back-off algorithm. The collision declaration and acknowledgment are done through the control channel. Since ordinary back-off control may across the border of CNT segment, a CNT segment counter is set so as to avoid the effects on other segments.

3.3   Dynamic Bandwidth Allocation: M-WDMA+

In M-WDMA with static bandwidth allocation, It is possible that some of the segments are over-loaded while some segments are partially filled, that results in low efficiency. Fortunately, in a M-WDMA, different classes of transmissions are *grouped* into a single frame, so the adaption on the bandwidth allocation can be easily realized by adjusting the segment sizes.

To accomplish this, a dynamic bandwidth allocation strategy is needed. Since the CBR traffic is connection oriented in nature, once a CBR connection is established, the connection is usually kept for a relatively long time, and the bandwidth required is known. For the VBR traffic streams using the reservation-based sub-protocol, the required bandwidth varies a lot because of the burstness in nature. However, the reservation sub-protocol requires the source node to reserve transmission request before the transmission, then every node can obtain the number of slots required for the RSV segments in each frame before hand. Having determined the TDM and the RSV segment lengths, we can leave the remaining slots of the frame to the CNT segment. With knowing the size of each segment of a frame, the bandwidth can be allocated efficiently. Our strategy is to assign priorities to the sub-protocol segments in the following order: TDM, RSV, and then CNT. That is, the CBR traffic are allocated (TDM), Next, we allocate the RSV segment. Finally, the remaining bandwidth, if available, is all given to the CNT segment.

Figure 2 shows the adaptability of the dynamic bandwidth allocation algorithm. The histogram is obtained using the following parameters: $L_{frame} = 30$, TDM bandwidth is 14, maximum RSV burst length is 25, and the normalized traffic load is 30%. From the histogram, we can see that more bursty data can be efficiently accommodated and more available bandwidth can be exploited by the contention-based sub-protocol. The highest priority sub-protocol, the TDM sub-protocol, just uses the bandwidth it needs.

4   Modeling of the M-WDMA Network

This section investigates the performance of the M-WDMA MAC protocol through simple mathematical models. We focus our attention on determining the packet transmission delays. In a M-WDMA MAC protocol, three sub-protocols coexist together, but they are not active simultaneously. When one of the sub-protocols is in use, the other sub-protocol are idle from the view of channels and nodes. Given that the bandwidth (sub-protocol segment sizes) is statically allocated, the three sub-protocols can be thought of as if they operate using three different networks. We can assume that the three classes of traffic streams are independent mutually, which is termed as *protocol independent assumption*. With this assumption, the three sub-protocols can be modeled separately.

Apparently, it is reasonable to apply a polling system analysis [3, 4]. We assume that all the nodes in the M-WDMA network have equal probability to generate packets and also have equal probability to be the destination of a packet. Let λ be the network normalized traffic load, and λ_{TDM}, λ_{RSV}, and λ_{CNT} be the mean traffic loads for the individual segments of the sub-protocols, respectively.

For a queue i, The period between two consecutive visits to queue i is named *i-cycle*. Let W denote waiting time, Y be duration of a i-cycle, and R be the forward residual time after service time in a i-cycle. Our purpose here is to get the mean

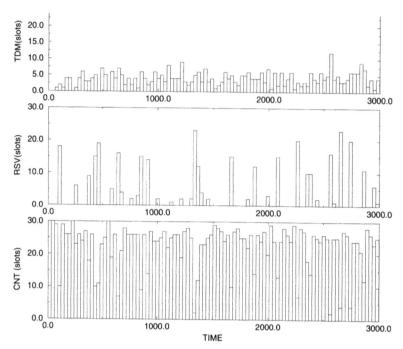

Figure 2: A bandwidth occupation of M-WDMA+.

delay, $E[W_i]$, in queue i in steady state. Let X_i denotes the number of packets present in queue i at an arbitrary moment. The waiting time of an arbitrary packet at queue i consists of the following two components: 1) The time since the packet arrives until the next visit of the server to queue i, that is, R_i. 2) The time required for the server to serve the X_i packets found at the queue during the last visit time.

Then we have:

$$E[W_i] = E[R_i] + E[X_i] \tag{7.1}$$

By Little's Law we get:

$$E[X_i] = \lambda E[W_i] \tag{7.2}$$

This is true according to the PASTA (Poisson Arrivals See Time Averages [4]) property. When an arbitrary packet arrives at an arbitrary time, the number of packets ahead of it in the queue is also considered the mean number of packets in the queue.

We approximate $E[R_i]$ as follows [4]:

$$E[R_i] = \frac{E[Y_{b,1}]}{E[Y_{b,i}]} E[R_1] \tag{7.3}$$

Consequently, we can get a general form for the mean packet delay which is given by:

$$E[W_i] = \frac{E[Y_{b,1}]E[R_1]/E[Y_{b,i}]}{1 - \lambda_i} \qquad (7.4)$$

Next, we apply this general form onto the individual sub-protocols of M-WDMA network to finalize our mathematical model.

In the TDM sub-protocol, the transmission is organized according to a pre-fixed schedule table as shown in Figure 1. In addition, the cycle time is fixed to $(N-1) * T_{frame}$. Since the schedule for transmission operates in a round-robin fashion, each queue has a fair chance (i.e., pre-allocated bandwidth) to transmit packets and the TDM segment is of fixed length L_{TDM}. Hence, when an arbitrary packet arrives at an arbitrary time, $E[R_i] = (N-2) * T_{frame}/2$. Consequently, the mean packet delay using the TDM sub-protocol is given by:

$$E_{TDM}[W_i] = \frac{(N-2) * T_{frame}}{2(1-\lambda)} \qquad (7.5)$$

In the RSV sub-protocol of M-WDMA network, the *i-cycle* is no longer fixed. It depends on the transmission details of the sub-protocol. When a node gets a token, it may occupy all the slots of the RSV segments in the current frame, and may continue to use the RSV segment in the next frames. In case few or no other nodes use this channel, the token may come back again. According to the suggestion given in [4], the $E[Y_{b,i}]$ can be derived using the following recursive formula:

$$E[Y_{b,i}] = b_i + \sum_{i \neq j} min(1, \lambda E[Y_{b,i}])b_j + s \qquad (7.6)$$

where s is the overall switch over time. Since we have fixed the frame length, $E[R_1]$ can be chosen in the same way as in the above description. Combining these results, the $E_{RSV}[W_i]$ can be easily obtained.

The CNT sub-protocol in a M-WDMA network is a random access protocol. Every node can access the CNT segment of each frame, so the *i-cycle* time is T_{fame}. But due to collisions, Packets' re-transmissions are needed. As a result, the network load is no longer equal to just λ_{CNT}. Many mathematical models have been proposed for such a protocol [1]. In our case, we follow Dowd's model [1] which exploit the *semi-Markov process* model. According to the model, the average number of packets in the system is given by: $E[N] = \sum_{i=0}^{2(Q+1)} E[N_i]P_i$ where P_i is the probability of being in state S_i, i.e., there are i packets residing in the buffer. Q is the capacity of the buffer. By Little's law, the mean delay is given by:

$$E[X_i] = \frac{E[N]}{\Gamma_s} \qquad (7.7)$$

where $\Gamma_s = \gamma \sum_{i=1}^{(B+1)} P_i$, and γ is the probability of successful transmission. Given $E[R_i] = T_{frame}/2$, we can obtain the CNT mean packet delay .

5   Simulation

We study the M-WDMA based on intensive simulation. In the simulation study, we assume data rate of each channel is 1Gb/s, slot size is 53Byte, frame size is 30 slots, tuning time is 20 slots. Network parameters include number of nodes N, number of channels C. Large enough buffer capacity is assumed.

For CBR traffic streams, delay jitter is mainly investigated. The missing rate of CBR is the ratio that the delay jitter exceed the given limitation. For VBR1 and VBR2 traffic sources, the missing rate is defined as the fraction of packets where their transmission delay exceed their given delay deadline. VBR1 has a relatively more strict delay deadlines that VBR2. VBR2 has large variations in their deadline specifications.

Figure 5 show the mean delay of a M-WDMA network. These results are obtained using our mathematical model and using simulation. The number of nodes is $N = 10$ and the number of channels $C = 10$. We also assume that the frame size is $L_{frame} = 30$, and the sub-protocol segment sizes are $L_{TDM} = 10$, $L_{RSV} = 10$ and $L_{CNT} = 10$.

As can be seen from the figures, our simulation and mathematical model results are close to each other. This is an indication of the accuracy of our simple mathematical models for the M-WDMA MAC protocol.

Improvement from the M-WDMA to the M-WDMA+ in terms of mean delay is illustrated in Figure 5. We can see that the performance of CBR streams using the M-WDMA and the M-WDMA+ MAC protocols are more or less the same since both of them guarantee the bandwidth required for the CBR traffic streams. The performance of the VBR1 traffic streams is improved since the M-WDMA+ can accommodate longer data burstness than in the "static" M-WDMA. Because all the un-used bandwidth are left to the VBR2, the enlarger bandwidth result in lower collision rates, and thus better efficiency.

Figure 5 through Figure 5 illustrate the superiority of integrating various protocols into a single network (M-WDMA) when compared with any individual conventional protocols (the ITDMA, Multiple Tokens and ISA). For a fair comparison, exactly the same traffic patterns and proportions are loaded onto both networks, and the same node configurations are also applied, i.e., in ITDMA, the transmitters are also pipelined. The mean delay and loss rate for both networks are shown in Figure 5 and 5.

The CBR traffic performance is more or less same for both networks, since our M-WDMA+ MAC protocol takes advantage of the ITDMA MAC protocol for this type of traffic. But for the other types of traffic streams, VBR1 and VBR2, they are much better served by our M-WDMA+ network. In terms of loss rate (delay deadline missing), we can draw similar conclusions.

Now we compare the performance of our M-WDMA+ protocol with a reservation-based MAC protocol namely MT-WDMA [6]. The MT-WDMA stands for the Multiple Token WDMA which is essentially a token passing protocol. By examining Figure 5 and Figure 5, it is obvious that the M-WDMA performs better for all types of traffic streams. Again, this is an affirmation of the superiority of using an integrated

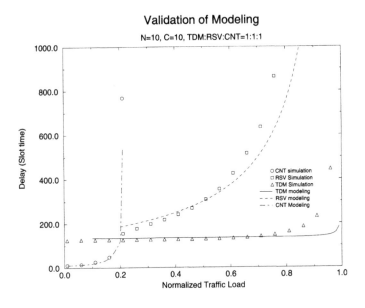

(a) Delay of M-WDMA

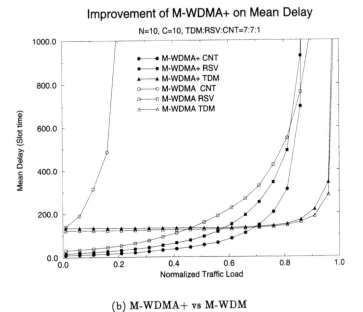

(b) M-WDMA+ vs M-WDM

Figure 3: Delay of M-WDMA and M-WDMA+

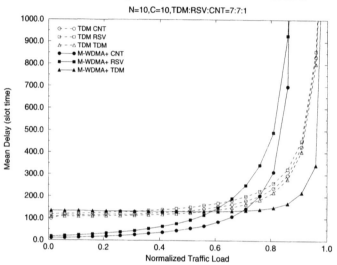

(a) In terms of mean delay

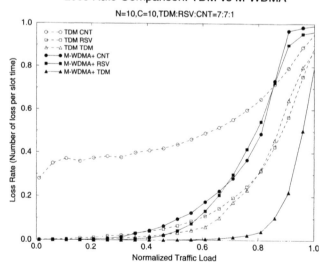

(b) In terms of deadline missing rate

Figure 4: M-WDMA+ and ITDMA.

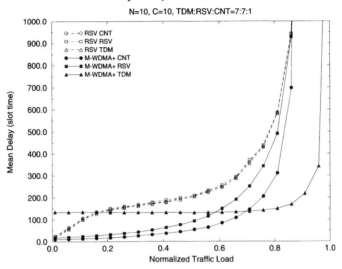

(a) In terms of mean delay

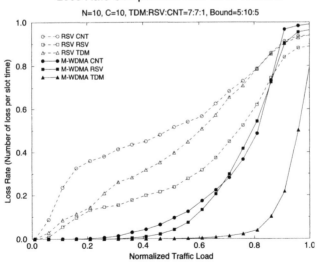

(b) in terms of deadline missing rate

Figure 5: M-WDMA+ vs MT-WDMA.

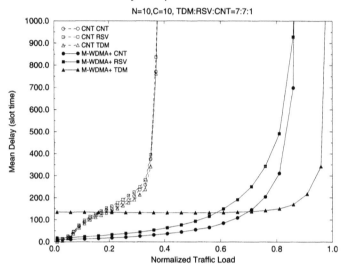

(a) In terms of mean delay

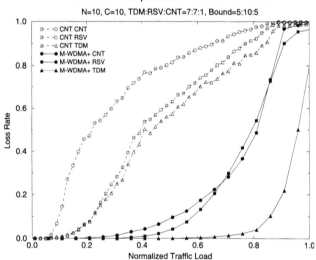

(b) In terms of deadline missing rate

Figure 6: M-WDMA+ vs ISA.

approach when designing MAC protocols for multimedia applications.

Figure 5 and 5 depict the integrated MAC approach for our M-WDMA+ with that of a single random access protocol, ISA [1]. ISA is implemented using the same network configurations as our M-WDMA+ protocol. Again, the differences is that in ISA, all types of traffic streams are processed under the same MAC protocol unlike the M-WDMA+ MAC protocol where each type of traffic stream is allocated to the proper sub-protocol. The results shown in Figure 5 and Figure 5 clearly illustrates the advantages of our integrated MAC approach in the M-WDMA.

6 Conclusion

This paper introduces a new approach that combines different types of MAC protocols into a single WDM network to better serves a wide variety of multimedia applications. Some of the goals of this approach are: 1) To keep the advantages of the individual MAC protocols with respect to specific types of traffic streams; 2) To efficiently support a large range of traffic streams with different characteristics and QoS requirements in a single WDM network; and 3) to dynamically allocate the network bandwidth to the different classes of traffic in order to boost the network performance. We have investigated the performance of our M-WDMA network, and it was clearly shown that it outperforms state-of-art MAC protocols for WDM networks in serving multimedia applications. As a result, we can reasonably expect that integrating various sub-protocols into a single protocol to have a good potential for meeting the QoS requirements of future integrated services WDM networks.

Bibliography

1) K. Bogineni, K. M. Sivalingam, and P. W. Dowd. Low-complexity multiple access protocols for wave-length-division multiplexed photonic networks. *IEEE Journal on Selected Areas in Communications*, Vol. 11, No. 4, pp. 590–604, (1993).

2) M. S. Borella and B. Mukherjee. Efficient scheduling of nonuniform packet traffic in a WDM/TDM local light-wave network with arbitrary transceiver tuning latencies. *IEEE Journal on Selected Areas in Communications*, Vol. 14, No. 5, pp. 923–934, (1996).

3) E. de Souza e Silva, H. R. Gail, and R. R. Muntz. Polling systems with server timeouts and their application to token passing networks. *IEEE/ACM Transactions on Networking*, Vol. 3, No. 5, pp. 560–75, (1995).

4) W. P. G. and H. Levy. Performance analysis of transaction driven computer systems via queueing analysis of polling models. *IEEE Transactions on Computers*, Vol. 41, No. 4, pp. 455–465, (1992).

5) F. Jia, B. Mukherjee, and J. Iness. Scheduling variable-length messages in a single-hop multichannel local lightwave network. *IEEE/ACM Transaction on Networks*, Vol. 3, No. 4, pp. 477–88, (1995).

6) B. Mukherjee. WDM-based local light-wave networks part i: Single-hop systems. *IEEE Network*, Vol. 6, No. 3, pp. 12–27, (1992).

7) B. Mukherjee. *Optical Communication Networks*. McGraw-Hill, (1997).

8) A. Yan, A. Ganz, and C. M. Krishna. A distributed adaptive protocol providing real-time services on WDM-based LANs. *Journal of light-wave technology*, Vol. 14, No. 6, pp. 1245-1254, (1996).

8

Priority Assignment for Multimedia Multipoint-to-point Communication

Mohammad Reza Ahmadi

Katsunori Yamaoka

Yoshinori Sakai

Tokyo Institute of Technology

ABSTRACT

This paper proposes a priority assignment method for multimedia multipoint-to-point communication. First, it discusses the performance degradation of multimedia communication caused by delay and proposes a new performance measure. Then it gives the priority assignment method based on the new measure. According to the analysis, it is shown that the proposed priority assignment increases the performance of the path with large performance degradation, at the expense of the decrease in performance of the path with small performance degradation.

1 Introduction

Due to the progress of high speed networks, digitized multimedia informations such as image and voice are transmitted through computer network in addition to computer data. In case of multimedia transmission, transmission quality of each media is deteriorated caused by network delay, where degradation in each media is different even for the same amount of delay. Priority control is an effective method to decrease the degradation caused by delay. This paper aims at obtaining the optimum priority assignment for multimedia multipoint-to-point communication. In section 2, we define a new quality degradation measure and formulate the problem. In section 3, the priority assignment method is proposed based on the new quality measure. In section 4, the performance of the proposed methods are shown.

2 Priority control for multimedia communication

2.1 Performance degradation measure

Effect of delay to each media is different. For example, in case of video transmission, if the variation of delay is more than 30ms, some data must be discarded at the receiver

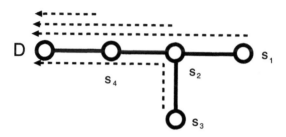

Figure 1: Multipoint-to-point communication

side; on the other hand, more than 100ms delay is allowed in facsimile transmission. In this paper, we define the media factor W_k for media k, and define $F_k = T/W_k$ as the new measure of quality degradation, where T is the average delay. Media factor W_k represents the sensitivity of media k concerning transmission delay. For example, if $W_1 = 2W_2$, it means that allowable delay of media 1 is twice as that of media 2.

2.2 Problem definition

In this paper, we focus on the multipoint-to-point communication as is shown in Figure 1, where S_i is source node, D is the destination node, P_i denotes the transmission path from node S_i to D. Each link is numbered from 1 to L, and is assumed to have two priority queues, high(H) and low(L). The set of source nodes issue the same traffic, with average of $\lambda packets/s$ on the average, to the destination node, D, at the same time. Priority of path $i(i = 1 - N)$ in link j is denoted as p_i^j, and can be assigned either as H or L independently. Further, it is assumed that delay is caused only by queuing delay. Let T_i be average delay of P_i and media factor in P_i be W_i, then $F_i = T_i/W_i$. Problem in this paper is defined as follows;

[Define evaluation function $E = f(F_1, F_2, ..., F_N)$. Find P_i^j which minimizes E.]

We have defined the average of F_i , $\bar{F}$, maximum of F_i among N paths, MAX$\{F\}$ and variance of F_i , VAR$\{F\}$ as the three basic quality measures and have defined complex measure E as follows;

$$E = a\bar{F} + bMAX\{F\} + cRVAR\{F\} \tag{8.1}$$

where, a, b, c are weighting constants, and RVAR$\{F\}$ denotes root of VAR$\{F\}$.

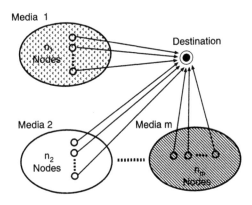

Figure 2: A con-cast communication model in multimedia environment

3   Priority assignment method

3.1   Conservation Low

In a multimedia environment, since each media (i.e. video, data, image, ...) has its own characteristic and delay constraint, we consider one constant value for each media. We define W_i as a constant value in media i that is a normalization factor for comparison of different media.

Theorem 1: In m multimedia environment, summation of average degradation caused by path delay multiplied by constants of each media is invariant.

$$\sum_{i=1}^{m} n_i \bar{F}_i W_i = constant \qquad (8.2)$$

where $\bar{F}_i$ is the average degradation, W_i is the constant value, and n_i is number of nodes in media i.

Proof: In a con-cast group with n source nodes and one destination node, we have n individual Virtual Paths form the set of source nodes to the destination node. We assume m different media such that media i contains n_i source nodes where $\sum_{i=1}^{m} n_i = n$. As is shown in Fig.2.

Based on Conservation law, for average delay in each link, we have

$$Link\ 1: \quad \sum_{j=1}^{l} S_1 \lambda_j T_1^j = r_1 \qquad (8.3)$$

$$Link \ 2: \quad \sum_{j=1}^{l} S_2 \lambda_j T_2^j = r_2 \tag{8.4}$$

$$\vdots$$

$$Link \ n: \quad \sum_{j=1}^{l} S_n \lambda_j T_n^j = r_n \tag{8.5}$$

where T_i^j is the delay of path j in link i, λ_j is traffic in path j, S_i is service time, and $r_1 \sim r_n$ are constant values. Note that, if a Virtual Path does not traverse through a link, the delay of that path in the link is zero.

If we calculate the total delay in each path, and assume $\lambda_j = \lambda$ we have,

$$T_1 + T_2 + \ldots\ldots + T_n = n \times \bar{T} = constant \tag{8.6}$$

also based on average path delay in each media we have,

$$n_1 \bar{T}_1 + n_2 \bar{T}_2 + \ldots\ldots + n_m \bar{T}_m = n \times \bar{T} = constant \tag{8.7}$$

where T_j is delay in path j, $\bar{T}_i$ is average path delay in media i, and $\bar{T}$ is the average total path delay in m media. On the other hand, in media k with n_k nodes and constant value of W_k, the path degradation and average path degradation are defined as follows

$$F_j = T_j / W_k \tag{8.8}$$

$$\bar{F}_k = \sum_{j=1}^{n_k} F_j / n_k \tag{8.9}$$

If we consider the average path degradation in m media, based on Eq.(8.6). we have

$$\sum_{j=1}^{m} \sum_{i=1}^{n_j} W_j (F_i / n_j) = constant \tag{8.10}$$

As a result, summation of average degradation multiplied by constants of each media is invariant, thus

$$n_1 \bar{F}_1 W_1 + n_2 \bar{F}_2 W_2 + \ldots\ldots + n_m \bar{F}_m W_m = constant \tag{8.11}$$

□

Based on this result, in a multimedia environment, with the aid of a suitable priority discipline, we can control the performance requirement of delay in a multipoint-to-point communication.

3.2 The priority assignment

The optimum priorities depend on constants a, b, and c in evaluation function(Eq.(8.1)). We have obtained the optimum priority assignment , in the case that $E = \bar{F}$, which means $b = c = 0$, and also the number of media is 2.

Theorem 2: Assume that W_i is W_h or W_l ($W_h < W_l$). The following priorities gives the optimum answer, in other word, minimizes E. If $W_i = W_h$, which means media in P_i is delay sensitive media, $P_i^j = H$. If $W_i = W_l$, which means media in P_i is delay tolerant media, $P_i^j = L$.

Proof: Let the set of paths where $W_i = W_h$ be S_h, and set of paths where $W_i = W_l$ be S_l. Eq.(8.10) can be written as

$$W_h \left\{ \sum_{P_i \in S_h} F_i \right\} + W_l \left\{ \sum_{P_i \in S_l} F_i \right\} = constant. \tag{8.12}$$

Average degradation $\bar{F}$ is

$$\bar{F} = \left[\left\{ \sum_{P_i \in S_h} F_i \right\} + \left\{ \sum_{p_i \in S_l} F_i \right\} \right] / N \tag{8.13}$$

Assume there is a path P_{i_s} which belongs to S_h ,where $p_{i_s}^k = H$. If we change $p_{i_s}^k$ from H to L, it follows that

$$\bar{F'}_{i_s} = \bar{F'}_{i_s} + dx \quad dx \geq 0 \tag{8.14}$$

As a result, from Eq.(8.12), other F_i decreases. Let total decrease in F_i of P_i which belongs to S_h be dh ($dh \geq 0$), and decrease in F_i of P_i, which belongs to S_l, be dl ($dl \geq 0$). Then,

$$- W_l dl + W_h(dx - dh) = 0 \tag{8.15}$$

Let $\bar{F}$ after the priority change be $\bar{F'}$, it follows

$$\bar{F'} - \bar{F} = dl \left(\frac{W_l}{W_h} - 1 \right) / N \geq 0 \tag{8.16}$$

Eq.(8.15) shows the average degradation $\bar{F}$ increase. On the other hand, it can be shown that $\bar{F}$ increases, if we change priority $p_{i_s}^k$ of the path P_{i_s}, which belongs to S_l, from L to H. As a result, the optimum priorities are

$$\begin{cases} P_i^k = L \ (P_i \in S_l) \\ P_i^k = H \ (P_i \in S_h) \end{cases} \tag{8.17}$$

□

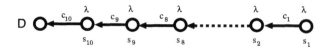

Figure 3: Line network model

On the other hand, it is difficult to obtain the optimum assignment method generally. We have proposed the following heuristic method. Heuristic method consists of initial priority assignment and local optimization procedure.

1. Initial priority assignment

    step1: Let all $p_i^j = L$, and E_0 be the minimum value of E. Obtain E under these priorities and $E_0 = E$.

    step2: Change all priorities with $p_i^j = L$ to $p_i^j = H$ one by one and obtain E as E_{ij}. Let $E_{i_m j_m}$ is the minimum of all E_{ij}.

    step3: If $E_{i_m j_m} < E_0$, let $p_{i_m}^{j_m} = H$, $E_0 = E_{i_m j_m}$ and go back to step2, else terminate the procedure.

2. Local optimization procedure
   Local optimization procedure applies the steepest decent method.

    step1: Initial values of E and p_i^j are determined by the initial priority assignment.

    step2: Change all priorities, p_i^j, one by one, where $p_i^j = H$ is changed to L, and $p_i^j = L$ is changed to H. Calculate E_{ij} for each change of p_i^j and the obtain the minimum value of E_{ij}. $E_{i_m j_m}$ is the minimum and $p_{i_m}^{j_m}$ is the priority which gives the minimum value.

    step3: If $E_{i_m j_m} < E_0$, let $p_{i_m}^{j_m}$ be the revised priority and $E_0 = E_{i_m j_m}$ and go back to step2, else terminate the procedure.

4   Performance analysis

Performance of the proposed method is analyzed concerning line network model which is shown in Figure.3 under the following condition.

- P_i: Defines a path from s_i to D

- Media type: 2 and 3

- Media factor W in 2 media case: P_2, P_3, P_5 have $W = 0.5$, the others have $W = 1$

- Media factor W in 3 media case: P_2, P_3 have $W = 0.5$, P_7, P_{10} have $W = 0.25$, the others have $W = 1$

- λ: Traffic of each path

- Packet size: 8000 bit

- Link capacity c_i: $c_1 = 1Mb/s, c_2 = 2Mb/s, c_3 = 3Mb/s, c_4 = 4Mb/s, c_5 = 5Mb/s, c_6 = 6Mb/s, c_7 = 7Mb/s, c_8 = 8Mb/s, c_9 = 9Mb/s, c_{10} = 10Mb/s$

Figure.4 shows the average $\bar{F}_i$, Figure.5 shows the maximum F_i and Figure.6 shows the variance of F_i in 2 media case. Figure.7 shows the average $\bar{F}_i$, Figure.8 shows the maximum F_i in 3 media case. The performance of the network without priority assignment is also shown. These figures show that proposed priority assignment method has the effect to decrease large F_i ,and as a result, decrease three measures of degradation.

5 Conclusion

In this paper, we have proposed a priority assignment method for multimedia multipoint to point communication. We have shown a conservation low for multimedia performance degradation and proposed the priority assignment method based on the new measure. It is shown that the proposed priority assignment has the effect to decrease the large quality degradation at the expense of increase in the small quality degradation. Here, we have assumed, delay is caused by the queuing in the network. Thus, the priority assignment discussed in this paper could apply to cell relay, frame relay and IP network. Further modification is necessary to apply to delay control in TCP/IP.

Bibliography

1) J. De Treville and D. Sincoskie, "A distributed experimental communications system", IEEE J. Select. Areas Commun., Vol. SAC-1, No.6, pp.1070–1075(1993)

2) C. Weinstein and J. Forgie, "Experience with speech communication in packet networks", IEEE J. Select. Areas Commun., Vol.1, No.6, pp.963–980(1993)

3) M. R. Ahmadi, K. Yamaoka, and Y. Sakai, "Network design and routing algorithm in convergence-cast communication", IEICE Transactions on communications, **E79–B**, No.2, pp.116–121(1996)

4) M. Garey and D. Johnson, "Computers and intractability", A guide to the theory of NP–Completeness. New York: W.H. Freeman and Co.(1979)

5) L. Kleinrock, "Queueing systems", John Wiley and sons. vol. 1 and 2(1975)

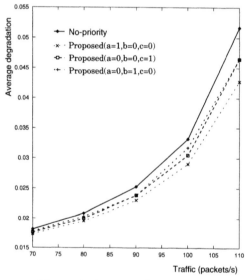

Figure 4: Average degradation
(2 media)

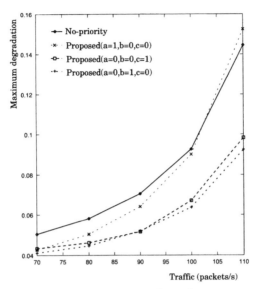

Figure 5: Maximum degradation
(2 media)

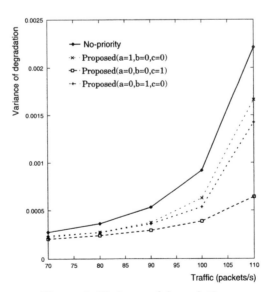

Figure 6: Variance of degradation
(2 media)

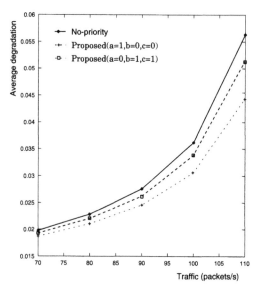

Figure 7: Average degradation
(3 media)

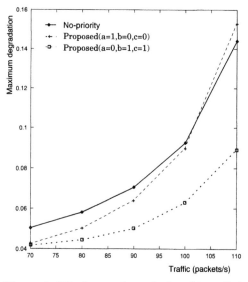

Figure 8: Maximum degradation (3 media)

9

Dynamic Rate Control Methods for Compressed Media Transmission

Jun Sato

Yukiharu Kohsaka

Toyo University

Koji Hashimoto

Yoshitaka Shibata

Iwate Prefectural University

ABSTRACT

In this paper, we introduce dynamic rate control method which consists of both a packet rate control method to reduce the packet loss, and a frame rate control method to maintain the frame rate constant. By combining these two different dynamic rate control methods, the user's QoS for video service can be dynamically controlled even if packets are lost or delayed as a result of increases of CPU loads at the client and video server, or network traffic. We implemented a prototyped packet audio/video system(PAVS) to evaluate performance of the suggested control methods when client CPU load and network traffic dynamically changed. Through the performance evaluation, the usefulness of our suggested control methods has been demonstrated.

1 Introduction

In order to provide continuous media services, such as video-on-demand over high speed networks, a suitable quality of service(QoS) requested by the user has to be guaranteed by taking into account of not only the characteristics of the media data being provided but also the bandwidth available, the network traffic load, and both the processing capabilities and load deviations of the client stations as well as the video servers. Therefore, the transmission system has to include mechanisms that guarantee end-to-end QoS from the application layer through the network layer. On the other hand, video compression techniques such as MPEG[1] are desired to reduce the amount of video data that needs to be stored and transmitted. However, since the amount of data of each video frame varies in time depending on the motion of the video content when the video compression methods are used, variable bit rate transmission is required to maintain the video frame rate constant.

In this paper, we introduce both a packet rate control method that reduces packet loss by adjusting the sending packets interval and a frame rate control method that maintains frame rate constant and keeps the time constraint needed for continuous media data, when MPEG compressed video data is transmitted using variable bit rate transmission. On both of the rate control methods adjust the packet interval and frame rate at the video server depending to the feedback messages sent by the client station. To evaluate the performance of these rate control functions, we implemented a prototyped packet audio/video system(PAVS) and compared temporal variation of the packet loss rate and frame rate with and without these suggested control methods when the client CPU load and network traffic load were dynamically changed. As a result, we found that these control functions could reduce the packet loss to acceptable levels and maintain the video frame rate constant while preserving the time constraint needed for continuous media data.

The rest of this paper is organized as follows. In section 2, we discuss the related works about the rate control based on feedback message for video transmission. In section 3, we introduce a PAVS architecture including dynamic rate control functions. In section 4, dynamic rate control methods which contain packet rate control and frame rate control are precisely described. In section 5, the prototype system for PAVS and the performance evaluation of dynamic rate control methods are discussed.

2 Related Works

So far there are several approaches[2)3)4)] for the rate control based on feedback information concerned with network traffic loads. These approaches estimate the state of the computing and network resources by monitoring the actual network loads, such as packet loss rate and throughput which are detected on the distributed networks. Sender station adjusts the packet transmission rate to adapt the conditions of the network and computer depending to the feedback information.

In the paper [2)], they suggested a rate control method which keeps the desired frame rate by adjusting the horizontal resolution of the video at the sender site depending of the network traffic condition. In order to adjust the horizontal resolution dynamically, however, they suggested a specific video coding method based on quadtree compression, which is not common to today's video format standard. On the other hand, the paper [3)], which uses H.261 video format and the paper[4)], which uses MPEG video format, adjust Q-factor to control sending data rate. In particular, the paper [4)] applies the priority scheme for each frame of MPEG.

In this paper, we use MPEG compression technique for video transmission, and assume the dynamic unpredictable extra load on the client station. We introduce both frame rate control and packet rate control to realize fine-grained adaptive rate control. By combining these two rate control methods, the transmitted data rate can be adapted to the load condition quickly and smoothly.

3   System Architecture

To realize continuous media service such as video-on-demand service, we introduce packet audio/video system(PAVS) which is based on client/server model architecture including three layers; synchronization layer, data transform layer and media flow control layer between the application and transport layers in the OSI reference model as showing in Figure 1[6].

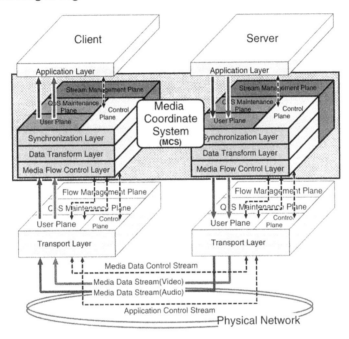

Figure 1: System Architecture

This system architecture contains the functions required to provide continuous media data to users and guarantee QoS from application through the network layer. Here we define these three layer as media coordinate system(MCS). The media coordinate system is further vertically divided into four planes; the user plane, the control plane, the QoS maintenance plane and the stream management plane. Our model is based on QoS architecture over ATM[5] which guarantees the network QoS under the media flow control layer. In the user plane, synchronization function between different media such as audio and video, data transform function between different media attributes and the media flow control function for both constant bit rate and variable bit rate transmission are realized. In the control plane, the connections between the client and the server are established and released and QoS of the media stream is negotiated and maintained. In the QoS maintenance plane, each entity is responsible for the fine-grained monitoring and maintenance of their associated protocol entities. In the stream management plane, the most suitable QoS parameter values on each protocol layer are determined depending on the user's QoS require-

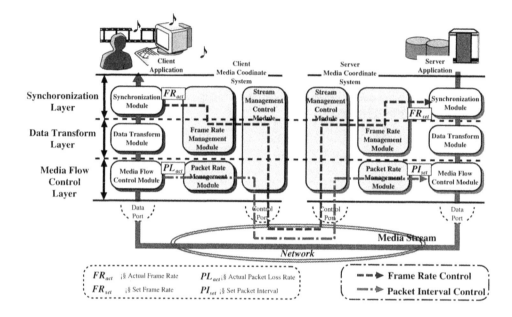

Figure 2: Functional Module Configuration and Flow of Rate Control

ments, the characteristics of the source media data, the attributes of the output device, and the available computing and network resources. We can regard frame rate, synchronization interval, packet interval, and packet loss rate as QoS decision factors.

Figure 2 shows the functional modules configuration of the PAVS necessary to realize the protocol functions of each layer. In the packet rate management module, the number of packets transmitted from server and received on client are managed. In the frame rate management module, the actual frame read from video server and displayed on client are managed. In the stream management control module, CPU loads on client and server, and network traffic load are periodically monitored and feedback messages between client and server are managed. The dynamic rate control functions are explained in detail in section 5.

4   Dynamic Rate Control Methods

Too much CPU loads of the client and server stations, and network traffic load cause packet loss, delay and jitter by packet buffer overflow and underflow at the client and server, and eventually the transmitted video frame rate is seriously influenced. In order to solve these problems, we introduce two dynamic rate control methods including packet rate control and frame rate control to adapt to these extra load conditions.

In the packet rate control, the inter-packet interval is controlled at the server station to reduce the packet loss rate under the admissible loss rate depending to feedback messages with the actual packet loss rate from the client station. In the frame rate control, the transmitted video frame rate is controlled on the server station to maintain the displayed video frame rate constant and to keep the time constraint needed for continuous media data, again depending to feedback message with actual value of frame rate from client station. The frame rate control is performed on the synchronization layer while the packet rate control is performed on the media flow control layer. By combining these two rate control methods together, audio/video quality can be adapted quickly and smoothly to the resource environment under the various extra load condition.

4.1 Packet Rate Control

In order to reduce packet loss rate under the admissible packet loss rate, packet interval PI is updated depending on the extra load conditions. When the packet loss rate, PL_{act} for a measurement interval, T is greater than the admissible packet loss rate, PL_{adm} then the packet interval, PI is immediately increased according to the characteristic curve which shows the relation between packet loss rate to packet interval as shown in Figure 3.

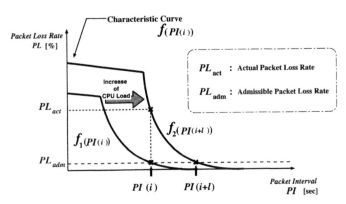

Figure 3: Characteristic Curve of Packet Loss Rate for Packet Interval

A priori to video service, this characteristic curve is measured in advance. The next packet interval $PI(i + 1)$ is decided based on the characteristic curve as follows : At first, the characteristic curve is shifted to the point which crosses the point at ($PI(i)$, PL_{act}). Here, $PI(i)$ is the set packet interval when PL_{act} was detected. The new packet interval $PI(i + 1)$ is determined by overlapping to the point which could limit under the PL_{adm} in the shifted characteristic curve.

When the extra load is reduced, the packet interval is reduced to the interval which is gradually adjusted as long as $PL_{act} < PL_{adm}$ is satisfied.

4.2 Frame Rate Control

To normally display the video frames, the source frame rate by which the video source was initially stored at the video server must be maintained during video session and displayed on the client station. When the source frame rate cannot be attained at the client, however, subsampling of frames must be carried out to reduce the source frame rate before the frames are sent from the video server.

The frame rate management module at the client periodically monitors the actual frame rate FR_{act} displayed and compares it with the set frame rate FR_{set}. If the FR_{act} is smaller than FR_{set} for the interval $T[sec]$, then the counter value for rate difference status, $Miss_{Cnt}$, is incremented. When $Miss_{Cnt}$ exceeds a threshold, $Miss_{Max}$, then the client station sends a rate control message telling by informing the frame rate management module at the server to reduce the current frame rate by ΔFR. The frame rate management module at the video server then dynamically updates the current frame rate by subsampling the source frame rate FR_{src}. The frame rate management module at the client station also updates the set frame rate FR_{set} to a new value, which has be sent to it by the frame rate management module at the server. Thus, the actual frame rate is maintained by periodically adjusting the set frame rate.

The priority of each video frame must be considered when MPEG compressed video is used. This is because MPEG video is consisted from I, P, B-pictures for the inter-frame prediction and has mutual relation to each video frame. It is obvious the priorities of I and P-pictures are higher than the B-pictures, because these pictures are required to predict the B-pictures. Therefore, when subsampling of the frames is required, some of B-pictures are subsampled first, then P-picture and finally I-picture depending on the condition of the CPU and the network loads.

For example, let consider the case where one GoP is consisted of N pictures and x frames are required to be subsampled. The B-pictures to be subsampled are determined by the following sequence numbers:

$$1, \frac{N}{x} + 1, \frac{N \times 2}{x} + 1, ..., \frac{N \times (x-1)}{x} + 1$$

For example, when $N = 8$ and $x = 3$, the equivalent sequence numbers are,

$$1, \frac{8}{3} + 1 = 3, \frac{8 \times 2}{3} + 1 = 6$$

Thus, the first, third, and sixth of B-pictures in a GoP could be subsampled while avoiding the I and P-pictures.

On the other hand, when extra load is reduced, the system determines whether the set frame rate can be increased or not by monitoring the computing CPU load conditions and the number of packets transmitted over the network. When the system confirms the extra load decrease, then the frame rate is updated to the original source frame rate gradually.

5   Prototype and System Evaluation

In order to evaluate the usefulness of our suggested dynamic rate control methods, we implemented prototyped packet audio/video system (PAVS) based on the combination of $100[Mbps]$ FDDI and $10[Mbps]$ Ethernet as shown in Figure 4.

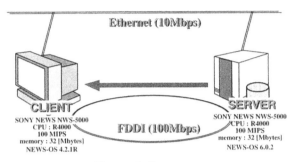

Figure 4: Prototype

In this prototype system, the processes for each layer including synchronization, data transform and media flow control layers for both audio and video are individually assigned. In Figure 2, the frame rate management module, the packet rate management module and the stream management control module of the client and server are implemented by one process as a QoS maintenance process. The system monitoring process which monitors the extra load conditions on the client, server and network is also realized by one process. Thus, the prototype system is consisted of 8 processes on client and server individually. In this experiment, we evaluated performance of rate control for only a video traffic. For the convenience, the audio processes are not executed in this evaluation. The inter-process communication(IPC) was used to exchange the control messages between these processes, and the shared memory scheme was also used to deliver the video data between these processes. TCP/IP protocol was used for message transmission between client and server. On the other hand, for video data transmission, UDP/IP protocol was used. As extra load on the client station, the number of the processes of MPEG-1 software decoder (mpeg_play) was executed on the client station during video data is transmitted. As network traffic load, continuous remote file transfer load which generates approximately $7.5[Mbps]$ traffic between the other workstations was intentionally executed during video data was transmitted. As a video source, we used a video source from the movie "Back to the Future" which was compressed by MPEG-1 format. The characteristics of the source video and the system parameters in PAVS are listed in Table 1 and 2.

We evaluated the following items :

1. The characteristic of packet interval and packet loss rate.

2. The packet rate control method.

3. The frame rate control method.

Table 1: System Parameters in PAVS

Extra Load	Client	Network
Physical Networks	FDDI	Ethernet
Packet Length[byte]	4K	1K
Average Video Bit Rate[Mbps]	5.0	1.5

Table 2: Transmitted Video Parameters

Compression Format	MPEG-1
Pixel Resolution[pixels]	640 × 480
Color Depth[bits]	24
Frame Rate[fps]	30
Number of Frames in GoP	N = 15
I,P Frames Cycle	M = 5

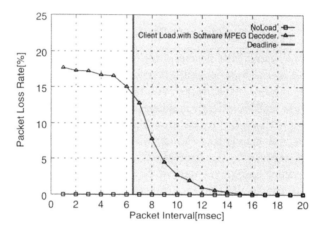

Figure 5: Relationship of Packet Interval and Packet Loss Rate

5.1   Packet Interval and Packet Loss Rate

To find out how the packet interval should be adjusted when the actual packet loss rate exceeds the admissible packet loss rate, the relation between inter-packet interval and packet loss rate was observed. The packet loss rate at various packet intervals was measured under two different CPU load conditions, namely no load and one load conditions when packets of a fixed length were sent from the video server to one of the client stations as shown in Figure 5.

The packet loss rate initially decreased gradually as the packet interval increased, but when the interval becomes more than 6.5[msec], the time constraint of the source video frame rate, 30[fps], could not be maintained. We define this time interval as the "deadline" packet interval. This is also the maximum packet interval which can guarantee time constraint needed for this video source. When the packet interval is greater than the deadline, the original frame rate cannot be maintained. Therefore, the source video must be subsampled and the packet interval must be controlled to maintain under admissible packet loss rate while keeping the frame rate as high as possible. Thus, this characteristic curve for packet loss rate, PL is approximately expressed as a function of packet interval, PI by the following characteristic equation:

$$PL = \begin{cases} -0.37 \times PI + 18.03 (PI < deadline) \\ -3.55 \times PI + 38.86 \ (PI >= deadline) \end{cases}$$

5.2 Performance Evaluation of Dynamic Rate Control Methods

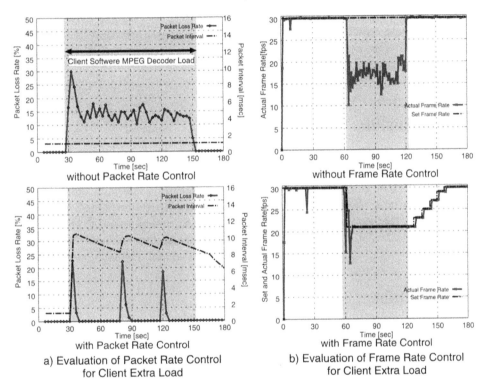

a) Evaluation of Packet Rate Control
for Client Extra Load

b) Evaluation of Frame Rate Control
for Client Extra Load

Figure 6: Evaluation of Packet and Frame Rate Control for Client Extra Load

Figures 6 a) shows the packet loss rate with and without packet rate control the extra CPU load on the client station were assigned. When the packet rate control was not introduced, the packet loss rate increased from 0[%] to about 13[%] while the packet interval was constant at 1[$msec$]. When the packet control function was introduced, on the other hand, the packet interval increased immediately to reduce the increased packet loss rate triggered when the extra load on the client station was given. The packet loss rate could be maintained quickly to the zero. However, the packet loss rate could not be completely regulated because the only feedback message with the current value of the packet interval from client station was used. It is required to improve the packet rate control under the admissible packet loss rate by combining this feedback message and change value of the CPU load conditions at the client.

Figures 6 b) shows the result of frame rate control when the client extra CPU load was given during video data transmission. In the case where the frame rate control function was not introduced, the actual frame rate was randomly influenced and decreased when CPU load on the client station was giving while the set frame rate was constant at $30[fps]$. On the other hand, in the case where the frame rate control was introduced, the set frame rate on the video server was immediately updated according to the feedback message from the client station. After that the actual frame rate could be maintained at constant $15[fps]$. After the CPU load was released, the frame rate increased gradually and again approached to the original $30[fps]$ frame rate.

Thus, through those performance evaluations, we could verify the usefulness of the suggested rate control functions.

6   Conclusions

Through this paper, we introduced packet rate control and frame rate methods that can be used to provide dynamic rate control when the client and network are subjected to extra loads. We implemented these rate control methods and evaluated their performance. As the result, the performance of the prototyped PAVS has demonstrated the usefulness of the suggested control methods under conditions in which the client CPU and network traffic loads change dynamically. In the near future, we will also evaluate of these rate controls when audio/video synchronization functions mechanism is implemented.

Bibliography

1) D. L. Gall, "MPEG: A Video Compression Standard for Multimedia Applications," Communications of the ACM, Vol.34, No.4, pp.46-58, Apr. 1991.

2) S. Chakrabarti and R. Wang, "Adaptive Control for Packet Video," Proc. of IEEE International Conference on Multimedia Computing and Systems, pp. 56-62, 1994.

3) J. Bolot and T. Turletti, "A rate control mechanism for packet video in the Internet," Proc. IEEE INFOCOMM'94, pp. 1216-1223, 1994.

4) H. Kanakia, P. Mishra and A. Reibman, "An Adaptive Congestion Control Scheme for Real-Time Packet Video Transport," Proc. of ACM SIGCOMM'93, pp. 20-31, 1993.

5) A. Campbell, G. Coulson and D. Hutchison, "A QUALITY OF SERVICE ARCHITEC-TURE," ACM SIGCOM Computer Communication Review, Vol. 24, No. 2, pp.1-27, 1994.

6) K. Hashimoto and Y. Shibata. "Performance Evaluation of End-to-End QoS Using Prototyped VOD System," Proc. of International Conference on Information Networking(ICOIN-12), pp.175-178, January 1998.

10

Analysis of a Kind of 2 Parallel Queueings with Precedence for Multimedia Network Communication

Wang Xin

Tadanori Mizuno

Shizuoka University

ABSTRACT

In multimedia network communication we should guarantee that the control information can be transmitted in time and as accurately as possible. First, we propose a parallel queueing model with precedence, which makes sure that the high priority packets are dealt with within constant time no matter how the traffic load is. On the other hand ,it ensures that the lost probability of the high priority packets is also very low. Next, we use MMM(mathemetic model method)to analyse the system and use SOR(successive over-relaxation method)to compute the state probability of the system. Then we compare the precedence queueing scheme and the conventional queueing scheme where all packets are serviced at the same priority level.Then a conclusion is drawn that the former one takes obvious advantage than the latter one in the fields of queue length distribution, average blocking probability, and average waiting time. We also give out how to realize this proposal in the real application and that is by looking up a table constructed before. Finally we provide simulation results to help verify the validity of analysis. It is shown that we can get very good performance of high priority packets while the performance of low priotity packets will not be very bad.

1 Introduction

Recently with personal computers widespreading into more and more families and the development of network techniques, multimedia network communication has been popular and widely used. More and more people communicate with each other through computer network while the resources are limited. Multimedia data, such as audio, video, image, although it is time-critical service its delay with mini-seconds is still tolerable[1]. Ref 3) introduced a deadline model to make sure that a packet which is close to a failing state is assigned a higher priority so as to improve its chances of meeting the deadline. This proposed dynamic priority assignment technique results in substantial reductions in the probability of dynamic failure without

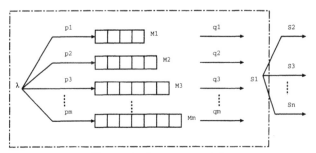

Figure 1: System model

greatly affecting the overall probability of miss. But control information, which probability is very small, generally will not appear deadline within several consecutive packets and should not be discarded, so the proposal above is unfit for this condition. In Ref 1) the arrival packets are divided into 2 kinds. They are wide band and narrow band. The WB packet is given higher priority of channel than the NB packet. In Ref 2) they proposed a protocol named NPP(Network Protocol with Performance), which provides best-effort soft time-critical-communication services. It uses the packet scheduling scheme to choose a packet among packets waiting for processing in an NPP queue, according to a precedent level and a time constraint of each packet. As to control information ,for example, playback indication, forward indication, audio muting, video freezing, and other kinds of signaling, the failure of it can have catastrophic consequences, therefore it must be transmitted in time and as accurately as possible. So it is reasonable that we process the control data with privileges. Here we deliver the control information a big processing probability and this means it is given higher priority of channel access than other types of data. The control information here mentioned is bursty and its probability is small. Differently from other proposals, we give the high priority packets(control data packets)a priorty, but it is just a probability very large, not equal to 1. This means that the priority of the high priority packets is fuzzy, not accurate. This maybe very useful in factual services.

Investigating traffic queueing models is very useful to know how to alter the system foundamental parameters to keep the system performance.

2   Model

The model we consider is as follows. We assume, in the source point every packet arrival process is assumed to have Poisson distributions with rate λ, and the respective service time has exponential distribution with rate $1/T$. Obviously the average service time of every packet is T. To ensure the stability of the system, we also assure that $\lambda < 1/T$. Since the arrival packets have different characteristics, such as different processing time limit, different error-corrected request and so on, all these characteriscs should be met so as to ensure the communication quality and efficiency. We divide all packets into several precedent degrees. This model is shown in Figure 1.

Figure 1 shows that there are total m precedent degrees and their probability is $p1, p2, p3, ..., pm$. We know that $p1 + p2 + p3 + ... + pm = 1$ holds. Then the relevant queueing buffer length is $M1, M2, M3, ..., Mm$. We deal with these kinds of packets at different probability $q1, q2, q3, ..., qm$, and of course $q1 + q2 + q3 + ... + qm = 1$ holds. Here we suppose that $p1 < p2 < p3 < ... < pm$. Certainly we get the following relationships: $M1 < M2 < M3 < ... < Mm$ and $q1 > q2 > q3 > ... > qm$. In figure 1 S1 means the source point, while S2,S3,...,Sn means the intermediate hops. So there is a traffic routing problem for every packet. Here we simplify the intermediate points to the source point. That is to say, the intermediate points provide the arrival packets with similar processing to the source point.

3 Analysis

In this paper for the simplification of analysis we suppose the system just has one service window. In this case, we define the high priority packets control information and the other multimedia data. In factual application, the control information is about how to control and deal with the multimedia data in the end point, such as playback indication, forward indication, audio muting, video freezing and other kinds of signaling.

When m equals 2 Fig.1 means the system we utilize. We know that a packet arrives at the rate λ. The probability of high priority packet is p1 and p2 means the possibility of the other multimedia data. M1 is the queueing buffer length for high priority packets and M2 is that of the low priority packets. Obviously the five equations following hold:

p1 + p2 = 1 ;

p1 < p2 ;

M1 < M2 ;

q1 + q2 = 1 ;

q1 > q2 .

Now we use a two-dimension vector (i, j) to denote the system state. Here i means the sum of the high priority packets queueing number and the number of the packets being served in the whole system. j is the low priority packets queueing number. Then Figure 2 shows the state transition diagram.

According to Figure 2, we have the following equation which holds while the system is in the balance state:

$$P_{i,j} \times (1/T + \lambda) = P_{i,j-1} \times \lambda \times p_2 + P_{i-1,j} \times$$

$$\lambda \times p_1 + P_{i,j+1} \times q_2/T + P_{i+1,j} \times q_1 1/T.$$

Here $P_{i,j}$ is an element of the state transition probability matrix P , while P has

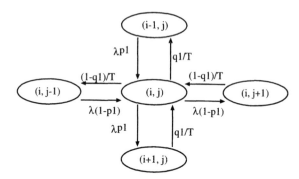

Figure 2: State transition diagram

the following format:

$$
P = \begin{bmatrix}
P_{0,0} & P_{0,1} & \cdots & P_{0,N} \\
P_{1,0} & P_{1,1} & \cdots & P_{1,N} \\
\cdots & \cdots & \cdots & \cdots \\
P_{M+1,0} & P_{M+1,1} & \cdots & P_{M+1,N}
\end{bmatrix}
$$

Taking the boundary limatations into consideration, we have the following equations:

$$P_{i,j} =$$

$$
\begin{cases}
P_{1,0}/\lambda/T & i = 0, j = 0 \\
0 & i = 0, N+1 > j > 0 \\
(P_{0,0}\lambda T + P_{2,0} + P_{1,1}q_2)/ & \\
(1 + \lambda T) & i = 1, j = 0 \\
(P_{i-1,0}\lambda p_1 T + P_{i,1}q_2 + & \\
P_{i+1,0})/(1 + \lambda T) & M+1 > i > 1, j = 0 \\
(P_{M,0}\lambda p_1 T + P_{M+1,1}q_2)/ & \\
(1 + \lambda p_2 T) & i = M+1, j = 0 \\
(P_{M+1,j-1}\lambda p_2 T + P_{M+1,j+1}\cdot & \\
q_2 + P_{M,j}\lambda p_1 T)/(1 + \lambda p_2 T) & i = M+1, 0 < j < N \\
P_{M+1,N-1}\lambda p_2 T + P_{M,N}\lambda p_1 T & i = M+1, j = N \\
(P_{i-1,N}\lambda p_1 T + P_{i+1,N}q_1 + & \\
P_{i,N-1}\lambda p_2 T)/(1 + \lambda p_1 T) & 1 < i < M+1, j = N \\
(P_{2,N}q_1 + P_{1,N-1}\lambda p_2 T)/ & \\
(1 - q_1 + \lambda p_1 T) & i = 1, j = N \\
(P_{1,j-1}\lambda p_2 T + P_{1,j+1}q_2 + & \\
P_{2,j}q_1/(q_2 + \lambda T) & i = 1, 0 < j < N \\
(P_{i-1,j}\lambda p_1 T + P_{i+1,j}q_1 + \lambda p_2 \cdot & \\
P_{i,j-1}T + P_{i,j+1}q_2)/(1 + \lambda T) & 1 < i \leq M, 0 < j < N
\end{cases}
$$

There are total $(M+2) \times (N+1)$ equations, of which there are $(M+2) \times (N+1) - 1$ equations irrelevant. So we select $(M+2) \times (N+1) - 1$ equations together with the equation $\sum_{i,j} P_{i,j} = 1$. By SOR(successive over-relaxation method), we can get the total state probability $P_{i,j}$. The SOR method is shown below:

We define a set of equations:
$$A \cdot x = b$$

Here ,
$$
\begin{aligned}
A &= \{a_{i,j}, 0 \leq i \leq n, 0 \leq j \leq n\}, \\
x &= \{x_i, 0 \leq i \leq n\}. \\
b &= \{b_i, 0 \leq i \leq n\}.
\end{aligned}
$$

Then we can get:
$$
\begin{cases}
\overline{x_i}^{k+1} = (b_i - \sum_{j=1}^{i-1} a_{i,j} x_j^{k+1} - \sum_{j=i+1}^{n} a_{i,j} x_j^k) \\
x_i^{k+1} = x_i^k + \omega(\overline{x_i}^{k+1} - x_i^k)
\end{cases}
$$

In SOR ω is the successive factor. The bigger ω , the quicker the computation converges. When k is near infinition, we get state probabilities of the system.

Since we have known the state probability, it is easy to get the average queueing length, the average waiting time, and the average packet loss probability. Of course, they are different according to the two kinds of packets.

Now we define L_A as the average queueing length for high priority packets. We have
$$L_A = \sum_{i>0,j} (i - L) P_{i,j}.$$

Similarly, L_D is defined as the average queueing length for low priority packets. We have
$$L_D = \sum_{i,j} j P_{i,j}.$$

On the other hand, we let T_A denote the average queueing waiting time of a high priority packet. We have
$$T_A = L_A / (\lambda p_1 (1 - pbA)).$$

Here we mainly consider the average time of services which is the queueing time, rather than the sum of the average queueing time and the average service time. That is to say, we suppose that the average service time for every kinds of packets is equal or the average service time can be omitted to the average queueing time. pbA is the block probability of a high priority packet.

Similarly ,we let T_D denote the average queueing waiting time of a low priority packet. We have
$$T_D = L_D / (\lambda p_2 (1 - pbD)).$$

Here pbD means the block probability of a low priority packet.

When pla is defined as the lost probability of a high priority packet, we have
$$pla = 1 - e^{-L_A/ThresholdA}.$$

Here ThresholdA means the wiating time limit of a high priority packet. Similarly when pld is defined as the lost probability of a low priority packet, we have
$$pld = 1 - e^{-L_D/ThresholdD}.$$

Here ThresholdD means the waiting time limit of a low priority packet.

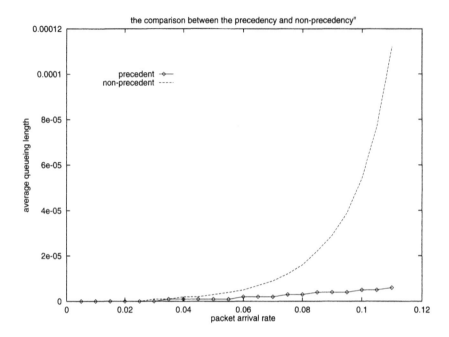

Figure 3: Average queueing length of high priority packets while $p1 = 10^{-5}$

4   Numerical Calculation and Computer Simulation

In this section we show our numerical results employed in the previous analysis.

4.1   System Parameters

Here we define some basic parameters the numerical calculations to be given. We let the buffer length 50 for either of the two kinds of packets. We suppose that the service time of a packet is 7 seconds. That is to say, $T = 7s$. Other parameters will be given when they are concerned.

4.2   The Average Queueing Length

Fig.3 shows the comparison of the average queueing length of the high priority packets under precedent condition(q1=0.999) and non-precedent condition($q1 = 10^{-5}$). Here we define $p1 = 10^{-5}$.

Fig.4 shows the comparison of the average queueing length of the low priority packets under precedent condition(q1=0.999) and non-precedent condition ($q1 = 10^{-5}$). Here we define $p1 = 10^{-5}$.

Fig.5 shows the comparison of the average queueing length of the high priority packets under precedent condition(q1=0.999) and non-precedent condition(q1=0.5) . Here we define $p1 = 0.5$.

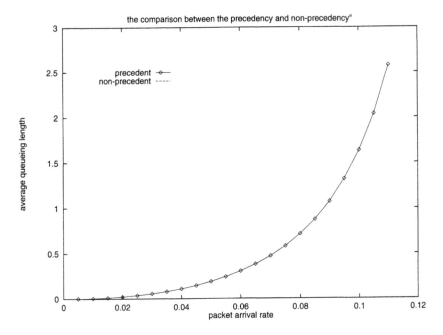

Figure 4: Average queueing length of low priority packets while $p1 = 10^{-5}$

Fig.6 shows the comparison of the average queueing length of the low priority packets under precedent condition(q1=0.999) and non-precedent condition (q1=0.5). Here we define $p1 = 0.5$.

4.3 The Average Waiting Time

Fig.7 shows the comparison of the average waiting time of the high priority packets under precedent condition(q1=0.999) and non-precedent condition($q1 = 10^{-5}$) . Here we define $p1 = 10^{-5}$.

Fig.8 shows the comparison of the average waiting time of the low priority packets under precedent condition(q1=0.999) and non-precedent condition ($q1 = 10^{-5}$). Here we define $p1 = 10^{-5}$.

Fig.9 shows the comparison of the average waiting time of the high priority packets under precedent condition(q1=0.999) and non-precedent condition(q1=0.5) . Here we define $p1 = 0.5$.

Fig.10 shows the comparison of the average waiting time of the low priority packets under precedent condition(q1=0.999) and non-precedent condition (q1=0.5). Here we define $p1 = 0.5$

4.4 The packet lost probability

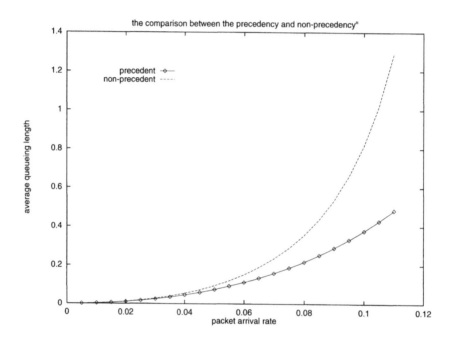

Figure 5: Average queueing length of the high priority packets while $p1 = 0.5$

Fig.11 shows the comparison of the average loss probability of the high priority packets under precedent condition(q1=0.999) and non-precedent condition($q1 = 10^{-5}$) . Here we define $p1 = 10^{-5}$.

Fig.12 shows the comparison of the average loss probability of the low priority packets under precedent condition(q1=0.999) and non-precedent condition ($q1 = 10^{-5}$.) Here we define $p1 = 10^{-5}$.

Fig.13 shows the comparison of the average loss probability of the high priority packets under precedent condition(q1=0.999) and non-precedent condition(q1=0.5) . Here we define $p1 = 0.5$.

Fig.14 shows the comparison of the average loss probability of the low priority packets under precedent condition(q1=0.999) and non-precedent condition (q1=0.5). Here we define $p1 = 0.5$.

4.5   Constant queueing lenth with priority

Fig.15 shows when λ is constant we adjust q according to the change of p to preserve the average queueing length of control information constant.

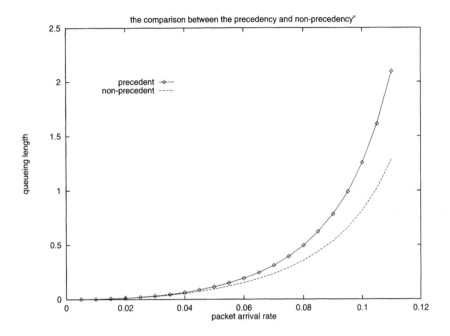

Figure 6: Average queueing length of the low priority packets while $p1 = 0.5$

Fig.16 shows when p is constant we adjust q according to the change of λ to preserve the average queueing length of control information constant.

p	0.0001	0.0002	0.0003	0.0004	0.0005	0.0006
q	0.000001	0.1229	0.2570	0.3969	0.5405	0.6867

Figure 15: q—p while λ is constant 0.02

p	&K	q
0.5	0.020	0.0001
0.5	0.0205	0.02069
0.5	0.021	0.3968

Figure 16:q—λ while p is constant

5   Conclusion

From Figure 3 and 4, we got when the probability of control information packets is very small, their average queueing length under precedent conditon is more less than that under non-precedent condition, while the average queueing length of low priority packets just increase very very little. Similarly, from Figure 7 and 8, from

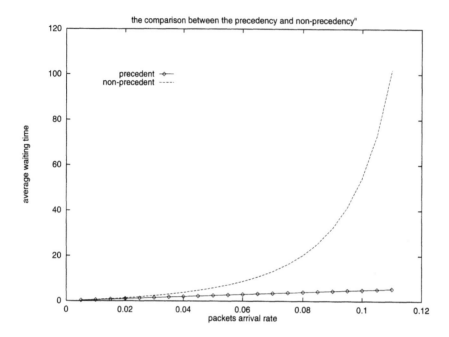

Figure 7: Average waiting time of the high priority packets while $p1 = 10^{-5}$

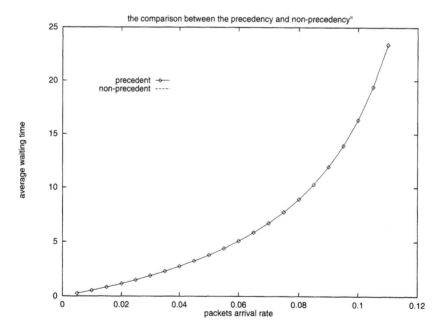

Figure 8: Average waiting time of the low priority packets while $p1 = 10^{-5}$

Figure 11 and 12, we see when the probability of control information packets is very small, their average waiting time and packet loss probability under precedent conditon are much less than those under non-precedent condition, while the average waiting time and packet loss probability of low priority packets just increases very very little. ¿From Figure 5 and 6, we get to know when the probability of control information packets is very big(equal to that of the multimedia data), their average queueing length under precedent conditon is more less than that under non-precedent condition, while the average queueing length of low priority packets increases less than the former decrease. Similarly, from Figure 9 and 10, from Figure 13 and 14), we see when the probability of control information packets is very big(equal to that of the multimedia data), their average waiting time and packet loss probability under precedent conditon are much less than those under non-precedent condition, while the average waiting time and packet loss probability of low priority packets increase less than the former decrease . The results mean that our proposal is obviously useful to keep the performance of the high priority packets, especially when their probality is very small. So this is exactly fit for the control information ,which probability is very samll in general.

We also realize keeping the performance of the control information processing constant, and it is done by looking up a table constructed before, just like in Figure 15 and Figure 16 . We can see that adjusting the value of q is effective while p changes, but it has not very obvious effect that we adjust q while λ changes.

We will go on studying the complicate condition, such as more service windows, more parallel queueings(ie. more precedent levels). The condition under more intermediate hops will also be taken into consideration, while the traffic routing will cost much time.

Bibliography

1) C. Chang and S. Wang :" Analysis of an Integrated Multiplexer with All Queueable and Fixed-Length Traffics in Intermediate Node,",IEICE TRANS.,E75-B,NO.7 (Jul. 1992)

2) K. Ohta, T. Watanabe and T. Mizuno:"A Proposal of Network Protocol with Performance for Multimedia Communication System",IEICE Trans. E79-D,NO.6 (Jun. 1996)

3) M. Hamdaoui, and P. Ramanathan :"A Dynamic Priority Assugnment Technique for Streams with (m,k)-Firm Deadlines,",IEEE Trans. on Comm.,VOL. 44 ,NO. 12, Dec. 1995

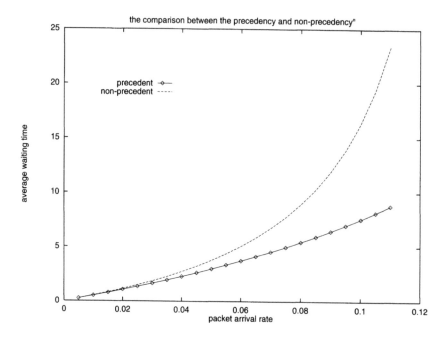

Figure 9: Average waiting time of the high priority packets while $p1 = 0.5$

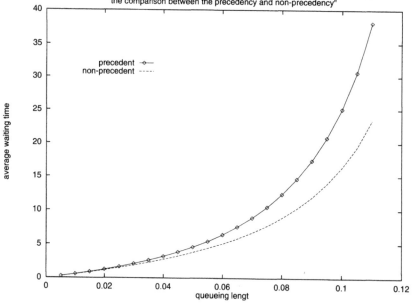

Figure 10: Average waiting time of the low priority packets while $p1 = 0.5$

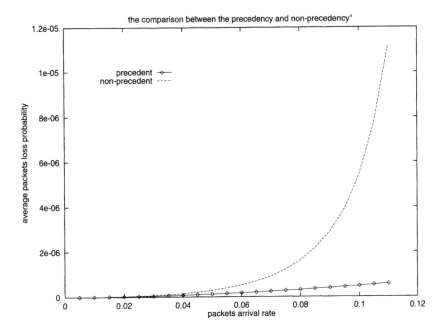

Figure 11: Average loss probability of the high priority packet while $p1 = 10^{-5}$

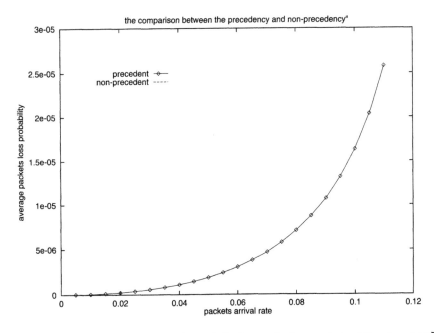

Figure 12: Average loss probability of the low priority packet while $p1 = 10^{-5}$

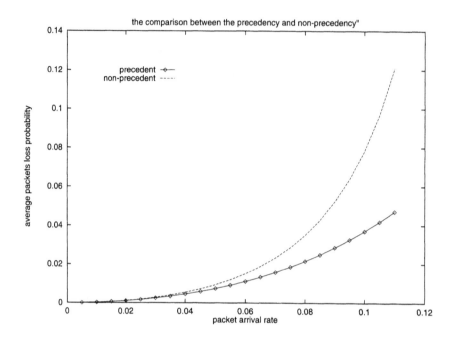

Figure 13: Average loss probability of the high priority packet while $p1 = 0.5$

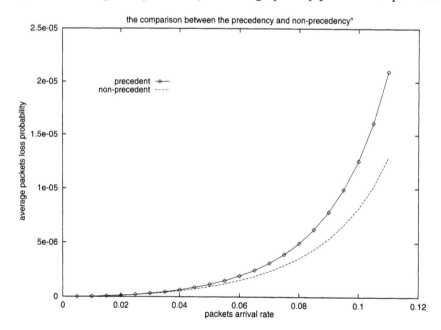

Figure 14: Average loss probability of the low priority packet while $p1 = 0.5$

11

The Prototype of Continuous Media File System, *CrownFS*

Se-Jin Hwang, Jin-Uok Kim, Myong-soon Park

Korea University

Oh-Young Kwon, Tae-Geun Kim

ETRI

ABSTRACT

The rapid movement of parallel computing environment from MPP to clustered workstations or high performance PCs, has strongly affected the track of multimedia data service. Currently, many multimedia or continuous media server system is under development on top of either workstations or high-end PCs clustered with high speed networking facilities.

In this paper, we introduce Crown, a continuous media server on clustered high performance PCs with Myrinet, fast network switching equipment, and then address CrownFS, a file system on top of Crown, to offer continous media streams to many subscribers at the same time. For easy and rapid tunning of the performance of CrownFS, we prototyped it. Prototyping requires less efforts and costs than direct implementation. Also, more reliable system optimization is obtainable rather than simulation. By using the prototype, we measured the scalability of CrownFS according to various disk access strategies.

1 Introduction

The remarkable improvement of microprocessor technology and the emergence of high speed network have strongly increased the popularity of clustered workstations as a desirable high performance computing environment. Workstation clustering technology brings the benefit of cost-effectiveness, flexbility and high scalability compared to MPPs[1]. Therefore, over the years, many researchers have attempted to use this technology to run applications requiring a great amount of system resources. Such trend has also made a great influence on the track of multimedia research as well, thus, recently, continuous media server by using many clustered workstations or high-end PCs has been actively researched and under development[2, 3, 4, 5, 7].

Crown(*C*lustered *r*esources *on w*orkstation *n*etwork) is our ongoing project to serve multiple continuous media streams to several dozens of subscribers. It is composed of a number of high performance PC, DEC *Kauai*[1] with one 200 MHz Pentium Pro[2] superscalar microprocessor and SCSI disks. *CrownFS(Crown File System)* is a file system to manage MPEG-1 file distributed over many disks in *Crown* and to simultaneously serve it to the subscribers. 9 Dec PCs are all currently connected with Myrinet high speed switching network, and one of them will play a role in the gateway bridging between many client nodes. *Linux* is equipped into all the PCs as an operating system for *CrownFS*. The rest eight PCs will keep the distributed MPEG-1 data streams. These DEC PCs will be caged into one cabinet, and internal physical network configuration with Myrinet will be strictly veiled, and, just Fast-Ethernet connector coming from the gateway node is revealed out of the cabinet for easy connectivity with client, subscriber.

Crown has conceptually three constituents, the eight storage server PCs containing the pieces of declustered MPEG-1 file, the gateway node bridging between clients and server nodes, and finally, client nodes for subscribers. The maintenance of such nodes is totally up to CrownFS, file system to pump continuous media streams from the eight storage servers, to multiple clients via the gateway at the regular rate.

To find out its bottleneck points ahead of implementation, we prototyped CrownFS. The prototype does not require whole system configuration, therefore we can have an advantage of the simplicity of validation. The prototype of Crown examines the usefulness of our strategy for servicing MPEG-1 data request from clients, and is implemented with good configurability for easy system designer's customization.

This paper is organized as follows. The next section enumerates the previous works related to file system for continuous media data management, and then, we introduce CrownFS continuous media file system for Crown implemented upon workstation clustering environment, and address its internal organization from section 3. Section 4 introduces the prototype of CrownFS, and then we show the performance variations of APIs supported by CrownFS at section 5. The section 5 also shows the problem of CrownFS shown after the performance measurement. Finally, we make conclusion at section 6, together with current situation of the project including future works.

2 Previous Works

The key technology of VOD system, continuous media server, is to design file system in order to pump media streams to many subscribers at the same time with satisfying the real-time requirement of the stream.

To this end, buffering strategy has been popularly employed in many continuous media servers[6] to prefetch some amount of streams into buffers located at clients or other intermediate components. The buffer is properly managed by file system generally dedicated to continous media stream service[4, 6]. Practically, the majority of the development of continuous media server is occupied by both the design of

---

[1] *Kauai* is a trademark of Digital Euipement Corporation.

[2] *Pentinum Pro* is a trademark of Intel.

buffer handling stategy of its file system and its real-time disk access technique.

The researchers in U. of Berkeley implemented a continuous media file system, *VFS*[4], for Berekeley VOD system. They support hierarchical data streaming and buffering at several levels in overall network topology. *Fellini*[7] was developed at AT&T Bell laboratory, which is a continuous media file system to support MPEG-1 streams. Here, the buffer struture is handled in the fashion of FIFO, exactly same to the physical access pattern of MPEG-1 byte streams. These were all implemented and optimized after directly realizing whole system architectures, therefore, its implementation cost is regarded as fairly high.

Oyang *et. al* did a exhaustive study on the storage system for a multimedia system with video-on-demand playback[2]. His work is highly concentrated on the analysis of upper bounds of various disk-seek algorithms. Song Bac Toh simulated the video-on-demand system with Simpack packages for simulation[3]. This work strictly relies on the functionality of software for only simulation use, Simpack, thus, the reliability of the simulation is hardly expected.

Therefore, we choosed a way of prototyping CrownFS to examine the bottleneck points of CrownFS and its correctness. It does not require high implementation cost rather than the direct implementation of whole system, but makes it possible to accomplish reliable system analysis compared to simulation. After addessing CrownFS itself at next section, we will switch to the discussion of prototype.

3   *CrownFS* : **Continuous Media File System**

Three conceptual components building *CrownFS* are *M-worker*, *S-worker* and *client library*. *M-worker*(Master *worker*) is a bridge node to govern stream arbitration between clients and storage server nodes, and accepts data requests from each client. The major role of M-worker is to deliver streams to the client by requesting them to the storage servers. The storage server nodes, 8 PCs are all called as *S-worker*(Slave *worker*)s, which keeps the pieces of declustered MPEG-1 files within disks. Figure 1 illustrates the Crown, continuous media server. Subscriber comes to access MPEG-1 file through client library APIs.

The main job of S-worker is to schedule the multiple requests from the M-worker and to drive disks by real time manner for retrieving the requested data. M-worker should have a knowledge of which pieces of data is stored in which S-worker, in order to exactly request data. Such requirement needs the presence of meta-data pairing S-workers with a specific portions of an arbitrary MPEG-1 file. MPEG-1 file is distributed over many disks within more than two S-workers in the fashion of round-robin, namely, simple striping.

Client library provides a set of APIs in Figure 1 to make application access MPEG-1 media data managed by CrownFS, so, it should be compiled and linked with the application in client node.

MPEG-1 data streams accessed with the APIs shown in Table 1 comes to be buffered in two hierarchies, both at the level of M-worker node and client library.

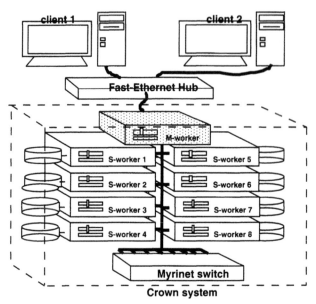

Figure 1: The configuration of *Crown* system (M-worker is connected both to Myrinet switch and Fast-Ethernet hub, threfore, two kinds of network card should be installed inside. PCs in dotted line are all DEC *Kauai.*)

The streams injected from S-workers travels via M-worker up to buffers in the client in a pipelined way.

Table 1. Supported APIs by CrownFS

API	*comments*
mf_creat	creates a meta-data for a new MPEG-1 file which will be distributed over disks in CrownFS
mf_open	opens a MPEG-1 file distributed over disks in CrownFS
mf_read	reads a declustered block of a MPEG-1 file from CrownFS
mf_write	writes a piece of a MPEG-1 file to CrownFS
mf_close	closes a MPEG-1 streams
mf_seek	changes a starting location to playback MPEG-1 file

M-worker should make a periodical contact with several S-workers to prefetch streams into its buffer. The stream retrieval of S-workers should be completed within a given time. To locate the exact position of requested data, *inode* structure for Crown file system is maintained as well as a disk partition dedicated to storing MPEG-1 media streams.

3.1 Buffer Management

Similarly other continuous media servers, CrownFS also uses buffer to satisfy the required bandwidth of network and disk in order to offer multiple MPEG-1 streams to many subscribers.

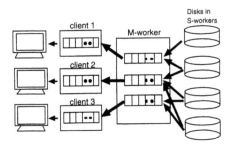

Figure 2: The buffer hierarchy of *CrownFS* (Here, 3 clients are being serviced of MPEG-1 streams, so M-worker is managing three buffers for each client.MPEG-1 file accessed by client 1 is distributed over two S-workers, and client 2 is accessing MPEG-1 over 3 S-workers)

MPEG-1 byte streams comes to be buffered in M-worker and client in advance of its playing time, if user would clicks *play* VCR operation.

The buffers are all managed in the fashion of FIFO with a royal obeisance to FCFS(First Come First Serve) policy. The hierarchical buffer structure is depicted in Figure 2. Buffer handling mechanism to service continuous MPEG-1 streams to many subscribers is based on a time-sliced round-robin way. The time for each client is called *service time*. CrownFS makes a proper action on five sorts of VCR operations, *play*, *stop*, *pause*, *resume*, *rewind*. Currently, *fast-forward* are not yet implemented, since it has a potential to make the internal architecture of CrownFS be complicated from the scratch.

The buffers are systematically filled and managed depending on VCR operations selected by subscribers via MPEG-1 media player in client node. Therefore, we can say that the buffer management strategy is how to manage subscriber's VCR operation. The following enumerates the buffer management in accordance with VCR commands, currently supported in CrownFS. VCR operations, *play*, *resume*, *rewind* spans more than two *service turn-around time*[3], since one service time slice is not long enough to complete their operations.

Play operation opens MPEG-1 file distributed over S-workers, and then, starts playing it immediately after filling buffers both within client and M-worker. These are executed by one *mf_open*, and the several invocation of *mf_read* to pre-fill the buffer in client and M-worker.

Both buffer filling and consuming comes to be repeated by the moment of the full. Such protocol can guarantee that some amount stream will be prepared as a few seconds to be played.

Pause operation temporarily stops playing MPEG-1 file, and then waits for the selection of *resume* VCR operation by user. This operation is simply achieved by stopping the issue of *mf_read* API till the click of *resume* button.

---

[3]It is equal to *service time* × (*maximum number of subscribers* - 1)

What the client does when a user clicks *pause* button, it prepares for the next stream of MPEG-1 which will be retrieved. Surely, client waits for the click of *resume* button.

Resume operation begins to playback the stream stored in the client buffer. After that, client jumped into the state of *play*. The second and third steps come to be repeated as descried before.

Stop terminates playing MPEG-1 file. Therefore, client buffer and buffer in M-worker are all freed. Such resource freeing happens by the invocation of *mf_close* API in client node.

Rewind operation takes the longest time among five VCR operations. Invoking *mf_seek* is all that we have to do for positioning the file pointer to the beginning of the file.

On playing MPEG-1 byte streams, client intermittently requests MPEG-1 streams not yet fetched from M-worker as much as the empty space of buffer in the client node. This request is serviced by M-worker at the associated service time slice.

Simple glance at the steps of each VCR operation can clearly reveal the fact that the longest work is accomplished at the third step in *play* operation. Therefore, we decided that one service time for one client takes as long as both sending contents of buffer in M-worker to client and getting streams injected from S-worker under requests.

Since MPEG-1 file is simply distributed over more than two disks of S-workers in round-robin fashion, both requesting each pieces of the file to one S-worker and sending the requested data from another S-worker can be overalapped.

3.2   Disk Management

Each distributed block of MPEG file is stored in a specific disk partition dedicated to CrownFS, called *RawDisk*. RawDisk partition is created by a raw disk management mechanism[7]. This area is not under control of traditional UNIX file system, therefore, we can save the time consumed by traditional UNIX file system to handle buffer cache or to manipulate inode structure, etc. To keep track of all declustered blocks of MPEG file, the beginning of RawDisk partition contains superblock and a set of inode strutures. Superblock records the status of each block in RawDisk partition as either *used* or *free*, and designates the starting offset of inode information. Inode structure is not identical to that of traditional UNIX file system, though, it keeps information of blocks belongs to a certain MPEG file.

Declustering of MPEG file enables us to overlap at least two works of both requesting certain block to a S-worker, and accessing disks in another S-worker. Such overlap can comparably diminish the disk access time to fetch MPEG streams. M-worker is expected to wait for the arrival of requested blocks form each S-workers as long as the following intervals.

> *time taken to fetch streams from S-workers* =
> (*time to request a block to one S-worker* +
> *time to send a block to M-worker from S-worker*) ×
> ($\frac{number\ of\ S-workers}{2}$ + 1)

The equation expresses the overlap effect between requesting a block to a S-worker and the delivery of block from other S-workers. The time to send a block includes disk latencies to position disk arm to the track containing the requested block.

Since a MPEG file is distributed over several disks in S-workers, each scattered blocks should be collected and arranged to the form of consecutive streams for normal playback. Such arrangement takes place within M-worker. Depending on how well we collect each declustered pieces of the block, the scalability of CrownFS can be either good or bad. Therefore, we estimated the scalability with the variation of the disk access strategy to collct and to arrange declustered blocks by using its prototype.

4   Prototype of *CrownFS*

The major reason of building a prototype is to do an accurate validation test of service routine which we designed, and to estimate the scalability of CrownFS. By using the prototype, we could also find a bottleneck points of the performance.

The prototype is currently installed and runs on three Sun 10 W/Ss. It treats the continuous MPEG-1 streams as described at previous subsection, and conceptually, it also configures M-worker, S-workers, and client. The used network facility is Ethernet, neither Myrinet and Fast-Ethernet, because of the lack of such network equipments at the launch of building the prototype. Ethernet networking can be used instead of Myrinet to relatively evaluate the performance of networking since latencies of the two equipment is linearly proportional to the increment of packet size. SCSI disks is also just simulated on the file created with a very large empty space in traditional UNIX file system area.

The client MPEG-1 player software was implemented by modifying *mpeg_play* freely distributed by U. of Berkeley. It was recompiled and linked with client library routine which can make it communicate with the prototyped M-worker daemon process, *mwd*. Since it does not drive harware MPEG decoder, it is nearly imposssible to continuously spread out realistic MPEG frames. *Mwd* module fetches MPEG streams via the interaction with *swd*, prototyped S-worker module.

The exclusion of screen manipulation routine to display the consecutive shot of MPEG image is also available by simply switching on a command line option. Such functionality can help us estimate the validation of our routine by eradicating potential side-effects by screen handling and by mouse focusing within X-window frame generated by *mpeg_play*.

The important feature of the prototype system is free and easy configurability. Simply put, if a user wish to alter the size of the declustered block in S-worker, and

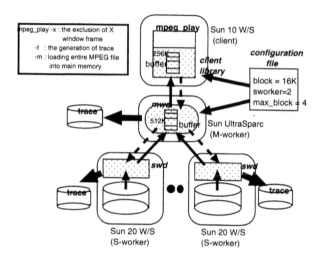

Figure 3: The strucure of the prototype of CrownFS.(*mwd* works as M-worker, *swd* as S-worker, *client library* is for the interaction between client and M-worker. Bolded rectangular box explains the command line options to switch on/off the functionality of CrownFS. We put *mwd* and *mpeg_play* into one Sun W/S due to the lack of W/Ss.)

the amount of buffer in M-worker, it can be easily done by modifying a configuation file shown in Figure 3. The configuration file keeps all parameters relevant to system resources. The file also contains information of system resources of target environment of Crown, therefore, it enables user to predict how fully it can utilize the system resources, and how much well it can promise the non-stop MPEG byte streams.

5   Evaluation

We estimated the scalability of CrownFS under two kinds of S-worker access strategies. The increment of the number of S-worker has been also considered.

MPEG-1 streams are distributed over many disks within S-workers in the fashion of simple striping, therefore, we have to gather them into a continuous streams for normal plackback. To collect the distributed blocks, we should take two steps. First, we have to request the blocks to S-workers, and then S-worker should respond it. In collective mode, M-worker sends only one block request to one S-worker. The request packet describes all blocks to which M-worker wants to refer within that S-worker. Then, the S-worker sends the blocks within a big packet containing all requested blocks. In the other case, non-collective mode, M-worker sends requests for every distributed blocks. Therefore, less communication overhead does we can take by using collective-mode request. However, more intelligent and complicated arrangement of data deliver from S-worker should be supported. Better scalability of CrownFS could be possible rather than non-collective mode.

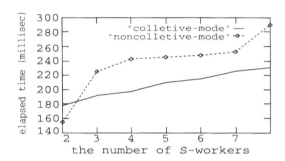

Figure 4: The variation of service time to fetch a stream as much as 128K bytes from S-workers according to S-worker access methodology.

Underlying network environment was based on Ethernet. Six W/Ss are connected to the Ethernet, and two of them operate as M-worker and client respectively. The remaining four W/Ss played a role of S-workers, and disk partition dedicated to CrownFS is only emulated on top of a big file as much as several megabytes. All workstations are all the family of Sun Sparc, one Sparc-10, two Sparc-20s, three Ultra-Sparcs. Used benchmark is a horror movie 'psycho', and we averaged all traced elapsed service times during plackback for about 20 minutes. The network protocol between client and M-worker is TCP, meanwhile UDP protocol is employed for the communication between S-workers and M-worker. Client perodically requests streams to M-worker, and then, M-worker appropriately requests the blocks to several S-workers according to its distribution. We applied two kinds of the request by M-worker to CrownFS, both collective request and non-collective one. The amount of request size from client is up to 128K bytes. Each MPEG file had been distributed as 8K bytes.

Figure 4 shows the variation of the service time in milliseconds for one stream access according to S-worker access strategies by M-worker. Here, diamond line designates the time to access 128K byte block in non-collective communication way, simple line in collective communication way. The vertical axis is guaged in millisecond, and horizontal axis means by the number of S-worker's which we used.

In Figure 4, with the increment of S-workers, the collective communication shows better performance rather than non-collective communication, that is, point-to-point communication. More than 8 S-workers were not estimated, since 8 S-workers are our maximum number of S-workers in the specification of Crown. To meet with the customer's acceptable price , we strictly limit the maximum number of S-workers. The second thing is S-workers are all implemented virtually within practical two workstations. Evenly, 4 *swds* are competitively executed within a node in case of 8 S-workers. Then, more than 4 S-worker daemon's called *swd*, makes great burden of the workstation, thus, extra unpredicted impacts will greatly make it irregular system performance by adding more *swds*.

6 Conclusion

This paper introduces a continous media file system, CrownFS to support multiple MPEG-1 streams to many subscribers. Also, to find a bottleneck point of CrownFS, we prototyped it.

For the sake of easy customization of the prototype we made it have high configurability and easy installation. Currently, it is implemented on top of three Sun W/Ss connected by Ethernet.

By using the prototype, we estimated service time under two kinds of S-worker access strategies with the variation of S-workers. Collective communication shows better scalability rather than non-collective communication between S-workers and M-worker. Then, some kind of difficulties might arise when we try to implement this technique on top of Myrinet networking substrates. Myrinet networking just support small size networking buffer and data travels on top of it without interrupt notification to operating system itself. That implies that sophisticated network buffer control to correctly catch up the flowing packets sould be supported in the future.

Bibliography

1) Thomas E. Anderson, *"Serverless Network File Stystem"*, Technical Report, Berekeley, 1995.

2) Yen-Jen Oyang, Meng-Huang Lee, Chun-Hung Wen and Chih-Yuan Chen, *"Design of Multimedia Storage System for On-Demand Playback"*, Proc. of the 11th International Conf. on Data Engineering.

3) Song Bac Toh, *"Simulation of a Video-on-Demand System"*, PCS-TR95-260, Dartmouth Computer Science, 1995.

4) D. James Gemmell, Harrick Vin, Dilip Kandlur, P. Venkat Rangan, and Lawrence A. Rowe, *"Multimedia Storage Servers: A Tutorial"*, IEEE Computer, May, 1995.

5) Craig Fedeighi and Lowren A. Rowe, *"A Distributed Hierarchical Storage Manager for a Video-on-Demand System"*, Symp. on Electronic Science and Techniques, Feb. 1994.

6) P. V. Rangan and H. M. Vin, *"Design File System for Digital Video and Audio"*, Proc. of the 12th ACM Symp. on Operating Systems, 1991.

7) C. Martin, P. S. Narayan, B. Ozden, R. Rastogi and A. Silberschatz, *"The Fellini Multimedia Storage System"*, Journal of Digital Libraries, 1997.

8) David Kotz, *"Disk-Directed I/O for MIMD multiprocessors"*, Technical Report PCS-TR94-226, Dartmouth College, 1994.

12

QoS-based Flexibility in Distributed Systems

Tetsuo Kanezuka

Hiroaki Higaki

Makoto Takizawa

Tokyo Denki University

ABSTRACT

This paper discusses how to make a distributed object system flexible so as to satisfy applications' requirements in change of the system environment. The change of the system is modeled to be the change of not only types of service but also quality of service (QoS) supported by the objects. We discuss equivalency and compatibility relations among operations on the basis of QoS. By using the QoS-based relations, we newly discuss a QoS-based compensating way to recover the object from the less qualified state. Finally, we discuss a QoS-based way for replicating objects to make required QoS available. Be using these QoS-based way, we can reduce time and cost for making the system flexible.

1 Introduction

Units of resources in distributed systems are referred to as *objects* [4]. An object is an encapsulation of data and operations for manipulating the data. CORBA [4] is getting a general framework to make distributed applications interoperable. The system is required to be *flexible* in change of the system environment and the applications' requirements in addition to supporting the interoperability. One of the major changes in the system is *fault*. There are two approaches to realizing the fault-tolerant system; replication and checkpointing. The active [5] and passive [2] replications are discussed so far. The applications can get the service of the object as long as some number of the replicas are operational. In the checkpointing protocols, the object is rolled back to the consistent checkpoint if the object is faulty. Tanaka and Takizawa [7] discuss an object-based checkpoint which allows orphan messages to exist but which is consistent from the object point of view.

In addition to the object fault, other properties of the system like the response time change. The service supported by the object is characterized by the parameters showing QoS. Yoshida and Takizawa [8] model the *movement* of the mobile object to be the change of QoS supported by the object. It is critical to discuss how to support QoS which satisfies the application's requirement in change of QoS supported by the objects. The object o_i supports the application with service through the operations. Relations among the operations are discussed so far with respect to the states of the objects. For example, two operations are compatible if the states obtained by applying the operations in any order are the same [1]. The applications can view QoS of the object only through the operations. For example, suppose that a multimedia object m supports higher quality image data and a *display* operation. Here, the application can only get the lower quality image if *display* can output only lower quality image. We define QoS-based equivalency and compatibility among the operations in terms of views obtained by applying the operations to the objects.

Effects done by operations computed have to be removed if applications' requirements are not satisfied, e.g. the system is faulty. The effects can be removed by the *compensating* operations [3, 6] of the operations computed. In multimedia applications, it takes time to restore a large volume of high-resolution video data. We can reduce time for recovering the system if data with lower resolution but satisfying the applications' requirement is restored instead of restoring the high-resolution data. In this paper, we discuss a compensating method where an object o_i may not be rolled back to the previous state which o_i has taken but can be surely rolled back to a state supporting QoS which satisfies the applications' requirement.

An object can be replicated in order to increase availability. Since huge volume of storage and expensive devices are required to realize multimedia objects, it is expensive, maybe impossible to replicate the objects. The less qualified the state of object is, the less volume of storage is required. Hence, the replicas may support different levels of QoS. Applications can use a subset of replicas which support enough QoS. This is a QoS-based replication to be discussed in this paper.

In section 2, we present a system model. In sections 3 and 4, we discuss relations among the operations and the compensation on the basis of QoS, respectively. In section 5, we discuss QoS-based replications.

2   System Model

2.1   Objects

A system is composed of objects o_1, ..., o_n interconnected by reliable networks. Each object o_i is an encapsulation of the data and a collection of abstract operations op_{i1}, ..., op_{il_i} only by which o_i can be manipulated. Let $op_{ij}(s_i)$ denote a state of o_i obtained by applying op_{ij} to a state s_i of o_i. $[op_{ij}(s_i)]$ denotes the response data obtained by $op_{ij}(s_i)$. $op_{ij} \circ op_{ik}$ means that op_{ik} is computed after op_{ij}. Here, a conflicting relation [3] among operations is defined as follows: for every pair of operations op_{ij} and op_{ik}, op_{ij} *conflicts* with op_{ik} if $op_{ij} \circ op_{ik}(s_i) \neq op_{ik} \circ op_{ij}(s_i)$, $[op_{ij}(s_i)] \neq [op_{ik} \circ op_{ij}(s_i)]$, or $[op_{ij} \circ op_{ik}(s_i)] \neq [op_{ik}(s_i)]$ for some state s_i of o_i. For example, *record* conflicts with *delete* in the *movie* object. op_{ij} is *compatible* with op_{ik} unless op_{ij} conflicts with op_{ik}. If op_{ij} and op_{ik} are compatible, both the same state and the same response data are obtained independently of the computation order of op_{ij} and op_{ik}. We assume the conflicting relation is symmetric but not transitive.

2.2 Quality of service (QoS)

The service supported by an object o_i can be obtained by issuing an operation to o_i. Each type of service is characterized by parameters like levels of resolution, number of frames, and number of colors. The parameters show quality of service (QoS). Even if a pair of objects o_i and o_j support the same types of service, they may provide different levels of QoS.

The *scheme* of QoS is given in a tuple of attributes $\langle a_1, ..., a_m \rangle$ where each attribute a_i shows a parameter. Let $\mathrm{dom}(a_i)$ be a *domain* of a_i, i.e. a set of possible values to be taken by a_i. For example, $\mathrm{dom}(resolution)$ is a set of numbers each of which shows the number of pixels for each frame. A QoS *instance* q of the scheme $\langle a_1, ... a_m \rangle$ is given in a tuple of values, i.e. $\langle v_1, ..., v_m \rangle \in \mathrm{dom}(a_1) \times ... \times \mathrm{dom}(a_m)$. Let $a_i(q)$ show v_i in q. The values in $\mathrm{dom}(a_i)$ are partially ordered by a precedent relation $\preceq \subseteq \mathrm{dom}(a_i)^2$. A value v_1 *precedes* v_2 $(v_1 \succeq v_2)$ if v_1 shows better QoS than v_2. For example, $120 \times 100 \preceq 160 \times 120$ [pixels] for the *resolution* attribute. Let q_1 and q_2 show QoS instances of a scheme $\langle a_1, ..., a_m \rangle$. q_1 *totally dominates* q_2 $(q_1 \succeq q_2)$ iff $a_i(q_1) \succeq a_i(q_2)$ for every attribute a_i. Let A be a subset $\langle b_1, ..., b_k \rangle$ where $\{b_1, ..., b_k\} \subseteq \{a_1, ..., a_m\}$. A projection $[q]_A$ of q on A is $\langle w_1, ..., w_k \rangle$ where $w_i = b_i(q)$ for $i = 1, ..., k$. A QoS *instance* q_1 of a scheme A_1 *partially dominates* q_2 of A_2 iff $a(q_1) \succeq a(q_2)$ for every attribute a in $A_1 \cap A_2$. q_1 *subsumes* q_2 $(q_1 \supseteq q_2)$ iff q_1 partially dominates q_2 and $A_1 \supseteq A_2$. Let Q be a set of QoS *instances* whose schemes are not necessarily the same. q_1 is *minimal* in Q iff there is no q_2 in Q such that $q_2 \preceq q_1$. q_1 is *minimum* in Q iff $q_1 \preceq q_2$ for every q_2 in Q. q_1 is *maximal* iff there is no q_2 in Q such that $q_1 \preceq q_2$. q_1 is *maximum* in Q iff $q_2 \preceq q_1$ for every q_2 in Q. $q_1 \cup q_2$ and $q_1 \cap q_2$ show a *least upper bound* (*lub*) and a *greatest lower bound* (*glb*) of q_1 and q_2 in Q on $\preceq$, respectively. $q_1 \cup q_2$ is some QoS instance q_3 in Q such that (1) $q_1 \preceq q_3$ and $q_2 \preceq q_3$, and (2) there is no q_4 in Q where $q_1 \preceq q_4 \preceq q_3$ and $q_2 \preceq q_4 \preceq q_3$. $q_1 \cap q_2$ is defined similarly to $\cup$.

Applications require an object to support some *requirement* QoS (*RoS*). An RoS instance $R \langle V_1, ..., V_k \rangle$ where each V_i is a value of an attribute a_i. Here, suppose an object o supports a QoS instance $q = \langle v_1, ..., v_m \rangle$ where each v_i is a value of a_i. Here, let A_R be the scheme of R and A_q be the scheme of q. q *subsumes* R $(q \supseteq R)$ iff q partially dominates R and $A_q \supseteq A_R$. If $q \supseteq R$, the applications can get enough service from o.

2.3 Invocation tree

An object is realized by using other objects. Thus, an operation op_{ij} of o_i may invoke another operation op_{kl} of an object o_k. op_{ij} successfully completes, i.e. *commits* if every operation invoked by op_{ij} commits. Otherwise, op_{ij} aborts. op_{kl} may further invoke other operations. Thus, the invocations of operations are *nested*. Here, suppose an operation op_i of an object o_i invokes operations $op_{i1}, \ldots, op_{it_i}$ $(t_i \geq 1)$. Some operation op_{ij} is issued to another object o_{ij}. Other operations are computed in o_i. The former ones are referred to as *public* and the latter ones are *private*. Each object supports two kinds of operations, i.e. private and public ones. The public operation can be invoked by other objects. However, the private ones cannot be used from the other objects. Here, op_i and op_{ij} are referred to as *parent* and *child*, respectively. In this paper, we assume that the child operations are invoked serially in a sequence $op_{i1}, \ldots, op_{it_i}$. This invocation is represented in an ordered tree form named an *invocation* tree.

2.4   Multimedia objects

In this paper, we consider multimedia objects. QoS of an object o_i has two aspects: *state* QoS which is obtained from the state s_i and *operation* QoS which is supported through the operations of o_i. For example, let us consider a video object *video* with a *display* operation as shown in Figure 1. A state s_i of o_i supports video data with a rate 30 fps, which is a state QoS. However, *display* can display the view $[display(s_i)]$ of the video data from s_i only at 20 fps. This is an operation QoS $Q([display(s_i)])$.

Let $Q(s_i)$ denote the state QoS of a state s_i of o_i. Let $Q(op_{ij})$ denote QoS supported by an operation op_{ij}. QoS of o_i can be viewed through the operation of o_i. Here, let $Q([op_{ij}(s_i)])$ denote QoS viewed by applying op_{ij} to the state s_i, which is given to be a minimum one of $Q(s_i)$ and $Q(op_{ij})$. Let $\langle s_i \rangle$ denote $\langle [op_{i1}(s_i)], \ldots, [op_{il_i}(s_i)] \rangle$, i.e. *view* of s_i. $Q(\langle s_i \rangle)$ is defined to be a tuple $\langle Q([op_{i1}(s_i)]), \ldots, Q([op_{il_i}(s_i)]) \rangle$, i.e. operation QoS. $Q(\langle s_i \rangle)$ shows QoS of o_i which the users can view through the operations. $Q(\langle s_i \rangle)$ *subsumes* $Q(\langle s_j \rangle)$ $(Q(\langle s_i \rangle) \supseteq Q(\langle s_j \rangle))$ iff there is some operation op_{ik} of o_i such that $Q([op_{ik}(s_i)]) \succeq Q([op_{ik}(s_j)])$ for every op_{ik} of o_j. QoS supported by o_i changes depending on the state of o_i and the types of operations supported by o_i. Let $maxQ(o_i)$ denote maximum QoS to be supported by o_i, i.e. maximum of $Q(\langle s_i \rangle)$ for every state s_i of o_i. Let $minQ(o_i)$ denote minimum QoS of o_i. Here, $minQ(o_i) \preceq Q(\langle s_i \rangle) \preceq maxQ(o_i)$ for every s_i of o_i.

[**Definition**] An object o_i *subsumes* o_j $(o_i \supseteq o_j)$ iff $Q(\langle s_i \rangle) \supseteq Q(\langle s_j \rangle)$ for every pair of states s_i of o_i and s_j of o_j. $\square$

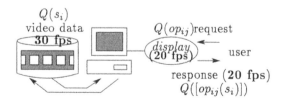

Figure 1: QoS of video object.

3 QoS-Related Operations

3.1 Equivalency

We discuss how operations op_1, ..., op_l supported by an object o are related with respect to QoS. A op_i is *equivalent* with op_j iff $op_i(s) = op_j(s)$ and $[op_i(s)] = [op_j(s)]$ for every state s of o. That is, op_i and op_j not only output the same data but also change the state of o to the same state. For example, suppose there are two versions *old-display* and *new-display* of a *display* operation supported by the *movie* object. *new-display* can display the same video image as *old-display* while *new-display* can display at a faster rate than *old-display*. *new-display* is equivalent with *old-display* because they output the same image data and do not change the state of *movie*. However, they support different levels of QoS, i.e. *new-display* is better than *old-display* with respect to the display speed.

[**Definition**] op_i is *QoS-equivalent* with op_j iff $Q(\langle op_i(s) \rangle) = Q(\langle op_j(s) \rangle)$ for every state s of an object o. □

That is, $op \circ op_i(s)$ and $op \circ op_j(s)$ support the same view for every operation op. op_i is *QoS-equivalent* with op_j if $Q(\langle op_i(s) \rangle) = Q(\langle op_j(s) \rangle)$.

Suppose that op_i invokes operations op_{i1}, ..., op_{it_i} as shown in Figure ??. It is sure that $op_i(s) = op_{i1} \circ \ldots \circ op_{it_i}(s)$ for a state s of the system. Here, $op_{i1} \circ \ldots \circ op_{it_i}$ is equivalent with op_i. A sequence $\langle op_{i1}, \ldots, op_{it_i} \rangle$ is *more expanded* than op_i, denoted by $(op_i)^1$. Each op_{ij} can be more expanded if op_{ij} is public and invokes operations op_{ij1}, ..., $op_{ijt_{ij}}$ $(t_{ij} > 1)$. That is, $\langle op_{i1}, \ldots, op_{i,j-1}, op_{ij1}, \ldots, op_{ijt_{ij}}, op_{i,j+1}, \ldots, op_{it_i} \rangle$. However, the private one cannot be expanded. The hth $(h \geq 0)$ expansion $(op_i)^h$ is defined to be $\langle (op_{i1})^{h-1}, \ldots, (op_{it_i})^{h-1} \rangle$ if op_i is public op_i, if op_i is private or $h = 0$. The full expansion $(op_i)^*$ of op_i is defined as follows:

1. $(op_i)^* = op_i$ if op_i is a private operation.
2. $(op_i)^* = \langle (op_{i1})^*, \ldots, (op_{it_i})^* \rangle$ if op_i invokes op_{i1}, ..., op_{it_i}.

$(op_i)^*$ shows a sequence of private operations computed in the objects. The less expanded operation shows the more abstract level of computation.

Let R be RoS which an object is required to support for an application. The application does not mind which operation *old-display* or *new-display* is used if the application does not care the display speed. The operations are considered to be equivalent if they support QoS subsuming R even if $Q(old\text{-}display(s_{movie})) \neq Q(new\text{-}display(s_{movie}))$ for a state s_{movie}.

[**Definition**] op_i is *RoS-equivalent* with op_j on R iff $Q(\langle op_i(s) \rangle) \cup Q(\langle op_j(s) \rangle) \supseteq R$. □

3.2 Compatibility

Next, we discuss in which order operations op_i and op_j supported by the object o can be computed in order to keep the state of o consistent. op_i *conflicts* with op_j if the result obtained by computing op_j and op_i depends on the computation order [1, 3]. op_i is *compatible* with op_j unless op_i conflicts with op_j. For example, suppose a *movie* object m is composed of an advertisement and a content. The advertisement part is removed from m by *delete*. An application does not care the difference between the original version and the updated version of m since the application is interested only in the content part of m. That is, the updated version of m supports the same level of QoS as the original version.

[**Definition**] op_i is *QoS-compatible* with op_j iff $Q((op_i \circ op_j(s))) = Q((op_j \circ op_i(s)))$ for every state s of an object o.$\Box$

The QoS-compatibility relation is symmetric. Unless op_i is QoS-compatible with op_j, op_i *QoS-conflicts* with op_j. For example, suppose an operation *delete* removes some frames from *movie*. The movie can be seen only by *display* with the low-level decoder. Here, the users can see the movie with the same quality even after *delete* is applied to the movie. Here, *delete* and *display* are QoS-compatible.

[**Definition**] op_i is *RoS-compatible* with op_j on R iff $Q((op_i(s))) \cup Q((op_j \circ op_i(s))) \supseteq R$, $Q((op_i \circ op_j(s))) \cup Q((op_j(s))) \supseteq R$, and $Q((op_i \circ op_j(s))) \cup Q((op_j \circ op_i(s))) \supseteq R$. $\Box$

Suppose an application is not interested in how colorful movies are. An *update* operation changes a movie from a colored version to a monochromatic one. Suppose *movie* supports a colored movie m. The colored movie m is seen by *display*, i.e. $[display(m)]$. If *update* is applied to m, the monochromatic version of m is seen. Since the application is not interested in the color of m, both versions are considered to satisfy the requirement QoS (*RoS*). Hence, $Q([display(m)]) \cup Q([update \circ display(m)]) \supseteq R$ and $Q(display \circ update(m)) = Q(update \circ display(m))$. *display* and *update* are RoS-compatible although they are not QoS-compatible because $Q([update \circ display(m)]) \neq Q([display(m)])$.

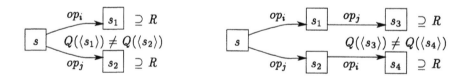

Figure 2: RoS-equivalent operations.   Figure 3: RoS-compatible operations.

3.3 Update operation

First, suppose an operation op_{ij} inserts some data d_{ij} to a state s_i of an object o_i. If $Q(s_i) \preceq Q(d_{ij})$, d_{ij} can be added to s_i. We consider case that $Q(s_i) \succ Q(d_{ij})$. If QoS of d_{ij} is worse than s_i, d_{ij} cannot be inserted in s_i. However, an application can get service from o_i through the operations of o_i. If QoS of d_{ij} viewed through an operation op_{ik} subsumes $Q(s_i)$, i.e. $Q[op_{ik} \circ op_{ij}(s_i)] \supseteq Q[op_{ik}(s_i)]$, the users do not mind even if d_{ij} is inserted in s_i as long as the users view o_i through op_{ik}.

4 Compensation

A traditional way to recover and restart an object o_i is to take a checkpoint. o_i is rolled back to a previous consistent state by restoring the state saved in the log l_i at the checkpoint. Many protocols for taking consistent checkpoints among multiple objects and restarting the objects are discussed so far.

Another way is to compute some operations to remove the effect done by the operations computed. An operation op_j is a *compensating* operation of op_i if $op_i \circ op_j(s) = s$ for every state s of an object o [3]. Let $\tilde{op}_i$ denote a compensating operation of op_i. Let s' be a state obtained by computing op_i on a state s of o, i.e. $s' = op_i(s)$. Here, o can be rolled back to s if $\tilde{op}_i$ is computed on s'. For example, *append* is a compensating operation of *delete*. Suppose a sequence of operations op_1, ..., op_m is computed on the object o. In order to undo op_1, ..., op_m, a sequence of the compensating operations $\tilde{op}_m$, ..., $\tilde{op}_1$ can be computed. That is, $op \circ op_1 \circ \ldots \circ op_m \circ \tilde{op}_m \circ \ldots \circ \tilde{op}_1 = op$ for every operation op.

A pair of states s and s' of o may be considered to be equivalent from the application point of view even if $s \neq s'$. For example, suppose there are two accounts A and B. First, $A = 100$ and $B = 50$ at a state s_1. Suppose $A = 110$ and $B = 40$ at s_2 after A and B are manipulated. If the application is only interested in the total amount of A and B, s_2 is considered to be equivalent with s_1.

Let us consider the multimedia object ME with two movies A and B, where it takes two hours to *play* each of A and B. This state is s_1. Suppose that A and B are *merged* into a movie C. Here, the state is s_2. Then, C is *divided* into two movies A' and B'. It takes one hour and half to *play* each of A' and B'. s_3 denotes this state. Each of A and B is composed of advertisement and content parts of the movie. A' and B' include only the contents of A and B, respectively. The advertisements of A and B are merged into AB. Here, s_3 is equivalent with s_1 since $Q(\langle s_3 \rangle) = Q(\langle s_1 \rangle)$. *divide* is a compensating operation of *merge*.

Here, suppose a state s_1 is obtained by applying an operation op_i to a state s of an object o. Let us consider how to roll o back to s from s_1. One way is to compute the compensating operation $\tilde{op}_i$ of op_i on s_1 since $op_i \circ \tilde{op}_i (s) = s$. Here, suppose there exists an operation op_j such that $op_i \circ op_j(s) = s_2$ where $s \neq s_2$ but $Q(\langle s_2 \rangle) = Q(\langle s \rangle)$. s_2 is not the same as s. However, s_2 is *QoS-equivalent* with s.
[**Definition**] op_j is a *QoS-compensating* operation of op_i iff $Q(\langle op_i \circ op_j(s) \rangle) = Q(\langle s \rangle)$ for every state s of an object o. □
Let $\tilde{op}_i$ denote a *QoS-compensating* operation of op_i.

Suppose one movie C is obtained by *merging* two movies A and B. Let s_1 show a state where A and B exist and s_2 indicate a state where there is C. Suppose the multimedia object ME supports an operation *divide2* which divides C into three parts A'', B'', and AB. A'' and B'' are the content parts of A and B, respectively, which are monochromatic. AB includes the advertisement parts of A and B. s_3 denotes a state where A'', B'', and AB are obtained from A and B. s_1 and s_3 are not the same. Furthermore, A and B are colored but A'' and B'' are monochromatic. That is, $A \supseteq A''$ and $B \supseteq B''$. Here, suppose an application just requires to see the monochromatic one as RoS R. Here, $Q(\langle s_3 \rangle) \supseteq R$ [Figure 4].

[**Definition**] op_i is an *RoS-compensating* operation of op_j on R iff $Q(\langle op_i \circ op_j(s) \rangle)$ $\cup Q(\langle s \rangle) \supseteq R$ for every state s of an object o. $\square$

For example, *divide2* is an *RoS-compensating* operation of *merge* in Figure 4.

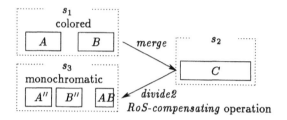

Figure 4: RoS-compensating operation.

Let us consider a *medical object* (MO) which supports medical operations as an example. Suppose an application AP_1 records medical operations in video data m of MO. m is a high resolution video data (1024 × 768 pixels). Suppose AP_1 displays m by an operation *display1* which can display video data with quality 1024 × 768 pixels. On the other hand, suppose an application AP_2 displays m through *display2* which can display video with 640 × 480 pixels. Here, suppose AP_1 would like to restore m after deleting m. A video data m' with 640 × 480 pixels which is less qualified than m is obtained by *undo*. AP_2 can display m'. *undo* is an *RoS-compensating* operation of *record*. It takes a shorter time to obtain m' by *undo* than restore m.

Suppose op_i invokes $op_{i1}, \ldots, op_{it_i}$ as shown in Figure **??**. In order to compensate op_i, $\tilde{op}_i$ can be computed as presented here. Since $(op_i)^1 = \langle op_{i1}, \ldots, op_{it_i} \rangle$ is equivalent with op_i, a sequence $\langle \tilde{op}_{it_i}, \ldots, \tilde{op}_{i1} \rangle$ can be computed to compensate op_i. Here, op_{ij} cannot be absorbed by $\tilde{op}_{ij}$ since $\tilde{op}_{ij}$ may be defined with the QoS-based relation. Here, $op \circ op_i \circ (op_i^1)^\gamma$ is QoS-equivalent with op. The full expansion op_i^* shows a sequence of all private operations directly and indirectly invoked by op_i. If every private operation op_i is compensated by the state log, $op \circ op_i \circ \tilde{op}_i = op$. Here, $op \circ op_i \circ (op_i^*)^\gamma = op$. $(op_i^*)^\gamma$ is defined as follows:

1. $(op_i^*)^\gamma = \tilde{op}_i$ if op_i is a private operation.
2. $(op_i^*)^\gamma = \langle (op_{it_i}^*)^\gamma, \ldots, (op_{i1}^*)^\gamma \rangle$ otherwise.

In the traditional compensation, $(op_i^*)^\gamma$ is computed to compensate op_i, i.e. every primitive operation computed in op_i is undone.

5   QoS-Based Replication

In the traditional systems, objects are replicated in order to increase the reliability, availability, and performance. However, it is expensive to fully replicate multimedia objects. In our system, replicas support different levels of QoS. The applications can use replicas which support enough QoS (RoS) required by the applications.

5.1 Retrieval operations

First, suppose that an application would like to get a snapshot $[op_{ij}(s_i)]$ from a state s_i of an object o_i by an operation op_{ij}. o_i has to support the application with not only $[op_{ij}(s_i)]$ which satisfies the qualification specified in op_{ij} but also enough QoS $Q([op_{ij}(s_i)])$. Here, let R denote the applications' requirement QoS (RoS) for the snapshot which the application derives from the object. If there exists some object o_i supporting an operation op_{ij} such that $R \subseteq Q([op_{ij}(s_i)])$, the application can manipulate o_i to derive the snapshot data by using op_{ij}. Otherwise, the application cannot manipulate any object. For example, suppose there are three objects o_1, o_2, and o_3 where $Q([op_1(s_1)]) \subset R$, $Q([op_2(s_2)]) \supseteq R$, and $Q([op_3(s_3)]) \supseteq R$. o_2 or o_3 can be manipulated by the applications because they satisfy R. If $Q([op_2(s_2)]) \supseteq Q([op_3(s_3)])$, o_2 is selected.

Suppose there are two objects o_1 and o_2 which support operations op_1 and op_2, respectively, and an application is manipulating o_1 though op_1. If o_1 is faulty or o_1 cannot support QoS subsuming RoS R, the application can no longer use o_1. Here, if o_2 supports enough QoS for the application, i.e. $Q([op_2(s_2)]) \supseteq R$ for a state s_2 of o_2, the application can manipulate o_2 on behalf of o_1.

[**Definition**] An object o_j is a *QoS-based replica* of o_i iff there is one operation op_j and state s_j of o_j such that $Q([op_j(s_j)]) \supseteq Q([op_i(s_i)])$ for every operation op_i and state s_i of o_i. □

Here, if $Q([op_j(s_j)]) = Q([op_i(s_i)])$ for every op_j and s_j of o_j, o_j is a *QoS-based full replica* of o_i.

[**Definition**] An object o_j is an *RoS-based replica* of o_i on R iff there is one operation op_j and s_j of o_j such that $Q([op_j(s_j)]) \supseteq Q([op_i(s_i)])$ and $Q([op_i(s_i)]) \supseteq R$ for every operation op_i and state s_i of o_i. □

Here, if $Q([op_j(s_j)]) = Q([op_i(s_i)]) \supseteq R$ for every op_j and s_j of o_j, o_j is an *RoS-based full replica* of o_i.

5.2 Update operations

The update operations can be considered to write some data to o_i. Here, let W be the applications' requirement QoS (RoS) of the data to be stored in the system. The RoS-based replicas o_1, ..., o_n of o_i have to be changed in order to keep the states of objects semantically consistent. The replicas are manipulated according to the following rules:

1. If $W \supset maxQ(o_i)$, the application writes the state with $maxQ(o_i)$ in o_i.
2. If $minQ(o_i) \subseteq W \subseteq maxQ(o_i)$, the application writes o_i with W in o_i.
3. If there is an object o_i such that $W \subset minQ(o_i)$, the application can write no object.

Suppose an application stores video data to three multimedia objects ME_1, ME_2, and ME_3. Suppose the application requires that each object support RoS R of 25 fps. Suppose ME_i supports QoS $(Q(\langle ME_i \rangle))$ as shown in Table 1. In this case, the application can store video data with 25 fps which satisfies R because each object satisfies $minQ(ME_i) \subseteq R$. However, ME_3 stores video data with 15 fps because $maxQ(ME_3) = \langle 15 \text{ fps} \rangle$. However, if RoS is 10 fps, ME_2 cannot store video data with 10 fps since $minQ(ME_2) = \langle 15 \text{ fps} \rangle$.

Table 1: Maximal and minimal QoS.

object ME_i	$maxQ(ME_i)$	$minQ(ME_i)$
ME_1	25 fps	10 fps
ME_2	30 fps	15 fps
ME_3	15 fps	5 fps

6　Concluding Remarks

This paper has discussed how to make the distributed system flexible with respect to QoS supported by the objects. We have discussed the novel equivalent and conflicting relations among the operations on the basis of QoS. We have also discussed the compensating method to undo the work done. A state equivalent with the previous qualified state with respect to QoS is obtained by computing the compensating operations of operations computed. We have also discussed the QoS-based replication to support required QoS in QoS change of objects.

Bibliography

1) Bernstein, P. A., Hadzilacos, V., and Goodman, N., "Concurrency Control and Recovery in Database Systems," *Addison-Wesley Publishing Company*, 1987.

2) Budhiraja, N., Marzullo, K., Schneider, B. F., and Toueg, S., "The Primary-Backup Approach," *Distributed Computing Systems*, *ACM Press*, 1994, pp.199–221.

3) Korth, H. F., Levy, E., and Silberschalz, A., "A Formal Approach to Recovery by Compensating transactions," *Proc. of the VLDB*, 1990, pp.95–106.

4) Schmidt, D. C., Gokhale, A. S., Harrison, T. H., and Parulkar, G., "A High-Performance End System Architecture for Real-Time CORBA," *IEEE Communications Magazine*, 1997, pp.72–77.

5) Schneider, B. F., "Replication Management using the State-Machine Approach," *Distributed Computing Systems*, *ACM Press*, 1993, pp.169–197.

6) Takizawa, M. and Yasuzawa, S., "Uncompensatable Deadlock in Distributed Object-Oriented Systems," *Proc. of IEEE Int'l Conf. on Parallel and Distributed Systems (ICPADS-92)*, 1992, pp.150–157.

7) Tanaka, K. and Takizawa, M., "Distributed Checkpointing Based on Influential Messages," *Proc. of the 4th IEEE Int'l Conf. on Parallel and Distributed Systems (ICPADS-96)*, 1996, pp. 440–447.

8) Yoshida, T. and Takizawa, M., "Model of Mobile Objects," *Proc. of the 7th Int'l Conf. on Database and Expert Systems Applications (DEXA'96)*, 1996, pp. 623–632.

13

Remote Joint Application Design Process using Package Software

Nobuhiro Kataoka

Information Technology Center, Mitsubishi Electric Corporation

Hisao Koizumi

Department of Computer and System Engineering, Tokyo Denki University

Norio Shiratori

Research Institute of Electrical Communication, Tohoku University

ABSTRACT

Corporate information systems, aiming at reduction of cycle times from order receipt to shipment, are increasingly based on integrated package software. In development of such a system, joint application design (JAD) plays an important role. In this paper, we propose a model of processes for the development of corporate information systems using integrated software packages, and also propose a method of CSCW to support determination of specifications. In this model, development tasks are divided into a number of stages, in each of which JAD activities are conducted with members located at remote sites. This methodology was actually applied to development processes, and evaluation results confirmed the usefulness of the method.

1 Introduction

In corporate information systems, such subsystems as accounting and production management must be integrated through a single database in order to reduce cycle times from receipt of orders until shipment. In light of these requirements, system development using integrated package software is attracting considerable attention.

In development such a system JAD (joint application design), in which the integrated package is used in prototyping and the users and developers cooperatively define requirements and determine specifications based on the prototyping, plays a vital role.

In JAD, the participation of key personnel in specification determination is required. But because these persons are not necessarily in the same physical location,

JAD activities with remote sites often become necessary. Such cooperative tasks can therefore be regarded as one mode of CSCW (computer-supported cooperative work).

In this paper, we propose a model for processes in the development of a corporate information system utilizing integrated package software, as well as a method for CSCW supporting determination of specifications. In this CSCW, development tasks are divided into several stages, and in each stage JAD activities are conducted with members at remote sites. This method was applied to an actual development process, and evaluation of the results confirmed the efficacy of the method.

2 Problems in Support for Specification

Using integrated package software, the various functions required in a corporate information system can be selected by setting parameters, so that systems can be developed far more efficiently than in the past. However, one problem faced in development of such a system is how to appropriately choose specifications for the system to be developed; and this in turn entails various other problems.

1) The need for remote cooperative activities
   The concerned parties may not necessary be in physically proximate locations, so remote arrangements enabling persons at distant locations to participate in a suitable manner can play a vital role.

2) Problems relating to description of specifications
   In traditional development, discussions are based on described documents, so that often discussions proceeded without the specifications having been conveyed in a suitable manner to participants. So, it is important that prototyping be used to actually operate a system.

3) Problems relating to modeling of specification determination processes
   Processes necessary for determining specifications must be based on such stages as identification of overall concepts, clarification of the overall flow, and specification of the individual functions. These processes must be established as a clear model.

3 Proposal of a Process Support Model Using Integrated Package Software

In development of corporate information systems using integrated package software, we refer to the tasks of specification definition, confirmation and finalization, which can be performed in an environment in which participants are in physically remote locations, as 'Remote JAD' activities. We here propose a model for development using remote JAD, as well as a model of process support for specification determination through remote JAD activities.

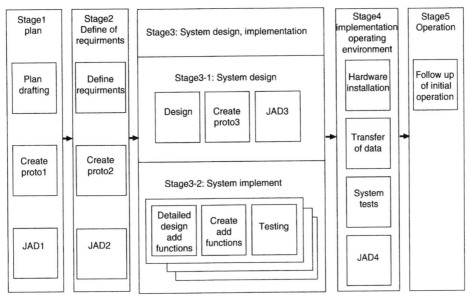

Figure 1: System development process using integrated package software.

3.1 Remote JAD environment

For remote JAD, an environment is necessary in which a prototype system using integrated package software can be operated, and the same task screens for this system can be viewed by participants at both local and remote sites while they exchange opinions orally. By using projectors to display the system screens on a large-format screen, the sense of presence of the participants can be enhanced. And, by displaying the images of participants as well as sharing task data among sites, cooperative activities can be further promoted.

3.2 Model of development process using an integrated package

Figure 1 illustrates a model of development using integrated package software. In the figure, the development processes are organized in stages consisting of the tasks described below.

- Stage 1: Plan drafting
  In this stage, a plan for system development is drafted, goals are clarified from the management perspective of system development, general system functions are elucidated, and processes, costs and other parameters are proposed. In this stage, prototype 1 is created, and remote JAD activities are conducted (JAD1). The contents of each JAD activities are indicated in Table 1.

- Stage 2: Definition of requirements
  In this stage, the system requirements are defined. Hearings are held on re-

Table 1: Contents of JAD Process.

	Purpose	Participants	Key aspects of JAD	Customization settings	Database settings M: master T: transaction
JAD 1	Examination of feasibility of package use	Upper managers, developers package experts	Confirm that package functions cover most of system functions	Adopt similar business systems as-is	Standard data
JAD 2	Definition of system required specs	Managers of practical affairs, developers, package experts	Determine subsystems to use Identify items for addition	Set general framework for this system	M: set for this system T: trial data
JAD 3	Set detailed system functions Design added specs	Key practical affairs personnel, developers, package experts	Determine/ extract detailed functions Design added specs	Set details for system	M: set for this system T: trial data(use data of current system in part)
JAD 4	Adjustment of system functions	Managers/ key personnel in practical affairs, developers, package experts	Tuning at system test stage	Adjustment of items already set	M/T: data transferred from existing system

quired specifications based on the rough specifications resulting from the JAD1 activities, and requirements are defined. Next, prototype 2 is created based on this, and JAD2 is conducted. The parameters of the integrated package are set according to the requirements defined above to determine the functions of prototype 2. Based on survey contents, the database fields and code system of the integrated package are mapped to those of the system under development, and data fields and code system settings for the prototype are chosen.

- Stage 3: System design and implementation

  a) Stage 3-1: System design: Based on required system specifications from stage 2, the settings of the package parameters are studied, additional modules for development are designed, and prototype 3 is constructed. This prototype 3 is created by adding to prototype 2 the minimum necessary functions, and by setting more detailed parameters for package customization. Using this prototype 3, JAD3 activities are conducted.

  b) Stage 3-2: System implementation: Here details of the additional functions are designed, programs are created and subsystem tests are conducted, including both additional modules and the integrated package modules.

- Stage 4: Implementation of the operating environment: System installation in actual hardware is performed and data is transferred from current systems. And system tests are also performed. JAD4 is conducted for adjustment of system function.

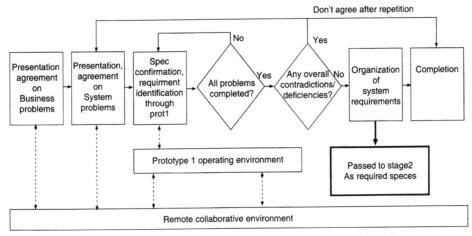

Figure 2: JAD1 process of consensus-building on use of package.

- Stage 5: System operation: This stage involves follow-up to the initial operation stage.

JAD participants include upper management, managers of individual divisions, key personnel in practical affairs, developers, and experts on the integrated package; these persons must participate at the proper times, and for this remote JAD, which is free from geographical constraints, is essential.

3.3   Modeling of processes in remote JAD

Next we discuss processes in different remote JAD activities. Each type of JAD has different goals and different participants, so processes will also be different.

3.3.1   JAD1

The process of remote JAD1 are as shown in Figure 2. In this process, initially the business problems which it is expected the system will solve are presented and agreed upon. Next, major functions–that is, system development goals–are presented and agreement is reached. Prototype 1 is operated to address each of these goals, it is confirmed that the current prototype specifications are in agreement with the general functions expected of the system, and if there are discrepancies, additional requirements are identified. The general specifications of each subsystem are also confirmed. After confirmation of each set of specifications is completed, JAD participants verify that there are no contradictions within the system and that no major functions are missing. If there are any problems related to these points, items for confirmation are again presented and agreement is again reached, and this process of specification confirmation is repeated. If no amount of repetition solves the problem, then use

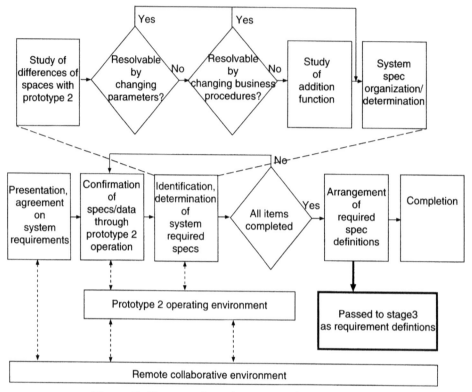

Figure 3: Process of requirement making by JAD2.

of the integrated package is abandoned. If there are no problems, requirments are passed on to stage 2 as rough required specification.

3.3.2   JAD2

The process of remote JAD2 are as shown in Figure 3. The purpose of JAD2 is to elucidate required specifications through prototype operation, rather than through documents. In JAD2, the system requirements that become the premises for construction of prototype 2 are first presented, and participants reach agreement on these requirements. Next the prototype specifications are confirmed through operation of prototype 2, and the validity of data fields set for this system in the database is verified. The process of determination consists of the following steps, as in the upper half of Figure 3.

1) Analysis of differences between required specifications and prototype 2

2) Analysis of the feasibility of absorbing differences through adjustment of the parameters of the integrated package

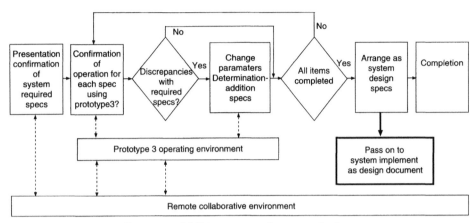

Figure 4: JAD3 process of system design.

3) If the above is not possible, analysis of the possibility of absorbing differences through modification of business procedures in accordance with the functions of the integrated package

4) If business procedures cannot be changed, study of the specifications of additional functions corresponding to the required specifications

3.3.3 JAD3

The process of remote JAD3 are as shown in Figure 4. Whereas the purpose of JAD2 was definition of required specifications, the aim of JAD3 is to determine the specifications of individual items in prototype 3, which is customized in greater detail, and also to determine the specifications of functions for additional development. Moreover, in prototype 3 the minimum necessary functions are added to prototype 2. Initially the required specifications representing the output of JAD2 are presented, and are confirmed by the JAD participants. In confirming operation, transaction data is input and the relevant subsystem started to confirm the specifications for the functions in question; if the JAD participants agree that there is no discrepancy with the required specifications, then that item is completed.

4 Application to System Development and Evaluation

4.1 Application to system development

4.1.1 Outline of the system for development

We here discuss the results of inspection in the development of a corporate information system for a certain company. The scope of system development included pro-

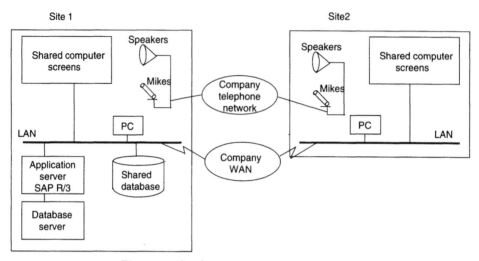

Figure 5: Verification system environment.

duction, material, purchasing, and accounting management. Approximately eleven months were required for development.

4.1.2   Remote JAD environment

The remote JAD environment of the verification system appears in Figure 5. This system employs a network in the company, connecting two points via PCs and using software with common screens.

The remote JAD participants project screen images on a large-format screen using a projector. A 10 Mbps Ethernet LAN connect the PCs; this LAN is connected to LANs at other sites via the frame relay of a company wide-area network. The frame relay transmission rate is 128 kbps. Voice transmissions employ an ordinary company telephone network. A Lotus Notes database can be used at both sites, and conference themes, the minutes of the previous conference are input in advance. In this study images of participants were not transmitted, so as to alleviate the load on the network.

4.1.3   Example of the contents of a remote JAD session

Of the remote JAD activities conducted in this study, we here describe one design process for the materials subsystem conducted as part of JAD3.

a) Participants

  · Site 1 (plant): Materials subsystem development leader four users of the materials subsystem; five persons total.

· Site 2 (System Development Division): Three persons of materials sub-system development, one expert on the integrated package; four persons total.

b) Details of the design process

- · Required specifications: Design of rules for inventory inquiry when an order is received

- · Specification confirmation (1): In the current prototype system, when an order is received, inventory inquiry is performed only for currently existing stock.

- · Differences with required specifications: It was pointed out that there is a need to include those issuing purchasing orders (orders issued by the purchasing department to parties outside the company) and those making purchase requests (sent from the production planning department to the purchasing department). (At this company, production in the company and purchases from outside the company are conducted in parallel.)

- · Modification of prototype parameters: In package parameter settings, it is possible to include items the purchase of which has been ordered or requested. However, there is some debate over whether such settings are appropriate–that is, over the accuracy of the delivery date for ordered items. We confirmed the operation of the system in these cases based on previous data.

- · Specification confirmation (2): Based on past data under assumptions similar to those for the existing system, it was discovered that when order receipt processing is performed, the delivery date response is earlier by five days. The number of days elapsing until actual order of items for which an order request was sent from the onsite division to the materials division fluctuated greatly between one and seven days, and it was pointed out that inclusion of this period in the delivery date response would be reckless. However, the new system links purchase request data to the materials subsystem in real-time and so only one-day elapses until the actual order. Thus purchase-request items were made to be regarded as usable stock, and parameters were modified.

4.1.4 Overall state of execution of remote JAD

The participants and average number of persons involved in JAD1, 2, 3 and 4 in the verification project, as well as the number of JAD sessions and average hour of each session, appear in Table 2. The effect of remote JAD was evaluated by comparing costs with the case in which all JAD activities were performed locally. The costs of local JAD sessions consist of participant costs, cost of participant movement, and losses involved in movement. Here participant costs are simply the number of JAD hours multiplied by the number of participants and by a unit cost per hour.

Table 2: Status of JAD execution(Cost unit is 10 Kyen).

	Average no. participants	Average JAD hours	No. JAD sessions (remote JAD)	Local JAD cost	Remote JAD cost	cost difference
JAD1	13	4.4	5(3)	328	176	152
JAD2	15	4.2	7(4)	492	257	235
JAD3	13	5.6	9(5)	624	624	372
JAD4	9	3.2	4(3)	194	89	105
Total				1638	894	744

Participant movement costs are the cost of movement (transportation) hours the number of persons, and transportation losses are the same unit cost per hour times the number of individuals, times the number of hours of movement. Remote JAD communication line and equipment costs consists of the respective unit costs times the number of JAD hours. Approximately half of the JAD participants participate from the remote site. From the table we see that remote JAD results in a cost reduction of approximately 7.4 million-Yen.

4.2 Evaluation and analysis

4.2.1 Evaluation of model of development process

JAD activities must be conducted at various levels corresponding to each stage of development. Hence the clarification of problems which is performed at the beginning of each process to determine specifications played a vital role in this development.

4.2.2 Evaluation of processes for specification determination

In this project, the appropriate members participated in each type of JAD activity, so that specifications were adopted in a highly efficient manner. This was due partly to the ability to secure the participation of the required members using remote JAD, and also because through system operation using historical data, as in the example of the JAD3 process, the participants were able to understand very clearly the significance of different parameters and their function within the system.

4.2.3 Evaluation of remote cooperative activities

Differences in costs due to use of remote JAD were shown in Table 2, from which we see that adoption of remote JAD produced a savings of about 7.4 million Yen. This is nearly one-tenth of the 95 million Yen total cost of the project, thus clearly demonstrating the efficacy of the remote JAD approach.

5 Conclusions

In this paper, we have proposed a model for development procedures when using integrated package software for software development, as well as a remote JAD method to support determination of specifications. On applying this method to the development of an actual system and evaluating the results, its effectiveness was confirmed. Themes for future research include the following: accumulation of experience in specification determination processes, and methods for reuse of this experience; estimation of productivity for system development by using JAD.

Bibliography

1) Koizumi *et al.*, "A Proposal of Decision-Making Process Support Methods and It's Implementation," *IPSJ Trans*, Vol. 37, No. 5, pp. 911-919 (1996).

2) Fukazawa *et al.*, "A group-ware Frame work -CCF for Cooperation of CSCW Applications," *IPSJ Group-ware workshop 18-5* (1996).

3) Grudin, "The History and future of CSCW and Group-ware: A Personal View," *IPSJ Group-ware workshop 12-6* (1995).

4) Tj Baldwin, " A design for multimedia desk-to-desk conferencing," *IEEE conference Publish (Inst. Electronics Eng.)*, No. 371, pp. 160-166 (1993).

5) Masui *et al.*, "Office system with group ware function," *EIC Trans.* Vol. D-113, No. 12 (1995).

6) Takagi, "Communication Architecture in group decision making meeting," *IEE Trans.*, Vol. C114, No. 3 (1994).

7) Itho, " Corporate information development using Interrogated Package software," *IPSJ Journal*, Vol. 37, No. 8 (1996).

8) James Martin, " Rapid Application Development," *Rictelecom* (1994).

14

Vicarious Certification and Billing Agent for Web Information Service

Chang Woo Yoon

Electronics and Telecommunications Research Institute, Korea

ABSTRACT

In this paper, we describe the concepts and implementation of agent providing vicarious certification and billing methods in World Wide Web. The object of vicarious certification is to provide open interface to users using World Wide Web information service. The billing agent has enhanced functions for usage based mini payment method, vicarious billing management instead of each CP (Content Provider), which gives reduction of costs needed for billing management. Our approach works with every WWW browser on every system. No additional software has to be installed at the user's computer or CP's server side.

1 Introduction

The World Wide Web is a document distribution system based on a client/server model.[1] The World Wide Web has experienced exponential growth over the last few years.[2] For example, in the first ten months of 1994 the amount of WWW traffic on the Internet doubled roughly in every 11 weeks. There are many reasons for the success: very low entry costs, freely distributed browser or free noncommercial use, free servers and not too difficult installation for anyone with reasonable computing skills.[3]

Although noncommercial usage has dominated the Internet for a long time, some commercial applications have emerged recently. The portion of commercial World Wide Web sites has increased. There are several types of commercial World Wide Web services: on-line shopping, education, information providing, etc.

The Information providing service is a sort of commercial Internet services. We call the information service provider a CP (Content Provider). The CP provides many sorts of valuable information to Internet users such as on-line newspapers, picture database, patent, etc. Many commercial CPs exist, but there are some problems to widen the web information service. The main problem is billing for information usage. Billing is an important aspect of World Wide Web, and there are several billing mechanisms that are well established for many years.[4] Most of the suggested billing methods require some actions to the service user side and server side. A certification method is required to support billing, for example, basic authentication method, secure protocol, SSL (Secure Sockets Layer), etc. The information service user has to maintain certification for each information provider. Recently, the certification agent server technique has emerged, because formal identification is required for commercial use of Internet services.[5] The most significant problem for billing is management. The CP must manage all processes of billing of their own. These processes require enormous efforts to collect the bill and to manage many service users.

In Korea, the INFOSHOP service was started on October 1995 by Korea Telecom. The INFOSHOP service is an open Value-Added Network (VAN) service concept that can provide a variety of value-added services such as videotex, facsimile mail, voice application, message switching, and information retrieval services.[6] INFOSHOP is the abbreviation of Information and Shop. The service users access the INFOSHOP service via telephone line. In the traditional service mechanism, the service users has to keep their passwords separately whenever they register new service providers, and could not easily access another VAN service system without redialing and it was difficult to know where the desired information was. From an information provider's perspective, he must keep the large subscriber database and has problems in charging for service usage rate and installation cost. From a common carrier's perspective, he experiences congestion and overload problems in PSTN (Public Switched Telephone Network) because of mixture of voice and non-voice traffic. To cope with these problems and support Infoshop service, the INFOSHOP service system has been developed. Korea Telecom manages advertising, information usage fee demand, receipt, and administration instead of each information provider. The information providers concentrate on the development of the content of information DB (DataBase). This is a vicarious billing for information usage.

The vicarious billing for information usage gives reduction of investment cost needed for collecting the bill. The small-scale information provider can easily start his information providing business.

2   Vicarious Certification and Billing Agent(VCBA)

2.1   Conceptual model of vacarious certifiaction

Typically, a WWW (World Wide Web) client (usually a web browser) sends a HTTP (HyperText Transfer Protocol) request directly to the target WWW server, and that server returns the response directly to the client. The certification between client and server is done by exchanging credentials according to the certification method. The HTTP is a very simple semantic based application level protocol. Internet is also an open network to the world, so the security mechanism is required for the exchange of credentials. There are several types of security mechanisms such as basic authentication in HTTP 1.0, S-HTTP (Secure HTTP), SSL (Secure Sockets Layer), and encryption methods such as DES (Data Encryption Standard)[7] and RSA[8]. The client must know the type of security mechanism and certification method. The user (client) has responsibilities to protecting from being hacked. This fact is troublesome to service user, if there are many sites that the service user must maintain.

For example, in many charged sites, the certification method that is adopted is the basic authentication method provided in HTTP version 1.0. In this method, the service user must have a username and password for using the charged information provider's web site. The service user must maintain each web site's address, username and password. It is very hard to maintain such information on many charged web sites.

The purpose of vicarious certification is to provide an open interface to users (clients). The service user can use CPs charged information without identification. The vicarious certification and billing agent (VCBA) has a role of giving credentials to CPs instead of service user.

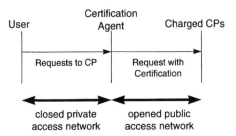

Figure 1: Conceptual model of Vicarious Certification

Figure 1 shows a conceptual model of vicarious certification. In this model, the certification agent has a role of vicarious certification. If the service user sends a request to charged CP, the vicarious agent sends credentials to the designated CP instead of the service user. There are no certification functions in the user (client) side. The service user can use the CP's information without any trouble to manage credentials for each charged CPs. To provide full security for use of certification agent, the network between the user and certification agent must be a closed private access network like VAN (Value-Added Network), PSTN, or PSDN (Packet Switched Data Network). This means the network must have a security mechanism or must provide network access restriction against public access.

The network between Certification Agent and charged CPs is open as a public access network like Internet. The certification agent must provide a security mechanism to protect from hacker's attack. All responsibilities for the security problem reside on the certification agent side. The role of certification is moved from the service user to the certification agent.

2.2 The concept of billing agent

The trends for billing in WWW information service are using credit card or bank transfer for information usage fee. The service user can use the CP's information from one week to several months according to the bill. This billing method burdens a user with plenty of bills, especially the users who want to use the information from time to time. This fact is one of the reasons that the service user cannot easily decide to use charged WWW service.

The current method cannot prevent illegal use of information. Credit card payment has a risk of appropriation, and a pre-paid method through bank transfer may cause rejection symptoms of users. A post-paid method may cause difficulties for receipt. The most significant problem of billing is that each CP must manage all of these billing management burdens.

To improve these problems, the billing agent has the characteristics as follows:

- Usage based mini payment method

- the billing agent takes care of billing management

On the CP side, the function of billing management is moved to the billing agent. This gives reduction of costs needed for billing management. A major role of prices is to present information for people on the true costs of their actions.[9] Usage-based prices can be used to prioritize usage of a congested resource like a WWW server so that those who value access most get the highest priority. The usage rate is calculated according to the used time or amount of used data.

2.3   The application

In the proxy technique, the WWW client sends the full URL (including protocol and server portions) to the designated proxy, which then connects to the desired server via the desired protocol, issues the request, and forwards the result back to the initial client. The key observation is that the client uses HTTP to communicate with the proxy, regardless of the protocol specified in the URL. There are some researches on using proxy for application level transducer.[10][11]

We use proxy HTTP daemon for VCBA. The request from the user is modified, and then transferred to Charged CP.

The interface between the user and billing agent is PSTN (Public Switched Telephone Network). The user is connected to the VCBA using PPP (Point-to-Point Protocol) over PSTN. The PSTN is a designated telephone line to an authorized user, so that it can provide the secured access to the VCBA.

There are several certification methods in the WWW. Currently, we provide the basic authentication method proposed in HTTP version 1.0 that is the standard WWW protocol. The system architecture of VCBA is independent from the authentication methods, and therefore, we can support any type of authentication methods. The service users do not mind what the method of authentication is.

Figure 2 is an example of Web Infoshop service system. In this system the VCBA has a function of vicarious certification and billing agent. The KORNET is one of the ISP's (Internet Service Provider) Internet access lines in Korea. As our open access method allows a user to access KORNET without identification, everyone who wants to be connected to the Internet can do it. The WACS (Web infoshop node ACcess Subsystem) is a telephone network processing system. When a user is connected to the Web Infoshop System through WACS, the WACS detects the telephone subscriber number of the user using R2 signaling and displays a welcome message on the user's PC. The detailed scenario is described in the next section. However, the detailed description of WACS is not within the scope of this paper. It works with a protocol converter from PPP to IP (Internet Protocol).

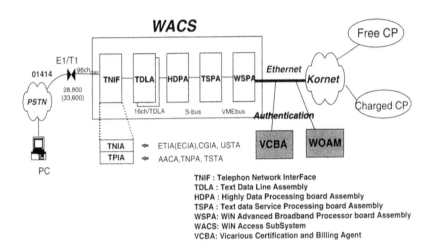

Figure 2: Web Infoshop Service System

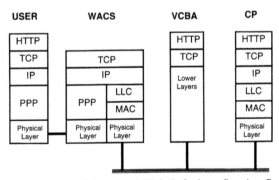

Figure 3: Protocol Stack of Web Infoshop Service System

Figure 3 is the protocol stack of Web Infoshop service system. The WACS act as an IP router, which transmits IP packet to the VCBA and Internet. The TCP (Transmission Control Protocol) layer in WACS is used to transfer operational data of service.

Our approach works with every WWW browser on every system. No additional software has to be installed at the user's computer or CP's server side.

2.4   Scenarios for vicarious certification

Figure 4 is the scenario of vicarious certification when the user sends a request to the charged CPs. Steps 1,2,3 show modem connection by a user. The user dials a special telephone number designated by the VCBA system. If the modem connection is successful, the VCBA displays the introduction to the usage of VCBA, then shows selection menus of protocols that can be supported by the VCBA system. Steps 4,5,6 show PPP connection. If the user selects PPP connection method, the system sets up the PPP connection, then gives IP address to the user. From this time, the user can use the Internet service.

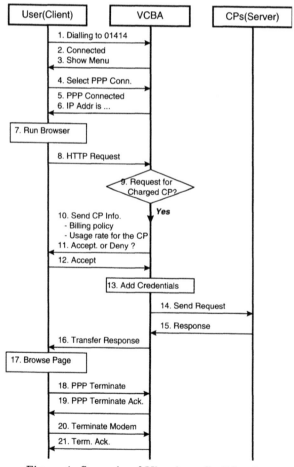

Figure 4: Scenario of Vicarious Certification

The user runs the web browser in step 7. At step 8, the user requests URL to the VCBA. The VCBA checks the URL whether the requested destination site is a charged CP. If the request is toward the charged CP, the VCBA sends notification to the user with billing information. If the user accepts the informed condition, then the billing agent adds the credentials for the designated charged CP and sends modified request to designated CP. The CP sends a response according to the request from VCBA. The VCBA finally responds to the user. Then the browser shows the information to the user.

2.5 Scenarios for billing

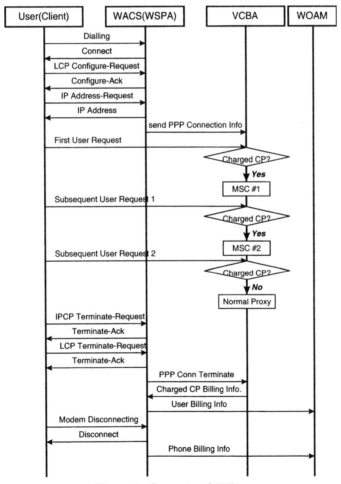

Figure 5: Scenario of Billing

The HTTP is a connectionless protocol, which makes TCP connection for each

request. It is hard to find the user status of WWW usage whether the request is
for the first time or not. To solve this problem, WACS sends the PPP connection
and disconnection information to the VCBA. The VCBA makes and maintains PPP
connection table using connection information, deletes the PPP connection table
according to PPP termination info. The VCBA determines whether the requirement
is the first request or not using the PPP connection table. Figure 5 is the scenario
diagram for overall scenario.

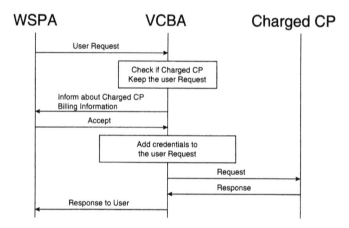

Figure 6: MSC#1: VCBA initial request scenario

MSC #1 is the scenario for processing initial user request. MSC #2 is the scenario
for processing subsequent user request.

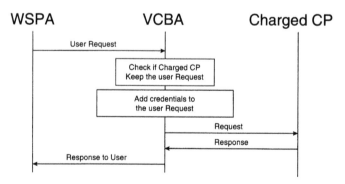

Figure 7: MSC#2: VCBA subsequent request scenario

When the user finishes the PPP connection, the VCBA calculates the billing data
for the user. When the user finishes the modem connection, the WACS calculates
telephone usage, and sends it to OAM sub-system.

3 Characteristics

3.1 Open access to charged CP and usage based billing

The Web service user does not think about the identification to the charged CPs. Vicarious certification gives convenience of WWW usage and reduces the burden of credential management of a user. The billing data can be calculated by the billing agent with the unit of used time or the amount of used data, that is usage based billing. The billing agent has all security responsibilities; there is no risk from hacker to user side.

3.2 Flexible billing architecture independent from CP's server

To use the billing agent, the CP must give credentials of their own to the billing agent's manager. According to the basic authentication method, the credential is a pair of username and password. There are no needs to change the architecture of CP's server or server software. These facts give flexibility to maintain CP's server program. Only one server is necessary to maintain the charged CP sites if the access methods are different, i.e., from the billing agent or public Internet lines.

3.3 Authentic billing management via PSTN

It is a problem to receive the usage fee using the current payment method, because there is not authentic billing method. In our billing agent system, the usage fee demand is linked to the user's telephone line. This guarantees the authentic billing management.

3.4 Convenient identification management to service users

If the user accesses the content provider in Internet without vicarious certification, the user must manage each identification values - username and password - of each CP. There is no problem if the number of managing sites is small. But as the number increases, the user may not remember each identification value. With the aids of vicarious certification, the user can access many Internet CPs with only one certification to web Infoshop system.

4 Conclusion

We developed an agent providing vicarious certification and billing methods. The Web service user can access the charged CP without identification, that is, open access method to the charged CP. We support a usage based billing method, which can reduce the user's billing burden. From the standpoint of CP, the billing management function is moved from each CP to the billing agent. There is no need to change the server architecture of the charged CP servers, which gives flexibility of server management.

Our system is best fitted to small-size electronic commerce on WWW Information providing services. For example, it is the special DB service, online publication, games, etc.

Currently, our system has a role of vicarious certification and billing, but the concept of agent is the application level HTTP gateway. In the application level HTTP gateway, the transformation of HTTP message can be done according to various application needs. It has a function of making the information to be value-added.

Acknowledgment

This work is a part of the project "Web Infoshop Service Node Development" sponsored by Korea Telecom.

Bibliography

1) Radhika Malpani, Jacob Lorcb, David Berger, "Making World Wide Web Chaching Servers Cooperate," Fourth International World Wide Web Conference, pp. 107–117 (1995).

2) O'Callaghan, D., "A central cashing proxy server for WWW users at the University of Melbourne," Proceedings of AusWeb95, the first Australian World Wide Web Conference, March (1995).

3) Gavin Thomas Nicol, "DYNA WEB Integrating Large SGML Repositories and the WWW," Fourth International World Wide Web Conference, pp. 549–558, December (1995).

4) Amir Herzberg, Hilik Yochai, "MiniPay: Charging per Click on the Web," Sixth International World Wide Web Conference, pp 239–253, April (1997).

5) Adam Cain, "SECURITY, AUTHENTICATION, AND PRIVACY ON THE WEB," Fourth International World Wide Web Conference, Tutorial notes pp 103–125, December (1995).

6) Dong Won Kim, Kyung Pyo Jun, Geun Teak Ryu, Hyeon Deok Bae, "Development of an Infoshop Service System," ICCE'96, June, (1996).

7) Feistel H., "Cryptography and Computer Privacy," Scientific American, May (1973).

8) Rivest R., Shamir A., Adleman L., "A Method for Obtaining Digital Signatures and Public Key Cryptosystems," Communications of the ACM, Feburary (1978).

9) Jeffrey K. MacKie-Mason, Hal R. Varian, "Some FAQs about Usage-Based Pricing," Second International World Wide Web Conference, pp. 302–311, December, (1993).

10) Charles Brooks, Murray S. Mazer, Scott Meeks, Jim Miller, "Application-Specific Proxy Servers as HTTP Stream Transducers," Fourth International World Wide Web Conference, pp. 539–548, December, (1995).

11) Louis Perrochon, Andrea Kennel, "W3-Access for Blind People," Fourth International World Wide Web Conference, Poster Session pp. 92–93, December, (1995).

15

Effectiveness of ATRAS Information Retrieval System in World-Wide Web

Kouichi Abe

Toshihiro Taketa

Yamagata University

Hiroshi Nunokawa

Iwate Prefectural University

Norio Shiratori

Tohoku University

ABSTRACT

In this paper, we introduce a new search system, called ATRAS (Agent-based Total Resource Access System), to solve the current Internet search problems. We also propose the Evolving Information Retrieval Agents (EIRA), which is based on Genetic Algorithms (GAs) and the Weighting Network (WN), to improve the ATRAS performance. The GAs are used to adjust the search parameters in different environments and for evolving the information retrieval agents. The WN is designed for more efficient information search in the information retrieval network. By implementation of EIRA and WN, the ATRAS information retrieval system has some biological characteristics which increase the ATRAS performance.

1 Introduction

The rapid spread of the Internet and the increase of the WWW have made possible the information exchange in all world. The WWW provides the framework to share information which is available to everyone from anywhere and at any moment. But, it is not easy for everybody to find out the necessary information in the WWW.

Many WWW search systems have been proposed and developed to solve Internet search problems[1, 2, 3, 4, 5]. Currently, many people use the search systems, called search engines, for information retrieval purposes. These search systems are very convenient to search the information. But, when the search systems have some troubles, everyone can't use their services. Other WWW search systems can be used, but the users cannot keep in mind all server's URL (Uniform Resource Locators). Furthermore, these search systems can't search the newest information, because they use the Web Robots to gather the information in the WWW, which cause the congestion of the network traffic.

We introduce a new search system called ATRAS to solve the above problems of the standard WWW search systems and to construct the new framework of the information retrieval. The ATRAS includes the self-organizing information retrieval network and the migration search. The first one is the function which indicates the network expanding when a new WWW server host will appear in the information retrieval network. The second one is the function which indicates that the information retrieval agents move from one to another WWW server host freely. To improve the ATRAS performance, EIRA and WN are proposed. The EIRA use GAs to adjust the search parameters in different environments. The WN is designed for more efficient information search by information retrieval agents in the ATRAS information retrieval network.

This paper is organized as follows. The detail of the ATRAS and the results of the experiments are explained in Section 2. The evolving information retrieval system is described in Section 3. The conclusions and future work are summarized in Section 4.

2   ATRAS

The ATRAS is an agent-based information retrieval system. By using the agents, the ATRAS has the following features: the self-managing WWW information, the migration search and the self-organizing information retrieval network. The ATRAS is described in the following.

2.1   ATRAS Agents

The agent is defined as a hardware or software-based computer system which has the autonomy, social ability, reactivity and pro-activeness properties[6]. In ATRAS, the agent is defined as a process which has the autonomy and the social ability. The autonomy means, the agent operates without the direct intervention of human or the other agents. The social ability means, the agent interacts with each other via some kind of agent-communication language. The other feature of the agent is the internal clock, which means that the agent changes its state by its life cycle. On the other hand, the standard agent changes its state by outside factors. This is one of the difference between the ATRAS agent and the standard agent.

The ATRAS has five kinds of agents, which cooperate together to make the information retrieval. The ATRAS agents are described in following.

InfoManager exists on the WWW server, and manages the information and creates the search catalog in the WWW server. The InfoManager acts as the WWW search server such as search engines.

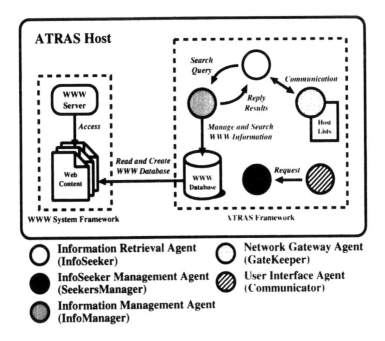

Figure 1: Self-managing information in the WWW host (the ATRAS host model).

InfoSeeker moves in each WWW server and searches the information, and also asks the InfoManager to search the information and gathers the search results. The InfoSeeker has the Search Termination Parameters (STP) and the Search Hosts List (SHL). The STP are the search condition. The SHL is the list of the searched host name.

SeekersManager manages the STP and the Identity Information (II) of the InfoSeekers. The SeekersManager receives the search request from the User Interface Agent (UIA).

GateKeeper secures the server host and manages the Connectable Host List (CHL), by which the GateKeeper routes the next search host for the InfoSeeker. The GateKeeper also organizes the information retrieval network. At first boot time, the GateKeeper gets the initial CHL from the default GateKeeper, which exists in the ATRAS information retrieval network.

Communicator is the user interface, and receives the search requests from the users. The Communicator also asks the SeekersManager to search for information and shows the search results to the users.

2.2 Self-managing Information

The self-managing information for the WWW is the basic feature of the ATRAS. This feature allows the WWW server host to manage its own information by itself and to act as search engines. To realize this function, all ATRAS agents are put in the WWW server host as shown in Fig.1. The self-managing information gives basis for the management and retrieval of the new information. For all practical purpose, the InfoManager manages the information and searches the database (search catalog) for search query. This host is called the ATRAS host.

2.3 Migration Search

The migration search is the information retrieval method in ATRAS. The mechanism is as follows. The InfoSeeker moves between the ATRAS hosts searching the information and gathering the search results. After the InfoSeeker finishes searching in the current host, it requests a decision of the next host to the GateKeeper. The GateKeeper receives the SHL from the InfoSeeker and decides the next host by using the SHL and the CHL. Then, the GateKeeper tells the next host to the InfoSeeker. At this time, the migrated GateKeeper checks whether the InfoSeeker is or isn't valid in order to secure the host from the invalid InfoSeekers which may enter in the host. A simple example is shown in Fig.2. After the InfoSeeker finishes the search in Host (B), it moves to next Host (A) with the search results. Then, in Host (A), the InfoSeeker begins the search. The migration search enables the users to search

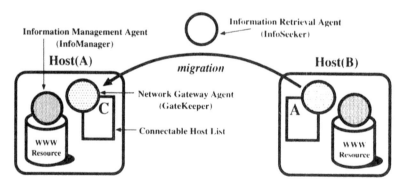

Figure 2: Migration search.

the necessary information without depending on the search server's URL, because the InfoSeekers can move between the ATRAS hosts and search the information. Moreover, the migration search can provide a parallel information retrieval by using multiple agents simultaneously.

2.4 Information Retrieval Network

The information retrieval network of ATRAS is constructed by the GateKeepers and the migration search. The ATRAS information retrieval network can self-organize the network by itself. The self-organizing mechanism is very simple. If the InfoSeeker comes from an ATRAS host, which isn't in the CHL, the GateKeeper adds the new

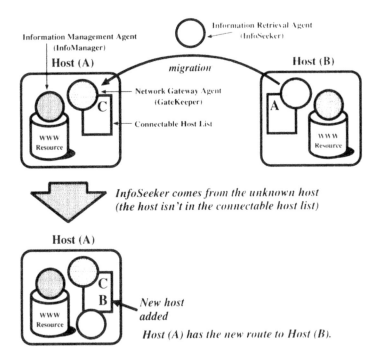

Figure 3: Mechanism of self-organizing information retrieval network.

host to the CHL (see Fig.3). The self-organizing information retrieval network allows the users to search the information even if the search servers have some troubles and also allows to search the newest information. In the standard WWW search systems, the users are connected direct to the search server in order to search the information. Therefore, the users can't search the information when the search server has some troubles. On the other hand, the ATRAS can provide the stable search for the users, because the InfoSeekers can search the information and avoid the troubled host in the information retrieval network. In ATRAS, if new WWW server host, which is an ATRAS host, appears in the information retrieval network, the ATRAS host connects to the network by the GateKeeper automatically. Therefore, the users can search the information in new ATRAS host.

2.5   Information Retrieval Mechanism

The ATRAS information retrieval mechanism is shown in Fig.4. In this mechanism, the user asks the Communicator for information retrieval (1). The Communicator makes a search request to SeekersManager (2). The SeekersManager orders the InfoSeekers to search for information (3). The InfoSeeker asks the GateKeeper for search host (4). The GateKeeper decides the next ATRAS host where the InfoSeeker should be migrated. At this time, the migrated host's GateKeeper checks that the

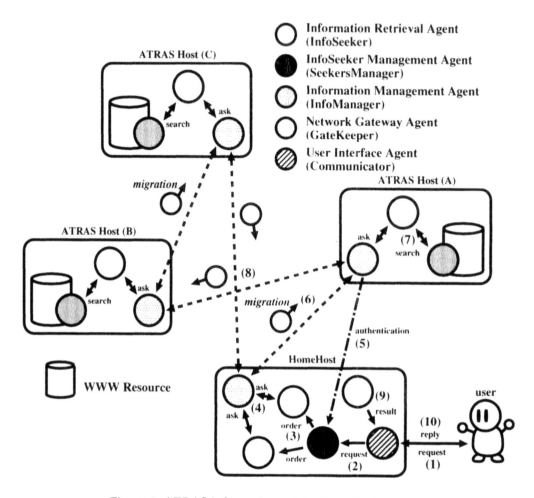

Figure 4: ATRAS information retrieval mechanism.

InfoSeeker is valid by the SeekersManager in the InfoSeeker's home host (5). The InfoSeeker migrates to the new ATRAS host (6). In the new host, the InfoManager searches for the information requested from the InfoSeeker and replies to InfoSeeker (7). The InfoSeeker repeats this search cycle until the search condition is satisfied (8). Then, the InfoSeeker returns to the home host and tells the search results to Communicator (9). Finally, the Communicator reports the search results to user (10).

2.6   Experiments in Prototype System

The purpose of the experiments is to investigate the ATRAS behavior. In order to test the ATRAS performance, a simple WWW network is constructed over the campus network, and the ATRAS agents are implemented in different hosts.

The experimental server hosts are the host walrus (which is a special host and has a default GateKeeper), eagle, miffy, cat, donkey, monkey, tiger and goose (which are the standard WWW server hosts). In Fig.5, the migration search which is the ATRAS basic function was observed. The migration search path was as following: the host walrus → cat → monkey → tiger → eagle and returned to the host walrus. In this experiment, the expand of the information retrieval network by the migration search was observed.

When a new WWW server host goose appears in the information retrieval network, the GateKeeper in the host goose requires the initial CHL to the default GateKeeper's host walrus automatically and the network is self-organized. This phenomenon was confirmed by the experiments. The migration search path also includes the new host goose.

In Fig.6, the GateKeeper in the host donkey was stopped to make the situation of the server trouble. In migration search, the InfoSeeker migrated from the host walrus to the host miffy and from the host miffy to the host monkey. The InfoSeeker tried to migrate from the host monkey to the host donkey, but failed because the GateKeeper was stopped in the host donkey. Nevertheless, the InfoSeeker avoided the host donkey and migrated from the host monkey to the host cat. This result shows that the users can search the information regardless of the search server condition.

Finally, the migration search was started from all hosts. It was checked whether the search was completed or not. The migration search was completed for all hosts. This results shows that the users can search the information without depending on the search server's URL.

3   Evolving Information Retrieval System

The ATRAS can solve the problems of the standard WWW search systems. But, the migration search has the following problems:

(1) takes a long time to search the information,

(2) has to adapt to the various environments and user preferences,

(3) gets different results because the migration search depends on the selected ATRAS host.

The ATRAS can solve the problem of item (1) by parallel information retrieval using multiple information retrieval agents. But using this method, information retrieval agents may move to the same ATRAS hosts. To solve this problem, we propose two methods. The first one uses the unique ID for search request. The second one selects the migrated host according to the individuality of agents such as STP. The problem of item (2) is solved by applying GAs to the information retrieval agents. GAs generate the information retrieval agents which have the best search parameters to adapt to the various environments. We also improve the ATRAS

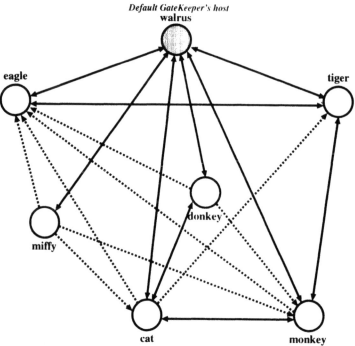

Figure 5: Information retrieval net (1).

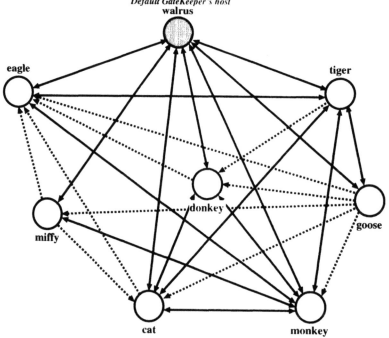

Figure 6: Information retrieval net (2).

to solve the problem of item (3) by WN. The WN is designed for more efficient information search of information retrieval agents and for more efficient selection of migrated ATRAS host. The WN enables the information retrieval agents to avoid the hosts with heavy CPU load, the hosts with few information and the hosts which have no search information.

3.1 GAs

GAs are search methods which solve optimization problems. The mechanism is based on the interaction between individuals and the natural environment. GAs comprise a set of individuals (the population) and a set of biologically inspired operators (the genetic operators). The individuals have genes which are the potential solutions for a problem. The genetic operators are crossover and mutation. GAs generate a sequence of populations by using genetic operators among individuals. As a result, only the most suited individuals in a population can survive and generate offsprings, thus transmitting their biological heredity to new generations[7, 8].

GAs operate through a simple cycle of four stages. Each cycle produces a new generation of possible solutions for a given problem. At the first stage, an initial population of potential solutions is created as a starting point for the search. In the next stage, the performance (or fitness) of each individual is evaluated with respect to the constraints imposed by the problem. Based on each individual's fitness, a selection mechanism chooses "parents" for the genetic operators: crossover and mutation. The crossover operator takes two chromosomes and swaps part of their genetic information to produce new chromosomes. The mutation operator introduces new genetic structures in the population by randomly modifying some of genes, helping the search algorithm escape from local minima's traps. The offsprings produced by the genetic manipulation process are the next population to be evaluated. GAs can replace either a whole population or its less fitted members only. The creation-evaluation-selection-manipulation cycle repeats until a satisfactory solution to the problem is found or some other termination criteria are is met.

3.2 Evolving Information Retrieval Agents

In ATRAS, the information retrieval agents have five search parameters: Maximum Search Host Number (MSHN), Maximum Search Item Number (MSIN), Search Information Acceptance Ratio (SIAR), Maximum Search Time (MST) and Maximum Migration Error Number (MMEN). The MSHN and MSIN are used for getting high quality results. To get high quality result, the information retrieval agents have to visit more ATRAS hosts and to gather more search results. The SIAR is a parameter to get appropriate results. The information retrieval agents gather search results which the information management agent selects according to the SIAR. The MST decides the search time for each information retrieval agent. The last parameter MMEN is used for avoiding the infinite migration loop.

These parameters have big effect for the search performance. The ATRAS hosts

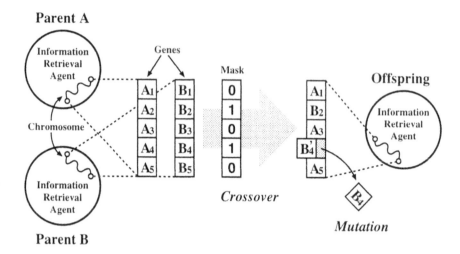

Figure 7: New information retrieval agent generated based on GAs.

don't have the same environments. The environments consist of the machine environment and the network environment. The machine environment has the number of users, the CPU power, the information quantity, the CPU load and the number of migrated agents. The network environment has the bandwidth, the network traffic and the property of line. Therefore, the ATRAS need to adapt to the various environments and user preferences. The search parameters must be different in all ATRAS hosts and have a suitable variation in order to adapt to each environment.

The information retrieval agents, which are based on GAs, are designed to adjust the search parameters in different environments. The search parameters are represented as the genes in chromosome. The genes in each agent varies with the evolution of the agents. The evolution of the agents is based on GAs cycle described in Section3.1. The genetic manipulation in GAs cycle generates the new information retrieval agent. The fitness of the information retrieval agent is evaluated by users, which decide the evaluation according to their satisfaction of search results. Then, the parents are selected based on each individual's fitness. There exist many selection strategies, but we use the rank selection strategy, because this strategy has the best performance compared with the statistical and probable strategy, the keeping elite strategy, the rank strategy and the tournament strategy. The rank selection strategy is that each individual is ranked by its fitness and is given new selection probability based on its rank and parents are selected according to new selection probability. Fig.7 shows the mechanism that new information retrieval agent is generated by the genetic operators.

GAs control five search parameters of the information retrieval agents. The information retrieval agents will adapt gradually to their environments and the search parameters will have a suitable variation. Therefore, in every ATRAS host, the information retrieval agents will have the best search parameters and the users will be able to search the information under the best search condition.

3.3   Weighting Information Retrieval Network

In the current ATRAS information retrieval network, the information retrieval agents cannot search the information efficiently, because the decision of next migrated host is selected randomly in the CHL and the information retrieval depends on the migrated host. In order to solve this disadvantage, the information retrieval network is weighted by the feedback of search results from information retrieval agents. In other words, the ATRAS host which has various information and fast information retrieval is given higher priority. The information retrieval agents move to such hosts and search the information.

For example, the information retrieval agent moves from host (A) to host (B). It searches the information and gets the search results in host (B), then transmits the feedback of search results to host (A). The connection between host (A) and host (B) is stronger by the weight which is calculated with the feedback of search results.

There are two kinds of methods for the weight calculation. In first method, the weight is calculated by Search Hit Number (SHN) and Search Time (ST). The SHN is the number of information which satisfies the search query. The ST is the total times for searching the information in an ATRAS host. The new weight (WT) is calculated by the following expression:

$$WT = F(SHN/ST). \qquad (15.1)$$

In second method, the weight is calculated by Quality of Information (QoI) and Search Speed (SS). The QoI is the standard which is calculated by Amount of Information (AoI) in the search catalog and SHN. The SS is the speed of information search which is calculated by the AoI and ST. The SS reflects not only the CPU power but also the host load, because the ST depends on the machine environment. In this method, the WT is calculated by the following expression:

$$
\begin{aligned}
WT &= F(QoI + SS) \qquad (15.2)\\
QoI &= SHN/AoI\\
SS &= AoI/ST.
\end{aligned}
$$

In expression (15.1) and (15.2), the F is the function which renews current WT based on previous WT.

The WN enables the information retrieval agents to move the ATRAS host which has various information. As the connection between ATRAS hosts is stronger, the information retrieval agents can be migrated to the hosts which have various information.

4   Conclusions

In this paper, we have presented a new information retrieval system, called ATRAS, for searching in the WWW. We also have proposed the EIRA and WN to enhance the ATRAS performance. By using the EIRA and WN, the ATRAS has the following improvements:

(1) the information retrieval agents have the best search parameters;

(2) the users will be able to search the information under the best search condition;

(3) the information search will be more efficient for the information retrieval agents.

The authors are planning to test the effectiveness of ATRAS biological characteristics (EIRA and WN) to investigate what search parameters (genes) can satisfy the user search request, and to implement new search parameters (genes) to the information retrieval agents.

Bibliography

1) C. M. Bowman, P. B. Danzig, D. R. Hardy, U. Manber and M. F. Schwartz, *"The Harvest Information Discovery and Access System"*, Proc. of the Second International World Wide Web Conference, pp.763-771, 1994.

2) R. Armstrong, D. Freitag, T. Joachims and T. Mitchell, *"WebWatcher: A Learning Apprentice for the World Wide Web"*, Proc. of the Symposium on Information Gathering from Heterogeneous, Distributed Environments, AAAI Press, pp.6-12, 1995.

3) M. Balabanovic and Y. Shoham, *"Learning Information Retrieval Agents: Experiments with Automated Web Browsing"*, Proc. of the Symposium on Information Gathering from Heterogenous, Distributed Environments, AAAI Press, pp.13-18, 1995.

4) F. Menczer, R. K. Belew and W. Willuhn, *"Artificial Life Applied to Adaptive Information Agents"*, Proc. of the Symposium on Information Gathering from Distributed, Heterogeneous Databases, AAAI Press, pp.128-132, 1995.

5) H. Lieberman, *"Letizia: An Agent That Assists Web Browsing"*, Proc. of IJCAI-95, pp.924-929, 1995.

6) M. Wooldridge and N. R. Jennings, *"Intelligent Agents: Theory and Practice"*, Knowledge Engineering Review 10(2), http://www.doc.mmu.ac.uk/ STAFF/mike/ker95.ps, Oct.1994.

7) M. Srinivas and L. M. Patnaik, *"Genetic Algorithms: A Survey"*, IEEE COMPUTER Society Press, pp.17-26, Jun.1994.

8) J. L. R. Filho, P. C. Treleaven and C. Alippi, *"Genetic-Algorithm Programming Environments"*, IEEE COMPUTER Society Press, pp.28-43, Jun.1994.

16

Extracting Structures of HTML Documents Using a High-Level Stack Machine

Seung-Jin Lim
Yiu-Kai Ng

Brigham Young University

ABSTRACT

Information on the Web, which are conglomeration of heterogeneous data such as texts, images and audio clips, are often accessed through documents written according to the HTML specification [?]. According to the HTML specification, HTML documents are semistructured in nature. We propose a *high-level stack machine* (HSM) which accesses an HTML document through its URL and constructs a *semistructured data graph* (SDG) of the document. The SDG of an HTML document H precisely captures the structure of the semistructured data embedded in H based on the dependency relationship [?] among the data objects in H. HSM is configurable to accommodate a user's interest with respect to the HTML elements in H to be considered during the construction process of the SDG of H.

1 Introduction

During the early days of the World-Wide Web (WWW or Web), users relied heavily on the mouse-button-click navigation method using hyperlinks provided by Web browsers to retrieve information of interest and soon found themselves lost somewhere in the midst of cyberspace [?]. Since then Web designers, as well as Web users, have been looking for better alternatives. Two recent approaches for retrieving information from the Web are (i) the keyword search method using index servers, and (ii) the method of using Web query languages, including SQL-like query languages [?, ?] and Datalog-like query languages [?].

To better understand this issue, we clarify three types of data, namely unstructured data, structured data, and semistructured data, with respect to their structures according to [?]. *Unstructured data* are data which is stored in files such as executable files, plain text files which contain no formatting code, and audio files. ([?] use the term *unstructured data* for any data of no rigid structure.) A typical example of *structured data* is tables in the relational database model. *Semistructured data* is anything between the two extreme types of data mentioned earlier. Examples of this type of data are text files that contain formatting codes, such as LaTeX and HTML files, and files which require strict inner structure but some of the structural components can be omitted, such as BIBTeX files, Unix environment files, etc.

Our view of information on the Web is a collection of heterogeneous data, such as HTML documents by and large and other types of data including images, sound, and video clips. HTML specification [?], which is the most widely used paradigm for posting information on the Web, does not require a uniform structure in HTML documents, e.g., an element which appears in an HTML document may be missing in other HTML documents. Hence, we treat an HTML document H as a textual representation of semistructured data embedded within H.

One of the benefits of using semistructured data is its flexibility in data representation [?]. A theory of semistructured data, however, is still missing [?], and there is no universally standardized definition on semistructured data. In this paper, we consider a finite set of data objects $\{o_1, o_2, \ldots, o_n\}$ as semistructured data D if (i) the structure of D is *irregular* or *incomplete* [?,?], (ii) the distinction between the schema of D and $\{o_1, o_2, \ldots, o_n\}$ is blurred and the schema may change dynamically [?], and (iii) o_i ($1 \leq i \leq n$) is not type-sensitive.

In this paper, we present an approach for extracting the structure of semistructured data embedded within an HTML document H on WWW, assuming that H is written in compliance[1] with the HTML specification [?] and referred by a given URL. (Additional URLs can be further obtained from the hyperlinks specified in H.) We first propose a graphical data model of semistructured data, called the *semistructured data graph* (SDG), and then present a tool, a *high-level stack machine* (HSM)[2], to extract the structures embedded in H.

The main contribution of this paper is three-fold. First, we extend the concept of *dependency relationship* among database components defined in [?] to capture the structure of the semistructured data embedded in an HTML document. Second, we design and implement a simple automaton HSM, using the *Java Language Environment*, to construct the SDG of an HTML document specified by an URL. Since HSM is built based on pushdown automata, HSM is fairly easy to implement using a stack without concerning about sophisticated functions such as rereading or replacing an input, or assuming unlimited auxiliary memory as a Turing machine does. Third, our HSM is easily configurable according to the user's need in terms of what HTML elements are to be included in an SDG. To configure HSM, a user simply provides a configuration file which contains a list of HTML elements in an HTML document H chosen by the user to be included in the SDG of H. Writing a configuration file does not require any knowledge on additional commands and their syntax, such as *get()*, *split()* and *_citytemp*[1 : 0] in [?].

This paper is organized as follows: In Section 2, we describe the details of SDGs. In Section 3, we propose HSM and demonstrate its application using a real-world example. In Section 4, we give the concluding remark.

---

[1] Note that erroneous HTML documents are not excluded from our consideration.
[2] HSM is a variation of the well-known pushdown automata (PDA).

2   The Data Model

The fundamental of our data model for semistructured data, SDG, is based on the notion of *dependency relationship* [?] among database objects.

Definition 1 An object o in a set S is a triple $\langle label, value, identifier \rangle$, where *label* is the textual (i.e., a string) description of o, *value* is a finite ordered set of strings (if *value* is empty, then o is called a *free* object; otherwise, o is called a *bound* object), and *identifier* is a non-empty string that uniquely defines o in S. □

In an SDG, the *identifier* and *label* of an object are static, whereas its *value* is dynamic. In other words, the identifier and label of an object do not change, whereas its value may change. We formalize and illustrate how the value of an object changes from *free* to *bound* in Definition 2 and Example 1. Also, type constraint is not straightly enforced on an object in an SDG, and hence the value of an object can be of any type. For instance, the value of object *Month* can be a string "January," an integer "1", or a string encoded using a character set other than ASCII. This relaxation is desirable in that whenever a query is posted for an object o using values of types different from o's, the system may gracefully fail to process the query rather than invoke an error [?]. For simplicity, we assume the value of an object is a set of strings since all the atomic and composite types, such as integer, real and boolean, and a set of objects of atomic type, can be represented as a string. In addition, we use *str* instead of $\{str\}$ for each singleton set $\{str\}$, and $\{A.B, A.C\}$ is written as $A.\{B, C\}$ where A, B, and C are strings.

In conjunction with the definition of an object, we define the utility functions $o.label()$ and $o.value()$ such that for each object o, $o.label()$ and $o.value()$ return the label and the value of o, respectively. In addition, we define the binary function *con*: $S \times S \to S$, where S is a set of strings and $con(arg_1, arg_2) = arg_1.arg_2$.

Definition 2 An object o_1 is said to *directly depend on* another object o_2, denoted $o_1 \leftarrow o_2$, if $o_1.value() := o_2.value()$. Dependency is transitive, i.e., $o_1 \leftarrow o_3$ if $o_1 \leftarrow o_2$ and $o_2 \leftarrow o_3$, and we say that o_1 *indirectly depends on* o_3, denoted $o_1 \leftarrow o_2 \leftarrow o_3$ or $o_1 \overset{*}{\leftarrow} o_3$. If $o \leftarrow o_1, \cdots, o \leftarrow o_n$, then $o.value() := o_1.value() \bigcup \cdots \bigcup o_n.value()$. □

Example 1 Given below is a set of objects and their data values in the form of object($o.label()$; $o.value()$; *a list of objects on which o directly depends*). A string which contains spaces is enclosed by double quotes, and '–' denotes an empty list.

Location (Location; (*free*); *Address*, "*Time Zone*"),
Address (Address; (*free*); "*Street Addr*," *City*, "*Zip code*"),
"*Street Addr*" (Street; (*free*); "*11 E. Pine Lane*"), *City* (City; (*free*); *Orem*),
"*Zip code*" (ZipCode; (*free*); *84057*), "*Time Zone*" (TimeZone; (*free*); *MST*),
"*11 E. Pine Lane*" ("11 E. Pine Lane"; "11 E. Pine Lane"; –),
Orem (Orem; Orem; –), *84057* (84057; 84057; –), and
MST (MST; "Mountain Standard Time"; –).

The dependency constraint of *Address* is *Address* ← "*Street Addr*" ← "*11 E. Pine Lane*", *Address* ← *City* ← *Orem*, and *Address* ← "*Zip code*" ← *84057*. Hence,

$$Address.value() = \{\text{``Street Addr''}.value(), \; City.value(), \; \text{``Zip code''}.value()\}$$
$$= \{\text{``11 E. Pine Lane''}.value(), \; Orem.value(), \; 84057.value()\}$$
$$= \{\text{``11 E. Pine Lane''}, \; Orem, \; 84057\}. \; \square$$

We now formally define the long label of an object and SDGs based on the dependency relationship of objects.

Definition 3 Given the dependency relationships among objects o_1, o_2, ..., o_N such that $o_1 \leftarrow o_2 \leftarrow \ldots \leftarrow o_N$, the *long label* of o_i, denoted $o_i.Label()$, $1 \leq i \leq N$, is defined as $o_1.Label() = o_1.label()$, and $o_i.Label() = con(o_{i-1}.Label(), o_i.label())$, $2 \leq i \leq N$. $\square$

Example 2 Consider the set of objects in Example 1. According to Definition 3, all the expressions listed below are valid.

$Location.Label() = Location.label() = $ Location
$Orem.Label() = (City.Label()).(Orem.label()) = (Address.Label()).(City.label()).Orem$
$\qquad = (Location.Label()).(Address.label()).City.Orem$
$\qquad = (Location.label()).Address.City.Orem = $ Location.Address.City.Orem
$\text{``Time Zone''}.Label() = $ Location.TimeZone $\square$

Definition 4 Given a semistructured data D, the *semistructured data graph* SDG[3] of D is a triple (V, E, g) which is a rooted, directed graph, where (i) V is a finite set of nodes and $V = \{V_R\} \cup V_I \cup V_L$, where $\{V_R\} \cap V_I \cap V_L = \emptyset$, and V_R with label 'D' is the root node of SDG which serves as the entry point of SDG and represents D, V_L is a finite set of leaf nodes, and V_I is a finite set of (internal) nodes other than V_R and V_L in SDG. $n \in (V_I \cup V_L)$, which is labeled by 'o', represents an object o in D; (ii) E is a finite set of directed edges; and (iii) $g: E \rightarrow V \times V$ such that $g(e) = (n_1, n_2)$ if and only if the object represented by $n_1 \in (\{V_R\} \cup V_I)$ depends on the object represented by $n_2 \in (V_I \cup V_L)$. $\square$.

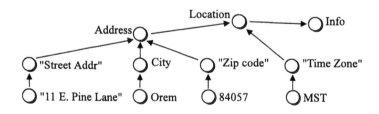

Figure 1: The SDG for *Info*

Example 3 Consider the object *Location* in Example 1 and suppose semistructured data *Info* is defined by *Location*. Given the dependency constraints for *Location* and its relevant objects, the SDG for *Info* is illustrated in Figure 1. A more comprehensive example of SDGs is presented in Section 3. □

Definition 5 Given the long label of an object o_N $(o_1.label()).(\ldots).(o_N.label())$ in an SDG, the *path expression*, *pe*, between o_i and o_i and between o_i and o_j $(1 \le i < j \le N)$ is a binary function $pe: S \times S \to S$ such that $pe(o_i, o_i) = o_i.label()$ and $pe(o_i, o_j) = con(pe(o_i, o_{j-1}), o_j.label())$, where S is a set of strings and o_1 denotes the root node of the SDG. □

It is easy to see that $pe(V_R, o) = o.Label()$, where V_R is the root node and $o \in (V_I \cup V_L)$ of the corresponding SDG.

An SDG precisely captures the structure and values of semistructured data graphically. Given below is the definition of the lexical representation of an SDG. The lexical representation of a semistructured data D is useful in some situations, e.g., finding an object in D using a textual path expression.

Definition 6 Given an SDG $= (\{V_R\} \cup V_I \cup V_L, E, g)$, the *lexical representation* L_o or *lexical SDG* of $o \in (\{V_R\} \cup V_I \cup V_L)$ is a textual representation of the subgraph S of SDG rooted at o such that $L_o = \cup_{\forall i} \{pe(o, o_i)\}$, where o_i is a leaf node in S. □

Example 4 Consider the SDG of *Info* in Figure 1. Listed below are a few path expressions and lexical representation of some objects in *Info*:

$$pe(Address,\ 84057) = con(pe(Address,\ \text{``Zip code''}),\ 84057.label())$$
$$= con(con(pe(Address, Address),\ \text{``Zip Code''}.label()),\ 84057)$$
$$= con(con(Address.label(),\ ZipCode),\ 84057)$$
$$= con(Address.ZipCode,\ 84057)$$
$$= Address.ZipCode.84057$$
$$pe(Address, Orem) = Address.City.Orem$$
$$L_{Address} = \{Address.Street.\text{``11 E. Pine Lane''}\}\ \cup$$
$$\{Address.City.Orem\}\ \cup$$
$$\{Address.ZipCode.84057\}$$
$$= Address.\{Street.\text{``11 E. Pine Pine''},\ City.Orem,\ ZipCode.84057\}$$

The lexical SDG of *Info* $L_{Info} = $ Info.Location.{Address.{Street.``11 E. Pine Lane'', City.Orem, ZipCode.84057}, TimeZone.MST}. □

Note that given an SDG $= (\{V_R\} \cup V_I \cup V_L, E, g)$, the lexical representation of the SDG is obtained by $\cup_{\forall i} \{pe(V_R, o_i)\} = \cup_{\forall i} \{o_i.Label()\}$, where $o_i \in V_L$. It is obvious that the lexical representation L of an SDG is not as easy to interpret as the SDG itself. To resolve this problem, L can be *formatted* using indentation and line feed. An example of the formatted lexical representation of the SDG for the semistructured data *Info* is given below:

Info.
    Location.{
            Address.{
                    Street."11 E. Pine Lane",
                    City.Orem,
                    ZipCode.84057}
            TimeZone.MST}

Definition 7 Given a semistructured data D and its corresponding semistructured data graph SDG $= (\{V_R\} \cup V_I \cup V_L, E, g)$, the *schema* S of D represented by SDG is $S = \cup_{\forall i}\{pe(o, o_i)\}$, where $o_i \in V_I$ and o is o_i's ancestor which is a child of V_R. $\square$

Example 5 Consider *Info* in Example 3 again. The schema S of *Info* is

$$
\begin{aligned}
S =\ & \{pe(Location, Location)\} \cup \{pe(Location, Address)\} \\
& \cup \{pe(Location, \text{``}Time\ Zone\text{''})\} \cup \{pe(Location, \text{``}Street\ Addr\text{''})\} \\
& \cup \{pe(Location, City)\} \cup \{pe(Location, \text{``}Zip\ code\text{''})\} \\
=\ & \{\text{Location}\} \cup \{\text{Location.Address}\} \cup \{\text{Location.TimeZone}\} \\
& \cup \{\text{Location.Address.Street}\} \cup \{\text{Location.Address.City}\} \\
& \cup \{\text{Location.Address.ZipCode}\} \\
=\ & \text{Location.}\{\text{Address.}\{\text{Street, City, ZipCode}\}, \text{TimeZone}\} \quad \square
\end{aligned}
$$

3 The High-level Stack Machine

In this section, we present a high-level stack machine (HSM) as a tool which extracts data structures embedded in an HTML document *H* and demonstrate the construction of the SDG for *H* specified by an URL using HSM[4]. See Figure 2 for an example of the HSM user interface.

To construct the SDG of a given HTML document, we propose HSM which processes HTML elements in the document. HSM is implemented in Java language environment as shown in Figure 2. The HTML elements, which are to be handled by HSM, can be determined by users using a configuration file as discussed earlier. The current version of HSM is implemented with a small set of HTML elements which are commonly used in HTML documents and is continuously being enhanced to handle more generic HTML documents.

As mentioned earlier, HSM is built based on pushdown automa (PDA). We are particularly interested in employing PDA since PDA is relatively easy to comprehend, design, and implement compared with Turing machines and has sufficient power to construct the SDGs for HTML documents.

With respect to the design of HSM, we classify the HTML elements in two types: (1) elements which begin with a start-tag and end with an end-tag, and (2) elements whose end-tags are either optional or do not exist. Most of the commonly used HTML elements are of type 1. Such elements include *document* element HTML, *head* element HEAD, *body* element BODY, *headings* H1 ... H6, *title* TITLE, *anchor* A, some of the block structuring elements such as *list* elements OL and UL, *block quote* BLOCKQUOTE, *preformatted text* PRE, *directory list* DIR, *menu list* MENU, *address* element ADDRESS, and *phrase markups* such as EM, B, I and STRONG. Examples of elements of type 2 are some of the *block structuring* elements such as *list* element LI, *definition lists* DT and DD, *line break* BR, and *horizontal rule* HR.

---

[4]SDG is constructed in various formats by using HSM, which are all equivalent with respect to the structure that SDG represents. The formats include the lexical SDG, a textual definition of the SDG using long labels of the objects or object identifiers, and a graphical display of the SDG on the screen. Each of these output formats can be chosen by the user.

Figure 2: An HSM user interface

Some HTML elements, such as IMG, do not accompany an end-tag, but the closing angle brackets indicate where the end of the elements are. Therefore, we categorize IMG as an element of type 1.

Besides the two types of HTML elements mentioned above, we treat some elements as 'unproductive' with respect to SDGs, i.e., they do not generate an output on an SDG in our current version of HSM, and are simply ignored by HSM. For instance, UPE, the set of unproductive elements, can be excluded from a user's configuration file. At the current version of HSM, elements such as HR, B, CITE, DIR, TT, DL, DT, DD, and *comments* <!... > are treated as elements in UPE. In addition, we treat the set of elements of type 2 as a proper subset of UPE. However, when we consider a query language for SDG in our future work, it may be appropriate to adjust UPE accordingly to give more weight to styled text than plain text. (The styled text is surrounded by character style tags such as <B>, <BIG>, <STRONG> and their corresponding end-tags.)

During the construction process of an SDG, the following two rules of HSM are applied to elements in an HTML document H: (1) Skip an element e if $e \in$ UPE. Also, no stack operation is necessary, and no changes occur in the SDG of H. (2) For an element e' of type 1, *push* the corresponding stack symbol γ (defined in Definition 8) of e' onto the stack whenever the start-tag of e' is encountered, and *pop* γ from the stack of HSM whenever the corresponding end-tag of e' is detected. In general, given the top of the stack symbol p and the SDG being constructed which includes a node o_p created for p, whenever a new stack symbol γ is pushed, γ is attached to the SDG as a child c of o_p with the edge from c to o_p. (It is assumed that *append*() is defined in HSM which appends a node or an edge to an SDG.)

Definition 8 HSM is a system $(Q, \Sigma, \Gamma, \delta, q_{BOF}, \epsilon, F)$, where

1. Q is a finite set of states: $q_{BOF}, q_1, q_A, q_{A\_ATTR}, q_B, q_{B\_ATTR}$, and q_{EOF}. State symbol q_{BOF} denotes the beginning-of-the-file state and q_{EOF} denotes the end-of-the-file state. States q_A and q_{A_ATTR} are used for anchors and APPLETs, and q_B and q_{B_ATTR} are used for processing the *IMG* and *META* elements. Also, when the machine is in state q_1, HSM is not currently processing the elements IMG, META, A, and APPLET.

2. Σ is a finite set of input symbols <HTML>, </HTML>, <HEAD>, </HEAD>, <META>, HTTP-EQUIV, NAME, CONTENT, <TITLE>, </TITLE>, <H1>, ..., <H6>, <BODY>, </BODY>, <MENU>, </MENU>, EOF, NT, <UL>, </UL>, <OL>, </OL>, <A>, </A>, <IMG, SRC, ALT>, <CAPTION>, </CAPTION>, <TABLE>, </TABLE>, <TR>, </TR>, <TH>, </TH>, <TD>, </TD>, <APPLET>, </APPLET>, ARCHIVE, CODEBASE, CODE, <ADDRESS>, and </ADDRESS>.

   NT denotes any input string symbol in an HTML document other than the rest of the input string symbols defined in (2).

3. Γ is a finite set of stack string symbols ϵ, *HTML*, *HEAD*, *TITLE*, *META*, *HTTP-EQUIV*, *NAME*, *CONTENT*, *BODY*, *OL*, *UL*, *TABLE*,

$CAPTION$, TR, TH, TD, $ADDRESS$, IMG, SRC, ALT, A, $HREF$, $APPLET$, $ARCHIVE$, $CODE$, $CODEBASE$, $MENU$, DES, and ", where DES denotes *Description* and ϵ denotes the empty stack symbol.

4. δ is a mapping from $Q \times \Sigma \times (\Gamma \cup \{\epsilon\})$ to $Q \times \Gamma^*$, where '*' denotes the *Kleene star*. '.' is used to separate different stack symbols in the following set of production rules of δ:

$\delta(q_{BOF}, \text{<HTML>}, \epsilon) = (q_1, HTML)$ $\delta(q_{BOF}, \text{<HEAD>}, \epsilon) = (q_1, HEAD)$

$\delta(q_{BOF}, \text{<BODY>}, \epsilon) = (q_1, BODY)$ $\delta(q_1, \text{</HTML>}, HTML) = (q_{BOF}, \epsilon)$

$\delta(q_1, \text{<HEAD>}, HTML) = (q_1, HEAD.HTML)$ $\delta(q_1, \text{</HEAD>}, HEAD) = (q_1, \epsilon)$

$\delta(q_1, \text{<TITLE>}, HEAD) = (q_1, TITLE.HEAD)$ $\delta(q_1, \text{</TITLE>}, TITLE) = (q_1, \epsilon)$

$\delta(q_1, \text{<BODY>}, HTML) = (q_1, BODY.HTML)$ $\delta(q_1, \text{</BODY>}, BODY) = (q_1, \epsilon)$

$\delta(q_1, \text{<TABLE>}, *) = (q_1, TABLE.*)$ $\delta(q_1, \text{</TABLE>}, TABLE) = (q_1, \epsilon)$

$\delta(q_1, \text{<CAPTION>}, TABLE) = (q_1, CAPTION.TABLE)$

$\delta(q_1, \text{</CAPTION>}, CAPTION) = (q_1, \epsilon)$ $\delta(q_1, \text{<TR>}, TABLE) = (q_1, TR.TABLE)$

$\delta(q_1, \text{</TR>}, TR) = (q_1, \epsilon)$ $\delta(q_1, \text{<TH>}, TR) = (q_1, TH.TR)$

$\delta(q_1, \text{</TH>}, TH) = (q_1, \epsilon)$ $\delta(q_1, \text{<TD>}, TR) = (q_1, TD.TR)$

$\delta(q_1, \text{</TD>}, TD) = (q_1, \epsilon)$ $\delta(q_1, \text{<OL>}, *) = (q_1, OL.*)$

$\delta(q_1, \text{</OL>}, OL) = (q_1, \epsilon)$ $\delta(q_1, \text{<UL>}, *) = (q_1, UL.*)$

$\delta(q_1, \text{</UL>}, UL) = (q_1, \epsilon)$ $\delta(q_1, \text{<A }, *) = (q_A, A.*)$

$\delta(q_A, \text{HREF}, A) = (q_A, HREF.A)$ $\delta(q_A, \text{NAME}, A) = (q_A, NAME.A)$

$\delta(q_A, \text{"}, HREF) = (q_{A\_ATTR}, DES.HREF)$ $\delta(q_A, \text{"}, NAME) = (q_{A\_ATTR}, DES.NAME)$

$\delta(q_{A\_ATTR}, \text{NT}, DES) = (q_{A\_ATTR}, DES)\dagger$ $\delta(q_{A\_ATTR}, \text{"}, DES) = (q_A, \epsilon)$

$\delta(q_A, \text{>}, HREF) = (q_A, DES)$ $\delta(q_A, \text{>}, NAME) = (q_A, DES)$

$\delta(q_1, \text{</A>}, DES) = (q_1, \epsilon)$ $\delta(q_A, \text{NT}, DES) = (q_A, DES)\dagger$

$\delta(q_1, \text{<APPLET }, *) = (q_A, APPLET.*)$

$\delta(q_A, \text{ARCHIVE}, APPLET) = (q_A, ARCHIVE.APPLET)$

$\delta(q_A, \text{CODEBASE}, APPLET) = (q_A, CODEBASE.APPLET)$

$\delta(q_A, \text{CODE}, APPLET) = (q_A, CODE.APPLET)$

$\delta(q_A, \text{"}, ARCHIVE) = (q_{A\_ATTR}, DES.ARCHIVE)$

$\delta(q_A, \text{"}, CODEBASE) = (q_{A\_ATTR}, DES.CODEBASE)$

$\delta(q_A, \text{"}, CODE) = (q_{A\_ATTR}, DES.CODE)$ $\delta(q_{A\_ATTR}, \text{NT}, DES) = (q_{A\_ATTR}, DES)\dagger$

$\delta(q_{A\_ATTR}, \text{"}, DES) = (q_A, \epsilon)$ $\delta(q_A, \text{>}, ARCHIVE) = (q_A, DES)$

$\delta(q_A, \text{>}, CODEBASE) = (q_A, DES)$ $\delta(q_A, \text{>}, CODE) = (q_A, DES)$

$\delta(q_A, \text{</APPLET>}, DES) = (q_1, \epsilon)$ $\delta(q_1, \text{<IMG }, *) = (q_B, IMG.*)$

$\delta(q_B, \text{>}, IMG) = (q_1, \epsilon)$ $\delta(q_B, \text{>}, SRC) = (q_1, \epsilon)$

$\delta(q_B, \text{>}, ALT) = (q_1, \epsilon)$ $\delta(q_B, \text{SRC}, IMG) = (q_B, SRC.IMG)$

$\delta(q_B, \text{SRC}, ALT) = (q_B, SRC)$ $\delta(q_B, \text{ALT}, IMG) = (q_B, ALT.IMG)$

$\delta(q_B, \text{ALT}, SRC) = (q_B, ALT)$ $\delta(q_B, \text{"}, SRC) = (q_{B\_ATTR}, DES.SRC)$

$\delta(q_B, \text{"}, ALT) = (q_{B\_ATTR}, DES.ALT)$ $\delta(q_{B\_ATTR}, \text{NT}, DES) = (q_{B\_ATTR}, DES)\dagger$

$\delta(q_{B\_ATTR}, \text{"}, DES) = (q_B, \epsilon)$ $\delta(q_1, \text{<META }, *) = (q_B, META.*)$

$\delta(q_B, \text{>}, META) = (q_1, \epsilon)$ $\delta(q_B, \text{>}, HTTP\text{-}EQUIV) = (q_1, \epsilon)$

$\delta(q_B, \text{>}, NAME) = (q_1, \epsilon)$ $\delta(q_B, \text{>}, CONTENT) = (q_1, \epsilon)$

$\delta(q_B, \text{HTTP-EQUIV}, META) = (q_B, HTTP\text{-}EQUIV.META)$

$\delta(q_B, \text{HTTP-EQUIV}, NAME) = (q_B, HTTP\text{-}EQUIV)$

$\delta(q_B, \text{HTTP-EQUIV}, CONTENT) = (q_B, HTTP\text{-}EQUIV)$

$\delta(q_B, \text{NAME}, META) = (q_B, NAME.META)$

$\delta(q_B, \text{NAME}, HTTP\text{-}EQUIV) = (q_B, NAME)$

$\delta(q_B, \text{NAME}, CONTENT) = (q_B, NAME)$

$\delta(q_B, \text{CONTENT}, META) = (q_B, CONTENT.META)$

$\delta(q_B, \text{CONTENT}, HTTP\text{-}EQUIV) = (q_B, CONTENT)$

$\delta(q_B, \text{CONTENT}, NAME) = (q_B, CONTENT)$

$\delta(q_B, \text{"}, HTTP\text{-}EQUIV) = (q_{B\_ATTR}, DES.HTTP\text{-}EQUIV)$

$\delta(q_B, ", NAME) = (q_{B\_ATTR}, DES.NAME)$

$\delta(q_B, ", CONTENT) = (q_{B\_ATTR}, DES.COMMENT)$

$\delta(q_{B\_ATTR}, \text{NT}, DES) = (q_{B\_ATTR}, DES)†$

$\delta(q_1, <\text{ADDRESS}>, BODY) = (q_1, ADDRESS.BODY)$

$\delta(q_{B\_ATTR}, ", DES) = (q_B, \epsilon\}$ $\delta(*, \text{NT}, *_1) = (*, *_1)$

$\delta(q_1, </\text{ADDRESS}>, ADDRESS) = (q_1, \epsilon)$ $\delta(*, \text{EOF}, *) = (q_{BOF}, \epsilon)$

† In this production rule, the current top-of-stack symbol is DES and nothing is pushed onto the stack, but NT is appended to the SDG.

Each rule of the form $\delta(state_1, INPUT, TOS_1) = (state_2, TOS_2)$ is interpreted as "the automaton is currently in state $state_1$ with the top-of-stack symbol TOS_1. After reading the input symbol $INPUT$, the automaton replaces TOS_1 by TOS_2, i.e., pop TOS_1 and push TOS_2 onto the stack, and enter state $state_2$." Note that '$*$' is a "syntactic sugar" used for simplifying notations such that '$*$' in $\delta(q_1, <\text{TABLE}>, *)$ denotes any stack symbol, and $\delta(q_1, <\text{TABLE}>, *) = (q_1, TABLE.*)$ is interpreted as "regardless of what the top-of-stack symbol is when the machine is in q_1 and the input string symbol is $<\text{TABLE}>$, push $TABLE$ onto the stack and remain in the same state." Furthermore, $*_1$ denotes any stack symbol except DES.

5. $Q_{BOF} \in Q$ is the initial state, $\epsilon \in \Gamma$ is the initial stack symbol, and $F \subset Q$ is the set of final states, i.e., $\{q_{EOF}\}$. □

Example 6 Consider the Web page of the CS Department at BYU whose URL is WWW.CS.BYU.EDU. The URL is created as the root node of the SDG, and the $<\text{HTML}>$ element directly depends on $<\text{HEAD}>$ and $<\text{BODY}>$. Furthermore, $<\text{HEAD}>$ directly depends on $<\text{TITLE}>$ which in turn directly depends on the string value "BYU CS Department Homepage" and the five $<\text{META}>$ elements, whereas $<\text{BODY}>$ directly depends on two $<\text{TABLE}>$ elements, five $<\text{A}>$ (anchor) elements, and one $<\text{ADDRESS}>$ element. The SDG of WWW.CS.BYU.EDU is shown in Figure 3. □

4   Conclusion

In this paper, we treat an HTML document H as the textual representation of the semistructured data embedded within H. We present a graphical data model, called *semistructured data graph* (SDG), which is based on the notion of the dependency relationships among the data objects in semistructured data D to describe the structure of D. The SDG of an HTML document precisely captures the structure of the semistructured data embedded in the document, and HSM, a high-level stack machine, is introduced as a tool to extract the structure of the HTML document. We continue to extend HSM so that it can handle more general HTML documents.

Bibliography

1) S. Abiteboul. Querying Semi-structured Data. In *Proceedings of the 6th International Conference on Database Theory*, 1997.

2) P. Atzeni, G. Mecca, and P. Merialdo. To Weave the Web. In *Proceedings of the 23rd International Conference on VLDB*, pages 206–215, August 1997.

3) P. Buneman, S. Davidson, M. Fernandez, and D. Suciu. Adding Structure for Unstructured Data. In *Proceedings of International Conference on Database Theory*, 1997.

4) P. Buneman, S. Davidson, G. Hillebrand, and D. Suciu. A Query Language and Optimization Techniques for Unstructured Data. In *Proceedings of ACM International Conference on Management of Data*, pages 505–516, 1996.

5) Network Working Group. HTML - 2.0. Request for Comments: #1866, November 1995.

6) J. Hammer, H. Garcia-Molina, J. Cho, R. Aranha, and A. Crespo. Extracting Semistructured Information from the Web. In *Proceedings of Workshop on Management of Semistructured Data*, June 1997.

7) D. Konopnicki and O. Shmueli. W3QS: A Query System for the World-Wide Web. In *Proceedings of the 21st VLDB*, pages 54–65, Sept. 1995.

8) L. Lakshmanan, F. Sadri, and I. Subramanian. A Declarative Language for Querying and Restructuring the Web. In *Proceedings of Post-ICDE IEEE Workshop on Research Issues in Data Engineering*, 1996.

9) S.-J. Lim and Y.-K. Ng. Vertical Fragmentation and Allocation in Distributed Deductive Database Systems. *Information Systems*, 22(1):1–24, 1997.

10) D. Quass, A. Rajaraman, Y. Sagiv, J. Ullman, and J. Widom. Querying Semistructured Heterogeneous Information. In *Proceedings of DOOD'95*, pages 319–344, December 1995.

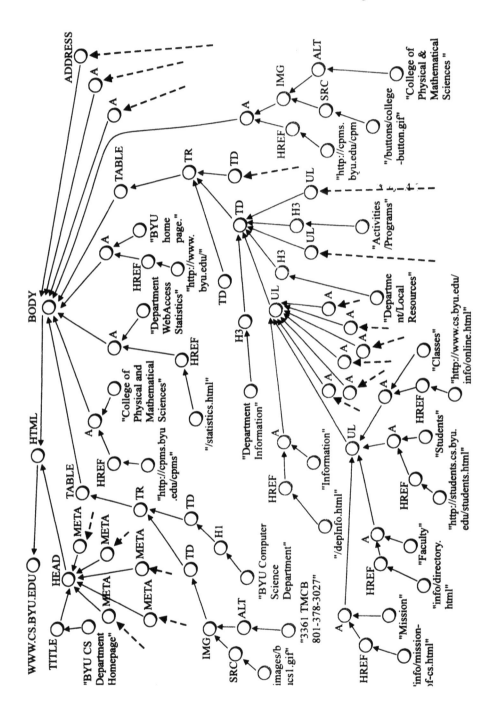

Figure 3: SDG of WWW.CS.BYU.EDU

17

Toward Zero Internet Administration Technology: Case Study of DNS

Cheng Soon Giap

Suguru Yamaguchi

Nara Institute of Science and Technology

Youki Kadobayashi

Osaka University

ABSTRACT

Knowledgeable network engineering practitioners are urgently needed in today's rapid growing networks. However, the community of these individuals is very small. In this paper, we discuss our Zero Internet Administration Technology which is one of the most important technology for today's network systems. This technology significantly reduces the load of network administrator in particular and computer user in general by eliminating repetitive tasks, e.g., application configuration job. Our approach has been bottom-up. We began by identifying requirement in formulating the methodology toward this technology by considering the case of DNS (Domain Name System). We also present our solutions by implementing an integrated tool with GUI called nssetup for managing DNS. Finally, we use this experience to identify the requirement in developing other applications for this technology.

1 Introduction

The Internet technology is making remarkable progress and rapidly growing, which in turn requires a lot of network administrators in many sites. In order to manage today's system effectively and to plan intelligently for the future use of network systems, system managers need an understanding of network management technology as well as a thorough grasp of the details of the existing and evolving standard. Network Administrators will be challenged with the amount of new information they have to learn in order to keep up with new technologies. Nevertheless, the number of knowledgeable network engineers are still quite limited. In general, learn to use it, manage it, debug it and keeping the net from overloaded by mismanagement are not easy tasks to everyone.

Hand-to-mouth style of knowledge transmission is currently prevailing in the
Internet community. Internet engineering cannot be a serious discipline based solely
on oral tradition [5].

The practical, detailed network information we have today, which is collected
through years of practical experience, is useless unless it can be put together into
uniform utilities and shared with others who need it. We strongly believe that the
main goal of Zero Internet Administration Technology is *to transform all the "hand-
to-mouth" style of management practices into easy to use applications.*

In this chapter, our approach has been bottom-up. We believe that the bottom-
up approach is crucial in identifying the necessary methodology towards Zero Internet Administration Technology. We began this chapter by considering the case of
DNS (Domain Name System). We have designed and implemented a software called
nssetup to handle DNS management. By showing the way we developed *nssetup*
that can help a user in managing DNS, we next use this experience to identify the
requirement in formulating the methodology.

However, our work with Zero Internet Administration Technology is not limited
to DNS. Our goal is to develop from this experience strong techniques that will
contribute to the development and acceptance of any other applications. Our long
term goal is to create a stable network infrastructure whose reliability and throughput
at various levels will be secured with a minimum configuration management.

2   Case Study: Domain Name System (DNS)

The Domain Name System, or DNS, is a network wide database. It is used by
TCP/IP applications to map between hostnames and IP addresses, and to provide
electronic mail routing information[7].

DNS name service software is conceptually divided into two components – a
resolver and a name server. Name server constitutes the server half of DNS's client
server mechanism. It contains information about some segments of the database and
make it available to clients, called *resolvers*. *Resolver* will communicate with name
server to access this database.

DNS uses a hierarchical approach. No single site on the Internet manage every
segment of overall database. Instead, one site maintains a portion of the database
and delegates responsibility to others for specific zones[1]

2.1   Problems in Managing DNS

Whenever a hostname is renamed or a new machine is connected to a network environment, database files in DNS must be modified. However, the syntax of DNS
files lends itself to making mistakes. In addition, it is not only one file needed for
modification but it includes multiple files.

---

[1]A zone is a subtree of DNS tree that is administered separately. Many top level domains will
divide their zone into smaller zones

Every DNS database file has a serial number. It must be incremented whenever the data in the database files is changed. Secondary name servers for a zone will not pick up the updated data (zone transfer) if this serial number is not incremented. Failing to increment serial number is the most common mistake made when updating a name server.

Some other mistakes includes syntax errors and inconsistencies in *BIND* database files. One common inconsistency is having an A(address) record for a host, but no corresponding PTR(pointer) record or the other way.

3   Our Implementation: *Nssetup*

Various utilities for managing DNS already exist. However, most of them are either not integrated or difficult to be used. Traditionally, multiple tools are required to perform different tasks. However, it is not easy for a beginner to know which utility is relevant. To overcome these limitations, we have developed *nssetup*, a *tcl/tk*-bases [3] tool which is meant to be useful, simple and integrated. The following sections illustrate some of the element we have considered while developing *nssetup*.

3.1   Task automation

The user should not be burdened with performing periodic maintenance tasks. These periodic maintenance tasks especially if it is repetitive, complicated or tedious are good candidates for both simplification and automation [8].

3.1.1   Configuring Name Server using host table

Host table of a unix machine (*/etc/hosts*) contains a list of IP addresses and the hostnames that they correspond to. For example, if the hostname of a machine is ryo2317.aist-nara.ac.jp with the IP address 163.221.154.66, then the */etc/hosts* would be:

```
127.0.0.1               localhost
163.221.154.66          ryo2317.aist-nara.ac.jp ryo2317
```

Setting up DNS server is almost well structured process for converting host table information into name server information.

In contrast to command line application, given the */etc/hosts* file, *nssetup* will analyze data in it and will guess the possible domain name which will be managed by the server to be configured. Most of the parameters which is necessary for configuring a name server can be found without provided manually. The problem of name server configuration is now reduced to the issue of confirming every piece of information provided in this interface. The GUI for this feature is shown in Figure 1.

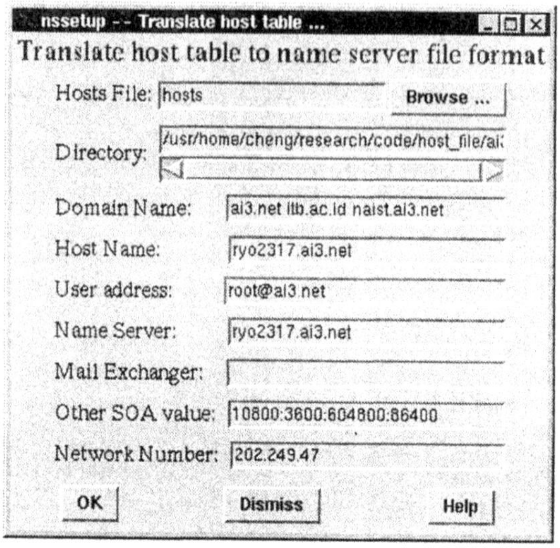

Figure 1: Translate host table into name server file format

3.1.2 Classless *in-addr.arpa* delegation support

One of the problems encountered when assigning address space on non octet bound-
aries is that it seems impossible for such an organization to maintain its own reverse
(*"in-addr.arpa"*) zone autonomously. An Internet Draft, [2] describe a reverse delegation method which solved the problem of assigning variable prefixes to unrelated
organization. However, the concept is not easy for most of the user to understand.

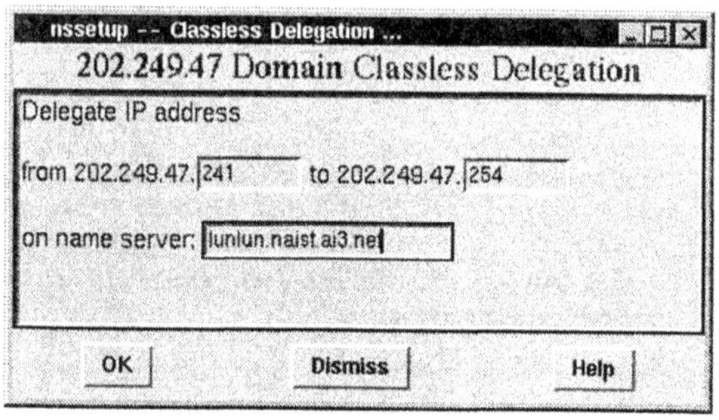

Figure 2: Classless in-addr.arpa delegation

By providing 3 necessary argument to the interface shown in Figure 2 , *nssetup*
will generate the necessary fields in the related file as shown in Figure 3.

```
...
70     IN    PTR     ait-iptv.ai3.net.
;
subnet241 86400    IN   NS    lunlun.naist.ai3.net.
241    IN    CNAME   241.subnet241.47.249.202.IN-ADDR.ARPA.
242    IN    CNAME   242.subnet241.47.249.202.IN-ADDR.ARPA.
243    IN    CNAME   243.subnet241.47.249.202.IN-ADDR.ARPA.
...
252    IN    CNAME   252.subnet241.47.249.202.IN-ADDR.ARPA.
253    IN    CNAME   253.subnet241.47.249.202.IN-ADDR.ARPA.
254    IN    CNAME   254.subnet241.47.249.202.IN-ADDR.ARPA.
...
```

Figure 3: This file, db.202.202.249 was generated using the classless delegation utility of nssetup

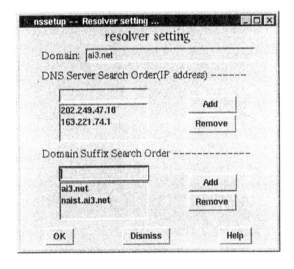

Figure 4: Resolver Configuration

3.2   Similar Outlook in Different OS Platform

3.2.1   *Resolver* Configuration

Setting a *resolver* is needed in any host connected to the network. Thus, similar outlook of the GUI in various OS platform is important to eliminate confusion.

Nssetup provide an interface as shown in Figure 4 to handle *resolver* configuration. We try to implement the interface to have almost similar outlook as provided by Window95 of Microsoft so that a user moving from Microsoft OS to Unix will not be reluctant to use the GUI provided.

3.3   Reconfiguration

3.3.1   Utility for updating the database

While the *resolver* configuration requires one configuration file, several files are used to configure name server as stated in section 3.1 Consequently, keeping consistency of all the files is very important. Without a utility to help automating this process, not only a lot of time have to be spent for inputing all the necessary data but also a lot of care have to be taken on the *BIND* database file syntax.

Figure 5 shows GUI for updating database of a name server in *nssetup*.

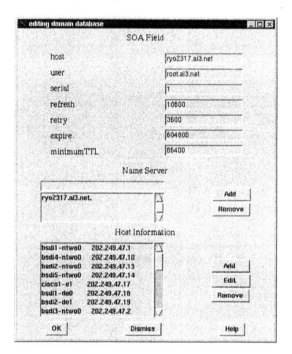

Figure 5: Detail of particular BIND database file

All parameters and data are extracted from database files. After adding or removing data using this GUI, the serial number of every database files which is related to this data will be updated automatically.

4   Evaluation

An experiment had been conducted in our laboratory to evaluate *nssetup*. The experiment requires participants to setup a name server for a domain consisting of about 10 hosts. A host table had been provided for generating the domain database. First of all, time was measured without any tool to help them. Following the first test, participant began to use a command line tool, *h2n* [6] to perform the same task.

Table 1: participants background

ID	Computer Use	Position	Background
1	work/research	Master 1st year(Computer Science)	Extensive use of PC and Workstation
2	work/research	Master 2nd year(Computer Science)	Experience in network management

Table 2: Time use for configuring a name server

	Time (minutes)	
ID	1	2
without any tool	600	120
using a command line tool	30	8
using *nssetup*	3	2

Finally *nssetup* was used for the same purpose.

There are 2 computer users participated in the experiment. The participant's experience with computers was distributed in terms of their experience in managing a network system. Table 1 provides a brief description of each participant.

The total time taken to complete each task is shown in Table 2. Our results show that the total time used for configuring a name server without using any utility is very long comparing to the other two approaches. The total time an experience user used for configuring a name server is about 5 times less than a user without any real experience in managing a network system. This is not surprising in view of the fact that a lot of typing and reference to technical documents on configuring *BIND* are required to perform all the tasks. To configure a single domain name server, we need at least 4 files to configure and also have to ftp one from the Internet. In addition, typing mistake and syntax error occurred very often and it takes time to debug it. The time are expected to be shorter with consistent practice or repetition.

Another remarkable fact from the table is that despite of the experience of participants, they took very short time to configure their server by using *nssetup*. Although utility like *h2n*, which is designed only for performing this task, also provide the same function to automate the configuration of name server, *nssetup* provide additional GUI to guide a user in using necessary arguments. In addition, most of the arguments are provided automatically in the GUI. *Nssetup* proved to be useful for both experienced and non experienced user.

5   Toward Zero Internet Administration Technology

The process of implementing *nssetup* was a Analysis – Design – Implementation development cycle. After examing the way we developed *nssetup*, we decided that it was necessary to first obtain a considerable amount of practical experience to build an application. This will ensure an application which is in the developing process actually work. Today, most of the technical knowledge/experience is available through various network administrative and technical staff at institutions. This "experience database" should be available to application designers, otherwise, assistance or technical cooperation from them is indispensable. Experience or pratical use of a software will make improvement to an application to be developed. Thus, practical experience must be involved in all the three phases in the cycle.

Also, our experience in creating *nssetup* led to the following observation:

- Network administrators could easily spend every minute of every day performing all periodic maintenance tasks unless they find a method of automation.

- Visualization of ideas is effective way for tackling the complex problems, especially when represented in colorful and comprehensible graphics.

- A system that provide necessary information to help a user in configuring or testing their system is important.

- Most of network administration software always require reconfiguration or update of its data.

The observations above suggest that the essential requirement in Design phase may contain the following components:

- **Informative,** an information management system will promote a better understanding of the output generated by a software.

- **Task Automation** is the key component in Design phase. Administration is simple as long as repeated or complicated tasks can be managed automatically. An interface that facilitates automation minimizes a user's effort required to plan what to do and formulate an action plan describing how to do it [4].

- **Graphical User Interface (GUI)** refers to the presentation to user. It will give users something better to work with and enable full interactive use. Without a GUI tool, configuring or managing even a simple system can be time consuming and error prone. In addition, to prevent a state of confusion, it is important to provide a single common GUI on different Operating System environment. Whenever possible, we opted for graphically oriented interface over text-based interfaces.

- **Ease of Reconfiguration**: Network environment change over time. For example, DNS database are updated as information changes. It is therefore important to create a design that supports the change of data and attributes. Ease of reconfiguration of a network is often desired in response to performance evaluation or in support of network upgrade, fault recovery, or security check [9].

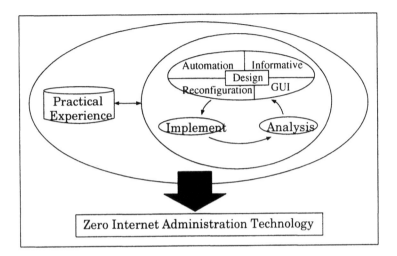

Figure 6: Toward Zero Internet Administration Technology

We summarize the disscussion above in Figure 6. It shows a methodical process which a designer can follow through while developing an application.

It includes a development cycle of Analysis – Design – Implementation. This process is a cycle and not in a linear fashion. The process is not completed by a simple three-stage process; rather the cycle continues. We also emphasize "Practical Experience Database" in this model. Also, recently gained knowledge/experience during the developing process cycle is made available so that it can be used as future experience database.

The requirement may change, depending on the future technology. Note that these requirements can be somewhat subjective. Thus, although they are described here, the intent is to use them as a starting point toward developing more objective requirements in the future.

6   Future work

Although our proposed approach toward Zero Internet Administration Technology is potentially beneficial, it is not particularly easy to achieve. It is still young in maturity and is the first step toward an integrated of concept and methodology into technology. Because there are too many fields that need this approach, we are now concentrating on 3 major applications. First, it is DNS which is described in this chapter. Second, we are also interested in automating the process of internet routing configuration and trouble shooting. And finally, we are also interested in managing the configuration of *sendmail* program, which is the daemon responsible for delivering electronic mail.

7   Summary and Conclusions

In this chapter, our objective was to clarify the importance and benefits of our proposed Zero Internet Administration Technology. We have described a bottom-up approach to formulate the methodology toward Zero Internet Administration Technology. We began by identifying requirement by considering the case of DNS. We have described *nssetup*, a *tcl/tk* application for managing the DNS. We used the experiences in developing *nssetup* to identify the requirement in developing applications for the Zero Internet Administration Technology.

Although it is not an easy task to transform all the hand-to-mouth style of knowledge into useful application that supports all aspects of a task well, the effort required to make it a reality is indispensable.

Still, there are areas we wanted to explore in our proposed Zero Internet Administration Technology such as automating the configuration of *sendmail* and internet routing.

As a final point, the ideas in *nssetup* should be applicable to other autoconfiguration applications. It is our foundation for integrating the concept and methology into technology. In the future, we expect to see more and more powerful applications that will fullfil the goal of this technology.

Bibliography

1) Craig Hunt, *TCP/IP Network Administration*, O'Reilly and Associates, Inc, 1993.

2) Havard Eidnes and Paul Vixie, "Classless IN-ADDR.ARPA delegation," *draft-ietf-dnsind-classless-inaddr*, April 1997.

3) John K.Ousterhout, *Tcl and the Tk Toolkit*, Addison-Wesley, 1994.

4) Kai H. Lim, Izak Benbasat and Peter A. Todd, "An Experimental Investigation of the Interactive Effects of Interface Style, Instructions, and Task Familiarity on User Performance," ACM Transactions on Computer-Human Interaction, March 1996

5) National Laboratory for Applied Network Research(NLANR), "Proposal for an Internet Engineering Repository," *http://www.nlanr.net/Iec/*, 1997.

6) Paul Albitz and Cricket Liu, *DNS and BIND*, O'Reilly and Associates, Inc, 1997.

7) P.Mockapetris, "Domain Names - Implementation and Specification," *rfc1035*, November 1987.

8) Unix System Administration Independent Learning(USAIL) Project, "Automating Tasks," *http://www.uwsg.indiana.edu/usail/index/automate.html*, 1996.

9) William Stallings, *SNMP, SNMPv2 and RMON*, Addison-Wesley, 1996.

18

Group Communication Protocol for Replicas in Transaction-Oriented Applications

Tomoya Enokido

Hiroaki Higaki

Makoto Takizawa

Tokyo Denki University

ABSTRACT

Group protocols imply larger computation and communication overhead to causally order all messages transmitted in the network. Transactions in clients manipulate objects in servers by sending read and write requests to the servers. In this paper, we define *significant* messages, which are to be ordered at the application level, by using a conflicting relation among the transactions. We newly propose an *object vector* to causally order only the significant messages. The scheme of the object vector is invariant in change of the group membership. We also show a TBCO (transaction-based causally ordered) protocol adopting the object vector.

1 Introduction

In distributed applications, a *group* of multiple objects are cooperating. Here, messages sent by objects have to be causally delivered to the destination objects. Group protocols[3, 11, 12] are discussed to causally order messages in the network. However, the protocols imply $O(n)$ to $O(n^2)$ computation and communication overhead[12]. Cheriton[4] points out that it is meaningless to causally order all the messages from the application point of view. Agrawal[9] discusses a rollback algorithm where only processes computing significant requests are rolled back if the senders of the significant requests are rolled back. Enokido and Takizawa[6, 7] define the *object-based causality* based on the conflicting relation among operations of objects in the presence of the nested invocation of operations. Raynal[1] discusses a way to relex the traditional message-based causality based on the write-semantics for replicas.

In this paper, we introduce a *transaction*[2] concept to define a causality among messages which are significant for the applications. A transaction T in a client processor issues *read* and *write* requests to server processors. The server sends back the responses to the client. Thus, a *subtransaction* of T in a server is a sequence of requests of T. A message m_1 may carry information in m_2 if a transaction sends m_1 after receiving or sending m_2. Thus, the messages received and sent by one transaction are related. Suppose a transaction T_1 sends m_2 after T_2 receives m_1 in the same processor. m_1 and m_2 are not related unless T_1 and T_2 manipulate same objects. The group is composed of multiple subtransactions and servers. In this paper, we define how read and write messages are causally related in a context of transactions. In addition, each object is replicated in order to increase the reliability, availability, and performance of the system. We define *significant* messages to be causally ordered based on the transaction concept.

The *vector clock*[10] is widely used to causally order messages. A group is required to be composed of subtransactions to causally order only messages significant for applications. However, the scheme of the vector clock is required to change each time a transaction is initiated and terminated. We newly propose an *object vector* whose size is given by the number of objects, not the number of transactions. We discuss a TBCO (transaction-based causally ordered) protocol which uses the object vector to causally order only significant messages.

We present transactions and messages in section 2. In section 3, we present the *object vector* and the TBCO protocol. In section 4, we evaluate the TBCO protocol.

2   Transaction Messages

2.1   Transactions

A system is composed of processors p_1, ..., p_N ($N \geq 1$) interconnected by a network. The objects are replicated in order to increase the reliability, availability, and performance of the system. Each replica o_a^t of o_a is allocated in one processor p_t. On receipt of a request message m with an operation op_a, o_a^t computes op_a and then sends back the response message to the sender of m. In the network, messages may be lost and may be delivered out of order.

A transaction T_i in one *client* processor p_s issues *read* and *write* requests to *server* processors to manipulate replicas of an object o_a. A processor p_s sends a *read* request to one processor which has a replica of o_a. p_s sends *write* to every replica of o_a. That is, the *read-one-write-all* principle is adopted. Here, $op_1 \rightarrow_{T_i} op_2$ shows that an operation op_1 precedes op_2 in T_i. T_i *commits* (c^i) or *aborts* (a^i) at the end of T_i. T_i commits if all the operations invoked by T_i complete successfully. Otherwise, T_i aborts. Thus, T_i is an atomic sequence of *read* and *write* operations[2]. Let $op_i^t(x)$ denote an instance of an operation op, r (*read*) or w (*write*), for a replica x in p_t which is issued by T_i. A subsequence of operations of T_i computed in p_t is named a *subtransaction* T_{it} of T_i in p_t. $op_1 \rightarrow_{T_{it}} op_2$ iff op_1 precedes op_2 in T_{it}. An interleaved computation of subtransactions in p_t is a *local history* H_t of p_t. op_1 *precedes* op_2 in p_t ($op_1 \rightarrow_{H_t} op_2$) iff op_1 is computed before op_2 in p_t. A global history H of T is a set of the local histories H_1, ..., H_N. op_1 precedes op_2 in H ($op_1 \rightarrow_H op_2$) iff op_1 $\rightarrow_{H_t} op_2$, $op_1 \rightarrow_{T_i} op_2$, or $op_1 \rightarrow_H op_3 \rightarrow_H op_2$ for some p_t, T_i, and op_3. Here, op_1

conflicts with op_2 iff op_1 and op_2 manipulate an object and the results obtained by computing op_1 and op_2 depend on the computation order of op_1 and op_2. T_i *precedes* T_j iff op_i issued by T_i conflicts with op_j issued by T_j and $op_i \rightarrow_{H_t} op_j$ in some p_t. H is serializable if all the transactions are totally ordered by the precedent relation[2].

2.2 Omissible messages

A processor p_t may not receive messages or may receive messages out of order. Hence, p_t has to *wait* for all messages causally preceding m after receiving a message m.

[**Example 1**] Suppose $w_t^1(x^t)$, $w_s^1(x^s)$, and $w_u^1(x^u)$ are initiated by a request message m_1, $r_t^2(x^t)$ is by m_2, $w_s^3(x^s)$, $w_t^3(x^t)$, and $w_u^3(x^u)$ by m_3, and $r_u^4(x^u)$ by m_4 as shown in Figure 1. $w_t^3(x^t)$ is computed after $r_t^2(x^t)$ in p_t. Hence, p_u has to compute $w_u^1(x^u)$, $w_u^3(x^u)$, and $r_u^4(x^u)$ in this sequence. $r_u^4(x^u)$ reads x from $w_u^3(x^u)$ but not from $w_u^1(x^u)$. Here, suppose $w_u^1(x^u)$, $w_u^3(x^u)$, and $r_u^4(x^u)$ are still stored in the receipt queue RQ_u of p_u due to the communication delay although the operations complete in p_s and p_t. Since $r_u^4(x^u)$ reads x^u written by $w_u^3(x^u)$, there is no need to compute $w_u^1(x^u)$. $w_s^1(x^s)$ can be omitted. Suppose $w_t^i(x) \rightarrow_H w_t^j(x)$. If there is no read $r_t^k(x)$ such that $w_t^i(x) \rightarrow_H r_t^k(x) \rightarrow_H w_t^j(x)$, p_t does not need to receive $w_t^i(x)$. Hence, p_t can reject $w_t^i(x)$ if p_t receives $w_t^i(x)$ after computing $w_t^j(x)$. Thus, some write requests can be omitted. □

[**Example 2**] Suppose p_t receives read requests r_t^i, r_t^j, and r_t^k from transactions T_i, T_j, and T_k, respectively. p_t reads a replica x and sends back the response with data each time p_t receives a read request. Here, p_t reads x three times. If p_t reads x once and sends the response back to T_i, T_j, and T_k, the number of read operations computed can be reduced. □

[**Definition**] A message m is *omissible* iff the following conditions hold :

- If $m = r_t^i(x)$, there is some read $r_t^j(x)$ in H such that $r_t^j(x)$ precedes $r_t^i(x)$ and there is no write $w_t^k(x)$ between $r_t^j(x)$ and $r_t^i(x)$ in H.

- If $m = w_t^i(x)$, there is some write $w_t^j(x)$ in H such that $w_t^i(x)$ precedes $w_t^j(x)$ and there is no read $r_t^k(x)$ between $w_t^i(x)$ and $w_t^j(x)$ in H. □

It is straightforward that the following theorem holds.

[**Theorem 1**] Let R_t be a sequence of messages received by p_t. Let R_t' be a subsequence of unomissible messages in R_t. Here, the state of p_t and the sequence of output values of read requests obtained by computing R_t' are the same as R_t. □

3 TBCO Protocol

3.1 Object vector

We discuss a TBCO (transaction–based causally ordered) protocol where only significant messages are causally delivered. Let $snd_t[m]$ and $rcv_t[m]$ denote sending and receipt events of a message m in a processor p_t, respectively. An event e_1 *happens before* e_2 $(e_1 \rightarrow e_2)$ iff e_1 precedes e_2 in a processor p_t, i.e. $e_1 \rightarrow_{H_t} e_2$, $e_1 = snd_s[m]$ and $e_2 = rcv_t[m]$, or $e_1 \rightarrow e_3 \rightarrow e_2$ for some event e_3[8]. A message m_1 *causally* precedes m_2 ($m_1 \rightarrow m_2$) iff $snd_s[m_1] \rightarrow snd_t[m_2]$[3]. p_t has to receive m_1 before m_2 if $m_1 \rightarrow m_2$. The *vector clock*[10] $V = \langle V_1, \ldots, V_N \rangle$ is used to causally order messages. Each element V_t is initially 0 ($t = 1, \ldots, N$). p_t increments V_t by one each time p_t sends a message m. m carries the vector clock V of p_t in a field $m.V$ when p_t sends m. On receipt of m, p_s changes V as $V_r = \max(V_r, m.V_r)$ for $r = 1, \ldots, N$ ($r \neq s$). $m_1 \rightarrow m_2$ iff $m_1.V < m_2.V$. If the group membership changes, the vector clocks of all the processors have to be resynchronized[3, 4, 8, 9, 10].

We consider a way to order only messages which are significant for transactions by using the conflicting and precedent relations among transactions.

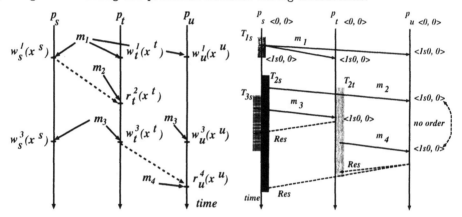

Figure 1: Omissible messages.   Figure 2: Message ordering.

[**Definition**] A request message m_1 *significantly* precedes m_2 iff

- m_1 is issued before m_2 by a transaction and the operations of m_1 and m_2 conflict with one another, or
- m_1 and m_2 are issued by different transactions T_1 and T_2, respectively, and T_1 precedes T_2. □

In order to significantly order messages, a group has to be composed of subtransactions and servers. In this paper, we newly propose an *object vector* $V = \langle V_1, \ldots, V_M \rangle$ to causally order only significant messages sent by transactions. Each element V_a shows a version number of an object o_a ($a = 1, \ldots, M$). Each replica o_a^t has a version number $v(o_a^t)$. $v(o_a^t)$ is updated each time o_a^t is written. Each operation op has a unique identifier $tno(op)$ which satisfies the following properties. We discuss how $tno(op)$ is calculated in the succeeding subsection.

- $tno(op_1) < tno(op_2)$ if op_1 is issued before op_2 by a transaction and one of op_1 and op_2 is write.
- $tno(op_1) < tno(op_2)$ if op_1 and op_2 are issued by different transactions T_1 and T_2, respectively, and T_1 starts before T_2 in the system.

Each replica o_a^t of o_a in p_t manipulates the version number $v(o_a^t)$ by using the operation identifier $tno(op)$ each time op is computed in o_a^t as follows:

- If $v(o_a^t) < tno(op)$, $v(o_a^t) := tno(op)$ if op is *write*.

- If $v(o_a^t) \geq tno(op)$, op is rejected.

Each processor p_t has an object vector $V = \langle V_1, \ldots, V_M \rangle$. If p_t has a replica o_a^t, V_a is $v(o_a^t)$. On sending a message m, p_t includes V in a field $m.V$. On receipt of a message m from p_u, p_t manipulates V as $V_a := \max(V_a, m.V_a)$ for $a = 1, \ldots, M$.

[Theorem 2] A message m_1 significantly precedes m_2 if $m_1.V < m_2.V$.

[Proof] Assume $m_1.V < m_2.V$ and m_1 does not significantly precede m_2. Suppose that p_s sends a write m_1 to replicas x^t and x^u in p_t and p_u. p_t sends a request m_2 to p_u. On receipt of m_1, the object vector V of x is changed and V_x is incremented. m_2 carries V. Here, $m_1.V < m_2.V$. According to the definition, m_1 significantly precedes m_2. It contradicts the assumption. $\square$

3.2 Operation identifier

We discuss how to realize the operation identifiers used in the object vector. Each transaction T_i has such a unique identifier $t(T_i)$ that $t(T_i) < t(T_j)$ if T_i starts before T_j in a processor or if a processor p_t initiates T_j after receiving a message from T_i. The transaction identifier is generated by using the linear clock[8]. Each p_t manipulates a variable tid showing the linear clock whose initial value is 0.

- $tid := tid + 1$ if a transaction is initiated in p_t.
- On receipt of a message from T_j, $tid := \max(tid, tid(T_j))$.

When T_i is initiated in p_t, $t(T_i)$ is a pair of tid and the processor number $pno(p_t)$ of p_t. Here, let $tid(T_i)$ denote tid given to T_i. $t(T_i) = \langle tid(T_i), pno(p_t) \rangle$. For every pair of transactions T_i and T_j initiated at p_t and p_u, respectively, $tid(T_i) > tid(T_j)$ if 1) $t(T_i) > t(T_j)$ or 2) $t(T_i) = t(T_j)$ and $pno(p_t) > pno(p_u)$. It is clear that every transaction T_i has a unique identifier $t(T_i)$ and $t(T_i) < t(T_j)$ if T_i precedes T_j.

Each event e occurring in T_i is given an event number $no(e)$ as follows :

- $no(e_1) = 0$ if e_1 is the initial event of T_i.
- $no(e_1) < no(e_2)$ if e_2 is *write* and $e_1 \rightarrow e_2$ in T_i.
- $no(e_1) = no(e_2)$ if e_2 is *read* and there is no *write* event e_3 such that $e_1 \rightarrow_{T_i} e_3 \rightarrow_{T_i} e_2$.

T_i manipulates a variable no_i to give an event number $no(e)$ to each event e in T_i. no_i is incremented by one each time a write event occurs in T_i. $no(e) := no_i$ when e occurs. Each event e in T_i is given a global event number $tno(e)$ as the concatenation of $t(T_i)$ and $no(e)$, i.e. $tno(e) = \langle t(T_i), no(e) \rangle$. Each operation op issued by T_i is given the global event number $tno(op)$ which is named an operation identifier.

3.3 Message transmission and receipt

A message m exchanged among processors is composed of the following fields :

$m.src$ = sender processor of m, i.e. p_s. $m.dst$ = destination processors.

$m.op$ = type of message, i.e. $op \in \{read, write, commit, abort, response\}$.

$m.tno$ = global event number $\langle m.t, m.no \rangle$, i.e. $tno(op)$.

$m.o$ = object to be manipulated by $m.op$. $m.V$ = object vector $\langle V_1, \ldots, V_M \rangle$.

$m.SQ$ = vector of sequence numbers $\langle sq_1, \ldots, sq_N \rangle$. $m.d$ = data.

Suppose a transaction T_h invokes an operation op_h to manipulate an object o_a. A processor p_s constructs a request message m as follows :

$\quad m.tno = \langle m.t,\, m.no \rangle := tno(op_h) = \langle t(T_h),\, no(op_h) \rangle;$

$\quad m.op := op_h; \quad m.o := o_a; \quad m.src := p_s;$

$\quad m.dst =$ some p_t with a replica of o_a if $op_h = read$, otherwise all the replicas.

A processor p_s manipulates variables $sq_1, \ldots, sq_N$ to send messages. Each time p_s sends a message to p_t, sq_t is incremented by one. m carries sq_u in a field $m.sq_u$ ($u = 1, \ldots, N$).

$\quad sq_t := sq_t + 1$ for every p_t in $m.dst; \quad m.sq_u := sq_u \,(u = 1, \ldots, N);$

A processor p_t has to detect a gap between messages received from p_s by checking the sequence number sq_t, i.e. messages lost or unexpectedly delayed. p_t manipulates variables $rsq_1, \ldots, rsq_N$ to detect the gap. On receipt of a message m from p_s, there is no gap between m and messages sent before m if $m.sq_t = rsq_s$. If $m.sq_t > rsq_s$, there is a gap m' where $m.sq_t > m'.sq_t \geq rsq_s$. That is, p_t does not receive m' which is sent by p_s. m is *correctly* received by p_t if p_t receives every message m' where $m'.sq_t < m.sq_t$. That is, p_t receives every message which p_s sends to p_t before m. p_t enqueues m in a receipt queue RQ_t. p_t manipulates the object vector V as $V_a = \max(V_a, m.V_a)$ for $a = 1, \ldots, M$.

If $m.op$ completes to manipulate a replica o_a^t, p_t sends back a response m' of m to p_s. If $m.op = read$, m' carries data derived from o_a^t in $m'.d$ and the version number $v(o_a^t)$ of o_a^t in $m.V$. The object vector V is updated as $V_a = v(o_a^t)$. The response message m' carries V including not only the current version number $v(o_a^t)$ but also the version numbers of the other replicas which p_t knows. If $m.op = write$, $v(o_a^t) := tno(op)$ as presented in the preceding subsection.

$\quad m'.tno := m.tno; \quad m'.o := o_a; \quad m'.op := response; \quad m'.V := V;$

3.4 Message delivery

A message m_1 significantly precedes m_2 if $m_1.V < m_2.V$. $m_1.V < m_2.V$ means that m_1 has to precede m_2 from the transaction point of view. Suppose that two transactions T_1 and T_2 issue requests m_1 and m_2 to replicas x^s in p_s and x^t in p_t. If $m_1.V = m_2.V$ or $m_1.V$ and $m_2.V$ are not comparable, p_s and p_t may compute m_1 and m_2 in different orders. If m_1 and m_2 are *write*, x^s and x^t get inconsistent. Hence, m_1 and m_2 have to be ordered if $m_1.op$ and $m_2.op$ conflict.

[Ordering rules] A pair of messages m_1 and m_2 are ordered as "m_1 precedes m_2 ($m_1 \Rightarrow m_2$)" if one of the following rules is satisfied ;

1. $m_1.V < m_2.V$.
2. $m_1.V = m_2.V$, and $m_1.t < m_2.t$ and $m_1.op$ conflicts with $m_2.op$.
3. $m_1.V$ and $m_2.V$ are not comparable and $m_1.o = m_2.o \,(= o_a)$, and
    a. $m_1.V_a < m_2.V_a$, or
    b. $m_1.V_a = m_2.V_a$, and $m_1.t < m_2.t$ and $m_1.op$ conflicts with $m_2.op$.

Messages received by p_u are stored in RQ_u in the order "$\Rightarrow$". If neither $m_1 \Rightarrow m_2$ nor $m_2 \Rightarrow m_1$, m_1 and m_2 are stored in RQ_u in the receipt order.

[**Example 3**] In Figure 2, $\langle \alpha, \beta \rangle$ shows values of an object vector $\langle V_x, V_y \rangle$ for objects x and y. Initially $\langle 0, 0 \rangle$ in every processor. Every processor has x and y in Figure 2. A transaction T_{1s} is computed in p_s. Here, $t(T_{1s}) = 1s$ where "s" is the processor number and "1" is the linear clock in p_s. T_{1s} sends a *write* request m_1 of x to p_s, p_t, and p_u. Here, $m_1.V = \langle 1s0, 0 \rangle$, $m_1.op = write$, and $m_1.o = x$. T_{2s} is initiated after T_{1s} completes in p_s. T_{3s} is initiated after T_{2s} is started, i.e. T_{2s} and T_{3s} are interleaved. In addition, p_t initiates T_{2t} after receiving m_1 from p_s. T_{2s} sends a *read* request m_2 of x to p_u. After T_{2s} sends m_2, T_{3s} sends a *read* request m_3 of y to p_t. After receiving m_3, T_{2t} sends a *read* request m_4 of x to p_u. Here, $m_1.V = m_2.V = m_3.V = m_4.V = \langle 1s0, 0 \rangle$. $m_2.op = m_3.op = m_4.op = read$. $m_2.o = m_4.o = x$ and $m_3.o = y$. In the traditional group protocols, $m_1 \rightarrow m_4$ since m_1 causally precedes m_2 ($m_1 \rightarrow m_2$) and $m_2 \rightarrow m_4$. p_u has to receive m_1, m_2, and m_4 in this order. The messages received in RQ_u are ordered by using the ordering rule. Here, m_1 precedes m_2 ($m_1 \Rightarrow m_2$) and $m_1 \Rightarrow m_4$ in p_u. Since $m_2.V = m_4.V$ ($= \langle 1s0, 0 \rangle$) and $m_2.t$ ($= 2s$) $< m_4.t$ ($= 2t$) but $m_2.op$ is compatible with $m_4.op$, neither $m_2 \Rightarrow m_4$ nor $m_4 \Rightarrow m_2$ in p_u by the ordering rule. □

This example shows that m_2 causally precedes m_4 although m_2 and m_4 are not ordered by the ordering rule. That is, p_u can deliver m_4 if p_u receives m_4 before m_2 due to the delay or loss of m_2.

[**Theorem 3**] Every pair of significant messages m_1 and m_2 are ordered in the same order $\Rightarrow$ in every common destination processor of m_1 and m_2 by the ordering rule. [**Proof**] From theorem 2, m_1 significantly precedes m_2 if $m_1.V < m_2.V$. If $m_1.V = m_2.V$ or $m_1.V$ and $m_2.V$ are not comparable, m_1 and m_2 are ordered by the identifiers of the transactions issuing m_1 and m_2. m_1 and m_2 are ordered by the transaction identifiers. □

A message m is a *top* message in RQ_t iff there is no message m_1 in RQ_t such that $m_1 \Rightarrow m$. The top message m_1 in RQ_t still cannot be delivered because p_t may not yet have received some message m_2 causally preceding m_1 due to the unexpected delay. We discuss what messages in RQ_t can be delivered. Let m be a message from p_u and stored in RQ_t. m is *stable* in p_t iff p_t had received a message m_1 from p_u in RQ_t where $m_1.sq_t = m.sq_t + 1$, and p_t correctly receives a message m_1 in RQ_t from every p_u where $m \Rightarrow m_1$. The top message m in RQ_t can be delivered if m is stable, because every message causally preceding m in RQ_t from the transaction point of view is surely delivered. A top message m in RQ_t is *ready* if p_t computes no operation conflicting with $m.op$ in a replica $m.o$. In addition, only significant messages which are not omissible in RQ_t are delivered by the following delivery procedure.

[**Delivery procedure**] While each top message m in RQ_t is stable and ready, m is dequeued from RQ_t; m is neglected if m is omissible, otherwise m is delivered;. □

If p_t receives read requests $r^1(x)$, ..., $r^h(x)$ ($h > 1$), p_t computes $r(x)$ once and then sends the response to all the source processors of $r^1(x)$, ..., $r^h(x)$. Thus, the number of operations computed can be reduced.

Each p_t has variables D_1, ..., D_M where each D_a shows the version number of an object o_a to deliver messages ($a = 1$, ..., M). Each time a message m is delivered, $D_a := m.t$ if $m.o = o_a$ and $m.t \geq D_a$. Here, if $m.t < D_a$, m is omitted.

If some p_u sends no message to p_t, messages in RQ_t cannot be stable. Hence, p_u sends a message without data to p_t if p_u had not sent any message to p_t for some predetermined δ time units. p_t considers that p_t loses a message from p_u if p_t does not receive any message from p_u for δ time units or p_t detects a message gap. Here, p_t requires p_u to resend m. p_u considers that p_t may lose m unless p_u receives the receipt confirmation of m from p_t in 2δ after p_u sends m to p_t.

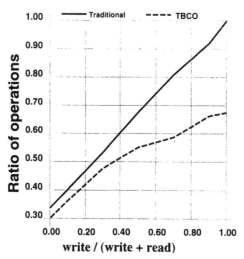

Figure 3: Ratio of operations ($N=3$).

4   Evaluation

In the TBCO protocol, only significant messages are causally ordered. We evaluate the TBCO protocol in terms of the number of messages causally ordered compared with the traditional message-based group protocol. The TBCO protocol is realized in threads of a Cray Super Server 6400 with 10 Ultra Sparc CPUs. Each processor p_t is bound to one CPU. TCP[16] is used to exchange messages among the processors. Each processor randomly creates transactions each of which randomly manipulates objects by *read* and *write*.

In the evaluation, three objects are fully replicated in all the processors ($M = 3$). Each processor randomly initiates totally twenty transactions each of which issues ten arbitrary types of operations on arbitrary objects. Figure 3 shows the total number of requests computed in the objects for the ratio of *write* requests issued by the transactions for three processors ($N = 3$). The more *write* requests are issued, the more messages are sent to the replicas. The figure shows that the more write messages are issued, the more messages can be omitted. For example, only 68% of the messages transmitted in the message-based protocol are transmitted in the

TBCO protocol in case that all the messages are writes, i.e. the write ratio is 1.0 while 50% for the write ratio 0.4 and 90% for the write ratio 0.0.

In Figures 4 and 5, the vertical axis indicates the ratio of the number of messages delivered to the number of messages transmitted for ten processors ($N = 10$) in the traditional message-based protocol. The dotted line shows TBCO and the solid line indicates the message-based protocol. Figures 4 and 5 show cases that 90% and 50% of the operations issued by each transaction are writes, respectively. These figures show that the number of messages delivered can be reduced by the TBCO protocol. About 30% and 20% of messages transmitted in the network are reduced for the write ratios 90% and 50%, respectively.

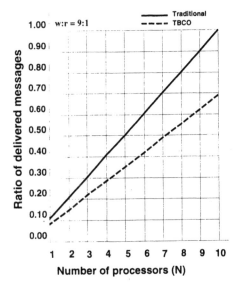

Figure 4: Ratio of messages.

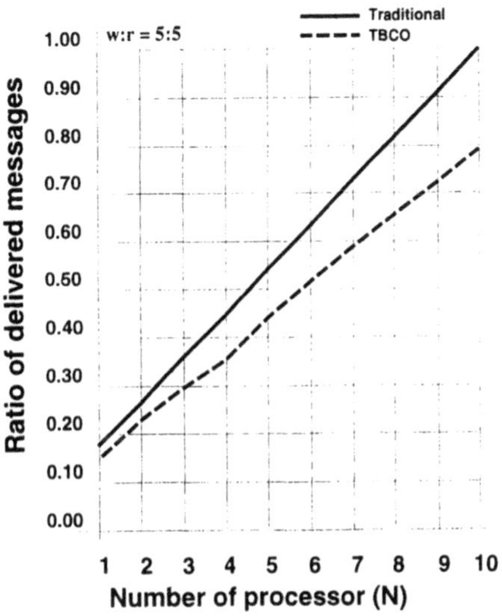

Figure 5: Ratio of messages.

5   Concluding Remarks

This paper has discussed what messages to be ordered in replicated objects with read and write operations from the application point of view. We have proposed the novel *object vector* for significantly ordering messages based on the transaction concept. The scheme of the object vector depends on the number of the objects. The object vector is invariant in change of the group membership, i.e. transactions. The TBCO protocol orders only the messages to be significantly preceded for the applications. We have also discussed a way for omitting insignificant messages. We have shown that the TBCO protocol implies fewer number of operations computed than the message-based protocols.

Bibliography

1) Ahamad, M., Raynal, M., and Thia-Kime, G., "An Adaptive Protocol for Implementing Causally Consistent Distributed Services," *Proc. of IEEE ICDCS-18*, pp. 86–93 (1998).

2) Bernstein, P. A., Hadzilacos, V., and Goodman, N., "Concurrency Control and Recovery in Database Systems," *Addison-Wesley*, 1987.

3) Birman, K., "Lightweight Causal and Atomic Group Multicast," *ACM Trans. on Computer Systems*, Vol.9, No.3, pp. 272–290 (1991).

4) Cheriton, D. R. and Skeen, D., "Understanding the Limitations of Causally and Totally Ordered Communication," *Proc. of ACM SIGOPS'93*, pp. 44–57 (1993).

5) Enokido, T., Tachikawa, T., and Takizawa, M., "Transaction-Based Causally Ordered Protocol for Distributed Replicated Objects," *Proc. of IEEE ICPADS'97*, pp.210–215 (1997).

6) Enokido, T., Higaki, H., and Takizawa, M., "Group Protocol for Distributed Replicated Objects," *to appear in Proc. of ICPP'98* (1998).

7) Enokido, T., Higaki, H., and Takizawa, M., "Protocol for Group of Objects," *to appear in Proc. of DEXA'98* (1998).

8) Lamport, L., "Time, Clocks, and the Ordering of Events in a Distributed System," *Comm. ACM*, Vol. 21, No. 7, pp. 558–565 (1978).

9) Leong, H. V. and Agrawal, D., "Using Message Semantics to Reduce Rollback in Optimistic Message Logging Recovery Schemes," *Proc. of IEEE ICDCS-14*, pp. 227–234 (1994).

10) Mattern, F., "Virtual Time and Global States of Distributed Systems," *Parallel and Distributed Algorithms* (Cosnard, M. and Quinton, P. eds.), *North-Holland*, pp. 215–226 (1989).

11) Melliar-Smith, P. M., Moser, L. E., and Agrawala, V., "Broadcast Protocols for Distributed Systems," *IEEE Trans. on Parallel and Distributed Systems*, Vol. 1, No 1, pp. 17–25 (1990).

12) Nakamura, A., Tachikawa, T., and Takizawa, M., "Causally Ordering Broadcast Protocol," *Proc. of IEEE ICDCS-14*, pp. 48–55 (1994).

13) Tachikawa, T. and Takizawa, M., "Significantly Ordered Delivery of Messages in Group Communication," *Computer Communications Journal*, Vol. 20, No.9, pp. 724–731 (1997).

14) Tachikawa, T., Higaki, H., and Takizawa, M., "Group Communication Protocol for Realtime Applications," *Proc. of IEEE ICDCS-18*, pp. 40–47 (1998).

15) Tanaka, K., Higaki, H., and Takizawa, M. "Object-Based Checkpoints in Distributed Systems," *Journal of Computer Systems Science and Engineering*, Vol. 13, No.3, pp.125–131 (1998).

16) Transmission Control Protocol, RFC793, pp. 1–26 (1981).

19

Predictive Method of Task Allocation in Stream-based Computing

Yoichi Aoyagi

Minoru Uehara

Hideki Mori

Toyo University

ABSTRACT

Static methods of task allocation have less overhead at run-time but they are difficult to adapt to the environment. We propose the predictive method in order to increase the adaptability of static task allocation methods. In this method, optimal allocations are decided by using system dependent factors which have been measured. In addition, we introduce stream-based computing which is suitable for data streaming used in real-time video. In this computing model, it is easy to predict computing costs. In this paper, we describe the evaluations of our predictive method in the case of applying it to stream-based computing.

1 Introduction

Recently, in the field of HPC, the importance of data streaming[2] is increased. The data streaming can be realized by pipeline processing. Therefore, in such fields, task allocation for pipeline processing is very important. Generally, dynamic task allocation does not fit a fine-grained process environment, because it prevents original processing due to runtime overheads. Static task allocation has very low runtime overhead, but it is difficult to provide portability of tasks. In this article, we propose the predictive method of task allocation in stream-based computing in order to increase the adaptability of static task allocation methods. This algorithm uses throughput prediction for deciding the optimal allocation. On task allocation, patterns for possible task allocations increase enormously as the number of processors and the number of parallel objects increase, therefore it is difficult to decide the most suitable allocation pattern. This method uses Genetic Algorithm(GA) in order to decide the approximated solution of the optimal allocation pattern among generated patterns efficiently. By applying GA to our method, the amount of computation for the task allocation has been extremely reduced, and the effectiveness of our method is proved.

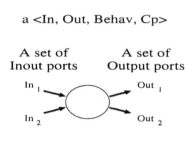

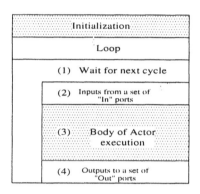

Figure 1: Composition of Actor.

This paper consists of the following sections. Section 2 introduces the Stream-based Computing model which is used as a basis of our predictive task allocation method. Section 3 proposes our task allocation method. Section 4 shows an evaluation of this algorithm for example application of a random task. Section 5 shows the conclusion of our predictive task allocation method.

2   Stream-based Computing Model

In this section, we introduce Stream Computing Model which is easy to analyze tasks and suitable for data streaming, pipeline processing, and so on. In this model, a task is represented as cyclic pipeline processes composed of actors and streams, and its execution cycle can be calculated by static analysis of actors' processing costs and streams' communication costs.

2.1   Definition of the Model

First, we show conceptual definitions of the basics of the stream-based computing model. The stream-based computing model is an extended macro data flow model that applies several optimizations mentioned below. This model features the allowance of simultaneous tokens on one stream as communication channels. And the sequence of each token's arrival will be preserved and guaranteed. Furthermore, this model consists of actors representing a primitive procedure and streams representing communication channels. The actor has two kinds of ports, one is for input, the other is for output. A stream is linked to those ports. In this model, a task is composed of one or more primitive actors. With this result, the task can be reconfigured easily without algorithm modification in order to adopt any number of processors.

2.2   Actor

An actor is an execution unit repeating a particular procedure and consists of one initialization part and one loop part. Both parts are painted in gray in Figure 1. The metrics model of an actor is represented as $\langle In, Out, Behav, C_p \rangle$, where In is the set of input ports, Out is the set of output ports, $Behav$ is the behavior of the actor, and C_p is the processing cost of the actor. The processing cost of an actor is defined as the period of an iteration. We assume that shared resources are not conflicted because each actor encapsulates a resource and maintains it. The loop part consists of the following sequence: (1) Waiting period for next cycle, (2) Input from a set of In ports, (3) Body of actor execution, (4) Output to a set of Out ports.

There are following kinds of primitive actors which based on data flow models: Operation actor, Conditional merge actor, Gate actor, and Switch actor. Users can define macro actors by combination of these primitive actors. For example, control structures are implemented by conditional merge actors and gate actors.

2.3 Stream

In this section, we give the measurement of communication cost. A stream is defined as a communication path from an Out port to an In port. The metrics model of a stream is represented as $\langle In, Out, Type, C_c \rangle$, where $Type$ is the data type of tokens in the stream, and C_c is the communication cost of the stream. A stream has the following features: (1) It is easy to analyze because communicating objects are fixed, (2) The order of tokens in a stream is guaranteed, (3) It is easy to optimize the granularity of communication by turning buffer size.

There is a large difference between local communication and remote communication in the distributed system. Local communication is often realized by means of memory-to-memory copy. On the other hand, remote communication is realized in a variety of methods such as message passing, shared memory and so on. In this paper, we employ message passing to realize stream communication.

In general, the message is divided into fixed size pieces called packets. The sending time T_s is shown as follows:

$$T_s = \alpha \cdot \lceil \frac{N}{Buf} \rceil + \beta \cdot N + T_t(N) \tag{19.1}$$

where N is the data size in a message, Buf is the size of a packet, $T_t(N)$ means a function giving transfer time and α, β are system dependent constants. The first term represents packet creation time, the second term represents data copy time to packet and the third term gives transfer time in the network. This transfer time is hidden in the case of asynchronous communication where this can be overlapped with other processing time. According to the investigation of the communication costs for AP3000[3], the costs are measured as shown in Figure 2. In this Figure, X axis is data size per a transfer, Y axis is the time of a transfer where the line labeled "Local" shows local communication cost and the line labeled "Remote" shows remote communication cost. From Figure 2, parameters in equation 19.1 are given from the segment and slope of the graph such as $Buf = 8192, \alpha = 0.14, \beta = 6.8 \times 10^{-6}, T_t(N) = 0.215$ in data size over 1024(Bytes). We assume that communication conflicts merely occur.

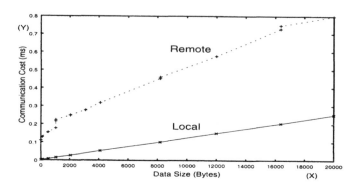

Figure 2: Communication Cost.

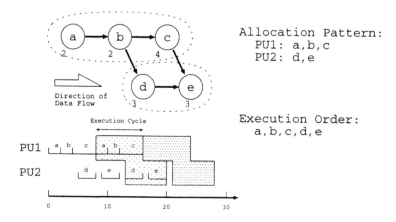

Figure 3: Timing chart and execution cycle of a task.

2.4   Throughput

Here, we describe the throughput which is an important factor in stream-based computing. In this paper, we define the throughput *th* as follows:

$$th = 1/T \tag{19.2}$$

where T is the execution cycle of the task.

Figure 3 shows how to get throughput of a task when one of possible patterns of the task allocation is given. The upper side in Figure 3 represents a sample task and one of its allocation pattern, and the under side represents a timing chart of the allocation pattern. The detail of generating allocation patterns is mentioned in section 3. In Figure 3, PU1, PU2 are processors and the symbols "a-e" are actors allocated into the processors. The under side in Figure 3 shows that actors are allocated according to the execution order "a,b,c,d,e" and the timing chart is drawn. This execution order is determined from the allocating order lists mentioned in section 3.2.2, and the allocating order is used as chromosome in GA. The detail of applying GA is described in 3.2.3. This allocating order list is sorted by communication dependencies of actors, and the first element of sorted lists is given as the execution order. The total process is represented as repeated blocks and the maximum execution period among all of them is the execution cycle of the task. In Figure 3, the execution cycle T becomes 8, and the throughput th becomes $1/8 = 0.125$.

3 Predictive Method of Task Allocation

3.1 Preparation of Task Allocation

The process of task analysis and allocation consists of following three stages:

1. System dependent Analysis. On the first time the stream-based computing model is implemented, or system configuration which affect system performance is changed, system dependent analysis is performed. Remote and local communication latencies are measured by evaluation programs. Then the parameter α, β in equation 19.1 are derived using the latencies. Thus communication cost for any data size can be calculated.

2. Compile Time Evaluation. Application dependent factors such as the behavior of a task are analyzed.

3. Pre-runtime allocation. Just before the executing the task, the number of available processors is given, then the task is executed with optimal allocation.

3.2 Task Allocation Algorithm

In this section, we explain the allocation method using knapsack algorithm[4] and Genetic Algorithm[7]. In the method, the task allocation is performed by allocating actors to processors.

3.2.1 Basic Algorithm of Task Allocation

In this section, we show the basic idea of our task allocation method in Figure 4. The allocation is decided by selecting the highest throughput allocation pattern among the patterns generated by using knapsack method.

In algorithm BA, allocation patterns are generated from all the permutation lists of allocating orders, and the best allocation pattern is selected by comparing predicted throughput of the allocation patterns. The example of allocating order lists are shown in right upper of Figure 3. The function "allocate(*Actors*)" allocates actors in order of the list *Actors* and save the allocation pattern to *al*. The detail of

Algorithm	BA // Basic Algorithm	$th_{best}=0$;
Actors	: an actor list representing	foreach *Actors* $\in \forall$ { $a_1..a_n$| a_i is an actor } {
	an allocation order	al = allocate(*Actors*);
al	: an allocation pattern	th = get_throughput(al);
al_{best}	: the best allocation pattern	if $th > th_{best}$ { // update
th	: throughput of *al*	$th_{best} = th$;
th_{best}	: the best throughput	$al_{best} = al$;
		}

Figure 4: Basic Algorithm of Task Allocation.

"`allocate(al)`" is described in the next section. The function "`get_throughput(al)`" returns the throughput of the allocation pattern *al* mentioned in section 2.4.

3.2.2 Generating Task allocation pattern using Knapsack Method

Generally, there are a lot of combinations of possible allocation patterns, but most of them are not suitable as a solution. So, in this allocation algorithm, allocation patterns are restricted as follows:

- Actors communicating with larger communication latency are placed into the same processor to reduce communication costs.

- The maximum processor load is limited to C in order to avoid an imbalance of processor loads. C is calculated as

$$C = e \cdot T_{ideal} \qquad (19.3)$$

where e is the coefficient(≥ 1) which depends on applications, and T_{ideal} is ideal execution cycle which is assumed that the task is equally divided into processors and there are no communication delays. It is calculated as

$$T_{ideal} = \sum_{i=1}^{n}(p_i)/d \qquad (19.4)$$

p_i : processing cost of actor i
n : number of actors
d : number of divisions

With this restriction, the allocated load to the processors gets closer to equal.

Figure 5 shows the process of actor allocation using Knapsack method, and Figure 6 is the algorithm of this method.

In algorithm `allocate`, allocation patterns are decided from the allocating order list *Actors*. The list is shown in the right upper of Figure 5. Figure 5 is a process of actor allocation and Figure 6 is the allocation algorithm which is a variant of a knapsack algorithm. Allocation pattern consists of actor location to processors and executing order.

Next, we explain an example of actor allocation procedure. Figure 5 is a process of actor allocation according to the allocating order:

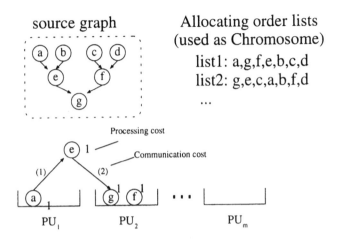

Figure 5: Knapsack Actor Allocation.

```
Algorithm allocate(Actors)
  Actors :   an actor list representing
             an allocating order
  {
    n_div :  number of divisions
    C :      capacity of processor load
    a :      an actor which is allocated
             to a processor
    th :     throughput of the generated
             allocation pattern
    p_alloc : the processor a is allocated
    p :      a processor
    al :     an allocation pattern
  }
```

```
foreach a ∈ Actors {
  // select the allocating processor p_alloc
  p_alloc = 1;
  foreach p ∈ { 2 .. n_div } {
    if gravity(a, p) > gravity(a, p_alloc){
      p_alloc=p if load_of( p ) < C;
    }
  }
  place(al, a, p_alloc); //put a into p_alloc
}
return al;
}
```

Figure 6: Actor Allocation based on Knapsack method.

list1: a,g,f,e,b,c,d
('a'-'f' are actor names)

In this figure, actors 'a', 'g', 'f' are already allocated to processors and 'e' is in the process of being allocated. To make the explanation simpler, all the actors' processing costs are assumed to be 1. At this time, the sum of load in PU_1 is 1, and in PU_2 is 2. The allocating actor 'e' is pulled by both 'a' and 'g', and the gravity (communication latency) to 'g' is stronger, so 'e' is placed into PU_2 which has 'g'. Then the sum of the load of PU_2 becomes 3. If the load of PU_2 is over the limit, 'e' is placed into PU_1 which has extra space to take 'e'.

In Figure 6. the function "gravity(a, p)" returns the sum of remote communication costs between allocating actor a and other actors in the processor p. The function "load_of(p)" returns the current load of the processor p. The function "place(al, a, p_alloc)" places an actor a into the processor p_{alloc}, and the current allocation status al is changed. Actors communicating with high communication latency are placed into the same processor with this grouping policy.

3.2.3   GA-based algorithm of Task Allocation

Task allocation in this computing model is considered as an NP complete problem. So we introduced GA in order to get the approximated solution in a practical time. GA is applied as follows:

1. Generate chromosome. Chromosome is defined by allocating order of actors, and it is used in the Knapsack method in section 3.2.2.

2. Repeat the following steps:

   (a) Generate allocation patterns from chromosome by using the Knapsack method.

   (b) Calculate the fitness of the allocation patterns as the evaluation of GA. Fitness is defined by the proportion of the predicted throughput to the ideal throughput T_ideal in equation 19.4.

   (c) Perform the GA operations: selection, crossover, and mutation.

4   Evaluations

Here, we present the evaluation of our predictive method of task allocation, the validity of throughput prediction and the degree of efficiency of GA-based allocation.

4.1   Comparison between Prediction and Measurement

Figure 7 shows the comparison between predicted throughput and the actual throughput on the Fujitsu AP3000 system [3](CPU: UltraSparc 143MHZ × 8, Memory: 128 MB). In this case, we employ a task which is generated at random as a sample application.

In Figure 7, X axis is the number of processors used in allocation, Y axis is the data transfer rate [ms], and Z axis is the reciprocal number of throughput. As Data transfer rate depends on architectures, communication latency is changed as a parameter to show this allocation algorithm is applicable on other systems. Data transfer rate is the communication cost for sending a constant amount of data, and it is calculated in equation (19.1). At this time, parameter e in equation (19.3) is set to 1.5, and the number of processors n_p is set in the range from 1 to 20. The thick line in Figure 7 is drawn to connect the best throughput points for each number of divisions. As shown in this figure, the predicted throughput is close to the measured throughput.

4.2   GA based Improvement

BA is classified as an NP complete problem. In this section, we consider how to improve our method. In such problems, GA is usually used to reach a practical

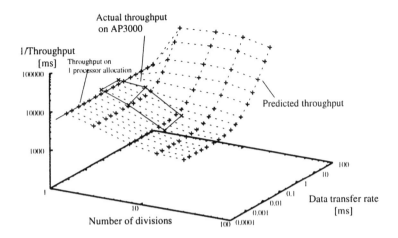

Figure 7: Comparison between Prediction and Measurement.

Table 1: Number of trials of GA operations for deciding the optimal allocation.

n_p	GA		BA	
	n_{trial}	speedup	n_{trial}	speedup
1	1	1	1	1
2	60	1.89	40320	1.93
	120	1.93		
4	60	3.02	40320	3.06
	120	3.06		

n_p: number of processors
n_{trial}: number of trials of GA operations
speedup: throughput(n_p)/throughput(1)

throughput(n_p): throughput of the allocation on n_p processors
throughput(1): throughput of the allocation on 1 processor

solution. So we evaluate the efficiency of GA by applying our method. In order to apply GA to our allocation method, we define the list of allocating order as chromosome. The list of allocating order is used in the Knapsack allocation method in section 3.2.2, and the list is shown in the top right side of Figure 5. The initial generation set of the allocation order lists (e.g list1,2 in Figure 7) is given at random. Then the next generation sets are created by applying crossover, mutation, and so on.

Table 1 is the comparison of average number of trials for deciding the allocation pattern between the GA based algorithm and BA algorithm described in 3.2.1. In this comparison, 8 actors are generated with random connection of streams. Actors' processing cost is given as exponential random numbers with average 100 ms, and data size of the stream is set to 100 Bytes.

In table 1, *speedup* is the effect of speedup by increasing the number of processors n_p. The *speedup* implies, the closer the value of *speedup* to n_p is, the higher the throughput is. In BA method, n_{trial} is the factorial of number of actors and the required n_{trial} becomes 8! = 40320. On the other hand, in our GA method, in order to get the same *speedup* of BA, n_{trial} is only 120. In GA, n_{trial} varies to the condition of convergence judgement and number of initially generated chromosomes. From this table, the trial number of GA is improved to that of BA's. So, the efficiency of applying GA on task allocation is proved.

Our objective for this algorithm is not to solve the actual optimal allocation but the practically optimal one. The role of throughput prediction is an evaluation function, so if you can get the practical solution by using anything else beside throughput, it can be used as a new metric in our method.

5   Conclusions

In this paper, we proposed the predictive method of task allocation. This method consists of three stages of analysis and the Knapsack allocation method. We employed GA in order to reduce the number of computations for deciding the allocation. We evaluated the random task allocation in order to certify the validity of this algorithm. Using our predictive method and GA to the task allocation in stream-based computing, the optimal task allocation can be obtained efficiently.

Bibliography

1)   Message Passing Interface Forum, "Document for a Standard Message-Passing Interface", Technical Report No. CS-93-214 (revised), Apr. 1994.

2)   Patrick T. Gaughan, "Data Streaming: Very Low Overhead Communication for Fine-grained Multicomputing", In Pro eedings of 7tk IEEE Symposium on Parallel and Distributed Processing, Oct. 1995.

3)   Hiroyuki Oyake, Yuji Iguchi and Tsunemi Yamene, "Operating System of AP3000 Series Scalar-Type Parallel Servers", FUJITSU Sci. Tech. J.,33,1,pp.31-38,June 1997.

4)   Yoichi Aoyagi, Minoru Uehara and Hideki Mori, "A Case Study on Predictive Method of Task Allocation in Stream-based Computing", The 12th International Conference on Information Networking(ICOIN-12),IPSJ,IEEE Tokyo and Taipei, pp.316-321, Jan. 1998.

5)   Minoru Uehara and Mario Tokoro, "An Adaptive Load Balancing Method in Computational Field Model", ACM OOPS Messenger, Vol. 2, No. 2, Apr. 1991.

6)   Gustav Pospischil, Peter Puschner, Alexander Vrchoticky and Ralph Zainlinger, "Developing Real-Time Tasks with Predictable Timing", IEEE SOFTWARE, pp.35-44, Sep. 1992.

7)   Zbigniew Michalewicz, "Genetic Algorithms + Data Structures = Evolution Progrtams", Springer-Verlag, 1994

20

Test Generation of a Communication Protocol in an EFSM model

Tae-hyong Kim, Ik-soon Hwang, [†]Min-seok Jang, Jai-yong Lee and Sang-bae Lee

Yonsei University, [†]Kunsan National University

ABSTRACT

In this paper, we generate conformance test cases for a communication protocol modeled in an EFSM(Extended Finite State Machine) by a transition-based fault coverage analysis. As the analysis model, we choose the expanded EFSM to resolve the inter-dependency problem between control and data flows within an EFSM. An expanded EFSM has several useful properties and makes it easy to generate test cases. For test case generation, at first we define data elements in the expanded EFSM. With the definition, we define some probable fault models in transitions of the expanded EFSM and discuss what test cases are needed for covering each fault model. The analysis shows that control flow test cases with full fault coverage and data flow test cases satisfying all-du-paths criterion are needed to guarantee high fault coverage in the expanded EFSM. A mass of generated test cases by high fault coverage is optimized through some steps. The result of a simple protocol shows the efficacy of this method.

1 Introduction

Lately the protocol model used for test case generation of conformance test is being changed from the FSM(Finite State Machine) model to the EFSM(Extended Finite State Machine) model, because the FSM model cannot fully specify communication protocols. As not considering data flows, control flow test using FSM model has also limited applicability, cannot detect any error of data flows, and moreover may be impractical for not considering executabilities of test sequences. The EFSM testing has both the control flow test part and the data flow test part. Its control flow test usually adopts the test methods used in FSM testing. In the data flow test part, the test sequences have been mostly used that can satisfy one of Weyuker's data selection criteria[8] based on data flow analysis of software testing[7]. But control flows and data flows are dependent each other and especially transitions in control flows gets decided executable by their data set. Lately some methods considering them have been proposed: EUIO(Executable-UIO)-method which considers data flows for generation of executable control flow test sequences[5] and a unified test sequence generation method whose sequences can test both control and data flows of IUT(Implementation Under Test)[3]. But the interdependency between control flows and data flows of an EFSM model of a protocol interferes with generation of each test cases having the desired test coverage. Some researches trying to solve this problem have been studied, one of which expands the EFSM by freeing predicate statements[10]. To resolve the state explosion, this method assumes finite and countable domains of the variables that occur in predicate statements. From the expanded EFSM, test sequences can be generated using classic methods. But the expanded EFSM is not a pure FSM but still an EFSM, so new test case generations method are needed to test the expanded EFSM properly with considering fault coverage.

In section 2, we define an expanded EFSM and explain its properties. A test case generation method by fault coverage analysis for the expanded EFSM is proposed in section 3. In section 4, we discuss an optimization scheme for both control and data flow test cases. Finally the empirical result of a real protocol and conclusions lie in section 5.

2   An Expanded EFSM and Its Properties

Conformance test of a protocol modeled in an EFSM is composed of the control flow test and the data flow test. Our concept of an EFSM is shown in Figure 1.

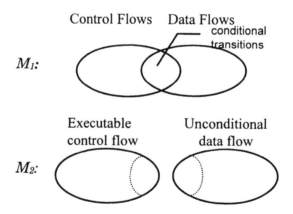

Figure 1: Transformation of EFSM structure

M_1 shows an outline of conventional EFSM structure. Control flows and data flows are mixed in conditional transitions, or transitions having predicate. This problem makes the fault coverage of each test not clear. So we will transform the EFSM to the expanded EFSM to separate control flows and data flows by eliminating predicates as shown in M_2. The properties of conditional transitions of the EFSM permeate both control flows and data flows, and the separated are functionally equivalent to the original. In addition, their independence makes it simple to generate their test cases. The generated expanded EFSM has more states than the original EFSM, but the number of states is finite if all the variables have a finite domain.

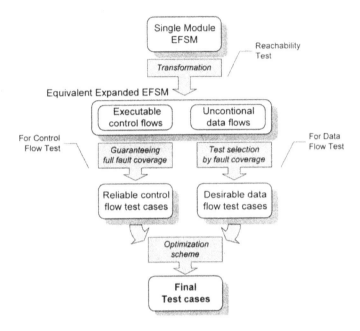

Figure 2: The test case generation procedure

Figure 2 shows our test case generation procedure for conformance testing of a protocol. It starts from a single module EFSM. A communicating multi-module EFSM itself is nearly impossible to analyze and to test, so the simplification is needed into the equivalent single module EFSM that has been a major issue in protocol testing. We already proposed a method to develop the loss-less transformation by the reachability analysis in another work before[11]. Our target for the control flow test part is to generate test cases satisfying full fault coverage if possible, which guarantee the reliability of data flow test cases. For data flow test part, we also try to select test cases for the required fault coverage. The generated reliable control flow cases and desired data flow test cases are optimized to the unified final test cases. We, first, define an expanded EFSM. It was defined in [10], but we modify it as follows.

Definition 1 A single module *expanded EFSM* is a 8-tuple $< \Sigma, \Omega, \Pi, \mathcal{V}, \mathcal{S}, \mathcal{I}, \mathcal{O}, \mathcal{T} >$, where Σ is a general state set, Ω is a global and local variable set, Π is a parameter set, $\mathcal{V}$ is a domain set of Ω, $\mathcal{S}$ is an extended state set which is $\Sigma \times \mathcal{V}$, $\mathcal{I}$ is a set of input declarations including the reset input ri and the delay input Δ, $\mathcal{O}$ is a set of output declarations including the null output $\emptyset$, and $\mathcal{T}$ is a set of transitions which is $\mathcal{S} \times \mathcal{I}$ and is expressed as $< I/I(\Pi : \mathcal{R}), \mathcal{M}, O(E) >$, where $I \in \mathcal{I}, O \in \mathcal{O}, \mathcal{R}$ is an input range of Π, E is an output parameter expression that is $f_O(\Omega, \Pi)$, $\mathcal{M}$ is an action block and is expressed as $\Omega \leftarrow (\Omega, \Pi)$.

An expanded EFSM can be considered a reachability-tested EFSM and can help the generation of test cases of control flow test and data flow test owing to the following properties.

1) All edges of an expanded EFSM are executable at any state.
2) The values of variables at each edge in an expanded EFSM are identical regardless of incoming paths.
3) The values of variables at each state in an expanded EFSM are identical regardless of incoming paths.
4) An expanded EFSM has no self-loop which has actions of variable.

3   Test Case Generation by Fault Coverage Analysis

In protocol testing and software testing, fault coverage of test cases has been a major issue. Because there is a trade-off relation between fault coverage and the length of test cases, how to select test cases by considering the relation is the policy of a tester like the selection of test purposes. Analyzing fault coverage of test cases, we think, can eliminate the redundant part of the test cases and make clear their detectability and undetectability of the probable faults. Fault coverage of control flow test cases of an FSM-modeled protocol has been mainly studied, but that of data flow test cases of an EFSM-modeled protocol has been rarely studied. The expanded EFSM can help the analysis of fault coverage.

We assume that the original EFSM representation of the protocol is deterministic and completely specified. Determinism and complete specification of an EFSM also mean that if there are predicates in an input declaration with parameters at a state, the regions satisfying the predicates are disjoint together and the union of the regions constructs the whole region.

3.1   Data elements in the expanded EFSM

The fault coverage of data flow test has been decided normally by using Weyuker's data selection criteria which use def-clear paths as test elements and define some test criteria by the test coverage of them[8]. As there is no *p-use* of a predicate statement in the expanded EFSM, data flow elements of Weyuker's should be modified for the expanded EFSM. We newly classify several *defs* and *uses* more clearly and redefine the meaning of a def-clear path to be fit for the protocol testing. The assumption that all the actions can be expressed as linear expressions would enable us to use matrix expressions.

Definition 2 An assignment, $\omega \leftarrow (\emptyset, \underline{\Pi})$ in an action block of an expanded EFSM contains an *i-def(independent-def)* of the variable ω where $\omega \in \Omega$ and $\emptyset \neq \underline{\Pi} \subset \Pi$. An assignment, $\omega \leftarrow (\underline{\Omega}, \underline{\Pi})$ in an action block contains a *d-def(dependent-def)* of the variable ω and a *u-use(unobservable-use)* of the variable $\underline{\omega}$ where $\omega \in \Omega, \underline{\omega} \in \underline{\Omega}, \emptyset \neq \underline{\Omega} \subset \Omega$, and $\emptyset \neq \underline{\Pi} \subset \Pi$. An output parameter expression $(\underline{\Omega}, \underline{\Pi})$ in an output declaration in the expanded EFSM contains an *o-use(observable-uses)* and an *i-def(independent-def)* of the variable $\underline{\omega}$, where $\underline{\omega} \in \underline{\Omega}, \emptyset \neq \underline{\Omega} \subset \Omega$, and $\emptyset \neq \underline{\Pi} \subset \Pi$.

Definition 3 We redefine a *def-clear path* of a variable as a path which starts an edge having an i-def of the variable and ends other edge having an o-use of the variable without passing any edge having another i-def of the variable in the expanded EFSM.

As Weyuker's test data selection criteria are based on software testing, its inclusion relation between criteria may not be valid for a protocol modeled in an EFSM. As an EFSM has many edges that do not have data flow element, the test cases satisfying *all-du-path* criterion may not have all edges in the EFSM. If we assume that the probability of faults is thought to be almost equal, untested edges reveal ineffectiveness of the test method. We, here, take the minimal and necessary assumption that all the faults can lie only in the edges constructing def-clear paths, which is acceptable to almost EFSM. By the above assumption, all the edges constructing any of def-clear paths must be tested. Therefore we have to select the all-du-path criterion for data flow test.

For control flow test, we will use the UIO(Unique Input Output) method that has been widely used for detecting faults in control flows. We will generate test cases for the state identification part and the transition identification part for the high fault coverage[2]).

3.2 Fault models in transitions of the expanded EFSM

In the general EFSM, faults of variables or parameters in data flows may exist in the following parts: input declarations with parameters, predicates, action blocks, and output declarations with parameters. There are two kinds of faults. One is the modification fault that the existing part is wrongly modified. The other is the addition fault that the unspecified part is wrongly specified. Each kind of faults may occur alone or both two kinds of faults may occur together. We assume that there is no fault in edges added only for completely specified condition for simplification. We classify the probable faults as follows.

Type I: The faults of the assignments, $\omega^* \leftarrow (\underline{\Omega}, \emptyset)$ in action blocks alone. In the expanded EFSM, these faults may create new states and edges.

Type II: The faults of the assignments, $\omega^* \leftarrow (\underline{\Omega}, \underline{\Pi})$ in action blocks alone. This type is the same as type I except that these faults are related with input parameters.

Type III: The faults of the parameters in input declarations alone. The parameters in the input declaration of an edge, to be meaningful, should be used in the edge.. These faults would mostly cause the faults of the action blocks or the output parameters in the edge. For the detection of this type of faults, therefore, we will check the faults of the action block with parameters, or type II faults, and the output declaration with parameters, or the next type IV faults.

Type IV: The faults of the parameters in output declarations alone. We assume that an expression with variables and parameters is allowed as an output parameter in an output declaration. We can detect these faults only by output declarations and values of their parameters. The faults of type I or II can be also detected by them. If we, therefore, consider type IV faults, the probable expression in an output parameter can be regarded as an extension of the action block of the edge. So we can regard this type of faults as those of type I or II.

Type V: The faults of the predicates not related with parameters. In case of modification faults, the executable region of the predicate is wrongly changed, which may cause the nondeterminism or incompleteness of the specification, but the problem is not our concern. If the regions are changed with holding our assumption that no fault will cause the nondeterminism or incompleteness, only the target states of the related edges are changed in the expanded EFSM. In case of addition faults, another partial executable region of the predicate can be created, which may cause the same problem as that of the modification faults. If all the modified executable regions of the edges hold the above assumption, the related edges will be divided into more than one edge. In the expanded EFSM, however, the edges are not divided but only their target states are also changed in the expanded EFSM, because there is no parameter in the predicate expression.

Type VI: The faults of the predicates having some relation with parameters. If the executable values of input parameters are unique each, this type can be treated as type V. But if not, their possible values firing the edge can be in closed or open region. In case of modification faults, their properties are the same as those of type V, except that they may create the target states of the related edges in the expanded EFSM. In case of addition faults, their properties are also the same as those of type V except that they divide the edges and may create the target states of the related edges in the expanded EFSM.

Type VII: The mixed faults of type I, II, and V of some edges. These faults may create many new states and edges in the expanded EFSM.

3.3   Test cases for the faults in transitions

Now, for each type of faults in transitions, we find out test cases fully covering the faults. Type I is the simplest. But these faults may increase the number of states and edges in the expanded EFSM. So, data flow test cases are needed. Test cases satisfying all-du-paths criterion will cover these faults. Even if test cases can not detect any fault, it does not matter because the faulty EFSM always works in the same manner to the original one.

Type II is a little more complicated. The defs of parameters of input declarations is different form those of variables in that the values of input parameters firing the edge may not be unique. We, the tester, do not know which value can surely detect this type of faults. To get feasible test cases covering these faults, we should assume the fault pattern of the implementation. If we assume that the action block, $\Omega \leftarrow (\Omega, \Pi)$ is expressed as the linear functions like $V = AV + BP + C$, where V is the variable matrix, P is the parameter matrix and A, B, and C are coefficient matrices, we can get the following theorem.

Theorem 1 In the expanded EFSM, if all assignments of action blocks are expressed linear functions and type I or II faults change the assignments to another linear expressions, two identical test cases having different values of the input parameter can cover the faults.

Proof By property 2 of the expanded EFSM, each variable in an edge has same value regardless of the previous paths. Therefore we can regard the action block of the edge, $V = AV + BP + C$ as $V = BP + C'$, where $C' = AV + C$. As this expression is a linear function of parameters, two different parameter values will determine the function. Therefore, two identical test cases having different values of input parameters can cover the faults.

Type V faults may cause wrong transitions without an addition of any extra edges in the expanded EFSM. This property clearly shows that these faults can be fully covered only by classic control flow test cases.

Test data selection of input parameters has been a major issue in software testing and protocol testing. The values of input parameters that make all the test cases executable may not be unique but may lie in closed or open region. The required test cases fully covering these faults, therefore, may not finite, so test data selection is necessary and it is the policy of the tester. Type VI faces this problem. Therefore we assume that there is no fault of type VI in the protocol implementation.

By the above analysis, we have only one combination type of faults, type VII faults. These faults are the most complex. Like type II, to surely get finite test cases, we should have the same assumption as that of type II faults. By the assumption, this type of faults can be also fully covered by the control flow test cases with the transition identification part and the state identification part and the data flow test cases satisfying all-du-paths criterion. Even if test cases can not detect any fault, it does not matter for the same reason as that of the type I fault.

4 A Unified Optimization Scheme

We tried to generate the test cases having high fault coverage. But the number of test cases needed for this purpose is tremendous, so the optimization of test cases is required. As there is generally a trade-off relation between the size of test cases and the fault coverage of test cases, optimizations may drop the fault coverage. We adopted an optimization scheme that can guarantee the desired fault coverage defined in the previous chapter. This optimization scheme is depicted in Figure 3.

Several implication checks at each step make test cases independent together as

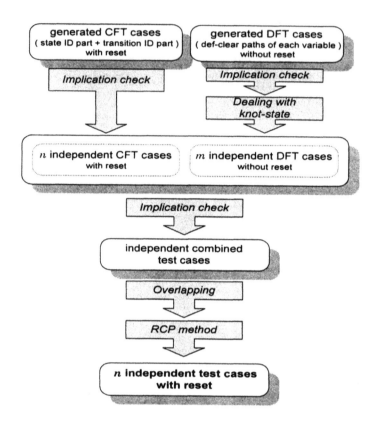

Figure 3: The proposed optimization procedure

shown in Figure 3. We adopted the overlap method and RCP method[1] for optimization. We do not use MUIO(Multiple UIO) method[6] because it needs another test cases for full fault coverage[2]. The serious defect of UIO method, not full applicability, can be almost overcome by applying properties of the expanded EFSM and adopting delay as an input declaration. Transitions with delay statements will keep the states from having their UIO sequences that have the same output declarations. In fact, however, the null output that outputs nothing is used as an output declaration in spite of the similar timing problem. Therefore we also use delay as an input declaration, which can extend the test coverage of control flow test cases.

The generated control flow test cases for both the state identification and the transition identification are checked if some test cases are implicated by others. The implicated test cases are discarded. Def-clear paths for all the variables compose data flow test cases, where the implication check is also run. In the EFSM, a major factor increasing test cases is the edges added for completeness of the specification, which have null actions and null output declarations. These edges are represented as loops in the expanded EFSM as well as in the normal EFSM. In the states having these edges or many incoming and outgoing edges, in fact most of states, the number of needed data flow test cases gets multiplied according to the number of edges. In the expanded EFSM, with the assumption of linearity, we solve the problem of those states as follows.

Definition 4 A state is called a *knot-state* if it lies in both more than 2 distinct incoming def-clear paths and more than 2 distinct outgoing def-clear paths in an expanded EFSM. A knot-state can have self-loops without data element.

Theorem 2 Let test cases have a common knot-state. When the knot-state connects m incoming def-clear paths and n outgoing def-clear paths and it has l self loops without data element, test cases having selected $m + n + l - 1$ def-clear paths among $m \times n \times l$ paths can satisfy all-du-paths criterion, if only linear faults are allowed in actions.

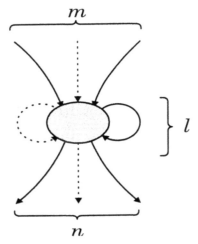

Figure 4: A model of knot-state

Proof If an edge in Figure 4 has a fault in one side, the upper side or the lower side, of the knot-state, a test case passing this edge may detect the fault. But the test case has another fault in the other side of the knot-state, it may not detect faults. Then another test case passing the edge having the latter fault may detect the fault. And the process can be repeated one after another. If test cases can not find any fault, this faulty specification is functionally equivalent to the original one. In other words, if all test cases can be connected in the edges without making any partition, they can find out the probable faults that can be detected by test cases satisfying all-du-paths criterion. A Loop at a knot state has the same property because it forms both incoming and outgoing edge except it is made of only one edge. The minimum number of needed paths that can connect the upper side having $n + l$ sub-paths and the lower side having $m + l$ sub-paths is $n + m + 2l - 1$. Because loops are counted twice there, the minimum number is $n + m + l - 1$.

In the expanded EFSM, knot-states are naturally connected together. In other words, test cases having linked def-clear paths can contain multiple knot-states. For this case, the following theorem is valid.

Theorem 3 Let a part of an expanded EFSM have p edges composing def-clear paths, q knot states dependent together and r o-uses of a variable. Then test cases having selected $p - q + r$ def-clear paths can satisfy all-du-paths criterion in the part, if only linear faults of the variable in the action block are allowed.

Proof In a knot state having n incoming edges, l loops and m outgoing edges, the number of needed test cases is $n + l + m - 1$. This can be regarded as the number of incoming edges of the following knot-state. If we repeat this process to all the knot-states with all the outgoing edges having o-uses, the number of required test cases will be $p - q'$ minimally where p is the number of edge composing the def-clear paths and q' is the number of knot-states which def-clear paths pass through. In the last knot-state, the number of needed test cases is $(p - q') + r - 1$. If we count the last knot-state, the number gets $p - q + r$, where $q = q' + 1$.

5   Empirical Results and Conclusions

To estimate the usefulness of the proposed method, we generated the test cases of a simple protocol, Inres[3] used often for the reason. Initiator module in Inres protocol is the target EFSM, where delay and reset are treated as input declarations. The original EFSM of Initiator module freed of edges for completely specified condition has 4 states and 14 edges. The complete specified transformed expanded EFSM has 18 states and 147 edges, but the number of edges freed of the edges added for completeness of the specification is 57. Among them one edge should not be omitted, because it is a part of a UIO sequence. We finally generated 46 test cases for control flow test and 3 test cases for data flow test by the proposed optimization scheme. This result shows that most of test cases for detecting faults of data flows is transferred to control flow test cases by the proposed method. 3 data flow test cases are linked to the control flow test cases by RCP method.

By now, there has been little study on the fault model for data flows and the optimization of data flow test cases for conformance testing of communication protocols. The major reasons are the complexity of data flows and inter-dependence between control and data flows. To resolve these problems, we transformed an original EFSM into the equivalent expanded EFSM that is good to analyze without being interfered by those problems. With the advantages of the expanded EFSM, we proposed a test case generation method by transition-based fault coverage analysis. The analysis shows that control flow test cases with full fault coverage and data flow test cases satisfying *all-du-paths* criterion are needed to guarantee high fault coverage. We also proposed an optimization scheme with some assumptions. The optimization scheme can cope with frequent knot-states in the expanded EFSM. The result of a sample protocol showed the efficacy of this method and applying it to real protocols like B-ISDN protocols can give it more applicability and reliability.

Bibliography

1) Alfred V. Aho *et al.*, "An optimization technique for protocol conformance test generation based on UIO sequences and Rural Chinese Postman Tours," *Protocol Specification, Testing and Verification*, Atlantic City, USA, pp.75–86 (1988).

2) Ricardo Anido *et al.*, "Guaranteeing full fault coverage for the UIO-based testing methods," *Int. Workshop on Protocol Test Systems '95*, Evry, France, pp.221–236, (1995).

3) Samuel T.Chanson *et al.*, "A unified approach to protocol test sequence generation," *IEEE INFOCOM '93*, San Francisco, USA, pp.106–114, (1993).

4) Do Young Lee, Jai Yong Lee, "A well-defined Estelle specification for the automatic test generation," *IEEE trans. on Computer*, Vol.4, No.4, pp.526–542, (1991).

5) Xiangdong Li *et al.*, "Automatic generation of extended UIO sequences for communication protocols in an EFSM model," *Int. Workshop on Protocol Test Systems '94*, Tokyo, Japan, pp.213–228, (1994).

6) Y. N. Shen *et al.*, "Protocol conformance testing using multiple UIO sequences," *Protocol Specification, Testing and Verification '90*, Ottawa, Canada, pp.131–143, (1990).

7) Hasan Ural *et al.*, "A test sequence selection method for protocol testing," *IEEE trans. on Comm.*, Vol.39, No.4, pp.514–523, (1991).

8) Elain J. Weyuker *et al.*, "Selecting software test data using data flow information," *IEEE trans. on SE*, Vol.11, No.4, pp.367–375, (1985).

9) Byungmoon Chin, Taehyong Kim, Minseok Jang, Iksoon Hwang, Jaiyong Lee, Sangbae Lee, "Generation of Reliable and Optimized Test Cases for Data Flow Test with a Formal Approach," *ICOIN-11*, Taipei, Taiwan, (1997).

10) O. Henniger *et al.*, "Transformation of Estelle modules aiming at test case generation," *Int. Workshop on Protocol Test Systems '95*, Evry, France, pp.45–60, (1995).

11) Iksoon Hwang, Taehyong Kim, Minseok Jang, Jaiyong Lee and Sangbae Lee, "A Method to Derive a Sing-EFSM from Communicating Multi-EFSM for Data Part Testing," *Int. Workshop on Testing of Communicating Systems '97*, Cheju, Korea, (1997).

21

Asynchronous Distributed Recovery with Multiple Checkpoints

Hiroaki Higaki

Makoto Takizawa

Tokyo Denki University

ABSTRACT

This paper proposes a novel protocol for taking checkpoints and asynchronously restarting the processes for recovery in asynchronous distributed systems. In the protocol, only the minimum number of processes take checkpoints. The amount of execution of application program wasted by the recovery is also the minimum. Each process is asynchronously restarted at most once to recover from a failure of process. Hence, the livelocks can be avoided. Only $O(l)$ messages are transmitted where l is the number of channels in the system. Moreover, garbage collection to discard obsolete checkpoints is discussed.

1 Introduction

Information systems become distributed and are getting larger by including various kinds of component systems and interconnecting with various systems, e.g. by the Internet. The distributed systems are designed and developed by using widely available products rather than specially designed ones. These products are not always guaranteed to support enough reliability and availability for the applications. It is important to discuss the mechanism to make and keep the systems so reliable and available that even fault-tolerant applications could be implemented.

Distributed applications are realized by cooperation of multiple processes in multiple processors. Checkpointing and recovery are well-known time-redundant fault-tolerant techniques. Every process takes checkpoints by recording the state information in the logs while executing the applications. If some process fails, the processes are rolled back to the checkpoints by restoring the saved state information and then restarted to execute the applications from the checkpoints. Here, the system can tolerate *transient* failures, e.g. hardware errors, process crashes, transaction aborts, and communication deadlocks. These failures are unlikely to recur after the recovery.

The system has to be kept consistent even after the recovery. A *global checkpoint* is a set of checkpoints taken by all the processes in the system. A *consistent global checkpoint* of the distributed system is formalized by Chandy and Lamport

[3]. Many papers [3, 7, 8, 12, 14] have proposed so far protocols for taking a consistent global checkpoint and for restarting the processes. The conventional checkpointing protocols require all the processes in the system to take checkpoints synchronously. However, in large-scale distributed systems, each process only communicates with a subset of the processes. Hence, a checkpointing protocol that allows the subset of the processes to take the checkpoints is necessary. On the other hand, the processes are required to be synchronously restarted. However, the recovery procedure may be slow down due to the synchronization. If checkpoints are taken in a subset of the processes to take a consistent checkpoint and the processes are asynchronously restarted, the recovery procedure may continue forever, i.e. a livelock may occur. In this paper, we propose a protocol for a livelock-free asynchronous recovery where only a subset of the processes are restarted.

In section 2, the conventional checkpointing and recovery protocols are reviewed and we show how the livelock occur while the system is asynchronously restarted from a consistent *regional* checkpoint. In section 3, a livelock-free asynchronous recovery protocol is proposed. The evaluation of the protocol is presented in section 4.

2   Checkpoint and Recovery

2.1   Consistent state

A distributed system is composed of multiple processes interconnected by channels, i.e. $S = \langle V, L \rangle$ where $V = \{p_1, \ldots, p_n\}$ is a set of processes and $L \subseteq V^2$ is a set of channels. $\langle p_i, p_j \rangle$ is a channel from p_i to p_j. In a process, three kinds of events occur: message-sending event $s(m)$ of a message m, message-receipt event $r(m)$ and local events. The *happens before* relation among the events is defined as follows:

Definition (happens before) An event e *happens before* another event e' ($e \to e'$) iff one of the following conditions is satisfied [9]:
- e occurs before e' in the same process.
- $e = s(m)$ and $e' = r(m)$ for a message m.
- There is an event e'' where $e \to e''$ and $e'' \to e'$. □

A state of a process p_i is changed each time an event occurs in p_i. Messages are transmitted from p_i to p_j via a channel $\langle p_i, p_j \rangle \in L$. Here, $\langle p_i, p_j \rangle$ is named a *channel of* p_i. If there is a channel $\langle p_i, p_j \rangle$, p_j is referred to as a *neighbor* of p_i.

A checkpoint c^i is taken in p_i by recording the state of p_i in the log. A global checkpoint $C = \{c^1, \ldots, c^n\}$ is a set of checkpoints taken by all the processes in V. If the processes take the checkpoints and are restarted independently of the other processes, there may exist two kinds of inconsistent messages: *lost messages* and *orphan messages*. Here, suppose that p_i sends a message m to p_j. m is a lost message iff $s(m)$ occurs before c^i and a $r(m)$ occurs after c^j. m is an orphan message iff $s(m)$ occurs after c^i and $r(m)$ occurs before c^j. By recording the received messages in the log after p_j takes c^j, lost messages can be received by taking them out of the log after p_j is restarted. However, if there exist orphan messages, the system becomes inconsistent after the recovery, even though p_j records m in the log

at $s(m)$. Therefore, C is defined *consistent* iff there is no orphan message [5]).
Theorem 1 A global checkpoint C is consistent iff $\forall c^i, c^j \in C$ $c_i \not\to c_j$. $\square$

2.2 Checkpointing

There are two approaches toward taking a consistent global checkpoint C: *asynchronous* checkpointing and *synchronous* one. In the asynchronous checkpointing [2, 6]), each process takes checkpoints independently of the other processes. If some process fails, all the processes are coordinated to determine C. This approach implies less overhead during the failure-free execution. However, *domino effects* may occur in the recovery [12]). On the other hand, in the synchronous checkpointing [3, 7, 8, 12, 14]), all the processes are coordinated to take C. Here, additional messages are transmitted and the processes are blocked during the synchronization [1]) while no domino effect occurs. Our discussion is based on the synchronous checkpointing.

In the conventional synchronous checkpointing [3, 6, 8, 12, 14]), additional messages are transmitted to take a consistent global checkpoint and the execution of the applications is blocked during the checkpointing procedure. Moreover, all the processes in the system are required to take the checkpoints simultaneously. However, in a large-scale distributed system, each process only communicates with a subset of the processes in the system. Hence, we define a *regional* checkpoint $\tilde{C}$ and a *consistent regional checkpoint* in $S = \langle V, L \rangle$.

Definition (regional checkpoint) A *regional* checkpoint $\tilde{C}(W)$ of a subset $W \subseteq V$ is defined as a set $\{c^i | p_i \in W\}$ of checkpoints. $\square$

Definition (consistent regional checkpoint) $\tilde{C}(W)$ is consistent iff there is no orphan message in every channel of every process $p_i \in W$. $\square$

Theorem 2 $\tilde{C}(W)$ is consistent iff $\forall c^i, c^j \in \tilde{C}(W)$ $c^i \not\to c^j$. $\square$

Theorem 3 Let s^i be a state of an operational process $p_i \in V - W$. A global state denoted by $\tilde{C}(W) \cup \{s^i | p_i \in V - W\}$ is consistent if $\tilde{C}(W)$ is consistent. $\square$

S can be recovered from a failure of a process in W iff $\tilde{C}(W)$ is consistent and only and all the processes in W are restarted from $\tilde{C}(W)$. Here, suppose that c^i is taken by $p_i \in W$. If a message m is the first message transmitted from p_i to p_j after c^i, m is referred to as a *checkpoint message* of c^i to p_j. In order to keep S consistent after S is restarted from $\tilde{C}(W)$, p_j has to take c^j and p_j has to be included in W.

[Regional checkpointing] If $r(m)$ of a checkpoint message m occurs in p_j, p_j takes c^j just before $r(m)$. $\square$

If some process in W fails, only and all the processes to be restarted take the checkpoints and are included in W. Since m can carry the information on whether m is a checkpoint message or not, no additional message is required to be transmitted.

2.3 Recovery

In the conventional recovery protocols [3, 6, 8, 12, 14]), the processes have to be synchronized to be restarted by the following procedure:

1) Request messages are transmitted from the *coordinator process* to all the other processes called *cohort processes*.

2) Each cohort is rolled back to the checkpoint. Reply messages are transmitted from every cohort to the coordinator.

3) The coordinator transmits restart messages to all the cohorts. Each cohort is restarted from the checkpoint.

In such *synchronous* protocols, all the processes are blocked and the additional messages are transmitted to synchronize all the processes. Thus, the recovery procedure is slow down and S becomes less available. In order to keep S highly available with the recovery, we propose an asynchronous recovery protocol.

c_s^i represents the sth checkpoint taken by p_i. $r_{s,t}^i$ represents the possible recovery event occurring in p_i after c_t^i is taken by p_i where p_i is restarted from c_s^i ($s \le t$). c_s^i is *active* if c_s^i is taken but $r_{t,u}^i$ where $t \le s \le u$ has not yet occurred. p_i may have multiple active checkpoints. If p_i fails, it is not sufficient to restart p_i from the most recent active checkpoint c_s^i because the messages sent by p_i after c_s^i is taken become orphan messages. Hence, S has to be restarted from a consistent $\tilde{C}(D_i)$ where a *recovery domain* D_i is a subset of the processes including p_i. Here, p_i has to identify which processes are included in D_i.

Definition (checkpoint precedence) Let c^i and c^j be active checkpoints taken by p_i and p_j, respectively. c^i *precedes* c^j ($c^i \Rightarrow c^j$) if there exist events e^i in p_i and e^j in p_j where $c^i \to e^i$, $c^j \to e^j$, and $e^i \to e^j$. $\square$

Definition (recovery domain) A *recovery domain* D_i of p_i is defined to be a following set of processes:

1) $p_i \in D_i$ if there is an active checkpoint in p_i.

2) $p_j \in D_i$ if $c_s^i \Rightarrow c_t^j$ where c_s^i is the most recent active checkpoint in p_i and c_t^j is an active checkpoint in p_j.

3) Only the processes satisfying 1) and 2) are included in D_i. $\square$

By the definition and Theorem 2, the following theorem is induced:

Theorem 4 $\tilde{C}(D_i)$ is consistent for every rollback domain D_i. $\square$

That is, a recovery domain is a region for the recovery. Suppose that p_i fails and is restarted from the most recent checkpoint c_s^i. If every process $p_j \in D_i$ is restarted from c_t^j where $c_s^i \Rightarrow c_t^j$, S is kept consistent. However, each process cannot know D_i completely. If p_j sends a message to p_k after c_t^j where c_s^i is the most recent checkpoint in p_i and $c_s^i \Rightarrow c_t^j$, p_j knows that p_k is included in D_i.

Definition (recovery view) A *recovery view* $W_i^j = \{p_k | p_j \text{ knows } p_k \in D_i\}$. $\square$

Now, S can be *asynchronously* restarted from $\tilde{C}(D_i)$ by the message diffusion [4].

[Asynchronous recovery]

1) If p_i fails, p_i sends a restart request R_{req} to every process $p_j \in W_i^i$ and is restarted from the most recent checkpoint c_s^i.

2) On receipt of R_{req} from p_k, each p_j also sends R_{req} to every process in W_i^j except p_k and is restarted from the checkpoint c_t^j where $c_s^i \Rightarrow c_t^j$.

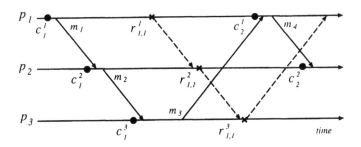

Figure 1: Livelock in recovery.

2.4 Livelock

Let us consider the scenario shown in Figure 1:

1) p_1 takes c_1^1 and sends m_1 to p_2. c_1^1 is active and $W_1^1 = \{p_1, p_2\}$.
2) p_2 receives m_1 and takes c_1^2. c_1^2 is active and $W_2^1 = \{p_1, p_2\}$. A recovery domain D_1 of p_1 is $\{p_1, p_2\}$ and $\tilde{C}(D_1) = \{c_1^1, c_1^2\}$ is consistent.
3) p_2 sends m_2 to p_3. p_3 receives m_2 and takes c_1^3. c_1^3 is active. $D_1 = \{p_1, p_2, p_3\}$ and $\tilde{C}(D_1) = \{c_1^1, c_1^2, c_1^3\}$ is consistent. p_1 does not know that $p_3 \in D_1$. $W_1^1 = \{p_1, p_2\}$, $W_2^1 = \{p_1, p_2, p_3\}$ and $W_3^1 = \{p_2, p_3\}$.
4) p_1 fails and is restarted from c_1^1. c_1^1 becomes inactive. p_1 sends $m_{restart}$ to p_2 and is restarted from c_1^1.
5) p_3 sends m_3 to p_1. p_1 receives m_3 and takes c_2^1. c_2^1 is active and $W_1^1 = \{p_1, p_3\}$.
6) On receipt of $m_{restart}$ from p_1, p_2 is restarted from c_1^2. Then, p_2 sends $m_{restart}$ to p_3 and is restarted form c_1^2.
7) p_1 sends m_4 to p_2. p_2 receives m_4 and takes c_2^2. c_2^2 is active and $W_2^1 = \{p_1, p_2\}$.
8) On receipt of $m_{restart}$ from p_2, p_3 is restarted from c_1^3. Then, p_3 sends $m_{restart}$ to p_1 and is restarted form c_1^3.

The recovery procedure may be continued forever, i.e. the livelock occurs. Now, we introduce a *generation* concept as follows:

Definition (generation of process) A generation $g(p_i)$ of p_i is assigned to s, i.e. $g(p_i) = s$ if the checkpoint most recently taken by p_i is c_s^i. □

Definition (generation of event) A generation $g(e)$ of an event e in p_i is assigned to s, i.e. $g(e) = s$ if $g(p_i) = s$ when e occurs in p_i. □

We assume that each process p_i takes c_1^i at the initial state. Each time p_i takes c_s^i, $g(p_i)$ is incremented by one. If a recovery $r_{s,t}^i$ occurs in p_i, p_i takes a checkpoint c_{t+1}^i just before p_i is restarted. Each time $s(m)$ occurs in p_i, $g(s(m))$ is piggied back by m. Suppose that an event e^i occurs in p_i and p_i receives m sent by p_j at $s(m)$ where $e^i \rightarrow s(m)$. If $r_{s,t}^i$ where $s \leq g(e^i) \leq t$ occurs in p_i, p_i has to discard m. If p_i accepts m, the livelock occurs as shown in Figure 1. This is realized by the generations of events. If $g(e)$ is piggied back by m and there has occurred $r_{s,t}^i$ where $s \leq g(e) \leq t$ in p_i, p_i has to discard m for the livelock-free recovery. In order to implement the livelock-free asynchronous recovery, generation vectors have to be piggied back by the messages transmitted among the processes.

3 Protocol

3.1 Assumptions

A distributed system $S = \langle V, L \rangle$ consists of a finite set $V = \{p_1, \ldots, p_n\}$ of processes and a set $L \subseteq V^2$ of channels. We make the following assumptions on S.

A1 Every channel in L is reliable and FIFO.

A2 S is asynchronous, i.e. the maximum message transmission delay is unbounded.

A3 Each process has a stable storage.

p_i records the state information in the log at each checkpoint. The sth checkpoint taken by p_i is denoted by c_s^i. Initially, every p_i takes c_1^i. p_i is restarted from one of the checkpoints taken by p_i if p_i fails or p_i receives a restart request. If $g(p_i) = t$ and p_i is restarted from c_s^i ($s \leq t$), the recovery is denoted by $r_{s,t}^i$. c_u^i is *active* unless there occurs $r_{s,t}^i$ where $s \leq u \leq t$ in p_i. c_u^i becomes *inactive* if there occurs $r_{s,t}^i$ where $s \leq u \leq t$ in p_i. c_u^i is *obsolete* if c_u^i is inactive or p_i will never be restarted from c_u^i. If p_i knows that c_u^i is obsolete, p_i can remove c_u^i.

An application message m contains the data $m.data$ and a generation vector $m.G = \langle m.g_1, \ldots, m.g_n \rangle$. A restart request R_{req} contains a generation vector $R_{req}.G = \langle R_{req}.g_1, \ldots, R_{req}.g_n \rangle$. A process p_i manipulates the following variables. Here, $Neighbor^i$ be a constant set of neighbor of p_i.

- A generation vector $G^i = \langle g_1^i, \ldots, g_n^i \rangle$ named a *checkpoint generation vector* in p_i. Every event e^i that will occur in p_i causally depends on an event e^j in p_j where $g(e^j) = g_j^i$, i.e. $e^j \to e^i$. Initially, $g_i^i = 1$ and $g_j^i = 0 (j \neq i)$.

- A set of generation $Inactive^i$. $u \in Inactive^i$ iff c_u^i is inactive, i.e. $r_{s,t}^i$ occurs in p_i, where $s \leq u \leq t$.

- A subset $Flow^i \subseteq Neighbor^i$. $p_j \in Flow^i$ iff p_i sends a message to p_j after the most recent checkpoint. Each time p_i takes a checkpoint, $Flow^i = \emptyset$.

- A sequence $Receive^i$ of messages received after the most recent checkpoint in p_i: Each time p_i takes a checkpoint, $Receive^i = \emptyset$.

Each time p_i takes c_s^i, $Flow^i$ and $Receive^i$ are recorded in the log with the state information as $Flow_s^i$ and $Receive_s^i$, respectively.

3.2 Failure-free execution

The protocol for taking consistent regional checkpoints is invoked each time a message-sending or message-receipt event occurs in a process. The protocol has to satisfy the following requirements:

R1 There is no orphan message even if S is restarted from one of the regional checkpoints.

R2 No message is lost.

R3 Each process p_i has the recovery view W_i^j if p_i recovers from the failure of p_j.

R4 No pretended checkpoint message is accepted.

For the requirements, the generation vector is manipulated as follows:

1) Each time $s(m)$ of m occurs in p_i, $G^i = \langle g_1^i, \ldots, g_n^i \rangle$ is piggied back with m as $m.G$, i.e. $m.g_j \leftarrow g_j^i$ for every j.

2) Each time $r(m)$ of m occurs in p_i, $G^i = max(G^i, m.G)$. $G' = max(G^i, G^j)$ is defined as $g_k' = max(g_k^i, g_k^j)$ for every k.

If $r(m)$ occurs in p_i where $g(p_i) = s$ and m is a checkpoint message from p_j, p_i takes c_{s+1}^i just before $r(m)$. Suppose that c_t^j is the most recent checkpoint in p_i. If $m.g_k \leq g_k^i$ for every process p_k, p_i is not required to take a checkpoint. p_i is also restarted from c_s^i for the consistent recovery if p_j is restarted from c_t^j. On the other hand, if $g_k^i < m.g_k$ for some p_k, p_i has to take a checkpoint c_{s+1}^i. Unless p_i takes c_{s+1}^i, m becomes an orphan message if p_j is restarted from c_t^j. Hence, R1 is satisfied.

To assure that no message be lost, if p_i receives m, m is added to $Receive^i$. Each time p_i takes c_{s+1}^i, the messages in $Receive^i$ are moved to $Receive_s^i$ and $Receive^i = \emptyset$. If $r_{s,t}^i$ occurs in p_i, every message m satisfying the following conditions is received:

1) $m \in Receive_u^i (s \leq u < t)$ or $m \in Receive^i$

2) $m.g_j < (g_j^i)_s$ for some p_j where $G_s^i = \langle (g_1^i)_s, \ldots, (g_n^i)_s \rangle$ is assigned to c_s^i.

Hence, R2 is satisfied.

If p_i sends an application message to a neighbor p_j at $s(m)$, p_j is added to $Flow^i$. Each time p_i takes c_{s+1}^i, the processes in $Flow^i$ are moved to $Flow_s^i$ and $Flow^i = \emptyset$. If $r_{s,t}^i$ occurs in p_i, p_i sends a restart request message R_{req} to every neighbor p_j where $p_j \in \cup_{s \leq u < t} Flow_u^i$ or $p_j \in Flow^i$. Hence, R3 is satisfied.

S has to prevent from the livelocks caused by the asynchronous recovery. By the generation vector, p_i never accepts phantom checkpoint messages. Each time $r_{s,t}^i$ occurs in p_i, $Inactive^i$ is updated to $Inactive^i \cup \{u | s \leq u \leq t\}$. Let m be a message taken out of the channel $\langle p_j, p_i \rangle$ where $m.G = \langle m.g_1, \ldots, m.g_n \rangle$ is piggied back.

[Livelock-free message receipt] On receipt of m from p_j, p_i discards m if $m.g_i \in Inactive^i$. Otherwise, p_i accepts m. □

If $m.g_i \in Inactive^i$, there exists an event e^i such that $g(e^i) \in Inactive^i$ and $e^i \to s(m)$. Since e^i is canceled by one of the recovery which occurred in p_i, $s(m)$ also has to be canceled, i.e. m is a phantom checkpoint message. Thus, m is discarded and R4 is satisfied, i.e. the recovery becomes livelock-free.

3.3 Recovery

If a process p_i fails, the recovery procedure is initiated. p_i is restarted from the most recent checkpoint c_s^i where $s = g(p_i)$. To keep S consistent, every process p_j in which an event e^j occurs where $c_s^i \to e^j$ also has to be restarted. This is realized by using $Flow^i$ and the message diffusion [4]. p_i has to send restart requests to every process p_j to which p_i sends an application message m after c_s^i. Here, p_j has to be restarted from the checkpoint before $r(m)$. In our protocol, only and all the processes to be restarted are recorded in $Flow^i$. Thus, p_i sends a restart request to each $p_j \in Flow^i$. Moreover, every message m received after c_s^i has to be accepted by the application again. Since $s(m)$ satisfies $c_s^i \not\to s(m)$, m becomes a lost message unless p_i accepts m again after the recovery. Thus, all the messages in $Receive^i$ are put into the buffer in

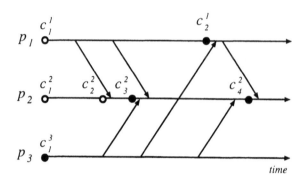

Figure 2: Garbage collection.

p_i. p_i accepts the messages again in the recovery procedure. Here, the failed process p_i is restarted asynchronously.

On the other hand, if an operational process p_i receives a restart request, p_i also has to be restarted. At first, p_i finds the most recent checkpoint c_s^i to keep S consistent. This is realized by piggying back a generation vector $R_{req}.G = \langle R_{req}.g_1, \ldots, R_{req}.g_n \rangle$ named a *recovery vector* by each restart request R_{req}. If p_j is restarted from c_t^j, the value t is assigned to $R_{req}.g_j$ and p_j sends R_{req} to all the processes in $Flow^j$. Now, p_i finds the oldest checkpoint c_s^i such that $R_{req}.g_j \leq (g_j^i)_s$ for every p_j. After that, p_i sends the restart requests and puts the received application messages to be accepted again after the recovery into the buffer as the failed process. Here, an operational process p_i is also restarted from c_s^i asynchronously.

Each process p_i in which a recovery $r_{s,t}^i$ occurs adds $\{s, \ldots, t\}$ to $Inactive^i$. If p_i receives an application message m where $m.g_i \in \{s, \ldots, t\}$, p_i discards m. According to this procedure, no livelock occurs even in the asynchronous recovery procedure.

3.4 Garbage collection

In order to reduce the storage used for the information at checkpoints, a garbage collection procedure has to be executed to remove the obsolete checkpoints. If p_i would never be restarted from c_s^i both for recovering from the failure of p_i and for keeping the system consistent even in the failure of any $p_j \neq p_i$, c_s^i has to be discarded. Here, we also use the generation vector. Let $G_s^i = \langle (g_1^i)_s, \ldots, (g_n^i)_s \rangle$ be the checkpoint generation vector of c_s^i and $G^i = \langle g_1^i, \ldots, g_n^i \rangle$ be the generation vector manipulated in p_i. If $s \leq t$ for every t where $(g_j^i)_t = g_j^i \neq 0$ for some j, p_i is restarted from c_s^i when p_j fails. Otherwise, p_i is never restarted from c_s^i and p_i discards c_s^i.

For example, in Figure 2 $S = \langle V, L \rangle$ where $V = \{p_1, p_2, p_3\}$. The checkpoint generation vectors for every c_s^i are as follows: $c_1^1 = \langle 1, 0, 0 \rangle$, $c_2^1 = \langle 2, 0, 1 \rangle$, $c_1^2 = \langle 0, 1, 0 \rangle$, $c_2^2 = \langle 1, 2, 0 \rangle$, $c_3^2 = \langle 1, 3, 0 \rangle$, $c_4^2 = \langle 2, 4, 1 \rangle$, $c_1^3 = \langle 0, 0, 1 \rangle$. If p_1 fails, p_1 and p_2 are restarted from c_2^1 and c_4^2, respectively. If p_2 fails, p_2 is restarted from c_4^2. p_1, p_2 and p_3 are restarted from c_2^1, c_2^2 and c_1^3, respectively, if p_3 fails. Since c_1^1, c_1^2 and c_2^2 are obsolete, they have to be discarded.

By using the garbage collection procedure, p_i has only one checkpoint from which p_i is restarted if p_j fails and p_i and p_j are in the same recovery domain.

Theorem 5 There are at most n active checkpoints in each p_i. □

4 Evaluation

In the proposed protocol, since p_i discards any phantom checkpoint messages, p_i is restarted from the checkpoint at most once for a failure of process. Hence, the protocol realizes the asynchronous livelock-free recovery. Here, $O(l)$ restart requests are transmitted for the recovery from the failure of p_i where l is the number of processes included in D_i.

Now, we evaluate the overhead for the checkpointing procedure and the recovery procedure in the proposed protocol and the conventional synchronous protocol [8]. The conventional protocol is based on the two-phase commitment protocol both in checkpointing and recovery procedure. Thus, the number of the additional messages is $O(N)$ where N is the number of processes in S and the required time is $O(D)$ where D is the diameter of S. In our protocol, no additional message is transmitted in the checkpointing procedure. In the asynchronous recovery procedure, only $O(n)$ additional messages are transmitted where n is the number of processes included in a recovery domain of a failed process. The required time is $O(d)$ where d is the diameter of the recovery domain. Since $n \ll N$ and $d \ll D$ in a large-scale distributed system, our protocol reduces the overhead.

5 Conclusion

This paper has proposed the protocol for taking consistent regional checkpoints and restarting the processes asynchronously in a distributed system. In the checkpointing procedure, no additional messages are transmitted and no process is blocked. The number of processes required to take a checkpoint is the minimum. Each process keeps at most n checkpoints where n is the number of processes. If some process fails, the minimum number of processes are restarted from the checkpoints asynchronously. Since the process is restarted at most once for a failure of process by discarding phantom checkpoint messages, the recovery protocol is livelock-free. To realize the recovery, each message contains a n-size vector of generation and only $O(l)$ messages are transmitted where l is the number of channels. Hence, the reliable and available large-scale distributed systems can be easily and effectively developed and operated by using the protocol proposed in this paper.

Bibliography

1) Bernstein, P. A., Hadzilacos, V., and Goodman, N., "Concurrency Control and Recovery in Database Systems," *Addison-Wesley*, pp. 222–261 (1987).

2) Bhargava, B. and Lian, S.R., "Independent Checkpointing and Concurrent Rollback for Recovery in Distributed Systems," *Proc. of the 7th International Symposium on Reliable Distributed Systems*, pp. 3–12 (1988).

3) Chandy, K. M. and Lamport L., "Distributed Snapshots: Determining Global States of Distributed Systems," *ACM Trans. on Computer Systems*, Vol. 3, No. 1, pp. 63–75 (1985).

4) Dijkstra, E. W. and Scholten, C. S., "Termination Detection for Diffusing Computation," *Information Processing Letters*, Vol. 11, No. 1, pp. 1–4 (1980).

5) Higaki, H. and Takizawa, M., "Group Communication Protocol for Flexible Distributed Systems," *Proc. of the 3rd International Conference on Network Protocols*, (1996).

6) Juang, T. T. Y. and Venkatesan, S., "Efficient Algorithms for Crash Recovery in Distributed Systems," *Proc. of the 10th Conference on Foundations of Software Technology and Theoretical Computer Science (LNCS)*, pp. 349–361 (1990).

7) Kim, J.L. and Park, T., "An Efficient Protocol for Checkpointing Recovery in Distributed Systems," *IEEE Trans. on Parallel and Distributed Systems*, Vol. 4, No. 8, pp. 955-960 (1993).

8) Koo, R. and Toueg, S., "Checkpointing and Rollback-Recovery for Distributed Systems," *IEEE Trans. on Software Engineering*, Vol. SE-13, No. 1, pp. 23–31 (1987).

9) Lamport, L., "Time, Clocks, and the Ordering of Events in a Distributed System," *Communications of the ACM*, Vol. 21, No. 7, pp. 558–565 (1978).

10) Manivannan, D. and Singhal, M., "A Low-Overhead Recovery Technique Using Quasi-Synchronous Checkpointing," *Proc. of the 16th International Conference on Distributed Computing Systems*, pp. 100–107 (1996).

11) Perterson, S. L. and Kearns, P., "Rollback Based on Vector Time," *Proc. of the 12th International Symposium on Reliable Distributed Systems*, pp. 68–77 (1996).

12) Randell, B., "System Structure for Software Fault Tolerance," *IEEE Trans. on Software Engineering*, Vol. SE-1, No. 2, pp. 220–232 (1975).

13) Strom, R. E. and Yemini, S., "Optimistic Recovery in Distributed Systems," *ACM Trans. on Computer Systems*, Vol. 3, No. 3, pp. 204–226 (1985).

14) Tong, Z., Kain, R. Y., and Tsai, W. T., "Rollback Recovery in Distributed Systems Using Loosely Synchronized Clocks," *IEEE Trans. on Parallel and Distributed Systems*, Vol. 3, No. 2, pp. 246–251 (1992).

22

Object-Based Locking Protocol for Replicated Objects

Kyouji Hasegawa

Hiroaki Higaki

Makoto Takizawa

Tokyo Denki University

ABSTRACT

In object-based systems, the objects are replicated to increase the performance, reliability, and availability. We propose an object-based locking (OBL) protocol to lock replicas of objects supporting abstract operations by extending the quorum-based method to the abstract objects. Here, the number of the replicas locked is decided based on the access frequency and the strength of the lock mode. Unless two operations conflict, subsets of the replicas locked by the operations do not intersect even if the operations change the replicas. We newly propose a version vector to identify what operation instances are computed in a replica.

1 Introduction

In order to increase the reliability, availability, and performance of the system, objects are replicated in the system. The replicas of the object have to be mutually consistent. In the two-phase locking (2PL) protocol [1, 2], one of the replicas is locked for *read* and all the replicas for *write*, i.e. *read-one-write-all* principal is used. The method is not efficient for write-dominated applications. In the quorum-based protocol [3], some numbers Q_r and Q_w of the replicas are locked for *read* and *write*, respectively. Here, $Q_r + Q_w > a$ for the number a of the replicas. Q_r and Q_w are decided based on how frequently *read* and *write* are issued.

The distributed applications are modeled to be a collection of multiple objects which are cooperating. Object-based frameworks like CORBA [7] is widely used to develop distributed applications. The objects support more abstract operations like *Deposit* mode for *Deposit* operation in a *bank* object than *read* and *write*. Each object is locked in an abstract mode corresponding to the abstract operation. Two operations op_1 and op_2 supported by an object o conflict if the result obtained by applying op_1 and op_2 to o depends on the computation order of op_1 and op_2 [1]. In this paper, we propose a novel locking scheme for the replicated objects named

OBL (*object-based locking*) protocol. The *OBL* protocol is an extension of the quorum-based protocol to the replicas of the abstract objects. Before computing an operation op_t on an object o, some number Q_t of the replicas of o are locked in the abstract mode for op_t. Q_t depends on how *restricted* the lock mode of op_t is and how *frequently* op_t is invoked. The more restricted and frequently op_t is used, the fewer number of the replicas are locked. Suppose two operations op_t and op_u are issued to replicas of the object o. If op_t and op_u change the state of o, the traditional quorum-based protocol requires that $Q_t + Q_u > a$. That is, both op_t and op_u are guaranteed to be computed on at least one replica. If op_t and op_u are computed on replicas o^t and o^u, respectively, the states of o^t and o^u are different. Then, if op_t and op_u are computed on o^t and o^u, respectively, o^t and o^u get the same state if op_t and op_u are compatible. In the quorum-based method, there must be at least one up-to-date replica where every write operation is computed. However, there can exist replicas from which the up-to-date version can be constructed even if there is no up-to-date replica. In order to identify what operations are computed in o^t and o^u, we newly propose a *version vector*. In the *OBL* protocol, fewer number of replicas are locked than the traditional quorum-based protocols and $2PL$.

In section 2, we present the system model. In section 3, we discuss abstract lock modes for the objects. In section 4, we discuss the *OBL* protocol.

2   Replicated Objects

A system is composed of objects $o_1, \ldots, o_n$ ($n \geq 1$) which are cooperating by exchanging messages in a network. Each object o_i supports a set of operations $op_{i1}, \ldots, op_{il_i}$ for manipulating o_i. o_i is encapsulated so that o_i can be manipulated only through the operations supported by o_i. By using the network, o_i can send messages to o_j with no message loss in the sending order.

If a transaction T sends a request op_i to an object o_i, o_i computes op_i. Here, op_i may invoke an operation op_{ij} on another object o_{ij}. o_i sends the response of op_i back to T. T is an atomic sequence of operations. T *commits* only if all the operations invoked by T successfully complete, i.e. the operations commit. The operation op invoked by T commits only if all the operations invoked by op commit. op is also an atomic unit of computation. Thus, the operations are *nested* [6]. An operation which changes the state of the object is referred to as *update* operation.

Let $op(s)$ denote a state obtained by applying op to a state s of o_i. An operation op_{ij} is *compatible* with op_{ik} iff $op_{ij} \circ op_{ik} (s_i) = op_{ik} \circ op_{ij} (s_i)$ for every state s_i of o_j. op_{ij} *conflicts* with op_{ik} unless op_{ij} is compatible with op_{ik}. The interleaved and parallel computation of operations has to be *serializable* [1]. That is, if some operation op_i of a transaction T_i precedes op_j of T_j which conflicts with op_i, every conflicting *operation* of T_i precedes T_j. On an operation receipt of a request op_i, o_i is locked in a *lock mode* $\mu(op_i)$ in order to make the computation serializable. Here, let M_i be a set of lock modes of o_i. If operations op_1 and op_2 are compatible, $\mu(op_1)$ and $\mu(op_2)$ are compatible. Otherwise, the modes conflict. For example,

Dlock and *Wlock* denote lock modes of *Deposit* and *Withdraw* of the bank object B, respectively. *Dlock* and *Wlock* are compatible. After computing op_i, the lock $\mu(op_i)$ on o_i is released. Let $C_i(m)$ be a set of lock modes with which m conflicts in o_i, i.e. $C_i(m) = \{m' \mid m' \text{ conflicts with } m\}$. We assume that the compatibility relation is symmetric. Hence, m is in $C_i(m')$ for every m' in $C_i(m)$.

Suppose an object o_i is locked in a mode m and op_i would be computed on o_i. If $\mu(op_i)$ is *compatible* with m, op_i can be started to be computed on o_i. Otherwise, op_i has to wait until the lock of m is released.

3 Abstract Lock Modes

Replicas of an object o_i are locked in a mode $\mu(op_i)$ before op_i is computed. If o_i is already locked by modes conflicting with $\mu(op_i)$, op_i blocks. The more modes conflict with $\mu(op_i)$, the more often op_i blocks. A lock mode m_1 is *more restricted* than m_2 iff $C_i(m_1) \supseteq C_i(m_2)$.

[Example 1] Let *rlock* and *wlock* be lock modes for *read* and *write*, respectively, in a file object f. $C_f(rlock) = \{wlock\}$ and $C_f(wlock) = \{wlock, rlock\}$. Since $C_f(rlock) \subseteq C_f(wlock)$, *wlock* is more restricted than *rlock*. □

[Example 2] A *bank* object B supports operations *Deposit, Withdraw, Check*, and *Audit*. Let *Dlock, Wlock, Clock*, and *Alock* show modes $\mu(Deposit)$, $\mu(Withdraw)$, $\mu(Check)$, and $\mu(Audit)$, respectively. *Dlock* and *Wlock* are compatible. *Clock* conflicts with *Dlock* and *Wlock*. *Audit* gets the data on the accounts and stores them in B. Hence, *Alock* conflicts with *Dlock* and *Wlock*, but is compatible with *Clock*. $C_B(Dlock) = C_B(Wlock) = \{Alock, Clock\}$ and $C_B(Clock) = C_B(Alock) = \{Dlock, Wlock\}$. Since $C_B(Dlock) \cap C_B(Clock) = \phi$, there is no relation among *Clock* and *Dlock*. □

Let $\varphi(m)$ be usage frequency of a mode m, i.e. how frequently operations of m are issued to o_i. Here, $\sum_{m \in M_i} \varphi(m) = 1$. The *weighted strength* $\|C_i(m)\|$ of m is defined to be $\sum_{m' \in C_i(m)} \varphi(m')$ (≤ 1).

[Definition] A mode m_1 is *stronger* than m_2 ($m_1 \succeq m_2$) iff $m_1 \in C_i(m_2)$, $m_2 \in C_i(m_1)$, and $\|C_i(m_1)\| \geq \|C_i(m_2)\|$. □

Let m_1 and m_2 be modes $\mu(op_1)$ and $\mu(op_2)$ in an object o_i, respectively. If $\|C_i(m_1)\| \geq \|C_i(m_2)\|$, op_1 has a bigger blocking probability that op_i waits for the release of the lock conflicting with op_i than op_2.

In Example 1, *wlock* $\succeq$ *rlock* since $C_f(wlock) \subset C_f(rlock)$. In Example 2, suppose that the usage ratios of *Alock, Clock, Dlock*, and *Wlock* are 10%, 20%, 40%, and 30%, respectively, i.e. $\varphi(Alock) = 0.1$, $\varphi(Clock) = 0.2$, $\varphi(Dlock) = 0.4$, and $\varphi(Wlock) = 0.3$. $\|C_B(Clock)\| = \|C_B(Alock)\| = \varphi(Dlock) + \varphi(Wlock) = 0.7$. $\|C_B(Dlock)\| = \|C_B(Wlock)\| = \varphi(Clock) = 0.3$. Hence, *Dlock* $\preceq$ *Clock*, *Wlock* $\preceq$ *Clock*, and *Alock* $\preceq$ *Clock* since $\|C_B(Dlock)\| < \|C_B(Clock)\|$, $\|C_B(Wlock)\| < \|C_B(Dlock)\|$, and $\|C_B(Alock)\| \leq \|C_B(Clock)\|$.

The modes supported by o_i are partially ordered by the strength relation "$\preceq$". A mode m is referred to as *maximal* in o_i iff there is no mode m' such that $m \preceq m'$.

m is *maximum* iff $m' \preceq m$ for every mode m'. The *minimal* and *minimum* modes are similarly defined. m is a *least upper bound* (*lub*) $m_1 \sqcup m_2$ of modes m_1 and m_2 iff $m_1 \preceq m$, $m_2 \preceq m$, and there is no mode m' such that $m_1 \preceq m' \preceq m$ and $m_2 \preceq m' \preceq m$. The *greatest lower bound* (*glb*) $m_1 \sqcap m_2$ is similarly defined.

Next, we discuss how to lock replicas o_i^1, ..., $o_i^{a_i}$ in the cluster $R(o_i)$. We extend the traditional quorum-based protocol to the replicas in the object-based systems. Let N_{it} be a set of replicas to be locked by op_{it}, named a quorum set of op_{it}. Let Q_{it} be $|N_{it}|$ named a quorum number of op_{it}. The more replicas are locked, the more communication and computation are required. Hence, the more frequently op_{it} is invoked, the fewer number of replicas are locked. Q_{it} is decided depending on the probability that op_{it} conflicts with other operations of o_i.

[**OBL constraints**]

  1. If $\mu(op_{it})$ conflicts with $\mu(op_{iu})$, $Q_{it} + Q_{iu} > a_i$.
  2. $Q_{it} \geq Q_{iu}$ iff $\|C_i(op_{it})\| \geq \|C_i(op_{iu})\|$.

A transaction T locks replicas $o_i^1, \ldots, o_i^{a_i}$ of o_i by the following locking scheme before manipulating the replicas by an operation op_{it}.

[**Locking scheme**]

  1. First, a quorum set N_{it} is decided for op_{it}.
  2. Every replica in N_{it} is locked in the mode $\mu(op_{it})$.
  3. If all the replicas in N_{it} are locked, the replicas in N_{it} are manipulated by op_{it}.
  4. When T commits, the locks on the replicas in N_{it} are released. $\square$

4   Locking Protocol

4.1   Quorums on abstract operations

According to the quorum-based protocol, $Q_{it} + Q_{iu} > a_i$ for a pair of operations op_{it} and op_{iu} where a_i is the number of the replicas of o_i if op_{it} and op_{iu} are update operations. In the OBL protocol, $Q_{it} + Q_{iu} > a_i$ if op_{it} and op_{iu} conflict with one another. The OBL protocol satisfies the following properties.

[**Properties**] For every pair of conflicting operations op_{it} and op_{iu}:

  1) At least one replica computes both of op_{it} and op_{iu}.
  2) If two replicas o_i^h and o_i^k compute op_{it} and op_{iu}, o_i^h and o_i^k compute op_{it} and op_{iu} in the same order. $\square$

[**Example 3**] Replicas B^2, B^3, and B^4 of the bank object B support four operations *Deposit* (D), *Withdraw* (W), *Check* (C), and *Audit* (A) shown in Example 2. D is compatible with W. C is compatible with A. D and W conflict with C and A. D, W, and A are update operations but C is not. Let Q_D be 3 and Q_W be 2. Each replica B^i has a version number V^i whose initial value is 0. Hence, $Q_D + Q_W > 4$. Hence, D is issued to B^1, B^2, and B^3 and $V^1 = V^2 = V^3 = 1$. Then, W is issued to B^1 and B^4. Since $V^1(= 1) > V^4(= 0)$, W is computed on B^1 and $V^1 = 2$. B^4 is updated by sending the state of B^1. Here, $V^1 = V^4 = 2$ and $V^2 = V^3 = 1$. If the number of replicas to be locked is decided based on the conflicting relation among the abstract operations, we can reduce the number of the replicas to be locked but cannot decide which replica is up-to-date by using the version numbers. Here, $Q_{it} + Q_{iu} > a_i$ if op_{it} and op_{iu} conflict. For example, Q_D, Q_W, Q_C, and Q_A can be 2, 2, 3, and 3, respectively. First, suppose that D is issued to B^1 and B^2 and that W is issued to B^3 and B^4 since $Q_D = Q_W = 2$. Here, the version numbers of the replicas are changed to 1, i.e. $V^1 = V^2 = V^3 = V^4 = 1$. Then, C is issued to B^1, B^2, and B^3 since $Q_C = 3$. Here, the state of B^3 is different from the states of B^1 and B^2 although they have the same version number 1.

Since D and W are compatible, the replicas can be up-to-date if the instance of D computed on B^1 and B^2 is also computed on B^3 and B^4 and the instance of W computed on B^3 and B^4 is computed on B^1 and B^2. Then, C can be computed on one of the replicas, say B^1. Thus, the replicas can be up-to-date by computing operations which are not computed on the replicas but computed on the others. Problem is that the version numbers of B^1, B^2, B^3, and B^4 are 1 after D and W are computed. We cannot consider that the states of B^1 and B^2 are different from B^3 and B^4 by using the version numbers of the replicas. □

A replica o_i^h is considered to be newer than o_i^k if every operation computed in o_i^k is computed in o_i^h. We define a precedent relation "→" among the replicas to show which replica is newer.

[**Definition**] A replica o_i^h *precedes* o_i^k ($o_i^h \rightarrow o_i^k$) iff every update operation computed on o_i^k is computed on o_i^h. □

$o_i^h \rightarrow o_i^k$ means that o_i^k is obsolete since some update operations computed on o_i^h are not computed on o_i^k. The quorum-based method requires that every quorum set include at least one maximum replica o_i^h, i.e. $o_i^h \rightarrow o_i^k$ for every replica o_i^k. That is, if two update operations op_{it} and op_{iu} are issued, at least one replica o_i^h computes both op_{it} and op_{iu}. On the other hand, in our protocol, no replica may compute both of op_{it} and op_{iu} if op_{it} and op_{iu} are compatible even if op_{it} and op_{iu} are update ones. Hence, there may be no maximum replica but exist multiple maximal replicas. A cluster $R(o_i)$ is *complete* iff there is a maximum replica in $R(o_i)$. Although the $R(o_i)$ is complete in the quorum-based method, $R(o_i)$ may be incomplete in our protocol.

[**Definition**] Every pair of maximal replicas o_i^h and o_i^k are *unifiable* iff o_i^h and o_i^k get the same state if every update operation not computed on one of o_i^h and o_i^k is computed on the other replica. □

Let $\langle op_{h1}, \ldots, op_{hl_h} \rangle$ be a sequence π_{hk} of update operations computed on o_i^h but not on o_i^k. Let $\langle op_{k1}, \ldots, op_{kl_k} \rangle$ be a sequence π_{kh} of update operations computed on o_i^k but not on o_i^h. If every pair of op_{hu} and op_{kv} are compatible for $u = 1, \ldots, l_h$ and $v = 1, \ldots, l_k$, a state obtained by applying π_{hk} to o_i^k is the same as a state obtained by applying π_{kh} to o_i^h. The state obtained here is referred to as *least upper bound* (*lub*) of o_i^h and o_i^k ($o_i^h \cup o_i^k$) with respect to the precedent relation →. For example, suppose B^1 and B^2 compute D and B^3 and B^4 compute W in Example 3. Here, $\pi_{13} = \pi_{23} = \langle W \rangle$ and $\pi_{31} = \pi_{41} = \langle D \rangle$. The unifiable relation "≡" is equivalent. Let $U(o_i^h)$ be an equivalent set { $o_i^k \mid o_i^k \equiv o_i^h$ in $R(o_i)$ } for a maximal replica o_i^h. A cluster $R(o_i)$ is *consistent* iff $U(o_i^h) = U(o_i^k)$ for some pair of maximal replicas o_i^h

and o_i^k in $R(o_i)$. Here, $U(o_i^h)$ is referred to as *unifiable* set $U(o_i)$ of $R(o_i)$. In the consistent cluster, a least upper bound of $U(o_i)$ shows a possible maximum replica to be obtained in $R(o_i)$. In the quorum-based protocol, there exists a maximum replica. If $R(o_i)$ is inconsistent, the replicas cannot be consistent.

In an incomplete cluster $R(o_i)$, some operations computed on a maximal replica have to be computed later on other maximal replicas which have not yet computed the operations. *Incomplete* operations are defined to be update operations which are computed on some replicas but not on every replica in a unifiable set $U(o_i)$ of $R(o_i)$. In Example 3, D and W are incomplete operations. B^1 and B^2 are unifiable, i.e. $B^1 \equiv B^2$. $U(o_i) = \{B^1,\ B^2,\ B^3,\ B^4\}$. Every pair of incomplete operations not computed on the same replica are computed not on every replica. Complete operations are update operations computed on every replica in $U(o_i)$.

Let us consider how an operation op_{it} is computed on the replicas. op_{it} can be computed on a replica o_i^h in the quorum set N_{it} if every incomplete operation which conflicts with op_{it} is computed on o_i^h. However, there might not exist such a replica o_i^h in $R(o_i)$. Hence, op_{it} is computed as follows.

1. Before computing op_{it} on every replica in N_{it}, incomplete operations on each maximal replica in N_{it} are computed on the other maximal replicas in N_{it} as presented before. Here, every maximal replica is the newest one.

2. Then, op_{it} is computed on the maximal replicas.

3. If op_{it} is an update operation, the states of the replicas in N_{it} have to be changed. The non-maximal replicas in $R(o_i)$ compute every update operation computed in the maximal ones but not computed in the replicas. In another way, one of the maximal replicas sends the state to the other replicas.

Here, every replica in N_{it} is the newest one, i.e. maximum replica in $R(o_{it})$.

4.2   Version vector

In our protocol, it is critical to identify what operations each replica has computed. As presented before, the version number cannot be used to maintain the consistency among the object replicas. Because some pair of update operations may not be computed in any replica if they do not conflict.

We introduce a *version vector* to identify what operations are computed on each replica. Each replica o_i^h has a bitmap vector $BM_i^h = \langle BM_{i1}^h,\ \ldots,\ BM_{il_i}^h \rangle$ and a counter vector $U_i^h = \langle U_{i1}^h,\ \ldots,\ U_{il_i}^h \rangle$. Each element BM_{it}^h shows a version of o_i^h with respect to an operation op_{it} of o_i. BM_{it}^h is a bitmap $\langle BM_{it}^{h1},\ \ldots,\ BM_{it}^{ha_i} \rangle$ showing to which replica op_{it} is issued. The kth bit BM_{it}^{hk} is 1 if op_{it} is issued to o_i^k, otherwise 0 ($k = 1,\ \ldots,\ a_i$). Each U_{it}^h is a *version number* of o_i^h with respect to op_{it}. U_{it}^h is incremented by one each time op_{it} is computed on o_i^h and op_{it} is an update operation. For example, vectors BM_B^i and U_B^i of a replica B^i are $\langle BM_{BD}^i,\ BM_{BW}^i,\ BM_{BC}^i,\ BM_{BA}^i \rangle$ and $\langle U_{BD}^i,\ U_{BW}^i,\ U_{BC}^i,\ U_{BA}^i \rangle$, respectively, in Example 3 [Figure1]. Here, let V_{it}^h denote $U_{it}^h{}_{BM_{it}^h}$. For example, $V_{BD}^2 = 3_{1101}$ shows $BM_{BD}^2 = 1101$ and $U_{BD}^2 = 3$. This means that three instances of D are computed on a replica B^2 and

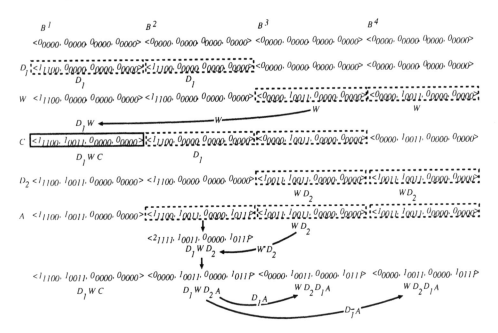

Figure 1: Version vector.

B^2 knows that the instances are also computed on B^1 and B^4. V_i^h is a version vector $\langle V_{i1}^h, \ldots, V_{il_i}^h \rangle$. Initially, $V_B^j = \langle 0_{0000}, 0_{0000}, 0_{0000}, 0_{0000} \rangle$ in each replica B^j for $j = 1, \ldots, 4$. Suppose D is issued to B^1 and B^2. $V_B^1 = V_B^2 = \langle 1_{1100}, 0_{0000}, 0_{0000}, 0_{0000} \rangle$. Then, W is issued to B^3 and B^4. $V_B^3 = V_B^4 = \langle 0_{0000}, 1_{0011}, 0_{0000}, 0_{0000} \rangle$. Suppose C is issued to B^1, B^2, and B^3. $V_B^1 = V_B^2 \neq V_B^3$. Since $V_{BD}^1 = V_{BD}^2 = 1_{1100}$ and $V_{BW}^3 = 1_{0011}$, B^1 and B^2 knows that D is issued to B^1 and B^2, and B^3 know that W is issued to B^3 and B^4. Here, any replica is not maximum because every replica has computed either D or W. One replica, say B^1 is selected. The instance of W computed on B^3 is computed on B^1. V_{BW}^1 is changed to be 1_{0011}, i.e. $V_B^1 = \langle 1_{1100}, 1_{0011}, 0_{0000}, 0_{0000} \rangle$. Then, C is computed on B^1. Since C is not an update operation, V_{BC}^1 is not changed. Suppose D is issued to B^3 and B^4. $V_B^3 = V_B^4 = \langle 1_{0011}, 1_{0011}, 0_{0000}, 0_{0000} \rangle$. Then, A is issued to B^2, B^3, and B^4. Since $V_{BD}^2 = 1_{1100}$ and $V_{BD}^3 = 1_{0011}$, B^2 and B^3 exchange the instances of D computed. In addition, $V_{BW}^2 = 0_{0000}$ and $V_{BW}^3 = 1_{0011}$. Here, the instances of D and W computed on B^3 have to be computed on B^2 to obtain the least upper bound (lub) version of B^2. Since D and W are compatible, D and W can be computed on B^2 in any order. Now, A is computed on B^2 after D and W are computed. $V_B^2 = \langle 2_{1111}, 1_{0011}, 0_{0000}, 1_{0111} \rangle$ and A changes the state of B^2. If the state of B^2 is sent to B^3 and B^4, B^3 and B^4 are updated with the state of B^2. $V_B^2 = V_B^3 = V_B^4$. Here, $V_{BD}^1 = V_{BD}^2 = V_{BD}^3 = V_{BD}^4$ (= 2_{1111}) is initialized to be 0_{0000} since the same instances of D are surely computed on every replica. In stead of sending the states, B^3 and B^4 can compute A. Then, B^2 can send a sequence of operation instances computed on B^2 to the other replicas.

Let BM_i^h and BM_i^k be bitmaps for o_i^h and o_i^k, respectively. BM_i^h is *included* in

BM_i^k ($BM_i^h \subseteq BM_i^k$) iff $BM_i^{kj} = 1$ if $BM_i^{hj} = 1$ for $j = 1, \ldots, a_i$. $BM_i^h \cup BM_i^k$ shows $\langle BM^1, \ldots, BM^{a_i} \rangle$ where $BM^j = 1$ if $BM_i^{hj} = BM_i^{kj} = 1$, otherwise 0 for $j = 1, \ldots, a_i$.

- $V_{it}^h \leq V_{it}^k$ iff $U_{it}^h \leq U_{it}^k$ and $BM_{it}^h \subseteq BM_{it}^k$.
- $V_i^h \leq V_i^k$ iff $V_{it}^h \leq V_{it}^k$ for every operation op_{it}.

If $BM_{it}^h \cap BM_{it}^k \neq \phi$, there is no ordering relation between V_{it}^h and V_{it}^k even if $U_{it}^h \leq U_{it}^k$ or $U_{it}^k \leq U_{it}^h$. For example, suppose $V_B^1 = \langle 1_{1100}, 0_{0000}, 0_{0000}, 0_{0000} \rangle$ and $V_B^3 = \langle 2_{1110}, 0_{0000}, 0_{0000}, 0_{0000} \rangle$. Here, $V_B^1 \leq V_B^3$. Here, if $V_B^2 = \langle 2_{0011}, 0_{0000}, 0_{0000}, 0_{0000} \rangle$, V_B^1 and V_B^2 are not compared. In a subset $N \subseteq R(o_i)$, V_i^h is *maximal* iff there is no version vector V_i^k of o_i^k such that $V_i^k \geq V_i^h$.

We define an operation $\cup$ for a pair of vector elements V_{it}^h and V_{it}^k on op_{it}:

- $V_{it}^h \cup V_{it}^k = \begin{cases} V_{it}^k & \text{if } V_{it}^h \leq V_{it}^k. \\ V_{it}^h & \text{if } V_{it}^h \geq V_{it}^k. \\ \langle U_{it}^h + U_{it}^k, BM_{it}^h \cup BM_{it}^k \rangle & \text{otherwise.} \end{cases}$
- $V_i^h \cup V_i^k = \langle V_{i1}^h \cup V_{i1}^k, \ldots, V_{il_i}^h \cup V_{il_i}^k \rangle$.

For example, suppose $V_B^2 = \langle 1_{0011}, 0_{0000}, 0_{0000}, 0_{0000} \rangle$ and $V_B^3 = \langle 1_{1100}, 1_{0011}, 0_{0000}, 0_{0000} \rangle$. $V_B^2 \cup V_B^3 = \langle 2_{1111}, 1_{0011}, 0_{0000}, 0_{0000} \rangle$.

[**Definition**] A version vector V_i^h is *equivalent* with V_i^k ($V_i^h \equiv V_i^k$) iff $V_{iv}^h = V_{iv}^k$ for every update operation op_{iv} conflicting with every pair of compatible operations op_{it} and op_{iu}. □

For example, D and W are compatible and conflict with A. Hence, $V_B^1 = \langle 1_{1100}, 0_{0000}, 0_{0000}, 2_{0101} \rangle$ is equivalent with $V_B^2 = \langle 0_{0000}, 1_{0011}, 0_{0000}, 2_{0101} \rangle$ since $V_{BA}^1 = V_{BA}^2 = 2_{0101}$. If $V_i^h \equiv V_i^k$, o_i^h and o_i^k can get the same state by computing compatible operations which are not yet computed on the replicas. For example, B^1 and B^2 get the same states if W is computed on B^1 and D is computed on B^2.

4.3 Locking protocol

We discuss a locking protocol by using the version vector. Suppose that op_{it} is issued to an object o_i. o_i^h has an operation log l_i^h for storing a sequence of operation instances computed on o_i^h. Let l_{it}^h be a subsequence of instances of op_{it} in the log l_i^h. For each operation instance op, let $op.BM$ be a bitmap showing replicas to which op is issued. U_{it}^h gives the number of operations in l_{it}^h.

[**Locking protocol**] An object o_s sends op_{it} to every replica in N_{it}.

1) All the replicas in N_{it} are locked in a mode $\mu(op_{it})$. Unless succeeded in locking the replicas, op_{it} aborts. Each replica o_i^h in N_{it} sends back a response with the version vector V_i^h and the log l_i^h to o_s.

2) On receipt of the responses from all the replicas in N_{it}, o_s obtains $V_s = \cup \{ V_i^k \mid o_i^k \in N_{it} \}$. Let $P_h(op_{it})$ denote a set $\{ op_{iu} \mid op_{iu}$ conflicts with op_{it}, $op.BM \neq \langle 1 \ldots 1 \rangle$, and o_i^h computes $op_{iu} \}$ of operations. o_s finds a replica o_i^h in N_{it} which is maximal with respect to operations conflicting with op_{it}.

3) If o_i^h is found at 2), o_s requires o_i^h to compute op_{it}. o_i^h computes op_{it}.

   3-1) If op_{it} is not an update operation, o_i^h sends a response to o_s.

3-2) Otherwise, o_i^h sends $P_h(op_{it})$ to a replica o_i^k in N_{it}. o_i^k computes every op_{iu} in $P_h(op_{it})$ unless o_i^k had computed op_{iu}. For every op_{iv} in $P_h(op_{it})$, $op_{iv}.BM := op_{iv}.BM \vee op_{it}.BM$. o_i^k sends a response back to o_s.

4) Unless o_i^h is found, o_s selects one maximal replica o_i^h in N_{it}. Let $P(op_{it})$ be { $op_{iu} \mid op_{iu}$ conflicts with op_{it} and op_{iu} is computed on some o_i^h in N_{it} }.

4-1) If op_{it} is an update operation, o_s sends $P(op_{it})$ to every replica in N_{it}. Each replica o_i^h in N_{it} computes every update op_{iu} computed in N_{it} which is not computed on o_i^h and then computes op_{it}. For every op_{iu} in $P(op_{it})$, $op_{iu}.BM := op_{iu}.BM \vee op.BM$ in o_i^h. o_i^h sends a response back to o_s.

4-2) If op_{it} is not an update one, o_s selects one maximal o_i^h in N_{it}. o_s sends $P(op_{it})$ to o_i^h. o_i^h computes every op_{iu} in $P(op_{it})$ if o_i^h had not computed op_{iu}. Then, o_i^h computes op_{it}. o_i^h sends a response back to o_s. □

Operations stored in the log have to be removed in order to reduce the size of the log l_i^h. The bitmap $op_{it}.BM$ in the log l_i^h shows that o_i^h knows that the instance op_{it} is computed on o_i^k if $BM^k = 1$. If $op_{it}.BM = \langle 1 \ldots 1 \rangle$, o_i^h knows that op_{it} is computed on every replica. However, o_i^h cannot remove op_{it} from l_i^h because another replica o_i^k may not yet know that every replica has computed op_{it}. Hence, an operation instance op_{iu} in l_i^h is removed as follows:

- op_{iu} is removed from the log l_i^h if $op_{iu}.BM = op_{iv}.BM = \langle 1 \ldots 1 \rangle$ for every operation op_{iv} in l_i^h which conflicts with op_{iu} and is computed before op_{iu}.

When BM_{it}^h gets $\langle 1 \ldots 1 \rangle$, the version number U_{it}^h and the bitmap BM_{it}^h are initialized again, i.e. $U_{it}^h := 0$ and $BM_{it}^h := \langle 0 \ldots 0 \rangle$. If $BM_{it}^h = \langle 1 \ldots 1 \rangle$ in some replica o_i^h, op_{it} is computed on every replica o_i^k in N_{it}. Thus, U_{it}^h shows how many instances of op_{it} are computed on o_i^t. If $BM_{it}^h \cap BM_{it}^k = \phi$ and ($U_{it}^h > 0$ or $U_{it}^k > 0$) for an update operation op_{it}, a sequence s^h of instances of op_{it} computed on o_i^h is different from a sequence s^k in o_i^k. s^h and s^k include U_{it}^h and U_{it}^k instances of op_{it}, respectively. In the OBL protocol, the sequences s^k and s^h are required to be computed on o_i^h and o_i^k, respectively. Then, BM_{it}^h and BM_{it}^k get $BM_{it}^h \cap BM_{it}^k$ and U_{it}^h and U_{it}^k get $U_{it}^h + U_{it}^k + 1$.

[**Proposition**] For every update operation op_{it}, $BM_{it}^h = BM_{it}^k$ and $U_{it}^h = U_{it}^k$ if $BM_{it}^h \cap BM_{it}^k \neq \phi$. □

[**Proposition**] For every update operation op_{it}, $U_{it}^h \leq U_{it}^k$ if $BM_{it}^h \subseteq BM_{it}^k$. □

[**Theorem**] For every update operation op_{it}, if $BM_{it}^h \subseteq BM_{it}^k$ and $U_{it}^h \leq U_{it}^k$, every instance of op_{it} computed on B_i^h is also computed on B_i^k. □

From the theorem and the properties of the OBL protocol, the following theorem holds.

[**Theorem**] If $V_i^h \leq V_i^k$, every pair of conflicting operation instances op_{it} and op_{iu} computed on o_i^h are computed on o_i^k in the same order. □

[**Theorem**] Every pair of maximal replicas o_i^h and o_i^k are unifiable to one unique replica.

[**Proof**] Assume op_{it} and op_{iu} conflict. If op_{it} is computed on o_i^h, op_{iu} is also computed on o_i^h. Otherwise, o_i^h is not maximal. Here, both of op_{it} and op_{iu} are computed on o_i^h or o_i^k or on none of them from the OBL properties. Operation instances which are computed on either one of o_i^h and o_i^k do not conflict. These operations can be computed in any order. Therefore, if operation instances computed on one replica are computed on the other replica, o_i^h and o_i^k get the same one. □

[**Theorem**] All the replicas are unifiable to one unique replica in the OBL protocol. □

5   Concluding Remarks

This paper has discussed the *object-based locking* (OBL) protocol on the replicas of the objects. The objects support more abstract types of operations than *read* and *write*. The strength relation among the lock modes is defined based on the conflicting relation and the usage frequencies of the operations. In addition, the version vector has been proposed to maintain the mutual consistency of the replicas. The replicas are not required to compute every update operation instance which has been computed on the other replicas if the operation instance is compatible with instances computed. By using OBL protocol, the efficient access to replicated objects can be realized in the distributed system.

Bibliography

1) P. A. Bernstein, V. Hadzilacos, and N. Goodman, "Concurrency Control and Recovery in Database Systems," *Addison-Wesley* (1987).

2) J. M. Carey and M. Livny, "Conflict Detection Tradeoffs for Replicated Data," *ACM TODS*, Vol. 16, No.4, pp. 703–746 (1991).

3) H. Garcia-Molina and D. Barbara, "How to Assign Votes in a Distributed System," *Journal of ACM*, Vol 32, No.4, pp. 841-860 (1985).

4) K. Hasegawa and M. Takizawa, "Optimistic Concurrency Control for Replicated Objects", *Proc. of the Int'l Symp. on Communications (ISCOM'97)*, pp. 149–152 (1997).

5) J. Jing, O. Bukhres, and A. Elmagarmid, "Distributed Lock Management for Mobile Transactions," *Proc. of IEEE ICDCS-15*, pp. 118-125 (1995).

6) J. E. Moss, "Nested Transactions : An Approach to Reliable Distributed Computing," *The MIT Press Series in Information Systems* (1985).

7) M. Silvano and C. S. Douglas, "Constructing Reliable Distributed Communication Systems with CORBA," *IEEE Communications Magazine*, Vol.35, No.2, pp.56-60 (1997).

8) T. Yoshida and M. Takizawa, "Model of Mobile Objects," *Proc. of the 7th DEXA (Lecture Notes in Computer Science, No 1134, Springer-Verlag)*, pp. 623–632 (1996).

23

The Algebra of Spatio-Temporal Intervals

Timothy K. Shih

Anthony Y. Chang

Yule-Chyun Lin

Tamkang University

ABSTRACT

The relations among temporal intervals can be used to model time dependent objects. We propose a fast mechanism for temporal relation compositions. A temporal transitive closure table is derived, and an interval-based temporal relation algebraic system is constructed. Thus, we propagate the time constraints of arbitrary two objects across long distances n by linear time. We also give a complete discussion of different possible domains of interval relations. A set of algorithms is proposed to detect time conflicts and to derive reasonable interval relations. The algorithms are extended for time-based media in an arbitrary n-dimensional space.

1   Introduction

Communication networks and multimedia applications usually contains a number of resources to be presented sequentially or concurrently. Temporal interval relations represent the timing among resources. These resources need to be analyzed to ensure that there is no time conflict among resources. Moreover, many of these resources, occupy period of time and screen space. These data can be heavily time-dependent, such as audio and video in a motion picture, and can require time-ordered presentation. The spatio-temporal relations among resources need to be computed and represented.

The importance of knowledge underlying temporal interval relations was found in many disciplines. As pointed out in [1], researchers of artificial intelligence, linguistics, and information science use temporal intervals as a time model for knowledge analysis. For instance, in a robot planning program, the outside world is constantly changed according to a robot's actions. The notion of "number three box is on the left of number two box" is true only within a temporal interval. The work discussed in [1] analyzes the relations among temporal intervals. However, the work [1] only states temporal interval relations. No spatial relation were discussed. We found that these relations can be generalized for spatial modeling.

Many researchers propose temporal modeling of multimedia objects. The work discussed in [3] presents a framework for data modeling and semantic abstraction of image/video data. Seven generalized n-ary relations were used to describe the temporal relations among n objects. The authors also defined spatial events in terms of these n-ary relations. A functional model extends media segments to include executable programs, live media streams and the links among them was proposed in [4]. Based on Allen's temporal interval relations, a set of directional and topological spatial relations were addressed in [5]. The authors also provided a set of spatial inference rules for automatic deduction. A methodology for spatial and temporal object composition under a distributed multimedia environment was proposed in [6]. A set of n-ary temporal relations with their temporal constraints were discussed in [7], which is an early result of the work addressed in [3]. The temporal model of reverse play and partial interval evaluation for midpoint suspension and resumption were also discussed. Algorithms for accessing objects in a database were presented. The work in [10] introduced a spatial and temporal model for actors of multimedia applications. A number of spatial and temporal operators were used to compose a presentation. The composition mechanism was defined in an extended BNF formal syntax definition. However, no discussion of the conflict situation among relations were found.

2   The Spatio-Temporal Relation Domains

According to the interval temporal relations intro-duced in [1], there are 13 relations ({ e, <, >, m, mi, d, di, o, oi, s, si, f, fi }), between two temporal intervals. We describe the symbolic constraint propagation. The general idea is to use the existing information about the relations among time intervals or instants to derive the composition relations.

The composition may result in a *multiple derivation*. For example, if "X before Y " and "Y during Z " , the composed relation for X and Z could be "before", "overlaps", "meets", "during", or "starts". If the composed relation could be any one of some relations, these derived relations are called reasonable relations in our discussion.

In some cases, relation compositions may result in a *conflict specification* due to the user specification or involved events synchronously. For example, if specifications "X before Y", "Y before Z", and "X after Z" are declared by the user, there exists a conflict between X and Z. When the specific relations are not found in derived reasonable set, the specification may cause conflicts.

We analyze the domain of interval temporal relations and use an directed graph to compute the relations of all possibilities.

Definition : An *user edge* denotes a relation between a pair of objects defined by the user. The relation may be reasonable or non-reasonable.

Definition : A *derived edge* holds a non-empty set of reasonable relations derived by our algorithm. The relation of the two objects connected by the derived edge can be any reasonable relation in the set.

3 The Finite Temporal Relations Group

Based on Allen's work, transitivity table for the twelve temporal relations showing the composition of interval temporal relations. Compo-sitions of three or more relations are computed using algorithms based on set operations, such as set union and intersection. These set operations are expensive. The compositions of three or more obtained directly from our table. Algorithm *ComputeTable*29 which consists of the compositions of 29 temporal relation sets. Based on the *Table*29, we found many properties of spatio-temporal relations.

The following table gives a summary of the 29 relation sets which contain all possible composition results:

Table 1: The 29 Relation Sets

ID	Relation Sets		Relation Sets		Relation Sets
1	{ < }	9	{ s }	17	{ oi, di, si }
2	{ > }	10	{ si }	18	{ <, o, m }
3	{ d }	11	{ f }	19	{ >, oi, mi }
4	{ di }	12	{ fi }	20	{ f, fi, e }*
5	{ o }	13	{ e }*	21	{ s, si, e }*
6	{ oi }	14	{ o, di, fi }	22	{ <, o, m, d, s }
7	{ m }	15	{ oi, d, f }	23	{ >, oi, mi, di, si }
8	{ mi }	16	{ o, d, s }	24	{ <, o, m, di, fi }*

25 { > , oi, mi, d, f }

26 { o, oi, d, di, s, si, f, fi, e }*

27 { <, m, d, di, o, oi, f, fi, s, si, e }

28 { > , mi, di , d, oi, o, fi, f , si, s, e }

29 { < , > ,m, mi, di , d, oi, o, fi, f , si, s, e }*

$Table29$ is generated by our program implemented based on the following algorithms.

Algorithm : *Relcomp*
Input : $rs_1 \in 29\,RelSet, rs_2 \in 29\,RelSet$
Output : $rs \in 29\,RelSet$
Preconditions : true
Postconditions : true
Steps :
$1. rs = \cup \forall r_1 \in rs_1, \forall r_2 \in rs_2 \bullet (r_1, r_2) \in rs_1 \times rs_2 Table13(r_1, r_2)$

Algorithm : $ComputeTable29$
Input : $Table13$
Output : $Table29$
Preconditions : true
Postconditions : relation composition is closed under I
Steps :
1. Construct a set of 13 atomic sets from the 13 relations,
assuming that this set is called I, which is an index set for table look up.
2. Let $Table29(i, j) = Table13(i, j), i \in I, j \in I$
3. $\forall Table29(i, j), i \in I, j \in I$, do
    3.1 if $k = Table29(i, j)$ and not belongs to I then
        3.1.1 $I = I \cup Table29(i, j)$
        3.1.2 $\forall m \in I$, do
            3.1.2.1 $Table29(k, m) = Relcomp(k, m)$
            3.1.2.2 $Table29(m, k) = Relcomp(m, k)$

Algorithm $ComputeTable29$ adds new relation sets computed by $RelcCmp$ to the index set I, and computes the new elements of Talble29. There are 2^{13} possible elements of I. However, from the computation of algorithm $ComputeTable29$, the cardinality of I results in 29. Based on this result, we argue that, for an arbitrary pair of temporal intervals, the possible relations between them must be an element of set I.

Table 2: The Temporal Transitive Closure Table

```
------------------------------------------------------------------------------------------
 o|01 02 03 04 05 06 07 08 09 10 11 12 13 14 15 16 17 18 19 20 21 22 23 24 25 26 27 28 29
------------------------------------------------------------------------------------------

01|01 29 22 01 01 02 01 22 01 01 22 01 01 01 22 22 22 01 29 22 01 22 29 01 29 22 22 29 29
02|29 02 25 02 25 02 25 02 25 02 02 02 02 25 25 25 02 29 02 02 25 29 02 29 25 25 29 25 29
03|01 02 03 29 22 25 01 02 03 25 03 22 03 29 25 22 29 22 25 22 25 22 29 29 25 29 29 29 29
04|24 23 26 04 14 17 14 17 14 04 17 04 04 14 26 26 17 24 23 17 14 27 23 24 28 26 27 28 29
05|01 23 16 24 18 26 01 17 05 14 16 18 05 24 26 22 27 18 28 22 14 22 29 24 28 27 27 29 29
06|24 02 15 23 26 19 14 02 15 19 06 17 06 28 25 26 23 27 19 17 25 27 23 29 25 28 29 28 29
07|01 23 16 01 01 16 01 20 07 07 16 01 07 01 16 22 22 01 28 22 07 22 29 01 28 22 22 29 29
08|24 02 15 02 15 02 21 02 15 02 08 08 08 25 25 15 02 27 02 08 25 27 02 29 25 25 29 25 29
09|01 02 03 24 18 15 01 08 09 21 03 18 09 24 15 22 27 18 25 22 21 22 29 24 25 27 27 29 29
10|24 02 15 04 14 06 14 08 21 10 06 04 10 14 15 26 17 24 19 17 21 27 23 24 25 26 27 28 29
11|01 02 03 23 16 19 07 02 03 19 11 20 11 28 25 16 23 22 19 20 25 22 23 29 25 28 29 28 29
12|01 23 16 04 05 17 07 17 05 04 20 12 12 14 26 16 17 18 23 20 14 22 23 24 28 26 27 28 29
13|01 02 03 04 05 06 07 08 09 10 11 12 13 14 15 16 17 18 19 20 21 22 23 24 25 26 27 28 29
14|24 23 26 24 24 26 24 17 14 14 26 24 14 24 26 27 27 24 28 27 14 27 29 24 28 27 27 29 29
15|24 02 15 29 27 25 24 02 15 25 15 27 15 29 25 27 29 27 25 27 25 27 29 29 25 29 29 29 29
16|01 23 16 29 22 28 01 23 16 28 16 22 16 29 28 22 29 22 28 22 28 22 29 29 28 29 29 29 29
17|24 23 26 23 26 23 14 23 26 23 17 17 17 28 28 26 23 27 23 17 28 27 23 29 28 28 29 28 29
18|01 29 22 24 18 27 01 27 18 24 22 18 18 24 27 22 27 18 29 22 24 22 29 24 29 27 27 29 29
19|29 02 25 23 28 19 28 02 25 19 19 23 19 28 25 28 23 29 19 23 25 29 23 29 25 28 29 28 29
20|01 23 16 23 16 23 07 23 16 23 20 20 20 28 28 16 23 22 23 20 28 22 23 29 28 28 29 28 29
21|24 02 15 24 24 15 24 08 21 21 15 24 21 24 15 27 27 24 25 27 21 27 29 24 25 27 27 29 29
22|01 29 22 29 22 29 01 29 22 29 22 22 22 29 29 22 29 22 29 22 29 22 29 29 29 29 29 29 29
23|29 23 28 23 28 23 28 23 28 23 23 23 23 28 28 28 23 29 23 23 28 29 23 29 28 28 29 28 29
24|24 29 27 24 24 27 24 27 24 24 27 24 24 24 27 27 27 24 29 27 24 27 29 24 29 27 27 29 29
25|29 02 25 29 29 25 29 02 25 25 25 29 25 29 25 29 29 29 25 29 25 29 29 25 29 29 29 29 29
26|24 23 26 29 27 28 24 23 26 28 26 27 26 29 28 27 29 27 28 27 28 27 29 28 29 29 29 29 29
27|24 29 27 29 27 29 24 29 27 29 27 27 27 29 29 27 29 27 29 27 29 27 29 29 29 29 29 29 29
28|29 23 28 29 29 28 29 23 28 28 28 29 28 29 28 29 29 29 28 29 28 29 29 29 28 29 29 29 29
29|29 29 29 29 29 29 29 29 29 29 29 29 29 29 29 29 29 29 29 29 29 29 29 29 29 29 29 29 29
------------------------------------------------------------------------------------------
```

Using $Table29$, when composing temporal relations, the set union operation is replaced by a table look up operation. Therefore, the time complexity of relation composition is reduced. The cost of memory used in $Table29$ is tolerable.

Theorem 3.1 : Let $< S, \circ >$ be a temporal algebraic system, and S be a set with a law of composition, then $< S, \circ >$ is closed.

Proof : Since function $\circ : S \times S \Rightarrow S$, and S is equal to 29RelSet, the function is closed to 29RelSet.

Theorem 3.2 : Let $< S, \circ >$ be a temporal algebraic system, and S be a set with a law of composition, then all $a \in S$, exists $b \in S$, such that $a \circ b = b \circ a = (A, \{e\}, A), b$ is called inverse of a.

Proof : Assuming that $a = (A, rs, B)$, where A, and B are interval names, and rs is a temporal relation set. We want to find a rs^{-1} for each rs. The following table shows the inverse relation sets rs^{-1} for each rs :

Table 3:   Inverse Relation Sets

rs	inverse	rs	inverse	rs	inverse
1	2	3	4	5	6
7	8	9	10	11	12
13	13	14	15	16	17
18	19	20	20	21	21
22	23	24	25	26	26
27	28	29	29		

Theorem 3.3 : Let $< S, \circ >$ be a temporal algebraic system, and S be a set with a law of composition, then $< S, \circ >$ has an unique identity (A,{e},A). i.e. all $a \in S, a \circ (A, \{e\}, A) = a = (A, \{e\}, A) \circ a$.

Proof : To prove the identity of function $\circ$, we need to show that $\forall tt \in TemporalTuple \bullet$
$a \circ a^{-1} = (A, \{e\}, A) \wedge a^{-1} \circ a = (A, \{e\}, A) \wedge$
$a \circ (A, \{e\}, A) = a \wedge (A, \{e\}, A) \circ a = a$

From the table lookup of $Table29$, we can easily verify that $\forall rs \in 29RelSet \bullet rs \circ \{e\} = rs \wedge \{e\} \circ rs = rs$. It is clear that $\forall a \in TemporalTuple \bullet a \circ (A, \{e\}, A) = a \wedge (A, \{e\}, A) \circ a = a$. Due to Theorem 3.2, and the inverse relation sets table given above, we can look at $Table29$ for the composition of each pair of rs and rs^{-1}, as well as for each pair of rs^{-1} and rs.

Theorem 3.4 : Let $< S, \circ >$ be a temporal algebraic system, and S be a set with a law of composition, then $< S, \circ >$ is associative. i.e. all $a, b, c \in S, (a \circ b) \circ c = a \circ (b \circ c)$.

Proof : Let L be an ordered list of relation sets obtained from I according to the order given in the 29 relation set table (i.e., $L = (1, 2, 3, \ldots, 29)$). We further define L_2 to be an ordered list of elements obtained from $Table29$ according to the row major order. L_2 has 841 (i.e., 29^2) elements. We can easily compute a table $T_{29 \times 841}$ from L and L_2 by :

$\forall X, Y, Z : TemporalTuple\bullet$
$X = (A, rs_1, B) \wedge rs_1 = L(i) \wedge 1 \le i \le 29 \wedge$
$Y = (B, rs_2, C) \wedge rs_2 = L^2(j) \wedge 1 \le j \le 841 \wedge$
$Z = (A, rs_3, c) \wedge rs_3 = T(i, j) \Leftrightarrow X \circ Y = Z$

4 Maintaining Time Constraints

Based on $Table29$, we propose a set of algorithms, using a directed graph, for fast temporal relation compositions. These algorithms can be used to compute the binary relation between an arbitrary pair of intervals. User edge conflicts are eliminated and derived edges and cycles without conflict are added.

Algorithm : $ComputeRD1$
Input : $G = (GV, GE)$
Output: $K_n = (K_n V, K_n E)$
Preconditions : true
Postconditions : $GV = K_n V \wedge GE \; UE \cup UE' \subseteq K_n E$
Steps :
$1 : G = EliminateConflicts(G)$
$2 : K_n = G \wedge pl = 2$
$3 :$ repeat until $|K_n E| = |K_n V| * (|K_n^V| - 1)/2$
    $3.1 : for each e = (a, b) \wedge e not \in K_n E \wedge a \in K_n V \wedge b \in K_n V \bullet$
      there is a path of user edges from a to b , with path length $= pl$
    $3.2 :$ suppose $((n_1, n_2), (n_2, n3), \ldots, (n_{k-1}, n_k))$ is a path with
$a = n \wedge b = n \wedge k = pl + 1$
    $3.3 : set e.rs = Table29((a, n_{k-1}).rs, (n_{k-1}, b).rs)$
    $3.4 : K_n E = K_n E \cup \{e\}$
    $3.5 : pl = pl + 1$

Algorithm : $EliminateConflicts$
Input : $G = (GV, GE)$
Output : $G'S = (G'SV, G'SE)$
Preconditions : G contains only user edges $\wedge G'S = G$
Postconditions : $G'S = G$, but the reasonable sets of edges in $G'S$ may be changed.

Steps :
1. for each $P = ((n_1, n_2), (n_2, n_3), \ldots, (n_k - 1, n_k))$ in $G'S$ with $n_1 = n_k \wedge k > 3$
   1.1 : for each $i, 1 \le i \le k - 2$
      1.1.1 : set $(n_i, n_{i+2}).rs = Table29((n_i, n_{i+1}).rs, (n_{i+1}, n_{i+2}).rs)$
   1.2 : $rs = Table29((n_k, n_{k-2}).rs, (n_{k-2}, n_{k-1}).rs)$
   1.3 : $if(n_k, n_{k-1}).rnot \in rs$ then
      1.3.1 : ask user to choose a $r'S \in rs$
      1.3.2 : set $(n_k, n_{k-1}).r = r'S$

Considering the five user edges, the algorithm computes derived edges until the last edge is added to K_n :

User edges :
$(A, B) = \{<\} = [1]$ $(B, C) = \{m\} = [7]$ $(C, D) = \{d\} = [3]$
$(C, E) = \{s\} = [9]$ $(F, D) = \{<\} = [1]$

Derivation based on user edges:

1. Path Length = 2
$(A, C) = (A, B) \circ (B, C) = [1] \circ [7] = [1] = \{<\}$
$(B, D) = (B, C) \circ (C, D) = [7] \circ [3] = [16] = \{o, d, s\}$
$(C, F) = (C, D) \circ (D, F) = [3] \circ [1]^{-1} = [3] \circ [2] = \{>\}$
$(D, E) = (D, C) \circ (C, E) = [4] \circ [9] = [14] = \{o, di, fi\}$
$(B, E) = (B, C) \circ (C, E) = [7] \circ [9] = [7] = \{m\}$

2. Path Length = 3
$(A, E) = (A, B) \circ (B, C) \circ (C, E) = [1] \circ [9] = [1] = \{<\}$
$(A, D) = (A, B) \circ (B, C) \circ (C, D) = (A, C) \circ (C, D) = [1] \circ [3] = [22] = \{<, o, m, d, s\}$
$(B, F) = (B, C) \circ (C, D) \circ (D, F) = (B, D) \circ (D, F) = [16] \circ [1]^{-1} = [23] = \{>$
$, oi, mi, di, si\}$
$(E, F) = (E, C) \circ (C, D) \circ (D, F) = (E, D) \circ (D, F) = [14]^{-1} \circ [2] = [15] \circ [2] = [2] = \{>\}$

3. Path Length = 4
$(A, F) = (A, B) \circ (B, C) \circ (C, D) \circ (D, F) = ((A, B) \circ (B, C)) \circ ((C, D) \circ (D, F))$
       $= (A, C) \circ (C, F) = [1] \circ [2] = [29] = \{<, >, d, di, o, oi, m, mi, f, fi, s, si, e\}$

5   Extending algorithms to Spatial Relations

Let rs denote a set of 1-D temporal interval relations (i.e., $rs \in 29\,Relset$). The relation composition table discussed in [1] can be refined (e.q., make each relation as an atomic set of that relation) to a function maps from the Cartesian product of two rs to a rs. Assuming that f^1 is the mapping function interpreting Allen's table, we can compute f^2, the relation composition function of 2-D objects, and f^3, the one for 3-D objects, from f^1. There are 13 relations for 1-D objects. A conjunction of two 1-D relations, which denotes a 2-D relation, has 13^2 variations. Similarly , there are 13^3 3-D relations.

$$f^1 = 29\,RelSet \times 29\,RelSet \Rightarrow 29\,RelSet$$
$$f^2 = 29\,RelSet \times 29\,RelSet \times 29\,RelSet \times 29\,RelSet \Rightarrow$$
$$29\,RelSet \times 29\,RelSet$$
$$f^3 = 29\,RelSet \times 29\,RelSet \times 29\,RelSet \times 29\,RelSet \times$$
$$29\,RelSet \times 29\,RelSet \Rightarrow 29\,RelSet \times 29\,RelSet \times 29\,RelSet$$

where $29\,RelSet \times 29\,RelSet \in \{\{<\} \times \{<\}, \{<\} \times \{>\}, \ldots, \{=\} \times \{=\}\}29\,RelSet \times$
$29\,RelSet \times 29\,RelSet \in \{\{<\} \times \{<\} \times \{<\}, \{<\} \times \{<\} \times \{>\}, \ldots, \{=\} \times \{=\} \times \{=\}\}$
Functions f^2 and f^3 are computed according to the following formulas :

$$\forall i_1 \times j_1, i_2 \times j_2 \in P(29\,RelSet \times 29\,RelSet)$$
$$f^2(i_1 \times j_1, i_2 \times j_2) = \Pi f^1(i_1, i_2) \times f^1(j_1, j_2)$$
$$\forall i_1 \times j_1 \times k_1, i_2 \times j_2 \times k_2 \in P(29\,RelSet \times 29\,RelSet \times 29\,RelSet)$$
$$f^3(i_1 \times j_1 \times k_1, i_2 \times j_2 \times k_2) = \Pi f^1(i_1, i_2) \times f^1(j_1, j_2) \times f^1(k_1, k_2)$$

where $\Pi A \times B = \{a \times b | \forall a \in A, b \in B\}\Pi A \times B \times C = \{a \times b \times c | \forall a \in A, b \in B, c \in C\}$
The functions are implemented as table mappings. Table generated by the above formula are stored in memory to reduce run-time computation load.

6 Conclusions

The main contributions of this paper is in building the algebra system of spatio-temporal interval relations and the set of enhanced mechanism for spatio-temporal relation composition. These algorithms deal with an arbitrary number of objects in an arbitrary n-dimensional space. We propose many properties of temporal interval relations and prove the correctness of these properties. We also argue that, many interesting researches in multimedia applications can benefit from using these spatio-temporal relations and our algorithms.

The algorithm proposed in this paper can be used in other computer applications. We hope that, with our analysis and algorithms, the knowledge underlying temporal interval relations can be used in many computer applications, especially in distributed multi-media computing and networking.

Bibliography

1)   James F. Allen , "Maintaining Knowledge about Temporal Intervals", Communications of the ACM, Vol. 26 , No. 11, 1983.

2)   Chi-Ming Chung, Timothy K. Shih, Jiung-Yao Huang, Ying-Hong Wang, and Tsu-Feng Kuo, "An Object-Oriented Approach and System for Intelligent Multimedia Presentation Designs" in Proceeding of the International Conference on Multimedia Computing and .Systems (ICMCS 'S95), Washington DC, U.S.A., pp 278-281 May 15-18, 1995.

3) Young Francis Day, et. al., "Spatio-Temporal Modeling of Video Data for On-Line Object-Oriented Query Processing" in Proceedings of the International Conference on Multimedia Computing and Systems, Washington DC,U.S.A., pp 98-105, May 15-18, 1995.

4) Cherif Keramane and Andrzej Duda, "Interval Expressions - A Function Model for Interactive Dynamic Multimedia Presentations" in Proceedings of the 1996 International Conference on Multimedia Computing and Systems, Hiroshima, Japan, pp 119-133, June 17-23, 1996.

5) John Z. Li, M. TamerOzsu, and Duane Szafron, "Spatial Reasoning Rules in Multimedia Management Systems" in proceedings of the 1996 Multimedia Modeling International Conference (MMM'S96),Toulouse, France, pp 119-133, November 12-5, 1996.

6) Thomas D. C. Little and Arif Ghafoor, "Spatio-Temporal Composition of Distributed Multimedia Objects for Value-Added Networks", IEEE Computer, October 1991, pp 42-50.

7) Thomas D. C. Little and Arif Ghafoor "Interval Based Conceptual Models for Time-Dependent Multimedia Data", IEEE Transactions on Knowledge and Data Engineering, Vol. 5, No. 4,1993, pp 551-563.

8) Timothy K. Shih, Steven K. C. Lo, Szu-Jan Fu, and Julian B. Chang, "Using Interval Temporal Logic and Inference Rules for the Automatic Generation of Multimedia Presentations" in Proceedings of the IEEE International Conference on Multimedia Computing and Systems, Hiroshima, Japan, pp 425-428, June 17-23, 1996.

9) Timothy K. Shih, Chin-Hwa Kuo, Huan-Chao Keh, Chao T. Fang-Tsou, and Kuan-Shen An, "An Object-Oriented Database for Intelligent Multimedia Presentations" in Proceedings of the 1996 IEEE International Conference on Systems, Man and Cybernetics, Beijing, China, October 14-17, 1996.

10) Michael Vazirgiannis, Yannis Theodoridis, and Timos Sellis "Spatio-Temporal Composition in Multimedia Applications" in Proceedings of the International Workshop on Multimedia Software Development, March 25-26, Berlin, Germany, pp 120-127, 1996.

24

Efficient Key Distribution Protocols for Large-Scale Networks

Wei-Chi Ku

Sheng-De Wang

National Taiwan University

ABSTRACT

As key distribution protocols (KDP) are usually the initial step for setting up a secure network-based service, they are very important in enabling the required security. Most of the existing KDPs make use of cryptographic algorithms, either secret key or public-key cryptography. However, it is also possible to employ secure keyed one-way hash functions (SKOWHF) in KDP designs. Though several works have been published in this area, they only focus on the small scale networks. In this paper, we first introduce the SKOWHF-based security trunks and security channels; then, two rules for KDP construction, KDR1 and KDR2, are described. Finally, a hierarchical KDP for large-scale networks is proposed.

1 Introduction

Before conducting a secure session using secret-key cryptographic technique, a secret key should be agreed upon by the communicants. To assure strict security, the secret key should be renewed for each session, i.e., it should be a session key, so that compromising one key will not divulge the contents of other sessions. The protocol for establishing a session key between the communicants is referred to as a key distribution protocol (KDP). As KDP is usually the initial process for setting up the secure network-based services, they are crucial in enabling the required security. To date, most KDPs employ either secret-key cryptosystems or public key cryptosystems. However, it is also possible to use one-way hash functions rather than encryption algorithms to construct KDP. Much research has been published in this area [2,3] [4,5,6,7,8]. Gong [2] presents the original idea of using a one-way hash function as the basic building block of a KDP. Later, Bull, Gong and Sollins [3] propose a KDP also based on one-way hash function. Another well-known instance is KryptoKnight [5,6], which is a family of KDPs developed by IBM. Compared with encryption algorithms, a one-way hash function is easier to be implemented for not having to provide the invertible property [2,5,6]. It also makes the object codes and the source codes of them exportable [2,3,5,6,7,8]. In particular, its computation is less complex [5)6)]. Maybe it is the reason why Global System for Mobile Communications (GSM) [1)] uses one-way functions in its security system.

However, it has been recognized that the characterization of the one-way hash function specified in the above mentioned works is not appropriate for the way they adopt it in a keyed manner [7)8)]. Berson, Gong and Lomas redefine the properties of the suitable one-way hash function for security use, labeled as secure keyed one-way hash function (SKOWHF). In addition, mix-up of confidentiality and authentication usually makes the design more difficult to be analyzed or to be implemented. To solve this problem, Boyd and Mathuria [8)] propose a systematic method for KDP construction by sharply distinguishing between the confidentiality and authentication channels. Most of the existing SKOWHF-based KDPs involve only one trusted key server (or key distribution center) for key distribution. Since the number of users of networks increases extremely, it is inefficient for a single key server to handle the key distribution [9)]. That is, suitable KDPs for large-scale networks are on demand. In this paper, we first introduce the method of constructing security trunks and security channels by using SKOWHFs. Base on the security channels, two approaches to KDP construction are proposed. The first approach provides more flexibility for key generation while the second approach requires fewer computations. Finally, we use three scenarios to demonstrate the usage of the proposed methods for constructing efficient KDPs in large-scale and administratively heterogeneous networks.

2   SKOWHF-based Security Trunks

In this section, we describe the method of using SKOWHF in the construction of security trunks. For a sequence of Z nodes X_1, X_2, ..., X_{Z-1}, X_Z (not necessary in geographical order), we assume that there exists a common key for each pair of adjacent nodes. That is, X_1 and X_2 have shared a common key CK_{12}, X_2 and X_3 have shared a common key CK_{23}, ..., X_{Z-1} and X_Z have shared a common key $CK_{(Z-1)Z}$.

For convenience, the definition of SKOWHF, which is proposed by Berson, Gong and Lomas [7)] is repeated here. A function f is a SKOWHF if it satisfies:
- f maps key k and a bit string x to a output string of fixed length.
- Given k and x, it is easy to compute $f(k, \{x\})$.
- Given k and $f(k, \{x\})$, it is computationally infeasible to compute x.
- Given k, it is computationally infeasible to find two values x and y ($x \neq y$) such that $f(k, \{x\}) = f(k, \{y\})$.
- Given pairs x and $f(k, \{x\})$, it is computationally infeasible to compute k.
- Without knowledge of k, it is computationally infeasible to compute $f(k, \{x\})$ for any x.
- The mapping from $k, \{x\}$ to $f(k, \{x\})$ is randomly chosen in the sense that it should not be possible to predict any portion of $f(k, \{x\})$ [8)].

Some researchers are convinced that an SKOWHF can be constructed by using existing unkeyed hash functions such as MD5 [10)], SHA-1 [11)] and Snefru [12)]. In the rest of this paper, f is used to represent an SKOWHF.

2.1 Confidentiality trunk

A confidentiality trunk for m from X_i to X_{i+1} $(1 \leq i \leq z - 1)$ ensures that only the authorized X_{i+1} will be able to read m sent by X_i and is denoted by
$$X_i\ (c) \to X_{i+1}:\ m.$$
This confidentiality trunk can be realized by using f accompanying with the one-time padding technique as follows:
$$X_i \to X_{i+1}:\ n_{X_i},\ f(CK_{X_i X_{i+1}}, \{n_{X_i}\}) \oplus m$$
where n_{X_i} is the nonce issued by X_i, i.e., this cannot be repeatedly used by X_i with the same key as $CK_{X_i X_{i+1}}$. By padding with $f(CK_{X_i X_{i+1}}, \{n_{X_i}\})$, X_i can send m to X_{i+1} without hesitating that it will be compromised to others. Note that a confidentiality trunk doesn't ensure that the messages will be obtained by the expected recipient.

2.2 Integrity trunk

An integrity trunk for m from X_i to X_{i+1} $(1 \leq i \leq z - 1)$ ensures that X_{i+1} can check that the received m, which is sent by X_i, has never been tampered and is denoted by
$$X_i\ (i) \to X_{i+1}:\ m$$
And, this integrity trunk can be realized by using f as in the following:
$$X_i \to X_{i+1}:\ m,\ f(CK_{X_i X_{i+1}}, \{m\}).$$
From another view, X_{i+1} can check to see whether m is (or was) actually sent by X_i. Note that an integrity trunk doesn't have to ensure that the received information is newly sent by the claimed sender. In other words, X_{i+1} doesn't need to verify the freshness of that message.

3 SKOWHF-based Security Channels

Now, we employ the previously described security trunks to build the security channels: confidentiality channel, integrity channel and authentication channel. Let X_1 and X_Z represents the end users of the security channel, in addition, the intermediate nodes between them, i.e., X_2, X_3, ..., X_{Z-1}, are trustworthy.

3.1 Confidentiality channel

The confidentiality channel for the message m from X_1 to X_Z is denoted by
$$X_1\ (c) \to X_Z:\ m$$
and can be constructed by orderly cascading the following confidentiality trunks:
$$X_1\ (c) \to X_2:\ m$$
...
$$X_{Z-2}\ (c) \to X_{Z-1}:\ m$$

$X_{Z-1}(c) \rightarrow X_Z$: m

and the following integrity trunks:

$X_1(i) \rightarrow X_2$: $\{m, ID_{X_Z}\}$

...

$X_{Z-2}(i) \rightarrow X_{Z-1}$: m, ID_{X_Z}

where ID_{X_Z} represents the identity of X_Z. Since the intermediate nodes X_2, X_3, ..., and X_{Z-1} are assumed to be trustworthy, X_1 can believe that only the authorized user X_Z will be able to read m.

3.2   Integrity channel

The integrity channel for the message m from X_1 to X_Z is denoted by

$X_1(i) \rightarrow X_Z$: m

and can be constructed by orderly cascading the following security trunks:

$X_1(i) \rightarrow X_2$: m

$X_2(i) \rightarrow X_3$: m, ID_{X_1}

...

$X_{Z-1}(i) \rightarrow X_Z$: m, ID_{X_1}.

The integrity channel for m from X_1 to X_Z ensures that X_Z can check that m is or has been sent by X_1. Moreover, each individual item contained in m cannot be modified alone unless the whole m is replaced with an old one ever sent by X_1.

3.3   Authentication channel

The authentication channel for the message m from X_1 to X_Z is dented by

$X_1(a) \rightarrow X_Z$: m

and can be constructed by directly using the integrity channel from X_1 to X_Z:

$X_1(i) \rightarrow X_Z$: $\{m, n_{X_Z}\}$,

where n_{X_Z} is a nonce issued by X_Z and is used as the freshness identifier for m. From this channel, X_Z should be able to check the freshness of m and the sender of m. If verified, X_Z can believe that m is newly sent by X_1.

Remark 1. The assumption of using trustworthy intermediate nodes between X_1 and X_Z will be reasonably justified later in the proposed hierarchical KDP, in which key servers rather than common users act these nodes.

4   Two Approaches to KDP Construction

In this section, two approaches to KDP construction are described. The major difference between these two approaches is the manner of generating a session key. In the first approach, the session key is generated by an independent random number generator. While in the second approach, the session key is generated by using an SKOWHF. Mutual confirmation can be achieved in both approaches so that one can check to see whether the peer end has obtained the right session key or not. In fact, Boyd and Mathuria omit such a function for simplification. However, for practical use, mutual confirmation should be considered in the KDP so that the resulting design can serve as a complete module for the adopted system. Symbols A (the originator) and B (the recipient) represent the two users who are going to establish a session key.

4.1 The first approach

A session key sk, which is independently generated, can be established between A and B using the authentication and confidentiality protocols according to the following key distribution rule.

KDR1:

(1) A sends n_A to B.

(2) B $(c) \rightarrow A$: $\{sk, y\}$ and B $(a) \rightarrow A$: $\{sk, y\}$.

(3) $A \rightarrow B$: y.

Nonce y is issued by B and is used for confirming A's knowledge of sk.

Theorem 1. According to KDR1, A and B can secretly share sk.

Proof: Since sk is independently generated by B, it implies that B believes it is a fresh session key. From the first part of (2), $\{sk, y\}$ can be sent to A confidentially. From the second part of (2), A can make sure that the retrieved $\{sk, y\}$ is newly sent by B. If succeeds, A can also believe that B has obtained sk. From (3), B can check to see whether the received y is equal to the one previously issued, if so, he believes A has obtained the right sk. Consequently, sk is secretly shared by A and B. □

4.2 The second approach

A session key can be generated by computing the session key generation formula (SKGF) rather than by a random number generator. With this approach, some SKOWHF computations can be mustered out.

KDR2:

(1) A sends n_A to B.

(2) Case I. If A and B have shared a common key CK_{AB}, B computes the SKGF, $\{sk, h_A, h_B\} = f(CK_{AB}, \{n_A, n_B\})$, and then sends $\{n_B, h_B\}$ to A. Next, A also computes the same formula as B does. Case II. If A and B don't share a common key, B computes SKGF, $\{sk, h_A, h_B\} = f(CK_{BW}, \{n_A, n_B, ID_A\})$ and then sends $\{ID_A, n_A, n_B, h_B\}$ to his adjacent node W. Next, W also computes $\{sk, h_A, h_B\}$ as B does. If the computed h_B equals the received one, W $(c) \rightarrow A$: $\{sk, h_A\}$ and W $(a) \rightarrow A$: sk, h_A.

(3) $A \rightarrow B$: h_A.

Handshake numbers h_A and h_B are used by A and B, respectively, for mutual confirmation.

Theorem 2. Following KDR2, A and B can secretly share sk.

Proof: In case I, CK_{AB} is only known to A and B, so no one else can obtain $\{sk, h_A, h_B\}$ using the SKGF. Furthermore, n_A and n_B are in the input of f and it implies that $\{sk, h_A, h_B\}$ is controlled by both A and B rather than by either one alone. On receiving n_B, A can compute the SKGF to derive h_B and then check to see whether it equals to the received one. If so, he believes that B has obtained the right session key. On receiving h_A in (3), B believes that A has obtained the right session key. In case II, a confidentiality channel and an integrity channel for $\{sk, h_A, h_B\}$ from A to W can be constructed. If the n_A received by W is fresh, a confidentiality channel and an authentication channel for $\{sk, h_A\}$ from W to A is subsequently constructed. From the characteristic of the authentication channel, a confidentiality channel and an authentication channel for $\{sk, h_A\}$ from B to A is constructed. In the meanwhile, A believes that B has obtained the right session key. On receiving h_A in (3), B believes that A has obtained the right session key. Hence sk can be secretly shared by A and B no matter in case I or II.   □

5   Practical Key Distribution Protocols

For practical use, we use the proposed key distribution rules to construct KDP for users within a large-scale network such as Internet.

5.1   Model

Because the number of network users increases drastically, it is inefficient for a single key server (or key management center) to execute key distribution. To reduce the management complexity, the system can be organized hierarchically [9]. A number of users are under the control of a domain key server and a number of domain key servers are under the control of a cluster key server, and so on. It is assumed that each entity has shared a common key, or mater key, with his control server. To provide more flexibility, entities of the same level are allowed to share a common key. It is economical when they frequently communicate. Let A and B denote the originator and the corresponding user of the protocol, respectively. MK_A, the master key of A, is used as the common key for A and his key server. Similarly, MK_B is the master key of B and is used as the common key for B and his key server.

5.2   Scenarios

Three scenarios are used to illustrate the described method of establishing session keys for the most common three spots in large-scale networks.

Scenario 1. A and B have already shared a common key CK_{AB}. (Involved key servers: none.)

[Scenario 1 proceeds according to KDR1]:

In this situation, A and B can directly construct the needed confidentiality channel and authentication channel without the help of any key server. The KDP is illustrated as follows:

Step 1. $A \rightarrow B$: n_A

B generates the session key sk using an independent key generator, e.g., a random number generator. Then, sk combined with another nonce y is transmitted back to A over the security channels where $f(CK_{AB}, \{n_B\}) \oplus \{sk, y\}$ forms the confidentiality channel and $f(CK_{AB}, \{sk, y, n_A\})$ forms the authentication channel.

Step 2. $B \rightarrow A$: n_B, $f(CK_{AB}, \{n_B\}) \oplus \{sk, y\}$, $f(CK_{AB}, \{sk, y, n_A\})$

Once all the received messages have been verified, A believes that sk is newly sent by B. However, B doesn't know that whether A has obtained the correct session key or not. Accordingly, a further confirmation from A to B should be conducted as follows:

Step 3. $A \rightarrow B$: y

In the protocol, A needs to perform two SKOWHF computations, and so does B.

[Scenario 1 proceeds according to KDR2]:

Clearly, the rule specified in case I of KDR2 can be directly used here.

Step 1. $A \rightarrow B$: n_A

On receiving n_A, B generates n_B and then computes the SKGF: $\{sk, h_A, h_B\} = f(CK_{AB}, \{n_A, n_B\})$. Next, B sends n_B and h_B back to A.

Step 2. $B \rightarrow A$: n_B, h_B

The handshake number h_B is used by B to inform his knowledge of sk to A. After retrieving n_B from the received message, A also computes the SKGF. Next, he compares the computed h_B with the second item of the received message, if equal, he believes that B has obtained the same session key as his own and then sends h_A to B.

Step 3. $A \rightarrow B$: h_A

h_A is used by A to inform his knowledge of sk to B.

In the protocol, A needs to perform one SKOWHF computation, and so does B.

Scenario 2. A and B don't share a common key but both are under the control of S. (Involved key servers: S.)

[Scenario 2 proceeds according to KDR1]:

Step 1. $A \rightarrow B$: n_A

Since S is the only intermediate server between A and B, there are two confidentiality trunks B $(c) \rightarrow S$ and S $(c) \rightarrow A$ and two integrity trunks B $(i) \rightarrow S$ and S $(i) \rightarrow A$ should be established first to construct the required confidentiality and authentication channels.

Step 2. $B \to S$: $n_B, f(MK_B, \{n_B\}) \oplus \{sk, y\}, ID_A, n_A, f(MK_B, \{sk, y, ID_A, n_A\})$

As MK_B is a common key between B and S, we can regard B's identity ID_B as being implicitly contained in the use of MK_B, i.e. it could be omitted.

Step 3. $S \to A$: $n_S, f(MK_A, \{n_S\}) \oplus \{sk, y\}, f(MK_A, \{sk, y, ID_B, n_A\})$

Note that ID_B is not transmitted in clear mode in the flow. Obviously, A should know the identity of B.

Step 4. $A \to B$: y

In this protocol, A and B need to respectively perform two SKOWHF computations while S needs four.

[Scenario 2 proceeds according to KDR2]:

   This could be regarded as the simplest instance of case II of KDR2. And, we will go into a more detail about the protocol. Similarly, sk is generated by computing the SKGF: $\{sk, h_A, h_B\} = f(MK_B, \{n_A, n_B, ID_A\})$.

Step 1. $A \to B$: n_A

Upon receiving this request, B generates n_B and then computes the SKGF to derive $\{sk, h_A\}$.

Step 2. $B \to S$: ID_A, n_A, n_B, h_B

On receiving the request from B in flow 2, S also computes according to the SKGF to derive $\{sk, h_A\}$ as B does. Then, he compares the h_A retrieved from flow 2 with the computed one. Once unequal, S quits the protocol. Otherwise, S transmits $\{sk, h_A, h_B\}$ to A through a confidentiality channel and an authentication channel.

Step 3. $S \to A$: $n_S, f(MK_A, \{n_S\}) \oplus \{sk, h_A\}, f(MK_A, \{sk, h_A, ID_B, n_A\})$

Next, A can verify sk and recognize B's knowledge of sk by checking the validity of the received messages. If correct, A sends h_A to B.

Step 4. $A \to B$: h_A

Then, B can recognize A's knowledge of sk by comparing the h_A retrieved from flow 4 and the one he holds. We can see that A authenticates S and B, and B authenticates S and A. However, S authenticate neither A nor B. In total, A needs to perform two SKOWHF computations, B needs one SKOWHF computation and S needs three SKOWHF computations.

Scenario 3. A and B don't share a common key. But their key servers S_1 and S_2 have shared a common key $CK_{S_1 S_2}$. (Involved key servers: S_2, S_1.)

[Scenario 3 proceeds according to KDR1]:

As S_2 and S_1 are the intermediate servers between A and B, there are three confidentiality trunks B $(c) \rightarrow S_2$, S_2 $(c) \rightarrow S_1$ and S_1 $(c) \rightarrow A$ and three integrity trunks B $(i) \rightarrow S_2$, S_2 $(i) \rightarrow S_1$ and S_1 $(i) \rightarrow A$ should be established first to construct the need confidentiality and authentication channels.

Step 1. $A \rightarrow B$: n_A

Step 2. $B \rightarrow S_2$: n_B, $f(MK_B, \{n_B\}) \oplus \{sk, y\}$, ID_A, n_A, $f(MK_B, \{sk, y, ID_A, n_A\})$

Step 3. $S_2 \rightarrow S_1$: n_{S_2}, $f(CK_{S_1 S_2}, \{n_{S_2}\}) \oplus \{sk, y\}$, ID_A, ID_B, n_A, $f(CK_{S_1 S_2}, \{sk, y, ID_A, ID_B, n_A\})$

Step 4. $S_1 \rightarrow A$: n_{S_1}, $f(MK_A, \{n_{S_1}\}) \oplus \{sk, y\}$, $f(MK_A, \{sk, y, ID_B, n_A\})$

Step 5. $A \rightarrow B$: y

[Scenario 3 proceeds according to KDR2]:

This protocol simply needs to establish two sets of security trunks should be established, i.e., S_2 $(c) \rightarrow S_1$, S_1 $(c) \rightarrow A$, S_2 $(i) \rightarrow S_1$, and S_1 $(i) \rightarrow A$. SKGF: $\{sk, h_A, h_B\} = f(MK_B, \{n_A, n_B, ID_A\})$

Step 1. $A \rightarrow B$: n_A

Step 2. $B \rightarrow S_2$: ID_A, n_A, n_B, h_B

Step 3. $S_2 \rightarrow S_1$: n_{S_2}, $f(CK_{S_1 S_2}, \{n_{S_2}\}) \oplus \{sk, h_A\}$, ID_A, ID_B, n_A, $f(CK_{S_1 S_2}, \{sk, h_A, ID_A, ID_B, n_A\})$

Step 4. $S_1 \rightarrow A$: n_{S_1}, $f(MK_A, \{n_{S_1}\}) \oplus \{sk, h_A\}$, $f(MK_A, \{sk, h_A, ID_B, n_A\})$

Step 5. $A \rightarrow B$: h_A

6 Conclusion

A class of efficient KDPs suitable for large-scale networks is constructed based on SKOWHF. From the number of required SKOWHF computations by each constituent in all the three scenarios, we know that the protocols constructed according to the second approach demands fewer computations. It may be an advantage of the second approach over the first approach especially when computation should be performed in a light-weight device such as a smart card. In contrast, the first approach provides more flexibility for session key selection because the session key can be chosen to have a specific structure. However, it is questionable that the session key should have such a feature. With hierarchical structure of key servers, the concept of using security trunks to construct security channels is practical and can also be applied to any system employing cryptographic techniques. It should be emphasized that no intermediate key server needs to authenticate the received messages. Instead, only the expected recipient (end user) should authenticate the messages. It is the reason why the authentication trunk is not discussed in this paper. Conscious reader may find that the sequence of protocol steps in each scenario forms a loop-around pattern. However, either proving its optimization or contriving another better design is a topic for our further investigation.

Bibliography

1)   Molva R., Samfat D., and Tsudik G., "Authentication of Mobile Users," *IEEE Network*, pp. 26–34 (Mar./Apr., 1994).

2)   Gong L., "Using one-way functions for Authentication," *ACM CCR*, Vol. 19, No. 5, pp. 8–11 (Oct., 1989).

3)   Bull J.A., Gong L., and Sollins K.R., "Towards security in an open systems federation," in Y. Deswarte, G. Eizenberg, and J.-J. Quisquater (Eds.): Computer security –*ESORICS 92'*, *Lect. Notes Comput. Sci.*, Vol. 648, pp. 3–20 (1992).

4)   Mathuria A., "Addressing weaknesses of two cryptographic protocols of Bull, Gong and Sollins," *Elect. Lett.*, Vol. 31, pp. 1543–1544 (1995).

5)   Bird R., Gopal I., Herzberg A., Janson P., Kutten S., Molva R., and Yung M., "Systematic design of a family of attack-resistant authentication protocols," *IEEE J. Select. Areas Commun.*, Vol. 11, pp. 679–693 (June, 1993).

6)   R. Bird, I. Gopal, A. Herzberg, P. Janson, S. Kutten, R. Molva, and M. Yung, "The KryptoKnight Family of Light-Weight Protocols for Authentication and Key Distribution, " *IEEE/ACM Trans. on Networking*, Vol. 3, No. 1, pp. 31–41 (Feb., 1995).

7)   T.A. Berson, L. Gong, and T.M.A. Lomas, "Secure, keyed, and collisionful hash functions," Technical report SRI-CSL-94-08, *Computer Science Laboratory*, SRI International Menlo Park, CA. (May, 1994).

8)   C. Boyd, A.Mathuria, "Systematic design of key establishment protocols based on one-way functions," *IEE Proc.-Comput. Digit. Tech.*, Vol. 144, No. 2, pp. 93–99 (Mar., 1997).

9)   T. Hwang and W.-C. Ku, "Reparable Key Distribution Protocols for Internet Environment," *IEEE Trans. on Commun.*, Vol. 43, No. 5, pp. 1947–1949 (May, 1995).

10) R. Rivest, "The MD5 Message Digest Algorithm," Internet Draft (July, 1991).

11) National Institute of standards and Technology, "Secure Hash Standard," *NIST FIPS PUB 180-1*, U.S. Department of Commerce (April, 1995).

12) R. C. Merkle, "A Fast Software One-Way Hash Function," *Journal of Cryptology*, Vol. 3 , No. 1, pp. 43–58 (1990).

25

A Purpose-oriented Access Control Model in Object-based Systems

Masashi Yasuda
Hiroaki Higaki
Makoto Takizawa

Tokyo Denki University

ABSTRACT

Distributed applications are realized by cooperation of multiple objects. Each object is manipulated through a method supported by the object and then the method may further invoke methods of other objects. Purpose-oriented access rules indicate what methods in objects can invoke methods of other objects. Information flow among the objects occurs if the requests and responses of the methods carry data. In this paper, we discuss how to specify purpose-oriented access rules so that the information flow occurring in the nested invocation is legal.

1   Introduction

It is significant to consider what subject s can access what object o by what operation t in the access control model[1]. The system is *secure* if and only if (*iff*) every object is manipulated according to the access rules. However, the access control model cannot resolve the confinement problem[4] where the information illegally flows among subjects and objects. The lattice-based model[1, 3] aims at protecting against the illegal information flow. One security class is given to each subject and object in the system. A *flow* relation among the security classes is defined to denote that information in one class s_1 can *flow into* s_2. In the *mandatory* model[1, 6], an access rule $\langle s, o, t \rangle$ is specified so that the flow relation between a subject s and an object o holds. In the role-based model[7, 9], a *role* shows a function or job in the application, which is given in a set of operations on objects. The access rule is defined to bind a subject to the roles.

Distributed applications are modeled in an object-based model like CORBA[5]. Each object is an encapsulation of data structure and methods. For example, a person s may withdraw money from a bank o in order to do house-keeping, but s cannot get money from o to go drinking. Thus, it is essential to discuss a *purpose* of s to manipulate o. In the *purpose-oriented* model[8], an access rule shows for what each subject s manipulates an object o by a method t of o so as to keep the information flow legal. That is, a purpose-oriented access rule is specified in a form $\langle s : u, \ o : t \rangle$, where u shows the purpose. In the object-based system, on receipt of a request op from an object o_1, o_2 computes op and then sends back the response of op to o_1. If the request and the response carry data, the data is exchanged among o_1 and o_2. Furthermore, the invocation of methods is nested in the object-based system, i.e. methods invoke further methods in other objects. Even if each purpose-oriented rule between a pair of objects satisfies the information flow relation, some data in one object may illegally flow to another object through the nested invocation. In this paper, we discuss what purpose-oriented access rules imply the legal information flow in the nested invocations.

In section 2, we present the purpose-oriented model in the object-based system. In section 3, we discuss the legal information flow.

2 Purpose-Oriented Models

2.1 Object-based model

The lattice-based model [1, 3] is proposed to keep the information flow legal. Here, subjects and objects are referred to as entities. Each entity e_i is given one *security class* $\lambda(e_i)$. A security class s_1 *can flow* to s_2 ($s_1 \rightarrow s_2$) *iff* the information in an entity of s_1 can flow into an entity of s_2. s_1 and s_2 are *equivalent* ($s_1 \equiv s_2$) *iff* $s_1 \rightarrow s_2$ and $s_2 \rightarrow s_1$. For every pair of security classes s_1 and s_2 in S, $s_1 \prec s_2$ *iff* $s_1 \rightarrow s_2$ but $s_2 \nrightarrow s_1$. Here, s_2 *dominates* s_1 ($s_1 \preceq s_2$) *iff* $s_1 \prec s_2$ or $s_1 \equiv s_2$. $s_1 \preceq s_2$ means that s_2 is more sensitive than s_1. $\cup$ and $\cap$ are the least upper bound (*lub*) and the greatest lower bound (*glb*), respectively. In the mandatory model [1, 6], access rules are defined so as to satisfy "$\preceq$". If s reads o, the information in o is derived by s, i.e. information in o flows to s. Hence, $\lambda(s) \succeq \lambda(o)$ is required to hold. If s writes o, $\lambda(s) \preceq \lambda(o)$ holds. Lastly, if s modifies o, $\lambda(s) \equiv \lambda(o)$.

In the object-based system, each object o_i supports more abstract level of data structure and methods than read and write. In addition, o_i is *encapsulated* so that o_i can be manipulated only through the methods supported by o_i.

First, methods are assumed to be unnested. An object s sends a request message q of op_i to an object o_i. On receipt of q, o_i computes op_i and sends the response r back to s. q and r carry the input and output of op_i, respectively. If op_i changes the state of o_i by using the input, the data in s may flow into o_i if q carries some data in s. If op_i derives data from o_i and then returns the data to s, the data in o_i may flow out to s if r carries the data derived from o_i by op_i. Thus, input and output of op_i have to be discussed to clarify the information flow relation between s and o_i. Each method op_i of o_i is characterized in terms of input (I_i), output (O_i), and state transition of o_i. The input I_i exists if some data flows from s to o_i, e.g. the request of op_i includes the data. The output O_i exists if some data in o_i flows out to s. In this paper, the communication among objects is assumed to be *secure*. Only data stored in o_i can flow out from o_i to s and the data in s can flow to o_i in

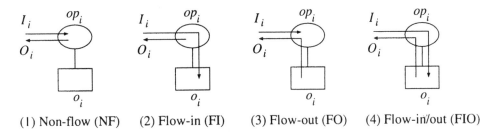

(1) Non-flow (NF)   (2) Flow-in (FI)   (3) Flow-out (FO)   (4) Flow-in/out (FIO)

Figure 1: Information flow.

the computation of the method of o_i.

Each method op_i is classified into one *flow* type $\tau(op_i)$ [Figure 1]: *non-flow* (NF), *flow-in* (FI), *flow-out* (FO), and *flow-in/out* (FIO). An NF method op_i implies no information flow from or to o_i. In addition, op_i does not change o_i. Even if the input data I_i exists, no information in s flows to o_i unless op_i changes o_i. Similarly, no data in o_i flows out to s unless the output data O_i is derived from o_i. An FI method op_i changes o_i by using I_i where data in s may flow into o_i. *write* is FI. In addition, o_i is updated without I_i. For example, a *count-up* method has no input but changes the *counter*. An FO method op_i does not change o_i. Since the output O_i of op_i carries data in o_i to s, data in o_i may flow to s. *read* is FO. An FIO method op_i changes o_i by using I_i and sends O_i including data in o_i back to s. Not only data in s may flow into o_i but also data in o_i may flow out to s. In *modify*, s first reads O_i in o_i and writes to o_i. FIO may not carry I_i like FI. The mandatory access rule is extended as follows[8]).

[**Extended access rules**] The subject s can manipulate o_i by op_i of o_i according to the following rules.

(1) $\tau(op_i) \in \{\text{NF, FI}\}$ only if $\lambda(s) \preceq \lambda(o_i)$.

(2) $\tau(op_i) \in \{\text{NF, FO}\}$ only if $\lambda(s) \succeq \lambda(o_i)$.

(3) $\tau(op_i) \in \{\text{NF, FI, FO, FIO}\}$ only if $\lambda(s) \equiv \lambda(o_i)$.□

The types of methods and the security class $\lambda(o_i)$ of o_i are specified when o_i is defined based on the semantics of o_i. Each time s invokes op_i, op_i is accepted to be computed on o_i if $\tau(op_i)$ and $\lambda(o_i)$ satisfy the access rules.

[**Example 1**] Suppose WWW[2]) server object w is manipulated by two hosts h_1 and h_2. Here, w supports GET and $POST$ methods. GET is an FO type method because the output data is derived from w. $POST$ is FI because w is updated by using the input data. If $\lambda(h_1) \preceq \lambda(w)$ and $\lambda(h_2) \succeq \lambda(w)$, h_1 can $POST$ but cannot GET data in w, and h_2 can GET but cannot $POST$ data in w. w can also support abstract methods like Common Gateway Interface (CGI). □

2.2 Purpose-oriented model

We assume a pair of methods op_1 and op_2 can exchange data only through the state of o_i. If data d flowing from an object o_i to o_j is neither derived from o_i nor stored

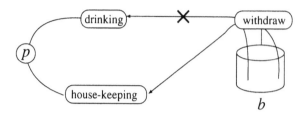

Figure 2: Purpose-oriented access control.

in o_j, it is meaningless to consider the information flow from o_i to o_j. If data derived from o_i is stored in o_j, the data may flow out to other objects.

Suppose a person p can withdraw money from a bank object b for the house-keeping. However, p cannot get money from b to go drinking. Thus, it is critical to consider a *purpose* for which s manipulates o_i by t_i.

[**Purpose-oriented (PO) rule**] An access rule $\langle o_i : op_i, o_{ij} : op_{ij} \rangle$ means that o_i can manipulate o_{ij} through a method op_{ij} invoked by op_i of o_i. □

op_i shows a *purpose* for which o_i manipulates o_{ij} by op_{ij}. Here, o_i and o_{ij} are named *parent* and *child* objects of the access rule, respectively.

[**Example 2**] If a person object p can withdraw money from a bank account b of p [Figure 2], an access rule $\langle p : house\text{-}keep, b : withdraw \rangle$ is specified. The method *house-keeping* of the object p invokes *withdraw* of b. Here, *house-keeping* shows the purpose for withdrawing money from b. □

3 Information Flow

3.1 Invocation graph

On receipt of a request op, an object o creates a thread of op named an *instance* of op. op may invoke methods $op_1, \ldots, op_l$ where each op_i is computed on an object o_i. In the serial invocation, op serially invokes $op_1, \ldots, op_l$. Hence, information carried by the response of op_{i-1} may flow to op_i. In the parallel one, op invokes $op_1, \ldots, op_l$ in parallel. Each op_i is computed on o_i independently of another op_j. This means information carried by the response of op_i does not flow to op_j. The invocations are represented in an ordered *invocation tree*. A parent-child branch ($op \rightarrow op_i$) shows that op invokes op_i. If op invokes op_i before op_j, op_i precedes op_j ($op_i \rightarrow op_j$). Suppose a user serially invokes two methods op_1 and op_2. op_1 invokes op_{12} and op_{13} in parallel after op_{11}. This is represented in an invocation tree as shown in Figure 3. "$\rightarrow$" shows the computation order of the methods.

An object o invokes a method op_i in o_i. op_i invokes methods $op_{i1}, \ldots, op_{il_i}$ where each op_{ij} is in o_{ij}. op_i in o_i communicates with o and o_{ij}. Hence, op_i is modeled to be a collection of inputs α_1, α_2, and α_3, and outputs β_1, β_2, and β_3 as shown in Figure 4. α_1 means the input I_i from o to op_i. For example, the request of op_i carries the input data α_1. β_1 means the output data to o, e.g. the response of op_i. β_2 shows that o_i is updated by using data carried by β_2. For example, the data of β_2 is stored

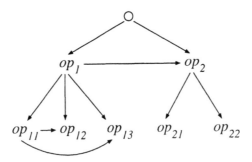

Figure 3: Invocation tree.

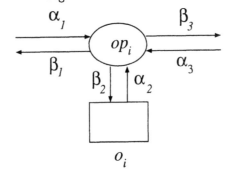

Figure 4: Input and output.

in o_i. α_2 means the data derived from o_i is stored in op_i. β_3 means some data is output to o_{ij}. For example, the request of another method op_{ij} with the input I_{ij} is sent to o_{ij}. α_3 shows that some output of o_{ij} is carried to o_i. For example, the response with the output data is sent from op_{ij}.

An *invocation graph* is introduced to show the information flow relation among methods. Each node indicates a method. There are two types of directed edges, i.e. *request* (Q) and *response* (S) edges. If a method op_i of an object o_i invokes op_j of o_j, there is a Q edge from op_i to op_j denoted by a straight arrow line. There are two points on the Q edges : (a) whether or not op_i sends data in o_i to op_j and (b) whether or not op_j changes the state of o_j. Hence, there are four types of Q edges as shown in Figure 5. A QNN edge means op_i sends o_i a request message op_j without data and op_j does not change o_j. That is, neither β_3 of op_i and α_1 of op_j nor β_2 of op_j carry data. No data flows from o_i to o_j. QON means op_i sends a request op_j with data to o_j but op_j does not change o_j. Although some data is derived from o_i, no data flows to o_j. QNI shows that op_j changes o_j while op_i does not send data to o_j. Some data flows into o_j but the data does not flow out from o_i. QOI indicates that op_i sends data to o_j and op_j changes o_j. Some data in o_i flows to o_j. α_2 and β_3 of op_i and α_1 and β_2 of op_j carry data.

Next, let us consider response (S) edges which show information flow carried by

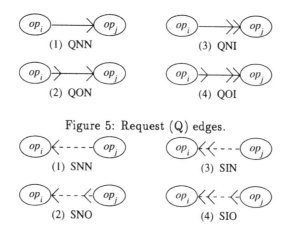

Figure 5: Request (Q) edges.

Figure 6: Response (S) edges.

the responses from o_j to o_i. S edges are indicated by dotted arrow lines. There are two points on the S edges ; (c) whether or not op_j sends data in o_j to op_i, and (d) whether or not op_i changes the state of o_i. There are four types of S edges as shown in Figure 6. SNN shows no information flow from o_j to o_i. SNO means op_j sends o_i the response with data derived from o_j, but op_j does not change o_i. SIN shows op_i changes o_i but op_j sends the response without data to o_i. SIO indicates op_j sends back the response with data derived from o_j to o_i and op_i changes o_i. That is, data in o_j flows to o_i.

If op_i invokes op_j, a *couple* of Q and S edges exist. One couple is denoted in a form α/β, where $\alpha \in \{QNN, QNI, QON, QOI\}$ and $\beta \in \{SNN, SNO, SIN, SIO\}$. Hence, there are sixteen possible couples for each invocation.

3.2   Flow graph and access rules

Suppose a method op_i invokes op_j in an invocation tree T. There are a Q edge Q_{ij} from a parent op_i to a child op_j and an S edge S_{ij} from op_j to op_i. Thus, each branch between op_i and op_j represents a couple of Q_{ij} and S_{ij} edges. Here, let *root* (T) denote a root of the tree T. In order to analyze the information flow among the methods, a *flow graph F* is introduced.

[Construction of flow graph]

(1) Each node in F indicates a method of the invocation tree T.

(2) For each node op_d connected to the parent by QNI or QOI edge in T, a path P from *root* (T) to op_d is obtained. For each node op_s in P, there is a directed edge $op_s \rightarrow op_d$ in F if there is a QON or QOI edge from op_s to a child node in P [Figure 7 (1)].

(3) For each node op_p in T, $op_{c_1} \rightarrow op_{c_2}$ if op_{c_1} and op_{c_2} are descendents of op_p in T, which are included in different subtrees of op_p, op_{c_1} has an SNO or SIO edge with the parent of op_{c_1}, and op_{c_2} has a QNI or QOI edge with the parent of op_{c_2} and op_{c_1} precedes op_{c_2} in T [Figure 7 (2)].

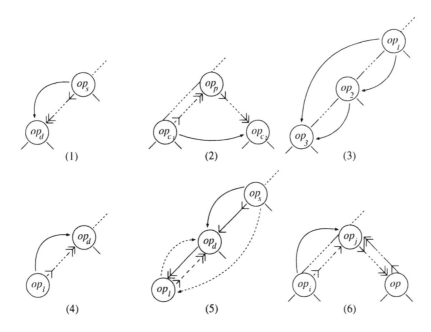

Figure 7: Directed edges.

(4) $op_1 \rightarrow op_3$ if $op_1 \rightarrow op_2 \rightarrow op_3$ [Figure 7 (3)].

A leaf node op_l in the invocation tree T does not invoke other methods. If op_l is invoked with some data and sends back the response, op_l may forward the input data carried by the request to the parent of op_l. Therefore, we have to consider the following additional rules for each leaf node op_l.

(5) For each node op_l connected to the parent by an SNO or SIO edge in T, a path P from $root$ (T) to op_l is obtained. For each node op_d in P, there is a directed edge $op_l \rightarrow op_d$ in F if there is an SIN or SIO edge from a child node to op_d [Figure 7 (4)].

(6) For each leaf node op_l, a path P from $root$ (T) to op_l is obtained. For every node op_s in P, $op_s \_\_ op_l$ if op_s is connected with the child in a QON or QOI edge. For each node op_d in P, there is a directed edge $op_l \_\_ op_d$ in F if op_d is connected to the child in an SIN or SIO edge. For each node op_s in P, there is a directed edge $op_s \rightarrow op_d$ if a) $op_s \_\_ op_l$ or $op_s \rightarrow op_l$ and b) $op_l \_\_ op_d$ [Figure 7 (5)].

(7) For each node op_i connected to the parent in SNO or SIO edge, a path P from $root$ (T) to op_i is obtained. If op_j in P is connected to the child in QNI or QOI and SIO or SIN edge, $op_i \rightarrow op_j$ [Figure 7 (6)]. □

[Example 3] Let us consider SSI commands [2] [Figure 8]. An $open$ method in a browser B accesses to an httpd server to GET a page P including two files F_1 and F_2. Suppose B invokes GET on P. After including these pages, B caches these data to a disk D. Figure 9 (1) and (2) show the invocation tree and the flow graph F,

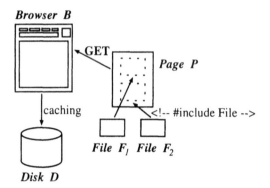

Figure 8: SSI–"include."

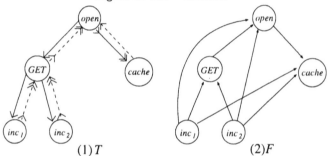

$(1)T$ $(2)F$

Figure 9: Flow graph.

respectively. The data in the files F_1 and F_2 can flow to the disk D from F. □

The flow graph F shows possible information flow to occur in the invocations of methods. Each purpose-oriented access rule $\langle o_i : op_i,\ o_j : op_j \rangle$ can be specified if the rule satisfies the information flow relation among the objects. A directed edge $\rightarrow$ among op_i and op_j is *legal* in F if the following rule is satisfied.

[**Flow rules**]

(1) $op_i \rightarrow op_j$ only if $\lambda(o_i) \preceq \lambda(o_j)$.
(2) $op_i \leftarrow op_j$ only if $\lambda(o_i) \succeq \lambda(o_j)$.
(3) $op_i \leftrightarrow op_j$ only if $\lambda(o_i) \equiv \lambda(o_j)$. □

op_i and op_j are referred to as *legally* related if every edge among op_i and op_j is legal. A rule $\langle o_i : op_i,\ o_j : op_j \rangle$ can be specified if all the directed edges incident to and from op_i and op_j are legal, i.e. op_i and op_j are legally related.

[**Example 4**] In the flow graph F of Figure 9, $GET \rightarrow open$ is legal only if $\lambda(P) \preceq \lambda(B)$, and $inc_1 \rightarrow GET$ is legal only if $\lambda(F_1) \preceq \lambda(P)$. That is, the rules $\langle B : open,\ P : GET \rangle$ and $\langle P : GET,\ F_1 : inc_1 \rangle$ are legal. However, $inc_2 \rightarrow GET$ is illegal if $\lambda(F_2) \succeq \lambda(P)$. That is, $\langle P : GET,\ F_2 : inc_2 \rangle$ is illegal. Illegal information flow between P and F_2 may occur if GET on P invokes inc_2 on F_2. Hence, $\langle B : open,\ P : GET \rangle$ is illegal and B cannot invoke GET on P through $open$. □

4 Concluding Remarks

In the distributed systems, objects support more abstract level of methods than *read* and *write*. The *purpose-oriented* access control model discusses why an object manipulates other objects in the object-based systems while the traditional access control model discusses if each subject can use an object by a method. In addition, the methods of the objects are invoked in a nested manner. The access rules have to satisfy the information flow relation among objects. In this paper, we have discussed how to validate the purpose-oriented access rules with respect to the information flow constraints.

Bibliography

1) Bell, D. E. and LaPadula, L. J., "Secure Computer Systems: Mathematical Foundations and Model," *Mitre Corp. Report* No. M74-244 (1975).

2) Berners-Lee, T., Fielding, R., and Frystyk, H., "Hypertext Transfer Protocol – HTTP/1.0," *RFC-1945* (1996).

3) Denning, D. E., "A Lattice Model of Secure Information Flow," *Communications of the ACM*, Vol. 19, No. 5, pp. 236–243 (1976).

4) Denning, D. E. and Denning, P. J., *Cryptography and Data Security*, Addison-Wesley (1982).

5) Object Management Group Inc., " The Common Object Request Broker : Architecture and Specification," Rev. 2.1 (1997).

6) Sandhu, R. S., "Lattice-Based Access Control Models," *IEEE Computer*, Vol. 26, No. 11, pp. 9–19 (1993).

7) Sandhu, R. S., Coyne, E. J., Feinstein, H. L., and Youman, C. E., "Role-Based Access Control Models," *IEEE Computer*, Vol. 29, No. 2, pp. 38–47 (1996).

8) Tachikawa, T., Yasuda, M., Higaki, H., and Takizawa, M., "Purpose-Oriented Access Control Model in Object-Based Systems," *Proc. of the 2nd Australasian Conf. on Information Security and Privacy (ACISP'97)*, pp. 38–49 (1997).

9) Tari, Z. and Chan, S. W., "A Role-Based Access Control for Intranet Security," *IEEE Internet Computing*, Vol. 1, No. 5, pp. 24–34 (1997).

26

Issues in Document Security Enforcement for Activity Execution in *CapBasED-AMS*

Kamalakar Karlapalem

James W. Gray, III

Patrick C. K. Hung

Hong Kong University of Science and Technology

ABSTRACT

Workflow systems are becoming very popular and are being used to support many of the day to day activities in large organizations. One of the major problems with workflow systems is that they often use heterogeneous and distributed hardware and software systems to execute a given activity (a set of tasks). This gives rise to decentralized security policies and mechanisms, which, in order to enable activity execution, give too many privileges to the agents (humans or systems) executing the work. The Capability-based and Event-driven Activity Management System (CapBasED-AMS) deals with the management and execution of activities. A Problem Solving Agent (PSA) is a human, or a hardware system, or a software system having an ability to execute activities. A task usually involves some processing of documents. Since many of the documents have sensitive information, document security issues have to be modeled, enforced, and managed by the activity management system. In this paper, we discuss three important issues for research in document security: least privilege, dynamic authorization of document access, and deduction of document privilege information from event observation.

Keywords: workflow system, activity management system, activity execution, document management, security control, least privilege, dynamic authorization.

1 Introduction

Workflow systems are becoming very popular and are being used to support many of the day to day activities in large organizations. These activities require interaction between humans and systems and among systems for their execution. The CapBasED-AMS (Capability-based and Event-driven Activity Management System), a workflow system, developed in [1, 2, 3, 4, 6, 7, 8, 9] deals with the specification, management and execution of activities. A Problem Solving Agent (PSA) is a human, or a hardware system, or a software system having an ability to execute activities. An activity consists of multiple in er-dependent tasks that need to be coordinated, scheduled and executed by a set of PSAs, where each task is an atomic activity executed by exactly one PSA. Since security is essential and integral part of activities, the activity management system has to manage and execute the activities in a secure way. In the CapBasED-AMS, threats, such as, unauthorized access or modification are identified as events. The security pilferage or illegal violation of privacy through accessing of specification time, compile time, or run-time data from activity management system and PSAs is monitored, controlled and reported. The activity execution is based on the occurrence of events. That is, a PSA after completion of a task (atomic activity) generates events which are captured by the activity management system, for initiating the execution of the next task.

In order to ensure integrity of activity execution, the detection of events and their transmission must be accomplished in an unambiguous, authentic and secure manner. A task can potentially involve some processing of documents, especially when executing document intensive task. Since many of the documents have sensitive information, document security issues have to be modeled, enforced, and managed by activity management system properly. We have developed a secure CapBasED-AMS (See Figure 1.) by taking into consideration the system infrastructure, secure match-making with additional security constraints, security policies, and secure PSA. Further, we developed a task coordination model for security document control and from the PSA viewpoint, organization viewpoint, task viewpoint, and activity viewpoint by adapting a role-based document security model, and protocols to facilitate event transmission and management for supporting the integrity of activity execution. In this paper, we discuss the issues for document security enforcement by considering the aspects of least privilege, dynamic authorization of document access and deduction of privilege information by event observation. The rest of the paper is organized as follows, section 2 describes the least privilege and the dynamic authorization of document access, section 3 describes the deduction of document privilege information from event observation, knowledge section 4 describes the case studies of additional issues in document security enforcement and section 5 presents the summary and future work.

2   Least Privilege Concept

Workflow systems are becoming very popular and are being used to support many of the day to day activities in large organizations. These activities require interaction between humans and systems and among systems for their execution. The CapBasED-AMS (Capability-based and Event-driven Activity Management System), a workflow system, developed in [1, 2, 3, 4, 6, 7, 8, 9] deals with the specification, management and execution of activities. A Problem Solving Agent (PSA) is a human, or a hardware system, or a software system having an ability to execute activities. An activity consists of multiple in er-dependent tasks that need to be coordinated,

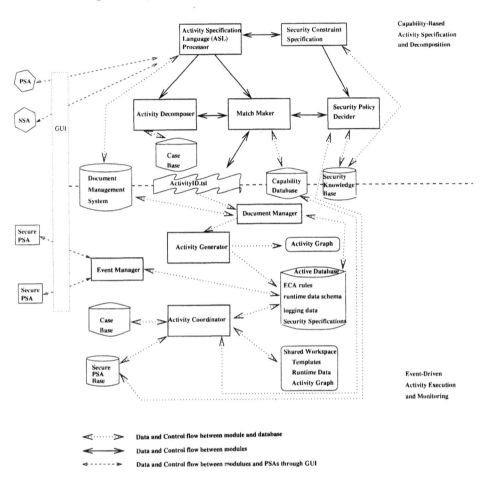

Figure 1: Architecture of Secure CapBasED-Activity Management System

scheduled and executed by a set of PSAs, where each task is an atomic activity executed by exactly one PSA. Since security is essential and integral part of activities, the activity management system has to manage and execute the activities in a secure way. In the CapBasED-AMS, threats, such as, unauthorized access or modification are identified as events. The security pilferage or illegal violation of privacy through accessing of specification time, compile time, or run-time data from activity management system and PSAs is monitored, controlled and reported. The activity execution is based on the occurrence of events. That is, a PSA after completion of a task (atomic activity) generates events which are captured by the activity management system, for initiating the execution of the next task.

In order to ensure integrity of activity execution, the detection of events and their transmission must be accomplished in an unambiguous, authentic and secure manner. A task can potentially involve some processing of documents, especially when executing document intensive task. Since many of the documents have sensitive information, document security issues have to be modeled, enforced, and managed by activity management system properly. We have developed a secure CapBasED-AMS (See Figure 1.) by taking into consideration the system infrastructure, secure match-making with additional security constraints, security policies, and secure PSA. Further, we developed a task coordination model for security document control and from the PSA viewpoint, organization viewpoint, task viewpoint, and activity viewpoint by adapting a role-based document security model, and protocols to facilitate event transmission and management for supporting the integrity of activity execution. In this paper, we discuss the issues for document security enforcement by considering the aspects of least privilege, dynamic authorization of document access and deduction of privilege information by event observation. The rest of the paper is organized as follows, section 2 describes the least privilege and the dynamic authorization of document access, section 3 describes the deduction of document privilege information from event observation, section 4 describes the case studies of additional issues in document security enforcement and section 5 presents the summary and future work.

The principle of least privilege for document access requires that each PSA in CapBasED-AMS be granted the most restrictive set of privileges (or lowest clearance) of document access needed for the execution of assigned tasks during a session. A session is a time interval during which a task of an activity gets executed. Least privilege with Discretionary Access Control (DAC) and Mandatory Access Control (MAC) set up tight domains of privilege in which specific PSAs can access to a specific document. The application of this preventive security principle limits the damage that can result from accident, error, or unauthorized use. In the next two subsections, we consider this principle from three perspectives: (1) static least privilege analysis of an activity specification, (2) dynamic least privilege enforcement during activity execution, and (3) dynamic evolution of least privileges.

2.1   Static Least Privilege Analysis

A practical problem with security controls is that they "get in the way" when people want to do their work. For example, when a PSA needs to edit a file, it is a significant annoyance if he does not have write permission for the file and must go to the file owner to be granted permission. As a result, file owners find it convenient to grant liberal permissions, e.g., read/write/execute permission to everyone. Thus, we see that user and PSA convenience is in direct conflict with the principle of least privilege. To address this concern, it would be useful to have a static analysis tool that identifies the least set of privileges that are sufficient for people to get their jobs done. More generally, document owners and security officers can work with the tool to identify a set of privileges that are sufficient for people to do their jobs, yet acceptable from the viewpoint of whether those people are trusted with those privileges (e.g., as determined by a personnel security background check). Such a tool is made possible using CapBasED-AMS specifications. Essentially, the task specifications provide the information about privileges are needed for PSAs to do their job. During the static specification of a task, the task creator or Security Officer specifies the set of documents and access privileges that the task requires to be executed successfully. Every task has both input and output event(s) (except the "START" and "END" task in the coordination plan as developed in [2, 8]), plus there may be documents embedded in events as shown in figure 2.

In Doc.1, ..., In Doc.N are the set of documents embedded in the input event(s). Also, some documents from *In Doc.* or *New Doc.* may be archived in the document system by the PSA. The output document *Out Doc.* includes the documents of the input document *In Doc.* and new document *New Doc.*, but does not include the document in the *Archives Doc.*, i.e., *Out Doc.* $\subseteq$ (*In Doc.* $\cup$ *New Doc.*) - *Archives Doc.*. There may be more than one output event of a task, in which case there may be more than one output document which carries semantic value to the next coordinated task as well, i.e., *Out Doc.1, ..., Out Doc.N*. For example, as shown in Figure 2, the output document of Task 1 is the input document of next coordinated Task 2, i.e. *Out Doc1.* → *In Doc2.*.

In addition to the static specification of tasks, an AMS specification includes specifications of PSAs and their capabilities. In particular, for any given task, it is possible to derive the set of PSAs who are *capable* (but not necessarily *permitted*) of performing the task. From this information, it is possible to derive a feasible assignment of PSAs to tasks. Such an assignment must take into account estimates of task completion times as well as inter-task dependencies. Finally, from such an assignment, the tool can derive the least set of privileges that would be needed to carry out all tasks. Note that the above analysis is done *statically*—at task specification time—and would be used to grant a set of privileges prior to task execution. Thus, we can employ a least privilege principle, while avoiding to the greatest possible extent the annoyance of have to consult document owners and/or security officers to grant new privileges at task execution time.

2.2 Dynamic Least Privilege Enforcement

In addition to the static identification and assignment of privileges, it is desirable to further restrict the privileges of PSAs dynamically, i.e., during task execution. For example, suppose a PSA is granted the privilege to write a particular file, say F, for the purpose of performing a particular task, say T. In this case, the PSA does not need to write F *before* he has started task T. Nor does he need to write F after T is *finished*. The principle of least privilege indicates that ideally, the PSA would be allowed to write F *only* while he is actively engaged in task T. Again, the use of an activity management system such as CapBasED-AMS allows us to implement such dynamic enforcement. The task needs to access various documents, like read and write, in order to be executed. The PSA who is assigned to the task dynamically (i.e., at runtime) will be granted the least privileges to the documents required for the execution of the task. Therefore, the PSA can access those required documents during the execution of task. This approach is called the execution time centralized PSA driven based document access control. These privileges will be revoked from the PSA after it has finished the execution. This policy will reduce the possibilities

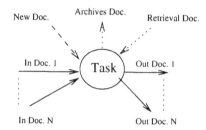

Document Flow within Task

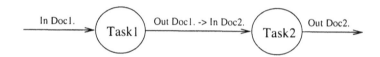

Document Flow between Tasks

Figure 2: Document Flow in Task

of information being released to third parties as the PSA is denied access to that information after the execution of the task.

2.3   Dynamic Evolution of Least Privileges

Owing to unforeseen requirements of a given task, a PSA may need to access more documents than those specified (statically) by the task creator. For example, the PSA may perform certain operations on input documents and create a set of new documents *New Doc.* with value added information. (See Figure 2.) Such exceptional cases will need to be handled by CapBasED-AMS. If the privilege has been granted to the PSA statically (e.g., in the context of another task), the privilege may be dynamically granted to the PSA in this exceptional case. This would be done for the convenience of the PSA and to avoid work delays; however, an alert would be sent to the task creator or system officer to inform them that the PSA is making use of his static privileges in an exceptional situation. Action could then be taken to investigate the matter, update the static privileges, etc, as appropriate. On the other hand, if the PSA does not have the required static privilege, human intervention is inevitable. Before proceeding, the task creator or security officer must be contacted to make a decision to grant or deny the privilege.

Besides exceptional requests for privileges, it may turn out that certain privileges that were specified by the task creator are *never used* during task execution. According to the principle of least privilege, such unnecessary privileges should not be granted to the PSA. Ideally, the activity management system would identify such un-needed privileges and after consulting the task creator or security officer (say, during a monthly review) these privileges could be revoked from the relevant PSAs.

To support such evolutionary development of access privileges, CapBasED-AMS is being designed to maintain a record of the runtime invocation of access privileges. When a PSA makes use of an access privilege in the context of a given task, CapBasED-AMS stores that fact. Thus, any reduction or expansion of the input and output document for the task can be identified and reflected back to the task creator or security administrator so that the static security specification of the task can be updated accordingly.

3 Document Privilege Detection

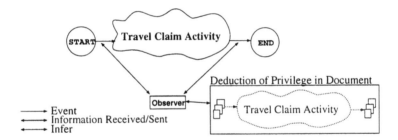

Figure 3: Deduction of Document Privilege Information By Event Observation

In many situations, the privilege information of document access can be deduced by third party, e.g., observer, by observing the events triggered during the execution of activity. The observer can also be a PSA involved in the activity, because no PSA will know other PSAs work and status, or communicate with other PSA directly during task execution in the same activity. In Figure 3 we present an example of "Travel Claim Activity". This activity is executed when the applicant submits the application form for travel claim. If the applicant is the observer, the observer can deduce privilege information through the flow of various documents during task execution. For example, the observer can deduce a set of privileges attached with his application form to the PSA who will execute this activity. After the execution of activity is finished, the observer may receive some documents from the result. Based on the information received, the observer can deduce partial picture of document flow in this activity as shown in Figure 3.

Furthermore, the observer can grasp more privileged information about document by sending detective event during the execution of activity as shown in figure 4. For example, the observer can keep on enquiring about the status of his application from the PSA involved. Then the observer may be able to grasp more information by invoking the detective event during the execution of activity.

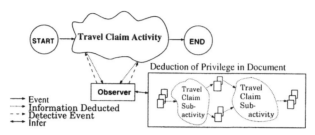

Figure 4: Deduction of Document Privilege Information By Detective Event

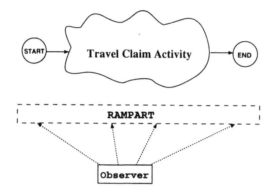

Figure 5: Prevention of Privilege Information Deduced By Cover Story

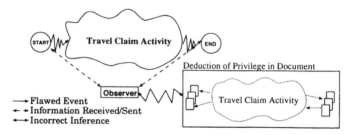

Figure 6: Prevention of Privilege Information Deduced By Noise

To prevent the observer from deducing the information for illegal or improper purpose. One way to prevent this situation to be from happening is to use cover story in order to hide all the information. In Figure 5, the "rampart" (guard) is used to prevent any information released to observer or only allow certain form of information to be released to observer. For example, in the "Travel Claim Activity", the activity will hide the name of the PSA has the right to approve the application from the applicant. In Figure 6, we present another method which is more destructive. The activity releases the noise (flawed event) to observer when some information needs to be kept highly confidential. This method is usually used for fudging highly confidential information. For example, a police officer investigates the crime and releases the flawed information to public in order to cover the status of investigation.

4 Additional Security Issues

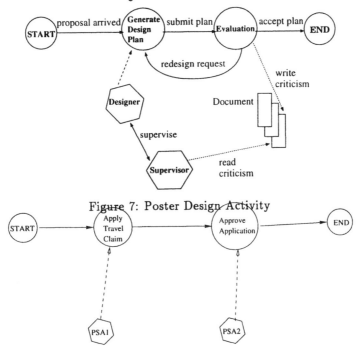

Figure 7: Poster Design Activity

Figure 8: Travel Claim Activity

In this section, we discuss two examples which present additional issues for in document security enforcement during the execution. In Figure 7 shows a "Poster Design" activity that involves the hierarchy of PSAs in a design company. When there is a proposal for poster design sought, the first task "Generate Design Plan" will be assigned to the PSA "Designer". The "Designer" will create the poster and submit the plan to next task "Evaluation" for approval. If there is nothing to change in the plan, then the whole activity will be finished. Otherwise, it will re-execute the task "Generate Design Plan" again until the plan is approved. In this company, the PSA "Supervisor" can view and read the documents involved in the whole activity according to the organization struc ure. For example, the PSA who executes the task "Evaluation" will write some criticism on the document for the design plan submitted by the "Designer". The "Designer" is allowed to see the criticism, but not the name of the PSA who did the evaluation, whereas the "Supervisor" is allowed to see both the criticism and the name. But the problem occurs when the "Designer" promoted to "Supervisor". The name of the PSA who wrote criticism of the "Supervisor" previous works should not be readable by this "Supervisor" even though "Supervisor" has the right to read it by default.

In Figure 8, it shows the other activity "Travel Claim". In this case, the PSA1 who submitted the application form in task "Apply Travel Claim" must not be the PSA2 who approve the claim in task "Approve Application". Therefore, the document "Travel Claim Application Form" can not be written and approved by the same PSA. This document access constraint also restricts the match making of the PSA to task in this case. This can be only supported by match making module.

4.1   Conflicts in Document Access

In some cases, the PSA may be able to access the same document by different privileges in different session. In Figure 9, it is possible that an identical PSA, like PSA1 executes Task1 and Task3 or PSA2 executes Task2 and Task4, execute more than one task in the same activity. If there are some security restrictions or constraints on the document that does not allow the same PSA to read and write the same document. This will have the security conflicts since PSA1 can write the document during the session of Task1 execution and it can also read and write the same document during the session of Task3 execution. In case of CapBasED-AMS, the Match Maker should be able to detect this conflict and assign these two tasks to different PSAs based on the security constraint imposed on the document. Furthermore, the same situation will also occur in multi activities environment as shown in Figure 10. In this case, the Match Maker should be able to detect the document access conflicts among different activities as well.

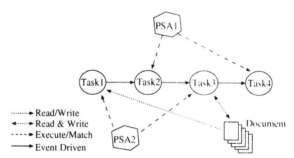

Figure 9: Document Access Conflict in Single Activity Environment

5   Summary and Future Work

The main focus of this paper is to raise some important issues for document security enforcement for the execution of activity. We introduce three important problems, namely, principle of least privilege, dynamic privilege enforcement, and deduction of document privilege information by event observation. And also, we raise the new concept in evaluation of security risk factor based on knowledge accumulation and dissemination factor. All these problems relate to maintaining security while providing less hindrance to the execution of the activities. The problem of least privilege is very challenging in an dynamic environment wherein the document needs of a task change over time. The intuitive notion of least privilege is not new. In

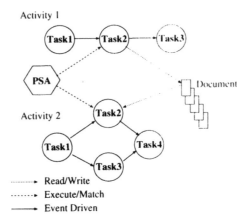

Figure 10: Document Access Conflict in Multi Activities Environment

fact, it has appeared in the (US government standard) "Trusted Computing Systems Evaluation Criteria" as far back as 1985. We are not aware of any current work that addresses these problems in the framework of an activity management system.

The goal of this paper is bring these three important problems to the notice of the researchers and promote further work in this challenging area of security enforcement in activity management systems. We have already addressed some basic issues by developing a framework of security enforcement in activity management systems and are currently enhancing the prototype implementation of CapBasED-AMS [6] to incorporate security features. Furthermore, we are also developing the web based secure CapBasED-AMS for use in Internet/WWW environments. Beyond this, we have been developing mechanisms for dynamic enforcement of least privilege, as well as a framework for exploring the tradeoff between security and fault resilience [5]. To date, our work has been in terms of the Secure CapBasED-AMS (Capability-based and Event-driven Activity Management System); however, we believe the work can be applied in other settings. In particular, the basic feature of the Secure CapBasED-AMS that makes it suitable for exploring least privilege is that it provides a vehicle to describe what needs to be done by the users of the system. It is the interaction between what the users need to do (what needs to be allowed) and the least privilege security requirement (what needs to be disallowed) that makes least privilege a difficult problem.

Bibliography

1) S. Chakravarthy, K. Karlapalem, S. B. Navathe, and A. Tanaka. *Database Supported Cooperative Problem Solving. International Journal of Intelligent and Cooperative Information System*, September 1993.

2) P. Hung. *A Capability-Based Activity Specification and Decomposition for an Activity Management System*. Master's thesis, The Hong Kong University of Science and Technology, 1995.

3) P. C. K. Hung and K. Karlapalem. Task Oriented Modeling of Document Security in CapBasED-AMS. In *IPIC'96, Rethinking Documents*, Boston, November, 1996.

4) P. C. K. Hung and K. Karlapalem. A Paradigm for Security Enforcement in CapBasED-AMS. In *Second IFCIS Conference on Cooperative Information Systems*, CHARLESTON, June, 1997.

5) P. C. K. Hung, K. Karlapalem, and J. Gray. A Study of Least Privilege in CapBasED-AMS. *Third IFCIS Conference on Cooperative Information Systems (CoopIS'98)*, 1998.

6) P. C. K. Hung, H. P. Yeung, and K. Karlapalem. CapBasED-AMS: A Capability-based and Event-driven Activity Management System (Demonstrations). *Proceedings of the ACM SIGMOD Conference on Management of Data*, June 1996.

7) K. Karlapalem and P. C. K. Hung. Security Enforcement in Activity Management System. In *Workflow Management Systems and Interoperability*, Turkey, August, 1997.

8) K. Karlapalem, H. P. Yeung, and P. C. K. Hung. CapBasED-AMS - A Framework for Capability-Based and Event-Driven Activity Management System. *Proceedings of the Third International Conference on Cooperative Information Systems*, 1995.

9) H. Yeung. *An Event-driven Activity Execution for An Activity Management System.* Master's thesis, The Hong Kong University of Science and Technology, 1995.

Index